The Cotton Patch Evidence

DALLAS LEE

The
Cotton Patch
Evidence

HARPER & ROW, PUBLISHERS
NEW YORK, EVANSTON, SAN FRANCISCO, LONDON
A Koinonia Publication

Scripture quotations are from The Cotton Patch Version, translated by Clarence Jordan and published by Association Press.

FIRST EDITION

LIBRARY OF CONGRESS CATALOG CARD NUMBER: 70-150593

Designed by C. Linda Dingler

To the Continuing Fellowship
at Koinonia Farm

"Never did Paul or Peter or Stephen point to an empty tomb as evidence of the resurrection. The evidence was the spirit-filled fellowship."

CLARENCE JORDAN

Contents

Sources and Acknowledgments

The Koinonia community involved deeply personal commitments and experiences, and asking its participants to speak of it was much like asking a family to reveal its secrets. Those who spoke openly and confidently with me made an invaluable contribution to this book. I must acknowledge in particular the investment of time and information made by Martin and Mabel England, Howard and Marion Johnson, and Conrad and Ora Browne.

Clarence Jordan's brother Frank enriched my understanding with thoughtful reflections and his strong sense of history, and other members of the family clarified and documented important experiences in Clarence's childhood. Florence Jordan stood with me as a reliable resource on virtually every aspect of the story, and as a patient, supportive friend.

I knew Clarence during the last year of his life, and interviewed him on two occasions for magazine articles. Tape recordings of his lectures over the years provided a major resource for this book. He drew heavily from the experiences at Koinonia Farm in his dramatic communications, and managed to remain reasonably accurate even in his best-spun yarns. P. D. East, the enduring editor of the *Petal Paper*, interviewed Clarence extensively in 1958, and I am grateful to him for making that information available.

Others on the periphery of the Koinonia experience were helpful, including Arthur Steilberg, friends at Forest River Colony and at Reba Place Fellowship, and several staff members at Southern Baptist Theological Seminary. A number of citizens of Americus, Georgia, though in total disagreement with Koinonia's past and present intentions, granted helpful interviews.

I am especially thankful for the research assistance of Carol Brink and the typing of Lori DiGilio, both of whom were among the first to respond to the dream of Koinonia Partners and help make it become reality. I am indebted, too, for the research contributions of Walker L. Knight, Jr., and to the people of the Oakhurst Baptist Church in Decatur, Georgia, who provided me with a place to work and with supportive friendship.

I express my deepest appreciation for those in fellowship at Koinonia Farm, who continue to inflame the imaginations of others who hunger for the integrity of faith rooted in action.

D. L.

The Cotton Patch Evidence

CHAPTER 1

Derailed

The promise of something wise or something funny or just something good to know danced in this man's eyes.

Tall, high-hipped, hands jammed into blue-jean pockets, floppy straw hat shading a grin—dusty from the peanut rows, greasy from the tractor shop, bespectacled from persistent study—the man was full of the unexpected, so you listened expectantly. He might talk about the time the city and county officials came out to the farm and pleaded with him to leave the area, or discuss the skills of winemaking, or describe in some detail the spider's intricate contribution to life on the planet (among other things, spiders snared the gnats in his study shack). Or he might talk about Jesus, a man who came alive in his drawl and walked the red roads of Georgia in his mind.

Clarence Jordan had a streak of magnetism best demonstrated by the contradicting virtues that marked him—he was a gentle man who thundered, a nonviolent man who was known to have stared down a Ku Kluxer or two, a man with much to say who listened patiently, a genuinely humble man who could walk into the home of an affluent person and say: "Nice piece of plunder you have here." He was a dirt-farming aristocrat, a good 'ole Georgia country boy with a doctor's degree, a teacher with manure on his boots, a scholar with working clothes on his mind.

In fact, the man was the essence of creative contradiction, a

1

high-flying visionary with his feet on the ground.

He was a romantic who dreamed aloud about the rich and the poor, the black and the white, the educated and the uneducated becoming partners in a new order, and at the same time he was a tough-minded realist who worked and suffered to flesh out the dream. He was a Bible-quoting Christian who thought the church had gone awhoring with Mammon, a country Baptist preacher who talked revolution, a New Testament Greek scholar who lived by the Sermon on the Mount.

He was said to be a man ahead of his time. But actually he was a man for his time, a forerunner who struggled to be actively faithful to values that many talked about but did not trust for a way of life. He was a bold experimenter, even when all the external forces of the age seemed to tell him: "Not now, dreamer, the time is not yet ripe for such foolishness."

The time was 1942. Southern boys were storming into the armed services, becoming the first conspicuous heroes of a world war, and confirming their own heady claim that the South was the toughest and the best. They had cursed Hitler when the rest of the nation still slumbered in isolationism. And now they were eager—so eager, an Alabama congressman boasted, that "they had to start the selective service system to keep our southern boys from filling up the army."

Some were saying the South was the poorest, most illiterate, most violent, most emotional section of the country. But it was wartime and the South was leading the nation in volunteer enlistments. Southern boys were patriotic, daring fighters, quick to volunteer, and the nation knew it and honored them. *Life* magazine carried an article in July 1942, "The Fighting South," and subtitled it: "It Knows That War Is Hell But That Hell Is Better Than Dishonor." If war was necessary, then southern boys would serve their country. After all, they were haunted by a consciousness of just how thoroughly fighting could settle matters.

The fever of patriotism chased other realities into the background. The Exalted Cyclops and Grand Dragons and Kleagles were herding along a modest upsurge in Ku Klux Klan activity. The presence of great multitudes of poor Negroes still distorted and tore at the white southerner's spirit and kept him on edge administering a fragile, tentative structure of unwritten law that held the Negro at bay. Floggings and beatings occurred frequently.

Although lynchings were at an all-time low across the South, down from several score to only four or five a year, the dark spirit manifested by the overt violence of the lynching was far from assuaged. It was visible still, brooding behind the nervous eyes of the leather-skinned rednecks who saw it as their community responsibility to keep the Negro iced with fear. It drawled insidiously from the cops who could not give a black man a traffic ticket without making sport of his humanity. And it foamed visibly around the mouths of the white supremacist politicians as they stood in the backs of pickup trucks in little crossroad towns, cursed the big cities, quoted the Bible, promised a return to white primaries, and discreetly raised The Negro Menace ("The federal government is gonna give your job to a nigger!").

That same dark spirit that once flashed openly in lynchings endured in the day-to-day routines of white Christians who would not even acknowledge the Negro as fully human. It was painfully present in those county school boards that refused to provide transportation for black children, and in the mind of one county superintendent who was known to say: "If we educate these niggers, who is gonna work on the farms?" And that dark spirit, in the shape of despair, was the one fact of life for the thousands upon thousands of sharecropping families—victims of legal peonage—who sought the city for restoration of hope.

But . . . it was 1942 and the heathen were raging in Europe and Asia. The oppressors had to be stopped. And these white southern boys were storming into the armed services, easily convinced that the risk and sacrifice of war abroad was essential to the preservation of freedom at home.

There were a few young men who recognized the same symptoms of cruelty and hate at home as were being opposed abroad, and so they could not be persuaded so easily to go so far to fight evil. A few even pursued their doubts to the conclusion that not only was war hell, it was also unjustified—absolutely, under any circumstances.

One such man was that open-faced, small-town boy Clarence Jordan. In 1942, while so many of Georgia's finest were marching gallantly off to fight a war overseas, this lanky, sandy-haired Georgian was striding in the opposite direction, into the middle of the state to make his stand against racism, greed, and exploitation down home.

He was not interested in fighting nazism in Europe with weapons; he was determined to fight facistlike oppression in Georgia with something that southerners were almost as familiar with as they were their guns: Christianity. The difference was, Jordan did not talk about the "Gee-zus" of the feverish radio evangelist, or the soul-saving Jesus of the crude highway sign, or even the slick Jesus of the sanctuary. He talked about Jesus the man, as if the guy actually worked and sweated, experienced love and hurt, and had about him all the shrugs and shuffles of a down-to-earth human being.

Jordan was just back from the Baptist seminary with a doctorate in Greek New Testament, and he had things to say about Jesus being a man who should be followed rather than a God who should be worshiped, about a man who initiated a movement that called people into revolutionary new ways of life now, rather than a God who was interested only in saving souls for the future. He was talking about Christianity as if it were a liberating movement rather than a sandbagged institution. Whatever other theological confusion clouded the faith, he was preaching that the ideas of the New Testament either had to be incarnated or rejected. It was unsafe to sit in the sanctuary and confess belief in ideas such as the fatherhood of God and the brotherhood of man, peaceful responses to evil, and a spirit of sharing. He who would profess the ideas but not give them expression would wind up a "busted-gut Christian," whose very life would convict him of taking God's name in vain.

Now Jordan was southern through and through, and he knew his culture before he knew his Bible. The Jordans, the Weavers, the Josseys, the Radcliffes, the Leonards, and so on—right on up the family tree—all were pure-bred Anglo-Saxon spirits who stalked Georgia, North Carolina, and Virginia as early as the seventeenth century. He looked southern, talked southern, walked southern, ate southern, dressed southern. He was the southerner of southerners. And yet in 1942, while most of the region physically and emotionally was marching off to war, Jordan stepped counter to virtually all that the South was or ever had been.

As if to ignore the little tyrant in Europe and the fiends in Asia, as if to disregard centuries of custom, as if to reject the best contemporary theology—in fact, as if he did not know better— Jordan established an experiment in Christian communal living on a farm in Sumter County, right in the heart of southwestern Georgia, and declared brotherhood, nonviolence, and economic sharing to be its fundamental guidelines.

As a southern Georgian might have put it: "Someone had gotten to old Clarence." He just did not come out right. All the proper ingredients were there to begin with, but he still came out marching the other way.

The trend of his later convictions was hinted at in his childhood and foretold in his later development. Clarence Leonard Jordan, born July 29, 1912, the seventh of ten children in a privileged Talbotton, Georgia, family, just seemed to grow up slightly out of cadence. He was not distinctly a maverick or conspicuously a rebel. It was more that he just seemed a little detached from the family. His brothers and sisters recalled that he was the only one of the children who would hold back from the headlong rush of play to listen to his nervous but sensitive mother chatter about her childhood in Talbotton and in Oregon. He was, in fact, clearly his mother's favorite, and he responded with a devotion that set him apart from the other children.

Clarence liked to be alone, and in his solitude he taught himself to play the piano and to type on his father's typewriter using all ten fingers. He participated in sports and other activities in school, but he was slow and dogged in his approach—"a plugger who was willing to pay the price," his eldest brother Frank said.

He seemed shy and retiring compared to the outgoing nature of his parents and his brothers and sisters, and yet he was a fighter —not physically, but intellectually. Of the seven children who survived infancy, Clarence was in the middle, with three older and three younger than he. Frank recalled: "Clarence would fight with anyone in the family. It didn't matter if he was going up the line or down the line. That was why we nicknamed him 'Grump.' "

He had such a capacity for verbal encounter, and such a reservoir of answers for every situation, that the family expected him to be a lawyer. His father, short and wiry (or "small and low" in hometown parlance), was an intense, puritanical businessman who started the Bank of Talbotton and a general store in the town of 1200. The bank and the store buildings were connected, and when Clarence and the other boys were supposed to be working in the store, J. W. Jordan would leave his cashier's window and slip silently into the store to check on them. He always worked standing up and he expected everyone else to do the same.

On one such occasion, he caught Clarence and two of his brothers sitting on the counter, loafing because no customers were in the store. After he chewed them out thoroughly and started back to the door, Clarence drawled out: "Dad, if you don't want to catch us sitting down, you ought to put hobnails on your boots."

The Jordans were loyal Baptists and the local Baptist church was a central part of their lives. Sunday School and stern preaching and hot nights at the August revivals were primary in the heritage of Clarence and his five brothers and one sister. All the children, in good tradition, made professions of faith and joined the church when they were about twelve.

Clarence, standing off just slightly from the experiences of the others, also seemed to take religion differently. In Sunday School he learned a little song that the children sang to the tune of "The Battle Hymn of the Republic": "Red and yellow, black and white, they are precious in his sight. Jesus loves the little children of the world."

Reflecting on that experience when he was in graduate school years later, Clarence wrote in his personal journal:

The question arose in my mind, "Were the little black children precious in God's sight just like the little white children?" The song said they were. Then why were they always so ragged, so dirty and hungry? Did God have favorite children?

I could not figure out the answers to these puzzling questions, but I knew something was wrong. A little light came when I began to realize that perhaps-it wasn't God's doings, but man's. God didn't turn them away from our churches—we did. God didn't pay them low wages—we did. God didn't make them live in another section of town and in miserable huts—we did. God didn't make ragged, hungry little boys pick rotten oranges and fruit out of the garbage can and eat them—we did. Maybe they were just as precious in God's sight, but were they in ours? My environment told me that they were not very precious in anybody's sight. A nigger was a nigger and must be kept in his place—the place of servitude and inferiority.

Whatever feeling troubled him at a young age, it probably was not as acute as his analysis in retrospect indicates. But the boy's simple registration of the discrepancy between what he was being taught and what he was seeing as fact derailed him at an early age from the mainline of tradition. When his father rebuked a Negro man for delivering the cleaning to the front door of their stately brick home, Clarence was embarrassed and angry with his father —and he expressed it.

The Talbot County jail was situated about 100 yards straight out behind the Jordan home, and a chain gang of convicted criminals was camped in the yard of the jailhouse most of the time. Clarence was fascinated by the rowdy, profane humanity of the men who lived out a portion of their lives there, and he began passing through the camp in the afternoons after school. He made friends with a number of the prisoners and with the cook, who gave him a slice of cornbread and fatback every afternoon. There he glimpsed again facts of life that seemed alien to what he was being taught in home and in church. He saw men with short chains locked between their feet to keep them from running, men bolted into the agonizing shame of primitive pillories, men beaten with whips or their bodies torn under the stress of the "stretcher" —a small frame structure in which a man could be placed with his feet fastened at the floor and his hands tied to ropes above him that extended out to a block and tackle on the outside. He saw that almost all these men were black.

"This made tremendous, traumatic impressions on me," he recalled. "It hit me the hardest a night or two after I joined the church during the August revival. I remember it was hot and I remember that the warden of the chain gang was singing bass in the choir. I'll never forget how carried away he got singing 'Love Lifted Me' that night.

"But the next night I was awakened by agonizing groans from the direction of the chain gang camp. I was sure I could recognize who it was, and I was sure I knew what was happening. Ed Russell was in the stretcher. I knew not only who was in the stretcher, I knew who was pulling the rope. The same man who only hours before was so carried away singing 'Love Lifted Me' was now lifting that man's body on the stretcher. That nearly tore me to pieces. I identified totally with that man in the stretcher. His agony was my agony. I got really mad with God. If He was love and the warden was an example of it, I didn't want anything to do with Him."

So Clarence Jordan, at 12, fresh from an August revival experience, was jolted into full recognition of the fact that the religion he aspired to and the life he was so much a part of simply did not jibe. He did not reject his church or raise a protest or risk his new understanding by exposing it to his family or friends. In fact, he may not have been capable of articulating all that he felt. And so it remained a secret, stuffed deep into the chemistry of his body and soul, where guilt abides, where fear is rooted, and where conviction slowly matures to action.

For a time thereafter Clarence responded to the impulse to be a lawyer, which pleased his family. He dreamed of going off to the state law school and then raging back into the county like a saviour to see that justice was done in the county jails and work camps. But this was a short-lived impulse, as he became increasingly aware that injustice and suffering were not confined to the chain gangs. The insidious fog of racism and greed, he began to see, was choking the whole county and the next, and the next, and the next. The victims of sharecropping—that system of legal peonage that enriched so many white farmers—huddled along every stretch of road. "I realized," he said later, "that most people are not stretched by ropes but by hunger, by oppression."

Toward the end of high school, he decided to be a farmer—a scientific farmer—and to try to lift the awful burden from the poor man's back by showing him how to get a lot from a little land. He would seek to work in partnership with the poor farmers. A volatile mixture of guilt and a rage for justice was stoking up a lifetime of pressure.

And so in 1929 he enrolled in the Georgia State College of Agriculture at the University of Georgia in Athens. His father, who may have been disappointed that Clarence did not choose law, chided him lightly: "If you want to be a farmer, why go to school? I'll buy you a mule and you can start right now." His father, however, supported him in school faithfully until his bank finally succumbed to the pressures of the Depression in March 1933.

If Clarence had been slow and a little withdrawn as a youngster, he finally began to come alive at the university. He joined everything in sight—fraternities, debating teams, drama clubs, the student agricultural newspaper, the band, the YMCA, the Baptist Student Union, the First Baptist Church, the Reserve Officers' Training Corps. He was a "good dancer and a lot of fun," according to a classmate, and soon was elected to leadership positions in the organizations he joined. He did well academically and was accepted into several honorary societies. He also came home his first year proudly displaying his boots and spurs, part of the outfit issued when he chose the cavalry instead of the infantry in the ROTC, which was required of male students for their first two years.

All this extracurricular activity combined with the discipline of the classroom tended to bury Clarence's most troubling religious struggles. He talked a time or two with D. B. Nicholson, the state and local Baptist Student Union director, about his growing convictions on the racial issue. But he did not create any confrontations or seek to convince too many others of his way. He plunged on through school with a popular image, perhaps more in step with the crowd than he ever had been—or ever would be.

By the time he was a senior, however, and had been elected statewide Baptist Student Union president and editor of the student agricultural newspaper, he began to search for a specific purpose in his life. What was he to do? The old passion to learn agriculture and share his knowledge seemed to have faded a little. Something was lacking. He said years later: "The thing that just bowled me over was the realization that whites seemed to have the very things that I wanted blacks to have, and the whites were living in such a hell. Why should I feel that blacks would be in any less a hell if they had these things. There had to be something extra somewhere. I was driven in a desperate search for spiritual resources."

At that point, Clarence responded to the inner urging to become a preacher. Nothing, it seemed, could have been further from the four-year investment in agricultural training that he was about to complete, but he seized upon it as God-provoked.

Convinced of his call to preach, he completed his bachelor of science degree in agriculture in the summer of 1933 and packed his ROTC uniforms and equipment for six weeks of summer camp in northern Georgia. He had volunteered for the last two years of ROTC, but now that he was about to complete the program, he was beginning to be confused by what seemed to be two distinct compulsions vying for his commitment. It had not occurred to him previously that what he was reading in the New Testament and what he was training himself to do were in conflict.

Now Clarence Jordan mounted on a bold black steed, a pistol in one hand and a saber in the other, was the fulfillment of a mysterious compulsion common to most sons of southern aristocracy. It was even a stronger image than, say, Clarence Jordan in a white suit, mounted on a wicker chair sipping mint juleps. The uniform, the discipline, the polished weapons, the horse—all the sights and smells and touches of gallantry came together and gushed with the snobbish masculinity of defending what was right and honorable. He was about to be commissioned as a second lieutenant in the U.S. Cavalry. There was no war to fight, no draft to dodge; this was strictly a voluntary act on the part of a Georgia son whose maternal grandfather reportedly had stolen a mule from Sherman's army.

But something new was tugging at him now. As he had grappled with his earlier convictions about the evils of racial oppression, and then the urge to preach, he had approached the Scriptures with fresh fascination. In fact, he had been memorizing long passages of Scripture that were particularly meaningful to him, primarily in chapters five, six, and seven in the Gospel of Matthew —commonly known as the Sermon on the Mount. He had become convinced that Jesus was not a religionist, but a revolutionary, and he was prepared to act on what he could learn about him.

And so he went to the ROTC camp, his ear finely tuned to what his growing awareness of conflicting commitments might be trying to say to him.

At camp early one morning he committed to memory passages in the fifth chapter of Matthew:

Ye have heard that it hath been said; An eye for an eye and a tooth for a tooth: But I say unto you, that ye resist not evil: but whosoever shall smite thee on thy right cheek, turn to him the other also. . . . Ye have heard that it hath been said, Thou shalt love thy neighbor, and hate thine enemy: But I say unto you, Love your enemies, bless them that curse you, do good to them that hate you, and pray for them which despitefully use you, and persecute you: That ye may be the children of your Father which is in heaven: for he maketh his sun to rise on the evil and on the good, and sendeth rain on the just and on the unjust.

Later Clarence told his friend P. D. East: "The class that day was a drill held on the edge of the woods. It was a mounted drill and I was on horseback. We were supposed to gallop through the woods with our pistols and sabers. We were to shoot our pistols. at the cardboard dummies and stick the straw dummies with our sabers. Every time I would shoot at one of those cardboard dummies, that verse, 'But I say unto you, love your enemies . . .' would flash through my mind. I tried to swap places in my mind, where I would be the dummy and he would be the one on the horse. At that moment I saw the conflict between the mind of Jesus and the mind of the commanding officer. It was crystal clear that this Jesus was going one way and I another. Yet I called myself his follower."

When Clarence broke out into the open on the other side of the woods, his choice seemed clear to him. He dismounted, approached the commanding officer, and announced he was resigning his commission. In the ensuing conversation, the officer suggested sympathetically that perhaps he would become a chaplain.

"I told him," Clarence said, "that that would be worse than ever. I could not encourage someone else to do what I myself would not do."

And so he abruptly ended his military career, instinctively making the choice between what he recognized to be incompatible inclinations. He returned to Athens and requested the First Baptist Church to license him to preach. His request was granted, and the statement he read before the congregation reflected his determination and his idealistic spirit:

If, according to popular opinion, being called to the ministry means spending all night in prayer, fighting constantly that voice which persistently speaks, being borne on the floods of passion, or having an "experience"—I repeat—if it means all that, I doubt very much that I have been called. But if being called to the ministry means lending an attentive ear to a simple statement, "My child, I want you to preach for me," then most assuredly I have been called to the ministry.

While I admit that God may choose the former method of speaking to those whom He wishes to preach, nevertheless I contend that it is not necessary, nor is it the only method. Behold a tree. Does it not speak to us thusly: "Don't you see that God is not working Himself into a frenzy in me? I am calmly, quietly, silently pouring forth my life and bringing forth fruit. Do thou likewise."

And so it was with me. No battle was fought. My heart and soul were not torn by doubt, for when His voice came I was sure of its source. My strength was never pitted against His. He spoke. I listened. I can still hear him just as vividly: "My child, I want you to preach for me." You wish my answer? Here it is: "Yes, Lord, whatever you say, just promise me that you'll go with me." "And lo, I am with thee always, even unto the end of the world." "Lead on, O Christ, I'll follow." And that's all there was to it.

And so Clarence completed his college years with two major convictions shaping his radical future. And though both convictions were cast more in a negative than a positive light—he would *not* participate in the subtle, tradition-defended oppression of the Negroes; he would *not* yield to the inclination to become a man trained to respond to evil with a more efficient evil—he knew at least that it would be as a preacher and teacher of the Gospels that he would make his push. And it was to this end that he moved next.

Louisville, Kentucky, would hardly be considered "north" from many perspectives. But from Talbotton, Georgia, 100 miles south of Atlanta and 300 miles south of the Kentucky line, Louisville loomed in Clarence's mind as a northern metropolis. It was the home of the Southern Baptist Theological Seminary.

He arrived in Louisville in the fall of 1933 with only a few dollars and the hope that he would work to pay for his seminary tuition. His father's bank and general store had crashed the spring before, leaving the Jordans with their home, a cabbage patch, and two hills of peas. Clarence was on his own.

For a time, he felt out of place on the campus. He was tall (6'2") and skinny, with a boyish face. He wrote in his personal journal: "At first I mistook the students for professors. Everyone looked so distinguished I thought surely he must be a prof."

His ease and gentle wit soon gained him a place in the fellowship of 400 or so students, however, and he settled down to serious grappling with Greek and Hebrew and comparative religions. (His appearance—long-legged, high-hipped—and his hometown, Talbotton, were parlayed quickly into the occasional nickname "Tall Bottom.")

As Clarence began the normal three-year master of theology degree, he made a discovery in the library that he returned to time and again. She was a tall, blonde librarian's assistant with large, ever-so-slightly slanted, pure blue eyes, named Florence Kroeger. He discovered, too, by mere chance, that she was a member of the Clifton Baptist Church. If he had harbored the slightest doubt about joining that church himself, he was now certain that he should.

Apart from the warmth of romance that then blossomed fragrantly around all those books he had to read, little in Clarence's early years at the seminary hinted of the radical departures from tradition that were beginning to take shape in him. In fact, the seminary seemed the last environment that would produce a young preacher who was to go against the strong forces of patriotism and preach a higher calling than the defense of the nation. The program of study was what the administration called "Bible-centered," with heavy emphasis on Greek and Hebrew and little or no word on the application of biblical principles.

The president of the school, J. R. Sampey, was a tall, straight, rigorous, military-looking man with long, hairy fingers who would bellow at the students in chapel: "Some of you low-down rascals ought to get up and go into the chaplaincy." And then he would talk about his hero, Robert E. Lee, "the greatest Christian since Paul." Later, during World War II, he was said to have promised a turkey dinner to the students at Thanksgiving and then reneged, saying that instead an offering would be sent to "that brave General MacArthur and our fighting boys in the Philippines."

On the matter of war, there was only one liberal hope on the faculty during Clarence's years at the seminary, and that was a young teacher who said: "If we go into war in Europe, let's at least not call it a holy war."

But Clarence was there to study, and he never lost his enthusiasm or took time to join any causes. Also, after working odd jobs for nearly a year, he was serving as pastor part time for a series of Kentucky churches—first the Knob Creek Church in Bullit County, then the Mt. Carmel Church on Wilson Creek near Lebanon Junction, and later, concurrently with the Mt. Carmel Church, the Clermont Baptist Church in Clermont.

And too, the blue-eyed assistant librarian occupied his mind at increasingly frequent intervals. At the end of three years, when Clarence was ready to receive his degree, he was confident enough to ask Miss Kroeger's parents for her hand. Her father, Fred Kroeger, a builder who had migrated from Germany around the turn of the century, gave his consent. Her mother, also of German origin but a native of Louisville, smiled and said it probably would not matter to the couple whether she and Mr. Kroeger gave their consent or not—but she approved.

In May 1936, Clarence received his degree, and he and Florence were married in July at her home, with the seminary's Librarian Thomas A. Johnson officiating. "They were a natural match," said seminary friend Peyton Thurman. "She always carried her head just a little higher and had just a little more substance than other girls."

She was, in a word, a strong woman who was quick to air her own opinions but solid in her willingness to do anything she could to give reality to Clarence's increasingly radical views.

The risk of adventure and commitment was there in Florence, and Clarence was encouraged by it. With her support, he moved on to further graduate studies and into deep contact with the Greek New Testament, where he began to discover theological foundations for the human impulses already alive in him. Supplementing his Greek New Testament major, he got involved in Louisville's teeming inner city and began to see firsthand the fragile life of the poor who had been driven off the land in desperation.

It was then that the old visions surfaced stronger than ever in his mind, and the dream of a radical experiment began to take shape that would send him marching counter to the cheering wartime crowds and place him in vigorous confrontation with his heritage.

CHAPTER 2

The Experiment

Clarence plunged hungrily into the strenuous discipline of Greek New Testament study, his imagination fired by Jesus' statement that "man shall not live by bread alone but by every word that proceedeth out of the mouth of God." He wanted the best understanding he could obtain about those "words," and the Greek language was the vehicle that could carry him closest to the original intent of the New Testament record.

Referring to the tedious exercises of conjugating verbs and illustrating points of syntax, he remarked to his friend Frank Stagg, a Greek New Testament major a year behind him: "There's a lot of dishwashing in this, but it keeps you reading the Greek New Testament."

At this point, Clarence accepted the opportunity to teach English New Testament at Simmons University, a Negro seminary in Louisville. His association with the black students led to his first showdown over the issue of brotherhood. In the spring of 1938, the prayer meeting committee at Mullins Hall on the Southern Seminary campus asked Clarence to invite several students from Simmons to conduct the weekly dormitory prayer meeting.

Clarence complied, and at the request of the committee, also invited them to eat supper in the dormitory—the custom with all prayer meeting speakers. But several days before they were to come, the committee informed Clarence that some of the seminary officials objected to the Negroes eating in the dining hall. Mr. Bullard, the business manager, for whom Florence was working as a secretary, was particularly outraged.

Bullard asked Florence about it, and, when she affirmed her support of the idea, he fairly exploded. Clarence and Florence decided then to avoid embarrassment for the guests and invite them instead to have supper in their apartment.

Clarence did confront President Sampey, however. "I reminded him," Clarence said later, "that I had heard him in a chapel talk say he had eaten dinner with a colored deacon in Brazil."

Sampey responded: "I'll do it in Brazil, but I won't do it in Birmingham, Alabama."

"I then told him," Clarence said, "that both my wife and I were working for the seminary, that we were living in seminary property, and that we had invited the Negroes to eat with us, and the seminary could be making up its mind what it would do with us."

The president asked if it were all right with Florence, and Clarence said: "Yes. In fact, she suggested it."

"Well," he said, "if she doesn't mind eating with them, it's your own home and you can do as you please."

When the student body got wind of this, a committee of fifteen or twenty students marched into Sampey's office to demand an explanation for what they considered unchristian conduct. He explained that the administration had been misinformed; it had understood that a Negro chorus had been invited and that the seminary could not afford to accommodate that many visitors at once. Assured that only a few of the black students had been invited, Sampey immediately consented to their eating in the dining hall, and added: "Go tell Jordan and his wife to come up and eat in the hall with them, too."

That fall, Clarence gave up his part-time pastorate at Clermont, Kentucky, in order to concentrate more fully on his studies during his last year of graduate school. Florence had given birth to Eleanor Kroeger Jordan in May, and the new father wanted time at home, too. He no sooner got well into the fall term, however, when a committee of the Long Run Baptist Association (of Southern Baptist Churches in metropolitan Louisville) asked him to take over direction of a little mission known as Sunshine Center in the predominantely black West End. The prospect was intriguing to Clarence, even though he dreaded the pressure it would put on his studies. He took the job, beginning in January 1939.

In the seamy West End area, literally jammed with people ill-equipped for the perils of city living, Clarence encountered the acrid odors and violent convulsions of compacted poverty. Much to his surprise, he discovered that hundreds of the rural families were from Georgia and Alabama.

The ghetto was far from the conscience of white America in 1939, and Clarence showed unusual insight. He changed the mission's name immediately from Sunshine Center to Fellowship Center, to get away from connotations of Little Black Sambo and harmless old darkies. And then he began a program of communication with the neighborhood, using movies and choirs and preachers from nearby Negro churches.

Clarence insisted from the beginning that a joint committee, consisting of the Long Run association's Committee on Negro Work and a similar group appointed by the black Louisville Minister's and Deacon's Meeting, be the governing body of the mission. He was most concerned about creating and advancing opportunities of fellowship between blacks and whites, and he set up such encounters as combined ministerial meetings and combined deacons' meetings between black and white churches.

He also began attending the Negro churches regularly, and eventually considered himself a member of the Virginia Avenue Church. Officially, however, his membership still was in a white Baptist church. When he approached the white Baptist pastor about transferring his letter of membership to the Negro church, he was floored by a storm of indignation. Were not the white Baptists paying his salary and was he not therefore responsible to them? Did not Jesus respect racial boundaries, and did not Paul maintain that he was a Hebrew of the Hebrews? Suppose a Negro were to apply for membership at his church, do you think he would be admitted?

Tension grew until eventually the chairman of the committee appointed by the Southern Baptist Association of Churches to oversee "Negro work" convinced Clarence that he should delay his decision. He agreed, but his notes in his personal journal reflected the resentment he felt:

It appeared to me that it would be just as well to have my [church] letter in the bottom of my trunk as to have it in a church where I never attended and never supported because my work carried me into other churches. This, however, did not matter. It was unethical and unchristian to join a Negro church because it was a Christian principle to abstain from meat if it caused your brother to stumble, and surely this would cause many to stumble. I guess it is also a Christian principle to tear out of the New Testament all those pages which proclaim the universality of the Christian brotherhood and which so terribly upset our complacent social traditions.

In the heat of this encounter, a special committee of the Long Run Baptist Association summoned Clarence to appear before them, and to his surprise, promoted him out of his predicament.

They asked him to become the first full-time superintendent of missions for the association, which meant he would direct all their other cooperative mission projects as well as the Fellowship Center.

Clarence accepted and was given an office in the Broadway Baptist Church, even though he protested that the associational offices should be put in the inner city, "where our preachers will have to wade through the shipwrecks of humanity to get there. I believe they would be better preachers."

Still pursued by the visions of hunger and depravity burned into his mind by previous experiences, Clarence proposed a project called "The Lord's Storehouse," which he hoped would help alleviate the more immediate, pressing problems of the poor as well as give the affluent a feasible way of sharing their abundance. The idea was simple enough. An inner-city store would be established by the churches, with both new and used clothing, appliances, fuel, food, and Bibles. Modest prices would be marked on each item, and the customers would pay all, part, or none, according to their ability to pay.

The churches could support the store with cash or products, and any profits would be plowed back into goods or into operating expenses. The plan, Jordan wrote in a proposal, would provide "a place where, in the name of Christ, destitute people might find enough to hold body and soul together during an emergency," and would create "a centralized outlet for the charities of stronger Baptist churches which might not have cases of acute need in proportion to their ability to meet them."

The idea generated much favorable response, but one key leader in the association opposed it on the grounds that it would put the churches in the mercantile business. He also felt people would not contribute items to be sold, only to be given outright. Though it was futile at the time, Clarence replied with a concept that was to surface again strongly in the last years of his life. As he wrote in his journal:

I was not successful in pointing out that everything would be given away, and that absolutely no pressure would be put on anyone to pay anything. The plan, as I see it, merely gives one an opportunity to contribute to others who might be in the same fix he is in; that is, to share his blessings with others. After all, is that not the plan the Lord uses in his dealings with us?

The storehouse plan was tabled, but the question of what influence a man's faith ought to have on his economic resources apparently continued to tumble end over end in Clarence's mind. An entry in his journal reflected the concept he finally settled on:

The Old Testament required a tithe, but in every instance in the New Testament where the Lord asked for anything, it was for all. Examples of this are: James and John, Peter and Andrew, Matthew, Zacchaeus, the poor widow, parable of the talents (all returned), rich young ruler, etc. Then after Pentecost they all sold their possessions, had all things common, and no one counted that he owned anything. Then when one had paid all into the Lord's treasury, a portion was returned to him "according as he had need." Thus, the basis of "pay" was not what responsibilities one had, nor what he knew, but what he needed. It was certainly possible for the janitor, if his need were greater, to be paid more than the pastor. Is this not the right way? What right has the pastor, for example, to wax fat on the leanness of the janitor? Should the man with one mouth to feed take bread from the man with five or six mouths? Surely our need should determine our income.

But who is to be the judge of our need? This will not be a great problem with those who love their neighbors as themselves, for everyone will not seek the things for himself but for his neighbor.

Clarence was deeply moved by the New Testament passages that referred to the nature of the early Christ followers' fellowship.

And all who believed were together and had all things in common; and they sold their possessions and goods and distributed them to all, as any had need. . . . Now the company of those who believed were of one heart and soul, and no one said that any of the things which he possessed was his own, but they had everything in common. And with great power the apostles gave their testimony to the resurrection of the Lord Jesus, and great grace was upon them all . . ." (Acts 2:44, 45: Acts 4:32, 33).

The coming together and the spirit of sharing, Clarence noted, were in radical proximity to the reference to bearing witness to the resurrection of Jesus. Those early apostles, in fact, were the resurrected body of Jesus—the new body still up to the old works, preaching, teaching, and healing.

"Never did Paul or Peter or Stephen point to an empty tomb as evidence of the resurrection," he said. "The evidence was the spirit-filled fellowship." His mind locked in on the channel of thought: "If that closeness of sharing in a common life exhibited the spirit of Jesus alive in those men, why not now. . . ."

Early in his new assignment, Clarence sought to involve more seminary students in the work of the Fellowship Center and the Negro churches. Bob Herndon, a friend of his who was several years younger, resigned his position as an assistant probation officer in the juvenile court to devote more time to direct mission efforts. Herndon and about a dozen others, including a student named Howard McClain and a young Japanese student named Jitsuo Morikawa, responded enthusiastically to Clarence's appeals.

They agreed to attend and participate in the Negro churches, and to do whatever the congregations called upon them to do. Several had opportunities to preach; a number taught Sunday School classes.

After several months, Clarence completed his doctoral program and began working full time. He was looked to for leadership by the group of students, most of whom were younger and less experienced. Those who continued to participate with him slowly and informally evolved into an on-campus group which met several times a month for study and discussion. Clarence began to toss out his ideas about pacifism, racial equality, and the radical stewardship of complete sharing. As the group became more cohesive, they sought to define themselves. Clarence offered the Greek word *Koinonia* (pronounced coy-no-neé-a).

Koinonia was used repeatedly in Greek New Testament manuscripts and depending on the context, was translated "communion" or "collection" or "fellowship." The word was ·used in the Book of Acts, for example, to describe the fellowship that developed among the early Christian followers when they pooled their possessions, shared their lives, and distributed their common resources to each as he had need. It was a word meant to communicate the fellowship of those who continued to participate in the life of Christ by seeking to carry on his ministry of reconciliation. The students, primarily under Clarence's leadership, were struggling to express the idea of being a fellowship in which individuals both gave to and received from the others in a spirit of sharing. And so they called themselves a koinonia.

They went so far as to establish a bank account into which each participant agreed to deposit any "excess" income. The fund would be available to any one of them in case of emergencies. It never grew by much, nor was it ever drawn on more than one or two times—the students just did not have any "excess."

Howard McClain recalled that Clarence shared with the group

his dream of establishing a farm in the South that could become a resource for the rural poor. And Clarence then added to that vision the prospect that the farm could sustain a fellowship of Christians who pledged themselves to peace and brotherhood and shared their belongings in a common life.

At this time Clarence was much aware of and influenced by the ministry of Walt N. Johnson, a pioneer in Southern Baptist stewardship who sought to catapult the idea of stewardship far beyond church fund-raising to a concept of faithful stewardship of all of an individual's or organization's resources. Johnson published a little shoestring newsletter from his office in Mars Hill, North Carolina, and in the summer of 1941, Clarence read a fascinating exchange of correspondence.

An American Baptist missionary to Burma, Martin England, had written to Johnson, who had published the letter. Skimming down the printed lines, Clarence's eyes were caught and held in the middle of the second paragraph:

I have not been able to explain away the Sermon on the Mount or the 13th chapter of First Corinthians, or lots of other passages in the New Testament, about loving your enemies. I must confess that there are situations in which I fall far short of the demands of the Gospel in that respect, but I do not feel that I can justify my failure by denying the validity or the applicability of Jesus' commands to any phase of life.

. . . as I read the New Testament it seems to me that He meant for those who believe in Him to begin living that way now, regardless of what the unbelievers do. If we are planning to be Christian only when the whole world or unbelievers agree to come in with us, then it will never come to pass.

Clarence must have done a double-take when he read further into the meat of the letter:

Here is what I am really trying to say: If the barriers that divide man, and cause wars, race conflict, economic competition, class struggles, labor disputes are ever to be broken down, they must be broken down in small groups of people living side by side, who plan consciously and deliberately to find a way wherein they can all contribute to the Kingdom according to their respective abilities. Suppose there were some Christian employees and employers, whites and Negroes, farmers and merchants, illiterate and school teachers, who were willing to enter into fellowship to make a test of the power of the spirit of God in eliminating the natural and artificial barriers that exist now—and let none deny they do exist!

The letter-writer took his supposition a step further and wrote:

Suppose each would commit himself fully to the principle that the strong must bear the burden of the weak (mainly by helping, teaching, and inspiring him to bear his own burdens as his strength in this fellowship grows) . . . "to each according to his need, from each according to his ability" in things material as in everything else . . . that each should trust in the spirit of God working in the group to take care of his needs in illness or old age and for his dependants . . . accepting the principle of stewardship and renouncing the anti-Christian and contradictory principle of ownership . . . accepting the principle of the obligation of the Christian to produce all he can and to share all above his own needs.

Whoever this missionary was, he was thinking in the same way that Clarence thought. The need was for experimentation with these ideas Christians had claimed for so long—for a demonstration plot in which the ideas could grow and develop to maturity.

As it turned out, Martin England had been on furlough from his missionary outpost in Burma since 1939. He had come to the United States for a year on leave after serving a full term, and when the war had broken out the American Baptist Board had refused his request to return to Burma without his family. Looking for a place to work out his commitments in the United States, England at first had gone to the University of Florida to audit courses in agriculture—a needed subject in the mission schools he directed—and then, intrigued by an experimental farmers' cooperative started by a Louisville businessman, he had moved to a little Kentucky crossroads called Wakefield in the fall of 1941.

That fall, Clarence met the slender, soft-spoken missionary at a meeting of the Fellowship of Reconciliation in Louisville. They talked, and then they arranged to talk some more—they were resonating on the same frequency.

"This was the tag end of the Depression," England said later, "and people were crowding into Louisville from farms all over the South. The feeling was heavy on Clarence that if something were done to help these people find fruitful lives on the farms they never would have to come to the city with its poor housing, welfare, uncertain employment, and despair.

"He was also concerned about better agricultural training. He didn't want to be a county agent or a professor of agriculture, but he knew he could interpret and demonstrate his knowledge to illiterate farmers. The agricultural experts, you see, never got around to the small farmers, the sharecroppers—these poorest of the poor who were crowding into Louisville. Clarence never seemed to be troubled by doubt or uncertainty at all. He seemed always to have the clearest sort of conviction."

Such resoluteness and confidence enchanted England and he began to share Clarence's dream. Clarence obviously needed a partner, and England was willing. He wanted the agricultural experience, he believed in the concept of community, and he had the free spirit and courage it took to pursue the dream of peace and brotherhood into the Deep South. They began to talk seriously and to determine certain aspects of their vision. The farm they would start would be in the South, because of the religious, social, and economic forces shaping its destiny—and because both men were southerners (England was a South Carolinian).

War was spreading across Europe and the Far East by then, but both men had already resolved not to be a part of the military. England was too old to have to register for the first peacetime draft, which had been enacted into law that summer. Clarence had sought to register as a conscientious objector, but he had been given an automatic ministerial deferment instead. As the two men's excitement grew over what they hoped to do on a farm in Alabama or Georgia, the Japanese struck Pearl Harbor and sprung the United States into the Second World War, stirring that great wave of southern volunteers.

Clarence, of course, continued to be superintendent of missions for the Long Run Baptist Association. One of the mission projects was a place called the Union Gospel Mission, similar in ministry to the Fellowship Center but located in the white poverty district known as the Haymarket. A board of directors was elected to administer the mission, and one of those directors— a Baptist layman named Arthur Steilberg—became intrigued with Clarence and his idealistic vision of starting a farming community in the South.

Steilberg was a maverick of sorts, a strongly individualistic man of German descent who made big money in erratic spurts and dispensed a good share of it in a similar pattern. He was a tender, compassionate man, and yet a loner, and on impulse he could give away money almost as fast as he made it. He started his business and later brought his father into it, calling it H. J. Steilberg & Son. ("I could hardly call it A. J. Steilberg & Father," he said.)

As an erratic member of the Shiveley Baptist Church, Steilberg was asked to be on the board for the Union Gospel Mission and he accepted in an impulsive moment. His encounter with Clarence moved him. "Clarence and I became close friends," he said. "I was attracted by his utter sincerity and by his idealism. He was an idealist like I had never met. He was never anything short of exuberant. He talked to me about Koinonia but said he didn't know how he would do it. I told him when I made money again, I would put a few dollars into it."

Steilberg already was in agreement with Clarence's pacifist position, and, despite his own incorrigible individualism, he was fascinated with the idea of community. He was, however, most fascinated with the man Clarence Jordan. "I was thrilled by Clarence's ideas," he said. "But a lot of it may have just been Clarence. He meant a lot to me. I agreed with his ideas in light of his life."

Early in 1942, H. J. Steilberg & Son won a job in Terre Haute, Indiana, building quartermasters' buildings for the Army. It was acceptable work from Steilberg's own peculiar pacifist view because the buildings were to be used for living quarters, clothing and fuel storage, and transportation equipment—not directly for combat.

He told Clarence that he was about to make some money and that he would make a contribution to his cause. Clarence and Martin immediately started looking for land, expecting that they would be able to raise a down payment with Steilberg's help. In the summer of 1942, they incorporated their dream as Koinonia Farm, Inc., and published a brochure which they mailed to about 500 people to announce their project to friends and to appeal discreetly for support. The brochure did not give priority to "community"—the intention of pooling possessions and sharing alike. This was in the minds of Clarence and Martin but as yet had not been defined as "community."

The brochure described the undertaking as a nonprofit missionary effort "which seeks to combine religious training with actual experience in community service. . . . Devoted to the proclamation of Jesus Christ and the application of his teachings, Koinonia Farm hopes to make a contribution to the lives of all those who suffer and are oppressed; who are bound by ignorance and sin; and who are desperately searching for a way in the wilderness. . . ."

Their intentions were to "relate, through a ministry to both individuals and community, the entire life of the people to Jesus Christ and his teachings. To undertake to train Negro preachers in religion and agriculture. To provide an opportunity for Christian students to serve a period of apprenticeship in developing community life on the teachings and principles of Jesus. To seek to conserve the soil, which we believe to be God's holy earth. . . ."

Clarence and Florence, and Martin and his wife Mabel, instigated a systematic search for land. They wanted an area that was fairly typical of the entire South, and finally decided on Alabama. They examined every rural county in the state from the standpoint of population, ratio of blacks to whites, income, soil types, tenancy, climate, spiritual resources, and so on. Clarence and Martin talked to government and college officials, county agents, and individual farmers.

"We looked at some of the best and some of the poorest land I've ever seen being farmed," England said. "One farmer showed us a pile of hoes and plowshares behind his barn that literally had been worn out on the land. There was little topsoil and a lot of rocks. The man said if corn sprouts up, you have to pull the rocks away from the stem with your hand. And then when it gets up any height, you have to put the rocks back to prop it up."

Tentatively, the two families decided that Chambers and Barbour counties, east of Montgomery on the Georgia line, offered the best opportunity for "typical" farming conditions in the South.

Florence and Mabel responded with amazing grace throughout this burst of enthusiasm and sense of adventure. Florence recalled: "Clarence had told me that he would never make money and never pastor a church again. And I had faith in him. Clarence was not just idealistic; he was also sound. No matter how little we had, I never worried about how we would live, because I knew Clarence could make whatever money was necessary. He worried some about not taking different job opportunities, about whether he was being fair to me and Eleanor, but I told him if he did what the Lord wanted, I knew we would be all right."

Mabel, who had been a partner to Martin during five and a half years in Burma and who had given birth to their three children there, was nothing short of eager to get on with the idea. "It sounded like a real adventure to me," she said.

Florence, however, had to call another time out for herself while the others sought to locate the right piece of land and close a deal. In September, she delivered the Jordans' second child, a healthy boy named James Frederick.

Clarence and Martin were about to settle on a piece of Alabama land when Clarence's eldest brother Frank, who was doing farm appraisal work for the Federal government, suggested that they not complete any deals until they looked in southern Georgia, particularly in the Sumter County area. They went to Sumter County and there, alongside Route 49 about eight miles southwest of Americus, were 440 ordinary-looking acres of soil, slightly eroded and virtually treeless. Through some power of hidden persuasiveness and sense of rightness that passes between man and earth, Clarence said: "This is it." Martin agreed, and they put a few dollars down to hold the property until the deal was closed.

Steilberg stunned them all with his response. He gave Clarence an envelope which Clarence confidently knew would contain as much as $400 or $500—Steilberg was generous that way. But when he opened the envelope his eyes snapped into focus on a considerably larger figure, the exact amount of the down payment on the mortgage, which was due in only a matter of days. Steilberg had prospered in Terre Haute, and he promised Clarence another substantial contribution before the end of the year.

And so with financial backing, an enriching partnership with each other, and the excitement of unpredictability mixed with the confidence of faithfulness, the Jordans and the Englands began mobilizing that fall for an experiment with peaceful ways at home while most of the nation moved full swing into war overseas.

CHAPTER 3

According to the KKK

Autumn does not come swiftly in the South. It wings in softly on subtle breezes behind warm rains and the harvest, gently fades the green to gold, and quietly appeases the fury of summer. The people, according to the measure of their inheritance, relax to enjoy their abundance or tense with the dread of another winter without warmth, while the tired old earth, unmindful of inequity among the stewards, just lulls itself toward winter sleep.

It was in this season, in November 1942, that Clarence Jordan and Martin England stood at the beginning of a pilgrimage and surveyed their portion of southern Georgia coastal plain soil. Large sections of fence were down; erosion scarred the rolling hills. The old sheet-metal barn and tool shed sagged with age. The ancient four-room farmhouse, which had a wide hall running straight through the middle, stood in disrepair.

But all this was good. They saw things that needed doing, they knew where to start, and what they did not know to do they could worry about later. What soured their enthusiasm was the presence of a gruff white tenant farmer and his family, who still occupied the farmhouse. He was to have moved on after the harvest—and he would, shortly, he growled. More bothersome than his skeptical presence was the fact that he acted as though imposed upon and moved with the slow air of authority, as if he owned the place and Clarence and Martin were unexpected and unwanted visitors.

Florence and Mabel had stayed behind with the children until the men could prepare a place for them, so Clarence and Martin accepted the discomforting arrangement and moved into one room of the old house. It was not long, however, before the tenant and his family left and Clarence and Martin could get on with the work of the house.

By Christmas, the house was passable enough for Mabel and the three England children to inhabit. Florence and the two Jordan children moved down to Clarence's home in Talbotton, 50 miles away, to wait until another dwelling could be built.

During the winter, the two men set about planning what and where they wanted to plant, repairing and moving fences, and planting trees—apple, pecan, peach, walnut, pear, plum, fig, apricot, nectarine, Chinese chestnut, Japanese persimmon. They borrowed a mule and a plow to break the ground for a vegetable garden planned for spring, and then—being without such sophisticated capital equipment for regular use—hitched one another to the plow to lay off the rows.

Two preachers in the fury of fresh commitment, panting both fore and aft the plow, aroused a little skeptical curiosity, and the two men began to meet their neighbors.

Clarence had graduated from agricultural school, and Martin had worked on farms as a boy. But managing a farm, much less starting one virtually from scratch, was a staggeringly different proposition. Clarence used to say that in those early days he got up on the rooftop every morning to see what his neighbors were doing. "If they were plowing," he said, "we plowed. If they were planting, we planted." (Clarence was encouraged one morning when shy, professorial Martin turned to him when they were pitching manure and said: "You know, I like the smell of this stuff.")

But their life-style, as well as their lack of experience, gained early visibility and attracted some curious hostility, too. For example, they hired a black farm hand, a former sharecropper whose family was forced to remain on his previous employer's land until his debts were paid. They took their meals together, and several neighboring farmers who came by to welcome them to the community witnessed this breach of tradition.

"We knew there would be hostility," Martin said. "I think what we hoped was that we could make a witness from the beginning and yet not completely alienate ourselves from our neighbors—that we could get to know each other as people. We knew there were some things we hoped eventually to do that we just couldn't do in the beginning. But we also knew there were some compromises we couldn't make. We knew, for example, that we couldn't set the precedent of eating apart from our black friend and then hope to do otherwise later."

Word got around quickly that those preachers were sharing their table with a black man. And one evening as Clarence was standing in the yard, a delegation arrived at the farm with the obvious intent of acting so utterly menacing that the two men would repent on the spot.

As they stepped from their car, one of the men looked at Clarence and said: "We're looking for Clarence Jordan." Clarence identified himself as the others gathered around him silently. He smiled and nodded toward each of them expectantly. No small talk broke the icy silence, however. The spokesman for the group looked Clarence square in the eye and said: "We understand you been taking your meals with the nigger."

Taken aback momentarily, Clarence replied softly. "Well, now, at lunchtime we usually eat with a man we've hired."

Having so deftly wrung a confession from Clarence, the spokesman for the group jumped right to the point and blustered out what they had come to say. "We're from the Ku Klux Klan," he stated, "and we're here to tell you we don't allow the sun to set on anybody who eats with niggers."

There was a tense pause while this soaked in, and Clarence took just a moment to glance at the horizon and note that the sun was ever-so-perceptibly moving on down to its setting position right then. Looking back into the leather-skinned face of his antagonist, which was still cocked with jutting jaw in the concluding gesture of his threat, Clarence cleared his throat and extended the pause to search for a meaningful response.

He knew these kinds of people. He was a southerner, and he was struggling now to make his living the same way they did. In a stroke of inspiration he reached out and seized the man's hand and began shaking it, saying with his best big brother grin: "I'm a Baptist preacher and I just graduated from the Southern Baptist Seminary. I've heard about people who had power over the sun, but I never hoped to meet one."

There was another pause, accentuated this time by the two hands pumping up and down in the air. The man gawked at Clarence in a petrified moment of disbelief, and then he said: "I'm a son of a—I'm a son of a Baptist preacher myself. . . ."

And so they talked and laughed and the old sun went right on down.

Martin faced a similar situation once when he was hoeing near the road. A car with two men, one of whom he knew to be hostile, stopped and called to him to get in for a chat. "I simply refused politely," Martin recalled, "and kept hoeing."

The good humor and poised politeness in the face of these early probes certainly did not imply that the two men knew no fear. That would be overestimating them and underestimating the potential terror of those who wanted to frighten them.

"It was not a question of whether or not we were to be scared," Clarence said, "but whether or not we would be obedient. The revelation in the New Testament that God is no respecter of persons, that he is a God blind to externalities, was clear. There was no quarrel about it, and yet the church had just set this idea aside. We felt that whatever we did, we had to give this project to God on his terms. We knew this flew in the face of the southern code. We knew white men could disappear just like black men. It scared hell out of us, but the alternative was to not do it, and that scared us more."

So, Koinonia Farm was suspect from the start, and the suspicion even extended to the children. The Englands' oldest son, John, was in the third grade, and his stamp collection, which included Burmese and Japanese stamps, aroused the suspicion of school officials. The rumor spread quickly among the school children that the Englands were about to be investigated as suspected spies.

Sure enough, one day as the rural letter carrier was at the Koinonia Farm mailbox to verify it, a dark blue car with a naval insignia on the side, driven by a man who was obviously an officer, turned into Koinonia's driveway. This had to be it. Mabel England, a little nervous about her hair being rolled up, called her husband in from the field and then rushed to greet the polite young Navy lieutenant. She showed him into the house and nervously began making small talk about the days in Burma. That, it turned out, was what he had come to hear.

"He was getting information about Upper Burma from a long list of people who had lived or worked there," Martin said. "The Japanese by that time had occupied that area, and little was known about it."

Although Martin stated at the outset of the conversation that what he knew could be found in a fifth-grade geography book, he did talk with the officer, hoping he was not inadvertantly revealing information that would assist a bombing mission. Later he received a letter written on unmarked paper, sealed in an unmarked envelope, that said if he were interested in a job with "strategic importance" he should write to a certain man at a certain box number. As mysterious as all this was, it seemed clear that the government was more interested in recruiting Martin than in prosecuting him. Martin, however, could not be wooed away from his more pressing responsibilities—he was in charge of the vegetable garden.

At about the same time that Clarence and Martin were refused a permit to build a new residence due to wartime shortage of materials, they did get permission to buy materials for a chicken house. They persuaded Florence, who was still commuting from Talbotton, that it was the government who imposed such priorities, not them.

Poultry was an early experiment. That section of Georgia imported most of its eggs and the two men felt that if poultry farming could succeed in the area, then small farmers and even sharecroppers could raise chickens and produce their own eggs. A friend donated 50 baby chicks, and later a Mennonite poultryman in Virginia who was impressed with Koinonia Farm's objectives sent 500 for a foundation flock.

A neighbor, Rob Hamilton, helped Clarence and Martin build a first-class chicken house. The hens must have been impressed —they produced beyond expectation, attracted the interest of farmers all over southern Georgia, and provided Clarence with the raw material for one of his favorite yarns.

The story goes that one of the farmers stopped by and walked silently and slowly through the chicken house, stooping and craning in his investigation. Then he turned to Clarence and drawled: "They told me you had some kind of a special nest with a chute under it that rolled the egg right out to a basket, and when the hen stands up and looks to see her egg, she thinks she hasn't laid one so she sits down and lays another."

About that new chicken house, Martin recalled: "We figured we could live in tumble-down houses, but if those hens were going to produce, they had to have good housing." Mabel added: "I begged them several times to put me in the new chicken house. It didn't leak, it was well heated, and it would seat 2,000!"

She probably did not consider the suggestion as farfetched as the men did. The old house she moved into that first winter—the original old four-room farmhouse—was run-down and crawling with insects, and in fact was referred to as the "rabbit hutch" after the Englands moved out two years later. The only running water was a pipe through the kitchen wall from the well. The fleas were steadfast roommates, and Mabel finally took an old farm woman's tip and scattered mothball flakes under the bottom sheets of the beds. The odor was irritating, but the fleas no longer were.

Housing was a problem, even though financially the project was on pretty stable ground. Steilberg's steady assistance covered more than half of the $11,000 purchase price, and many other friends were sending contributions in the amount of one acre of land ($25). But during those war years, building materials were scarce and building permits hard to come by. Florence, six-year-old Eleanor, and four-month-old Jim were kept waiting through the winter in Talbotton. Clarence finally decided to build a "shop"—a two-story frame building with an open-ended shop downstairs and living quarters upstairs. The idea qualified for a building permit, and early in 1943 he and Martin began construction. The house was completed in April and Florence finally became a resident member of the group again.

With the two families intact, they officially inaugurated community life. Martin suggested a family allowance format for handling family expenses. He had in mind that he and Clarence would estimate their income for the year and then budget a modest amount for each family, which then would be responsible for managing its own economic affairs. Clarence, whose idea from the beginning had been to pattern their community life after the sharing described in the second chapter of the Book of Acts, rejected this. He insisted instead on a "total community" concept in which all goods and income would be held in common and funds for individual needs would be meted out by the community. The others acquiesced and Clarence's way was implemented. They lived as one large family, discussing together all the major decisions, from buying clothing and groceries to making the capital investments for equipment necessary to launch a farming program.

Ministries to the rural Sumter County neighborhood were a primary concern from the beginning. The county had about 24,-oo6 residents, half of whom were black and either lived in "niggertown" in Americus or in old shacks rented from white farmers. Sharecropping, although on the decline since the depression years, was still common. The separate-but-equal school system was deplorable, if for no other reason than that the county did not provide transportation for the black children to get to school.

When the Jordans and the Englands managed to obtain extra wartime gas ration stamps to take Negro children to school, school officials actually protested to the rationing board. They were rebuffed, however. A county resident who actively opposed such interference by Koinonia then pulled a stunt that infuriated Clarence and caused him to lapse temporarily from his position against violence.

The resident wrote to Clarence's father in Talbotton, saying that Clarence was endangering his family by stirring up the Negroes and defying local custom. J. W. Jordan at this time was old and seriously ill. His wife had died of Bright's disease in 1935 and he had suffered a heart attack in 1940. In 1943 he was again in a state of deteriorating health, and he naturally was alarmed by the message from Sumter County. Unaware of this communication, Clarence stopped by Talbotton to visit his father on a return trip from a speaking engagement. He was greeted emotionally with expressions of concern about his family, and when the situation spun into focus for him, he left in a rage for Americus. He bombed into town, slammed to a halt at the resident's office and stormed in unannounced.

He recalled later: "That was, I suppose, one of the times I came nearest to losing my faith." He climaxed his presentation by saying: "I try to follow Jesus and he has taught me to love my enemies, but I don't see how I can do that in this case." Then, pushing forward his 6-foot-2-inch, 185-pound frame, he added for emphasis that if the man ever communicated with his father again: "I'll just have to ask Jesus to excuse me for about 15 minutes while I beat the hell out of you."

Koinonia accomplished gestures of goodwill in the neighborhood that were less intimidating to the white folks. They conducted vacation Bible school and Sunday School for neighboring children, mostly black. The poultry business thrived, and Koinonia shared its knowledge and helped a number of farmers establish their own flocks. Eventually, Koinonia set up an egg-grading and marketing cooperative when other farmers ran into difficulties. A half-dozen or so white farmers in the area participated.

Clarence developed the first mobile peanut harvester during those early war years when manpower was so crucial. By designing a way to attach an elevator, bin, and wheels to a stationary mechanical peanut-picker, he cut the needed work crew from sixteen to only three or four. His crude but workable improvisation again attracted the interest of farmers and engineers, but he sought no profit for Koinonia from the idea. Large farm implement companies were producing refined, economical models within a few years.

The Koinonians also established a cow library, from which large poor families could check out a milch cow free of charge, return her when she was dry, and check out another one. And they were among the first in the area to experiment with a hog-farrowing barn and a system of planned farrowing. As Koinonia gained economic stability, contributions of money that still were coming in were shifted to neighborhood concerns, such as a fund for a well at one of the Negro schools.

Clarence made frequent use of the sound motion picture equipment he had purchased for his work in Louisville and periodically showed films on agriculture, religion, cooking, mechanics, and so on. And always, Koinonia intentionally grew more vegetables and fruit for home consumption than it needed and shared the abundance with the neighbors who needed it most.

What was perhaps one of their best long-range ideas—the idea of establishing a seminary for local black pastors—never hatched. When they were in Louisville, Clarence and Martin had talked about combining classroom study of the Bible with agricultural training, thus helping the students not only to preach more knowledgeably but to offer some modern farming expertise to their parishioners. The farm and their other activities consumed their energies like a whirlpool, however, and Clarence was already in demand as a speaker and Bible teacher nationwide. And so they never pursued it.

The two families joined the little rural Rehoboth Baptist Church nearby and sought to make contributions as teachers, song leaders, and supply preachers. They were received well for a time, and their talents were used. Clarence preached frequently and often led the singing. He was a popular speaker in Sumter

County and the surrounding areas for several years, addressing church groups and graduating classes frequently until his radical messages finally undermined his charm and cut off invitations to speak.

Nationwide, however, he was in increasing demand as a Bible teacher. He was well equipped academically, and he had a down-home warmth and charisma as well as a thundering radicalism and a jolting earthiness: "We'll worship the hind legs off Jesus, but never do a thing he says." Student groups and pastors' conferences began calling on him regularly and his extensive lecturing began attracting student work teams to Koinonia Farm on week-ends and for summer months. A web of communication was beginning to develop that eventually generated such a momentum of interest that talking with visitors became one of the farm's major industries.

Clarence discovered later that he had seeded radical ideas of commitment into the minds of young men and women who later were to pitch their lives into the Koinonia experiment. In fact, one of those important contacts was made during the summer of 1942, when Clarence and Martin were still in Louisville playing armchair farmer.

Howard Johnson, a quiet, rangy Auburn University agricultural student from East Tallassee, Alabama, was peddling books in North Carolina that summer—a biography of General MacArthur and a family Bible. He worked his way to Asheville and then out several miles to the Ridgecrest Baptist Assembly, where he attended the Southern Baptists' student week activities. Clarence was there, teaching a seminar on the Sermon on the Mount, and his remarks about racial reconciliation jarred the Alabama boy.

"This was such an eye-opener," Howard recalled. "There was a terrific discussion in the final session, I remember, over whether or not Negro students should be invited to those conferences. I had already begun to question the compatibility of segregation with Christianity, but this was the first minister I had ever seen who stood up in public to take a position like this."

Clarence also described his dream of Koinonia Farm in the seminar, and Howard was intrigued. He promised to stay in touch. In August 1942, Clarence wrote to Howard giving him further details of his intentions: "At first we'll set up simply as farmers, trying to win the confidence of the people and establishing ourselves as good neighbors and citizens. When we feel that we are a part of the community, and are accepted as such, we'll try to bring in some of the principles we cherish. In this way, it will be a growth from within, rather than being a system imposed from without. As soon as conditions will permit, we want to bring in others, such as a doctor, nurse, agriculturists, mechanics, etc., so as to make the community self-supporting and dominated and pervaded by the Spirit of the Lord. We'll hold all things in common, distribution will be made to each according to his need, and every worker will be given equal voice in its government."

In February 1943, Howard and another Auburn student, Henry Dunn, visited Koinonia. ("I remember," Howard said with itchy nostalgia, "that we slept on the kitchen floor of that old farmhouse.") In March, however, Howard went into the Air Force "without questioning the decision." But Koinonia was on his mind.

Shortly after Howard's February visit, Clarence spoke at Religious Emphasis week on the campus of Stetson University in Florida. Harry Atkinson of Florida, a short, stocky, dark-complected, preministerial student, heard him speak.

"So many of us in those days had studied and been moved by the ideas of the New Testament," Harry said, "but we faced a real struggle in trying to live them out. Clarence came and I was really attracted to his brotherhood and peace themes. Even though I was exempt from the wartime draft, my conscience was not satisfied. After hearing Clarence, I began to define clearer positions for myself."

That summer, Harry encountered Clarence again, this time at the Ridgecrest Baptist Assembly's annual student week activities. "Friends of missionaries to Africa were visiting," Harry said, "but they were not allowed to stay on the assembly grounds. Clarence publicly raised sand over this, and it really pushed me to his position." Harry visited Koinonia before returning to school that fall, and his exposure to community life confirmed what he figured was already inevitable—he was coming back.

In 1944, an articulate, liberal young minister named Conrad Browne, a conscientious objector to the war, secured a job in Washington, D.C., with the National Service Board for Religious Objectors. A friend invited him to a revival meeting, a less-than-attractive offer for an outgoing young liberal. But his friend assured him that the visiting preacher, a Georgia farmer, was "something else." So Con gave in and attended the meetings at the Calvary Baptist Church. Clarence's preaching, and most particularly his persuasive comments about Christian life-style, captured Con's imagination. He went on the next year to the University of Chicago's divinity school without meeting Clarence again, but, as he put it: "I wrote so much about koinonia in my papers at the university of Chicago that one of the professors asked me if I couldn't write about something else."

Meanwhile, the Englands ended their partnership with Clarence and Florence. The American Baptist Mission Board had decided that the war was subsiding in the Far East, and they recalled Martin and Mabel in September 1944 for a period of training at Cornell University that was to precede their return to Burma. The work in Burma was their first commitment, and so they responded.

That same month, Harry Atkinson decided to drop out of school and spend the fall at Koinonia Farm. For one thing, he knew he could be of service, since Martin and Mabel were leaving and Clarence already had scheduled a full speaking itinerary. And for another, he wanted to take a closer look at this experiment in communal living.

The only other people on the place were the Candy Johnsons, a Negro family. Candy had wanted to work, but he had not been interested in community, so Clarence had set him up on a sharecropping arrangement and let him live in a house across the road that remained from earlier tenant days. A sharecropper usually came with nothing and the landowner was responsible for "furnishing" him—with food and a little cash—until he worked a crop. In fact, it was at this point that so many tenant farmers were exploited. They would be furnished by the farmers, and then at the end of the season, the farmers would deduct exorbitant costs from the tenants' income to cover the shacks and the modest provisions.

A man does not gain from year to year on that kind of deal, and so Candy had arrived emptyhanded and asked to be furnished. Meat had been especially scarce at the time, so Clarence had flushed a wild sow out of the swamp and shot her. Candy had gone to work with at least plenty of pork and fresh vegetables in his storehouse.

Harry stayed through the fall, went back to school for a quarter, and then returned to Koinonia in March 1945. He considered himself a part of the community, even though he was a little skeptical of the idea. There were no rules or membership requirements at that time, but Harry put what little money he had into the common purse.

In June he left for Southwestern Baptist Theological Seminary in Fort Worth, and Koinonia helped to pay his tuition. "I had come to Koinonia with very little assets," he said, "but I had given them. So the community was taking responsibility for me. I worked, but I had the assurance of knowing that I could write for money if I needed to."

Clarence sort of spoiled Harry's send-off to school by pestering him about an ill-fated romance at Stetson. When Harry was pulling out of the driveway, Clarence yelled: "Don't go out and marry the first girl you meet in Texas."

Harry recalled: "That really riled me up. I was sensitive about that. But the funny thing was, the first girl I met in Texas was Allene Griffin, who worked in the registrar's office at the school. I married her three years later."

While Harry was at school, the Jordans were alone for several years. Then they were joined by a young schoolteacher, Willie Pugh, who had heard Clarence speak when she was a student at Blue Mountain College in Mississippi. The Jordans' third child, Janet Elizabeth, also was born in December 1946.

In the winter of 1948, Harry returned from Texas convinced that he wanted to live at Koinonia Farm and bearing the news that he and Allene were to be married. He and Clarence cut pine trees and milled lumber for another house. (Mabel England's "rabbit hutch" had burned, unceremoniously and without regrets, by this time.) In April, with the house nearly complete, Harry went to Texas, returned with Allene, and they were married at the Rehoboth church.

Meanwhile, Howard Johnson had mustered out of the Army Air Corps and returned to complete his studies at Auburn. He had corresponded with Clarence during the war years, and Clarence had written him on one occasion in a prophetic vein: "Some day, maybe sooner than you think, you'll be in civilian life. No doubt you've given some serious thought as to how you will invest your life so that it'll count most for Christ and His Kingdom. I know neither your thoughts nor your plans, but I do want you to know that the door is wide open to you here at Koinonia. I believe we're on the trail of something, Howard, and it's not just a rabbit."

Back at Auburn, Howard maintained his contact through frequent visits and correspondence with Clarence. Clarence consulted him frequently by mail on knotty farming questions, and Howard kept Clarence supplied with up-to-date farm bulletins. In the spring of 1949, Howard completed school and decided to come to Koinonia Farm, giving warning, however, that he intended to continue commuting to Auburn on his big Harley-Davidson to court Marion Rutland, who still had another year of school.

The clincher in Howard's struggle for decision really had come after he went to Hawaii the summer before as a student summer missionary for Southern Baptists. "An editorial in the *Hawaii Herald* had really gotten after us," he said, "asking what business we had coming to teach Hawaiians about Christianity. There were 14 or so of us and we were shocked at this reaction from the newspaper. The races had lived together there for generations, the editorial said, and who were we to come in from the South and talk to them about how to live."

The editorial turned Howard upside down. "That was sort of a final straw," he recalled. "I was already convinced that I had to find a situation where compromise with segregation would not be involved. And I was a farmer. So I took off for Koinonia Farm. I didn't know if I was going to stay, but I felt it was the best expression I could find for what I believed. Aspects of the Gospel that had just been theory began to be real to me."

(Howard was blasting back and forth on his Harley-Davidson to court Marion, but he loaned the big motorcycle to Clarence for a trip or two. Clarence made a bold trip in January of 1950 on the bike to Bucknell College in Pennsylvania and nearly froze to death. It was like spring when he and a newcomer to Koinonia, Norman Long, left on the Harley, but the temperature plummeted as they roared north. After they had put on every piece of clothing they had with them, they finally stopped and bought a Sunday newspaper, went into a service station restroom, and stuffed their shirts and trousers with paper. When they arrived at the college president's home they looked like a couple of frosted scarecrows, their faces burned by the cold wind. "Even when I took my goggles off, it looked like I had them on," Clarence said. He parked the bike in the driveway of the president's home, only to discover the next day that the president had just recently banned motorcycles on campus.)

In the summer of 1949, Con Browne managed to get on a student team to represent the University of Chicago at an American Baptist Conference at the denomination's assembly in Greenlake, Wisconsin, unaware that Clarence was to be one of the featured teachers. If the idea of community had intrigued him before, it fairly floored him in this second encounter with Clarence. He told Clarence: "If my wife wants to come, I'll be down immediately. If she doesn't, I'll have to stay home long enough to make arrangements for her, and then I'll come."

He probably felt certain, however, that his tough little redheaded wife would be game for such an adventure. Ora Browne thought it was a good idea. "He had talked about community so much," she said, "and if he had gotten into a church situation, he would have had a hard time breaking away to try community. This was the ideal time."

During this time, other young men were going through traumatic experiences to get to Koinonia. The war and its aftermath had spun many into a web of disturbing moral questions, and they were looking for some new expression of life that would help heal the hurt that came from being swept off in directions they did not believe were right. "Misfits" was what they would be called eventually because they did not want to fight. But several of them found a place in this peculiar experiment in southwestern Georgia.

CHAPTER 4

War and the True Son

War had raged and then simmered during those years when Clarence and Florence were struggling to hold a dream together. Hitler had been crushed, the Japanese had been stunned into submission, and yet stability had not been achieved. In 1948, with the ring of the bombs and cannons of World War II only beginning to recede in the memories of the nation, the prospect of a Third World War arose and squelched the hope for an easing of tension.

It was then that the second peacetime military conscription fell upon the nation. The draft was a dangerous subject politically because senators and congressmen had to think about the families of those three to four million nonveterans who would be eligible, and about the families of those weary veterans. But the President and the Secretary of Defense shook the politicians to their senses. Their attitude was: Listen! Western Europe is virtually defenseless and Stalin looks hungry. We have only 100,000 troops in Europe facing nearly two million potentially hostile Soviet troops. We only have a handful of men in South Korea—and look what is happening in China . . . in Germany . . . in Finland . . . in Czechoslovakia . . . in Palestine . . . in Greece. . . .

What were the politicians to do? Obviously the nation's last retreat into isolationism had been blown back to reality at Pearl Harbor. Strength was necessary for peace. And so the draft, dreaded politically and spiritually, became a permanent reality in the United States in June 1948. That fall, men between 18 and 25, veterans and nonveterans alike, would register for their opportunity to become part of a peacetime conscript army.

By this time, of course, Clarence was 36 years old and beyond draftable age. He had applied for conscientious objection status in the 1940 draft, but he had been granted an automatic ministerial deferment instead. He had pestered his draft board through the war years until it had finally altered his status to III–A, which meant that eventually he could have been drafted and then made his stand for CO status. It never happened, however, and now another generation of young men faced a new draft. Clarence moved to support those who felt it compromised their beliefs to even register for a draft. He put his name to a petition signed by 300 ministers around the country that urged young men to refuse to register for the new Selective Service System.

He recognized the awesome responsibility of such a stand. Conscientious objection was a relatively new phenomenon in the country, much less a movement to refuse registration all together. The war years proved there was a little sympathy in the nation for those who refused to serve. As World War II had moved into full tilt in Europe and in the Pacific, the plight of the conscientious objector had dropped from public discussion. In fact, from July 1943 to April 1945, only one of the widely read national publications printed an article about COs, and it reported only the "troublemakers."

Such coverage reflected the public's disinterest and contempt for the COs' position, but even more, it failed to communicate the authentic motivation of men, who, for reason of their faith, refused to support the military machine. Thousands of these men worked in soil conservation and volunteered for special projects, such as serving as attendants in mental hospitals to relieve an acute shortage of personnel. Some trained as smoke jumpers to fight forest fires, and hundreds of others served as human guinea pigs, drinking infected water, eating materials that included human waste, exposing themselves to malaria-bearing mosquitoes, and lying in bed for months in plaster casts to test medical theories about the dangers of immobilizing limbs. One large group braved a semistarvation diet with forced exercise, and then spent a year trying to recuperate.

All this, but the government paid no wages to COs, paid no allowances to dependants, provided no reemployment rights or educational benefits under the GI bill, and paid no discharge bonuses—fringe benefits that accrued to the COs who accepted noncombatant roles within the military. Many states, in fact, created laws banning the nonmilitary COs from civil service, and in some states such COs even lost the right to vote, to serve on juries, or to make contracts. In 1946, the Supreme Court upheld Illinois in its refusal to admit a lawyer to the bar because he was a conscientious objector. That same year some 3000 COs still remained in prisons, branded as felons for their refusal to cooperate with the Selective Service System.

The war years also revealed that COs could not count on main-line church groups for support. Early in World War II, as in the previous global conflict, church leaders had struggled to make a moral stand against the war, but as before, they had withered under the reports of atrocities and allowed the "just war" fever to infect them.

During these years, however, Clarence's thoughts about war had radicalized. Despite the atrocities of the Nazis, he still would accept no rationalization for war.

"Nowhere is it immoral to be killed," he said, "but it is immoral to kill." You love your enemies, he said, because that is what it is to be a son of God—not because it would save the nation or convert the enemy. The nature of a "son of the spiritual Father" is not determined by the reaction of the enemy but by his relationship to the Father. Sons will increasingly become partakers of the Father's nature, he said. If the Father loves all men regardless of what they are, if he is a Father of steadfast love and redemptive purpose, can the true son hold to a lesser ideal?

Clarence could raise a storm of discussion at any gathering, as he did on one occasion when he asserted that being king or president was ruled out for the Christian. Such an official, he argued, had to transfer all his allegiance to the wrong deity.

"The President is Commander in Chief of the Army and Navy, isn't he?" he asked. "What, then, in the name of Jesus, is he going to command the Army and the Navy to do?" Clarence's position was that he would cooperate with the health department and other areas of government, but not with the military structure. "I'll render unto Caesar what is Caesar's," he said, "but I'll not render unto Caesar what is God's." When a government wants to hand a man a gun and order him to shoot another human, he argued, it is conscripting a man with God's image stamped on him and asking him to shoot another made in the same image.

Asked what he would do if he were a Christian German during Hitler's reign who was hiding Jews in his home, and German soldiers banged on his door, Clarence replied: "If you were a Christian in Germany during those times and you knew what was happening to the Jews, and you waited until the soldiers came and banged on your door to make a decision, I would question your commitment. The loving thing to do would have been to put the Star of David on your own arm and get in the concentration camp with the Jews. If more Germans had done that, the concentration camps would have had to be different."

"God's revelation of himself is a terrifying thing, because we can no longer plead ignorance," Clarence stated. "A soldier is not trained to go and die for his enemies. There is no redemptive purpose in it [soldiering] and there is no analogy with the incarnation and crucifixion."

Clarence taught that the Bible revealed a graduated level of understanding about violence. In the Old Testament, the "life for a life, eye for an eye, tooth for a tooth" attitude represented a law of limited retaliation that was a giant step beyond the unlimited, destructive retaliation that might characterize a jungle. And then, the "limited love" expressed in "love your neighbor but hate your enemy"—in other words, forgive one of your own kind if he harms you, but retaliate against an outsider—was a step beyond limited retaliation. Jesus, Clarence said, was the final revelation in word and deed of the nature of the Father when he demonstrated and preached unlimited love: not only do you love your friends, you love your enemies also. To a student who used the Old Testament as a foundation for an argument that the Bible teaches a just use of violence, Clarence replied: "Any man who has looked on Calvary cannot live like he is looking on Sinai."

Told by a friend about a headstone in Mississippi that reads: "Here lies J. H. S. In his lifetime he killed 99 Indians and lived in the blessed hope of making it 100 until he fell asleep in the arms of Jesus," Clarence said in one lecture: "Now you could kill 99 Indians in Mississippi and fall asleep in the arms of Jesus and be buried in the Baptist cemetery. But if you killed one white man in Mississippi you fell asleep in the noose. It's all right to drop a bomb on Nagasaki or Hiroshima and obliterate 250,000 people of color, but you kill one American and you don't get a medal like the fellow who dropped the atomic bomb—you get the electric chair.

"We've learned to limit our love to our own race, to our own people, and we think it's not murder beyond that," he said. "But Jesus takes us beyond that to unlimited love. Now, if you are going to love your enemies and your friends, there is no one left to hate. This is not practical, this does not convert the enemy. Jesus is simply saying, 'I want you to love your enemies so you can be sons of the Father.'

"It seems to me that we Christians have an idea here that the world is in tremendous need of. We need to say that we know the way, the way of love and peace. We will not confront the world with guns and bombs, but we will confront the world with our utter helplessness except for the strength of God."

Clarence enjoyed using as an illustration of this subject his own embellished account of the time an old farmer stated to him with obvious distaste: "I heard you won't fight."

Clarence replied: "Who told you that? We sure will fight."

Surprised, the farmer said: "Well, you won't go in the Army, will you?"

Clarence said: "No, we don't fight that way. Let me explain. You see that mule over there? Well, if that mule bit you, you wouldn't bite it back, would you?"

"Nope," the farmer allowed, "I'd hit him with a two-by-four."

"Exactly," Clarence replied. "You wouldn't let that mule set the level of your encounter with him. You would get a weapon a mule couldn't use and knock his brains out. That's what Christians are supposed to do—they are supposed to use weapons of love and peace and goodwill, weapons that the enemy can't handle."

(According to one of Clarence's children, Clarence had another experience with a mule that he never used as an illustration. The story goes that Clarence walked past the mule one day and it kicked him. In a burst of anger, he turned and kicked the mule back—and the mule never kicked him again.

(Around 1965, with U.S. involvement in the Vietnam war escalating, Jordan wrote a satirical piece on the Selective Service

System in which he made a strong case for why we have to have the draft: "Most people today are too civilized to go to war voluntarily." He urged one change in the draft law, however, and called on the nation to draft the boys at 65.

(The 18- to 26-year-olds may be the best killers, but they're "too reckless, too flighty, and too sexy" and too much time and money has to be spent training them, he argued. Middle-aged men would be good, but they're too productive. They have to stay home and make the bombs and planes and napalm, "without which there can be no peace." But senior citizens? "They wouldn't even have to be drafted. If we gave them the opportunity they would volunteer in droves. No man is more anxious to fight than one who is sure he's too old."

(The advantages: At 65, a man would not likely have a weeping sweetheart, and this would cut down on the boom of war babies, an important factor in the population explosion. Wives would go with them to wash and iron and make them come home, so the elderly GIs would be less likely to turn a foreign city into a brothel and "burden its citizenry with illegitimacy." Too, men 65 or over have a passion for travel; the government would only have to equip them with camper-trailers "to have the world's most mobile military establishment."

(And perhaps most important, the morale of such an army would be boundless. "Unlike a youngster at 19, the senior citizen would have had long years to reflect on the bliss of private enterprise and the gross evil of communism. Without any hesitation, he would know what's worth dying for, and would gladly and eagerly spill his iron-poor blood." Many of the troops would be directors and chairmen of the boards of huge corporations with war contracts. "Given the opportunity to execute the wars they've helped plan and that have made them rich, their zeal would have no limits. Well may it be said of such a gallant soldier: 'His strength is as the strength of ten, because his heart's corrupt.' "

(Certain exceptions would have to be made to provide the greatest morale stimulus. The President, for example, even though not yet 65, should be allowed "to don his shorts and join his men and women in the field. Add to this the presence of the armed services committee and the appropriations committee, and morale would be at fever intensity." The House Un-American Activities Committee, too, "has repeatedly demonstrated its uncanny ability to detect with infallible accuracy all shades of communists, comsymps, and fellow travelers. Even though some of the members are not physically old enough for the draft-at-65, the services of the entire committee are so vital to the national welfare that it should be allowed to enlist as a body."

(The economic advantages are worth noting. Only two recruitment centers would be needed—one in Florida and one in California. Physical examinations could be eliminated since there would be almost universal disability. Salary would not be needed since the elderly GIs already would be on social security, old-age pensions, and annuities. "They could go at their own expense," Also, "if it could be so arranged that casualties would be quite high, there would be a sizable reduction in the cost of Medicare." The costly Veterans Administration probably could be eliminated too, since "a maimed man of this age would hardly consider it worth the effort to learn the use of artificial arms and legs. Nor would he likely want to go to college, or buy a house over a 40-year period. And because the crop of veterans would disappear so quickly, we could fight at least twice as many wars without overburdening ourselves with them." Expensive training centers also could be eliminated, "When a man is that old, he can be sent straight into action, because he's about as trained as he'll ever be."

(Another consideration is that when young men are killed off, the nation can never be sure of its loss—one of them might have been a future Einstein or Alexander Graham Bell. "When you kill a boy right out of high school or college it's like junking a new automobile fresh off the assembly line. We wouldn't long tolerate such waste. Wouldn't we insist on first getting some mileage out of the car? The same goes for our boys. Let's run them until they're at least 65 before junking them. Since elderly GIs would have already been fully depreciated, the generals could afford to be more lavish with them than with more valuable soldiers. If our casualty rates ran two, three, or even four times higher than the enemy's, so what? We might be losing men, but not valuable man-years."

(One final consideration: "This army would have no equal in the art of pacification. In its ranks would be retired bankers and insurance company executives who could completely rebuild the crude economic structure of any foreign country. . . . In mere weeks after storming the beaches, all these mighty architects of the American Dream, these wrinkled but wise GIs, would transform alien lands into prosperous territories ready for statehood. With prospects of such affluent bliss, most countries would actually invite us to invade them . . . It might be necessary to have a war waiting list . . .")

Clarence believed that it would be better for churches not to teach children the biblical lessons of loving their enemies and refusing to kill, rather than teaching such ideas and then complacently permitting their youngsters to be conscripted, trained, and sent out to do just the opposite. That sort of spiritual schizophrenia troubled many a returning soldier after World War II, and perplexed many other young men who were faced with the postwar draft registration. In 1947 there were two such young men at Mercer University, about 60 miles from Koinonia Farm—Jack Singletary and Millard Hunt.

Millard had knocked around Georgia Tech in Atlanta before being drafted in 1945 on the last day of the war. Ironically, he had tried to enter the Army right out of high school a few years earlier but had flunked the physical because of his eyes. Apparently the standards were lowered, because he was drafted at the end of the war and served 12 months before being discharged in December 1946. He entered Mercer University in Macon, Georgia, in the fall of 1947 as a preministerial student. His ambition was to be a youth worker or possibly a director of a Baptist Student Union on some college campus. It was at Mercer that he learned of the Koinonia experiment.

"Probably I heard of Koinonia from Jack Singletary," he said. "There were several of us who were interested in Christian community and we organized work parties on several weekends to visit Koinonia. But it was in the summer of 1948 when I read an article about 300 Christian ministers who were circulating a petition urging young men to refuse to register for the draft if the new Selective Service Act passed Congress and became law. This seemed way out and I remember wondering what Clarence would have to say. I went down especially to ask him about it. I remember we were sitting under a tree near his house when I asked him. He grinned characteristically and said: 'Well, I can't be against it—I'm one of the 300 ministers who signed it.' "

Before the summer was out, Millard and Jack had moved to the position of noncooperation. The Selective Service Act was passed into law and a timetable for registration was published. Jack already was notorious for having joined a black church, and was under pressure from the Ku Klux Klan, the police, and his landlord. What's more, his wife was pregnant, he was a student,and he was only nine days from being too old to have to register. (He had spent four years in the Navy during the war.)

Both men gave written statements to the local draft board,

stating that they refused to register on the grounds of their Christian faith. "They didn't know what to do from there, and neither did we," Millard said. "I went off to a Baptist student conference in northern Georgia. The whole thing hit the papers while I was gone. I was a candidate for president of the state Baptist Student Union, but that possibility ended abruptly."

Millard returned to the campus between the summer and fall quarters and helped produce a special issue of the Baptist student newspaper. When registration for the fall quarter began, he passed out the papers in the registration line, but when he attempted to register himself for classes, he was asked not to register. One of the religion professors arranged for Millard to meet with a school official.

"We didn't discuss the morality of any of it," Millard said. "He just indicated that it was bad enough to have someone join a colored church, but to have someone not even patriotic enough to fight for his country was just too much. He said for me not to step on campus again."

Meanwhile, Jack had been working in a service station and trying to keep his apartment. He did not try to register at the school. "It really wasn't my intention to return," he said. "I didn't feel like pushing the legal aspects of the case. I saw my involvement as part of a moral struggle to discover life for myself."

FBI agents arrested the two men in October, but the trial was not scheduled until the next April. Jack and his wife spent the interim at Koinonia Farm; Millard remained in Macon but visited Koinonia frequently.

In April, a friend of Jack's family, Charles Walker, stood with the men in Macon's U.S. District Court "as a friend who was an attorney." (Jack did not want to be represented officially by a lawyer, he said, because he was depending not on legal maneuvering but on his faith. He thought he could speak for himself. He accepted Walker's offer to "stand with them," however.) The trial was brief. The men gave statements referring to their uncompromising allegiance to Jesus' teachings against violence and their view that registration with the Selective Service System would constitute a tacit approval of war. Walker paraded several character witnesses by, including Clarence, and the "defense" rested its case.

The judge repeatedly expressed his appreciation of their sincerity, but on several occasions he strongly implied that the two young men had been "ill-advised." He stated, shortly before sentencing them: "I may be wrong, but I have a feeling that these young men may have been ill-advised. I am certain in my own mind that they did not and could not have taken this stand from their religious training and from the institutions that I know of. . . ."

Jack responded that he was "acting on the counsel of the Lord Jesus Christ." But a minister who was there to bear witness to the character of the two men declared that the "real culprits" were not in the courtroom, that he, as a former U.S. Army chaplain, had tried to dissuade them from this radical position, and that he had nothing but contempt for the 300 ministers who had advocated violating the draft law. Millard's father also made a statement expressing resentment of those who had influenced "these boys more than their parents." Millard recalled that the pastor's statement "wound up shattering any possibility of making our position sound Christian." They were found guilty and sentenced to a year and a day.

(The FBI did investigate Clarence for his role in the decisions of Jack and Millard, but both men had obviously begun moving toward their decisions before talking to Clarence. The investigation was apparently shelved.)

Jack and Millard entered the Tallahassee Federal Correctional

Institution on April 30, but they gained parole on September 10 after acting out a charade about registration. Legally, even after serving time for the offense, they would have been guilty again as soon as they hit the streets—unless they agreed to register. They were asked to sign a statement saying that they would obey all laws and not associate with criminals. They amended the statement to say that they intended to consort with one another and then signed it. Then the parole officer, who was obviously determined to set them free, told Millard he had filled out a Selective Service registration form for him, and began reciting the facts he had put in the blanks. When he read out the wrong birthday, Millard corrected him. He then responded: "Thanks, you've just assisted me in the registration." It must have meant something to the parole officer, because he then handed Millard his registration card and told him he could go. Millard kept it as a souvenir, but refused to carry it.

Jack was also issued a registration card, even though he refused to affix his signature to the forms. "I felt guilty about it," he said, "and I wrote a long letter to my parole officer and enclosed the card. Marion Johnson took the letter to mail. She pocketed the card and apparently never did mail the letter."

The two desperados were paroled to Koinonia Farm. Jack was reunited with his wife Jean, and Millard, whose Atlanta girl friend had waited for him, immediately applied to travel out of his parole district.

At about that same time, another young farming student from Auburn University, Gilbert Butler, refused to register for the new Selective Service Act, even though he, too, had served in the Navy during the war. He moved to Koinonia before his trial. Eventually he was tried in Birmingham and found guilty, but a sympathetic judge gave him what may be the shortest sentence on record for such an offense—60 days.

So, as Koinonia Farm approached the 1950s, a number of young, radically committed Christians had gathered there. Most of them knew little or nothing about the idea of community, but they were committed to the ideas of peace and love and sharing, and determined to incarnate these ideas in their lives. What lay ahead was the test of endurance, the painstaking task of giving definition to their new corporate existence and establishing the patterns of their life together. Questions flooded their minds: How were they to handle routine economic decisions? How was work to be assigned? Were they to take meals together, or was each family on its own? Who could be a member of the community, and what requirements were there, anyway?

Questions rolled forth like a mighty stream, and as the workload got larger the meetings grew longer. The Koinonia community, like any other new family, began its struggle toward maturity.

CHAPTER 5

Churched

By 1950, Koinonia Farm's population had boomed up to 14 adults, and more were on the way. Children were in the making. Visitors were beginning to stream in regularly, and adding to the pressure, the town's alcoholics discovered acceptance at Koinonia. What appeared to be a tiny community of people was suddenly pressed for space, food, and money—and faith, for a time, far exceeded efficiency.

Tension, confusion, and a measure of disillusionment were unavoidable as the group's supercharged ideals thudded into the heavy reality of economic survival. Some newcomers, hoeing under the blazing southern Georgia sun, worked out their commitments surprisingly fast; others recognized that the common pursuits of brotherhood, peace, and sharing were not definitive enough for a life together. They had come to join the revolution and found themselves in evolution. Form had to be found for life at the farm.

Their enthusiasm was strengthening, however. With at least the spirit of revolution, they began evolving a structure for a common life, thrashing their way through experiences that most of them viewed retrospectively with a sort of reverent and reserved hilarity. These were the days, after all, when their lives were turned upside down, the days of the new beginning, the days when they took everything so seriously.

"I remember," said Marion Johnson, "that 16 of us were using that one bathroom below the Jordans. I couldn't even leave a comb in there. The men would come in from the fields greasy and sweaty and use the comb, and if I complained, they would lecture me about sharing."

Howard's father donated a good used refrigerator, a welcome gift, it would seem, since there was only one refrigerator in the community. But no one was willing to have it in their home because it would seem unfair. So the refrigerator hummed its performance out in the shop, a monument to stingy generosity.

Alcoholics from the area found their way to Koinonia Farm about this time, not because of any formal rehabilitative effort, but because they knew they could get work and a bed and be treated like human beings. Most of them were good men, educated men who at one time or another had held responsible positions. One was an editor of a county newspaper who arrived at the Jordans' home one night when Clarence and Florence were struggling to put down a new sheet of linoleum on the kitchen floor, and he helped. Sitting on the floor exhausted when they finished, the three of them began a conversation, and Clarence volunteered to make popcorn. The editor, a sophisticated gentleman, sat there munching popcorn, and chuckled: "If my friends could see me now. . . ."

Several people showed up with varying degrees of misunderstanding about the Koinonia experiment and failed to carry their weight economically. "How many times," Con Browne sighed, "we would put time and money into getting a person or a family set to take care of themselves and then they would leave. We must have put $5,000 into one family with medical problems, and then one morning the guy is gone—and his family is still here. The Lord was always leading him off somewhere."

The fellowship jelled in these times, however, and relationships began to deepen. They were working together and worshiping together and becoming a part of each other's lives. For a time, they rose at 6 A.M. for a brief worship experience, and then later varied the daily worship period between a time after lunch and a half-hour before supper. Responsibility for the worship was shared. Sometimes it was a devotional, occasionally a Bible study, or now and then they would memorize hymns together. Often worship was simply a quiet time together.

Commitment to group decisionmaking was feverish. No one wanted to be in the position of lording it over the others, and they all expressed a reluctance at being "officers"—a word straight out of the old order. But a president, vice president, secretary, and treasurer finally were elected, to meet the requirements of the by-laws as much as anything else. There were no divisions between clergy and laity, and no officer had authority over the group.

As a matter of fact and not theory, however, Clarence, by virtue of tenure and farming experience and natural leadership capacity, was a sort of general manager of Koinonia Farm. He probably never would have won awards for patience in those days. The economic realities of their existence weighed heaviest on him at a time when so many of the others still were enthusiastically pursuing theological and personal questions about community life. Population growth meant land had to be purchased, and production had to improve regardless of whether or not the new members were farmers, preachers, teachers, or social workers. (Clarence did begin a series of land purchases when Harry and Howard arrived, eventually bringing the farm's total acreage to about 1100. By this time most of the land was paid for, but the arrival of more people, many inexperienced in farming, was creating new debt.)

"We were meeting almost every morning at 5 A.M. for breakfast and Bible study," Con recalled. "If it approached midnight in the evening meetings, Clarence would simply get up and go to bed. And he would be up and going while the rest of us were still dragging around the next morning."

Clarence was the work coordinator, the man responsible for assigning work details, because he knew the most about the work. He was viewed alternately as a dictator and as an indecisive administrator as he struggled for his own perspective on authority in a group committed to consensus. The men finally rose up and deposed Clarence as work coordinator, but the revolution did not solve the frustration and unpopularity that accompanied the job assignment responsibility.

"We sort of rotated the dictatorship after that," Con said. "We started out saying whoever had the job would keep it until he was dis-elected, so to speak. The first time I went on the job, I lasted two days and I said to hell with this. But then I got to where I could handle it for several weeks or even a month."

(Actually, Con had an amazing ability for selling eggs and so he was kept on the egg route. "Every time a new person came, I tried to get him on the egg route," Con said. "But every time, the market would disappear and I would have to go back in and build the darn thing back up again.")

Later on, the men got together and settled on a triumverate, with Norman Long, Howard Johnson, and Clarence forming a coalition for work administration. This broke down shortly thereafter when the three men came into the work detail meeting one morning shouting at each other. Finally, the community delegated responsibility around types of work and assigned work teams, one to field crops, one to cattle, one to equipment, and so on. The work coordinator, then, managed by exception—if one team needed help, he arranged for someone in another team to help, or if one team was caught up, he assigned them somewhere else.

The women and children were integrated into the work process, with women sharing shifts in housecleaning, laundry, cooking, canning, looking after the children, and secretarial work. Children were organized into teams for yard work, burning trash, caring for pets, and helping in the fields.

The children also were consulted on more important matters, such as when the adults became concerned over war toys. The children gathered in a community meeting and the adults explained their feeling that the toys symbolized violence and killing. After a loud discussion, the children agreed. In a special peace service, they tossed their toy weapons of war into a trash can to be burned and sat down to receive more tasteful toys and games from the community.

As far as membership in the community was concerned, there was one firm procedure: The new member either had to dispose of his possessions and cash before arrival or turn over such resources to the community. "We only passed the hat once," Clarence said, "and that was at the gate." From that point on, the individual or family looked to the group for even his most basic needs.

This was a powerful demonstration of commitment, but group decisionmaking on day-to-day economic matters had its drawbacks. A request for new shoes would escalate into a major discussion over whether or not the community should borrow money, and meetings, meetings, meetings would tumble on into the night.

Hours were spent discussing whether or not the single men needed more spending money in town than the others, or whether or not a mileage limit should be imposed on weekend dates. The women bravely trimmed their menus to pinch pennies, and then flinched as the men decided to spend another $10,000 on a tractor.

There were lengthy discussions about whether or not everyone should relinquish their insurance policies and count on the fellow-ship for insurance. And there were some who hedged when it came time to pool their cash. The Brownes, for example, had $100, and they wanted to designate its use before they let it go; they wanted a bathroom installed in the little white house Harry had built a few years earlier and where they were living at the time. (There was not much argument with that need; the bathroom was built.)

Eventually the shop below the Jordans' quarters was transformed into a community kitchen, and Jack Singletary donated a large institutional range. And the evolution extended to the matter of meals. Noon meals were taken together in the community kitchen, but to preserve some family privacy and unity, several approaches to evening meals were tried. For a time, until more kitchen facilities were added in the other frame houses being built, evening meals were prepared in the common kitchen and then carried into the homes on trays.

The proposal to have a nursery sprung another problem to the surface. There seemed to be some strain between the individual family units and the larger community "family." Single adults were especially prone to look on the community as "family," but the parents of young children were more inclined to protect and nourish the integrity of the individual family unit. This tension eased with time, however, and most of the parents began to consider the diversity of adult relationships experienced by the children one of the strengths of community.

Three other houses were built after the one that Harry and Allene originally moved into, one of which was built for an elderly Negro couple up the road and then later moved down to the little cluster of Koinonia buildings when the couple moved on. As each house was built, the discussion seemed to settle on the matter of family policy: Should a kitchen and dining room be included in the new house, or should families depend on the community kitchen except for breakfast? Is a living room needed or should the community kitchen and dining hall, as the larger "family's" gathering place, be the only provision? Each house, however, provided for individual family needs and kitchen facilities were built in or provided later.

It was the objective of the group from the beginning to administer the community money and goods on a basis of need, but somehow the factor of equality forced itself upon them—and proved to be a tough idea to administer. It became obvious, for example, that distributing food equally, rather than according to individual need, was foolish. And it seemed unreasonable that if a lover of music was granted a new record that everyone should get one, regardless of interest. A more relaxed, less legalistic approach based on need—and the availability of resources—eventually was returned to through the painful rites of long and frequent meetings.

Austerity was not the objective, of course. The group was working out its basic idea of modest but comfortable living and its common commitment to share the abundance with others around them. The life-style they were forming was not an exercise in self-denial, but liberation from a consuming concern for their own welfare, a freedom they believed would lead to an abundant and fulfilling life. Clarence, in the beginning of his vision, had been moved by Jesus' style of living, and the spirit of that way of life was what they sought to express.

"Jesus was not talking about a monastic or ascetic attitude toward possessions," Clarence said. "John the Baptist was, but not Jesus. Jesus loved the feast and feast means abundance. I think he loved abundance. He praised the woman who poured expensive perfume on his feet and he fed the multitudes. He took the attitude of abundance, but at the same time he rebuked those people who set their lives on possessions. He said the Father is full of abundance. And he said trust Him for it so you can be free to seek the God Movement."

So it all began to come together, hewn chip by chip out of the rock of consensus. Every proposition had to be made, balked at, and then pursued in some hybrid form. But the evolution began to produce some measure of stability and regularity.

As the fellowship was solidifying from within, however, an outside group, the little Rehoboth Baptist Church, was fuming its way toward an action that would clarify Koinonia's constantly discussed relationship as a church to a formally organized church.

Clarence and Martin had joined the Rehoboth Baptist Church shortly after their arrival in the fall of 1942. They had talked together then of Koinonia being the kind of fellowship that the New Testament referred to when it mentioned "church," but they also had felt a responsibility to the local church as expressed in traditional form. As the community expanded, however, the sense of responsibility to the local church was not shared by everyone. Some felt Koinonia should structure itself even more ecclesiastically and gear its outreach to "winning" people to its fellowship. Others simply felt the racism and affluence of local churches represented the antithesis of what they were trying to do in community, and so to participate was compromise.

The Jordans and several others, however, continued to participate faithfully at Rehoboth. Clarence often led the singing and played his trumpet, and he preached on occasion. Florence taught an adult Sunday School class, and Con Browne, though not a church member, participated regularly in the choir.

Actually, hostile signals from the church first intensified back in 1948, when Koinonia was just beginning to attract its first permanent residents. Perhaps it was becoming clear by then that

Koinonia was there to stay and not just some fly-by-night religious spasm after all. At any rate, as Koinonia's views on racial reconciliation and pacifism gained more expression, the deacons of the church began to apply pressure. Several of them suggested that the dozen or so Koinonians who attended the church withdraw voluntarily. This was quietly rejected. There may have been a movement behind the scenes to attempt to vote them out of the church, but Florence believed that the pastor discouraged such a move. The deacons then took the position, unofficially, that no one from Koinonia should be allowed to hold any place of responsibility in the organization.

Meanwhile, an agricultural student from India who was studying at Florida State University visited Koinonia Farm for a weekend, and he expressed an interest in attending an American Protestant worship service. The Jordans escorted him to Rehoboth, where the presence of his dark skin miraculously chilled the hot, humid southern Georgia atmosphere. Obviously Koinonia had disguised a "nigger", called him an Indian, and sneaked him into divine worship. The new pastor came out to Koinonia and told Clarence that Koinonians were the cause of disunity in his church.

"The man was dark, but he did not look like an American Negro," Florence said. "Actually, we thought the people would be delighted to meet him. He was not a Christian, but he had become interested and he wanted to go to church."

A group of men from the church came to the farm and confronted Clarence again with a plea for Koinonians to stay away from the church. Clarence said that he and the others would be willing to apologize before the congregation if they had done anything to offend anyone. He handed a Bible to one of the men and asked him to show, through the Scriptures, how any wrong had been committed. The man slammed the book down and said: "Don't give me any of this Bible stuff!" Clarence, who always geared down to a soft but confident tone in such encounters, replied: "I'm not giving you any Bible stuff. I'm asking you to give it to me." He then suggested to the deacon that if he could not accept the Bible as the "Holy inspired Word of God," that perhaps he should get out of the Baptist church himself. Exasperated, the men left.

The group at Koinonia commissioned Howard Johnson and Clarence to visit each of the deacons personally to attempt a reconciliation. They got around to three of the deacons, and then, on August 11, 1950, Clarence received a letter stating that the members of the Koinonia Farm could not be retained in the fellowship of the Rehoboth church.

The letter notified members of the Koinonia Farm that action would probably be taken on Sunday, August 13, and that possibly fellowship would be withdrawn from the group, and the names stricken from the church rolls.

Clarence immediately telephoned the pastor and told him that nearly all those concerned at Koinonia had previous engagements and would be unable to be at Rehoboth on Sunday, August 13. He asked for a postponement of one week, and the pastor said he would see what he could do. That Saturday evening, after Clarence already had left to keep a preaching engagement at the Dexter Avenue Baptist Church in Montgomery, one of the men from the church who worked with young people came to the farm.

"He wanted to know," Florence said, "how we would feel toward him personally if he did not vote to keep us in the church. I told him that as far as I knew our feelings toward him wouldn't change at all. He said he felt that if he sided with us, he would not be able to work with the young people, and yet he did not want to side against us. I told him not to worry about it, to do whatever he thought was right."

Florence reasoned from this encounter that the church was going to carry out its intentions on schedule the next day, despite Clarence's plea for a delay.

"You can imagine my feelings," she said. "Here I was, all by myself to face the church. So that night I prayed. I didn't know what in the world I was going to say. The next morning, in that half-awake stage, this Scripture came to my mind: 'When they bring you before judges, take no thought of what you will say.' That was the answer. I just forgot the whole thing and went on to Sunday School."

At the beginning of the morning worship service, Florence walked down front to the second row with her daughter Eleanor, seating herself where she could stand and face the church if necessary during the business meeting that would follow. At the end of the service the pastor called the church into business session and explained the absence of most of the Koinonians. He asked whether or not the church wished to proceed in their absence and a motion was made to proceed. It passed, and Deacon D. C. Sheppard rose to read the following recommendations from the board of deacons:

Whereas, Mr. & Mrs. C. L. Jordan, Miss Eleanor Jordan, Mr. & Mrs. Howard Johnson, and Miss Willie Pugh, members of Rehoboth Baptist Church, are also members of Koinonia Farm, an organization actively engaged in advocating views and practices contrary to those of other members of the Rehoboth Church, and

Whereas, representatives of this group have brought people of other races into the services of the Rehoboth Baptist Church, and have done this with the knowledge that such practices were not in accord with the practices of other members of Rehoboth Church, and

Whereas, said members do constantly visit Negro churches in the community, and have persisted in holding services where both white and colored attend together, and

Whereas, said members, because of these views and practices, have caused serious friction in our church, and have disrupted the Christian unity and spirit which had previously prevailed, and

Whereas, some members of Koinonia Farm have misbehaved, and created disturbances in our services, more than once, attempting to draw the attention of others, and

Whereas, the leaders of Koinonia Farm have made remarks that seemed unchristian, and have stated that they do not agree with certain doctrines and policies of the Baptist church, and they admit that they do not know what their relationship to the local church should be, and

Whereas, said leaders have stated that they are trying to convert individuals to their ideas and would like to see members added to their own group, we do not feel they are working for the best interest of Rehoboth Church, and

Whereas, members of Koinonia Farm have stated that the church is possibly operated under false doctrines (not holding the truth), and that it might be best for the present organization to collapse, and

Whereas, after much prayer and consideration, and after consulting many pastors and laymen of other Baptist churches, we feel that said members are no longer in full fellowship of our church, and that it will be to the best interest of the spiritual welfare and progress of our church to withdraw fellowship from them

Therefore, we recommend that the Rehoboth Baptist Church do on this 13th day of August, 1950, withdraw fellowship from any who are members of Koinonia Farm, and that their names be stricken from the church roll.

There was a heavy pause. Florence stood abruptly and punctured the stuffy tension with a clear voice. "I move," she said, "that the recommendations of the deacons be accepted as read."

Stunned, but still in control, the moderator called for a second to the motion. He was answered by absolute silence; gaping, confused silence. A deacon, who later said he had thought he was going to pass out, finally sorted out what was happening and rose to offer a second. No arguments on the motion came forth. The moderator called for a standing vote. There were movements, shuddering little gestures borne of confusion. About two-thirds of the people finally made it to their feet in favor of the motion.

"They supported the motion, but they didn't want to vote with me," Florence said. "Some remained seated and refused to vote. Some of them were literally neither up nor down."

Florence, in effect, had pleaded guilty to the "charges" outlined in the deacons' recommendations; they were mostly self-indicting, anyway. (The charge of creating disturbances, however, was confessed to by Con Browne. "Willie and I started that," he recalled. "What happened was that one Sunday we had worked all day in the chicken barn and we were so tired we shouldn't have gone to church. The minister got up and said that since this was Lent he and his wife were going to sing the most beautiful Christian song ever written. Well, they didn't hit two notes in harmony and Willie and I started snickering. Everytime we looked up we broke into gales of laughter, and we couldn't control it.")

Florence felt badly about the outcome, but she refused to worry about it. She had responded to a clear impulse, an imperative she recalls being as distinct as a whisper in her ear: "You make the motion!" When she explained to Clarence what had happened, he accepted her action "as a leading of the spirit." They talked over the matter, consulted the others, and then decided to return to the church as if nothing had happened.

On Sunday, August 20, the Koinonia group showed up at church as usual, intent to continue attendance "both as an evidence of our love for the church and to forestall any movement among other members to withdraw out of sympathy for us." (The latter was likely for only a few people.)

Representatives of the church promptly appeared at Koinonia Farm and, in so many words, expressed surprise that Koinonians had not gotten the message that they were not welcome. Clarence agreed that they would stay away from the church if they would be allowed to make a statement explaining why they no longer attended the services. (He often joked later that he told the pastor: "If we're sinners we need to hear the word; if we're saints, we need the fellowship—in any case, we ought to be there.")

The pastor consented, and on Sunday, August 27, one of the deacons made a motion that anyone connected with Koinonia in any way be requested to stay away from the church services. While the motion was being discussed, Clarence stood and read a statement that explained the scriptural basis of Koinonia's beliefs and said in part:

It is our desire . . . that it be clearly understood that our absence would be due, not to any malice or lack of forgiveness or willingness to attend on our part, but to the will and action of the church itself. We wish to extend to the pastor, the deacons, and the entire membership our sincere sympathy in these hours of suffering. We are grieved that it has become impossible for us to walk together as brethren in the Lord Jesus. Truly both you and we have broken His heart, and we all should penitently seek His forgiveness. It is our fervent prayer that all of us shall heed the command of our Lord Jesus to forgive each other "until seventy times seven"; to pray for one another, and to love those "who despitefully use you." May there be a ready willingness for a reconciliation which would involve no sacrifice of conscience or compromise of our Lord's truth.

One of the deacons appeared at Koinonia Farm some time later and confessed to Clarence that he had been haunted by his own participation in the Rehoboth purge. Tearfully, he told of how he would try to sleep and every time he dozed off, he dreamed someone was walking in his room singing. He asked for Clarence's forgiveness, and was told that he already had it. He said he was going to resign from the church; Clarence advised him instead to stay in the church and live in such a way "as to be kicked out." Clarence reported later that the old man was a divine irritant at Rehoboth for about a year until he died.

(The Rehoboth church's action was not the last word in Koinonia's struggle for relationships to white churches. The Jordans, the Johnsons, and Willie Pugh no longer sought to be a part of any other church, but Con and Ora Browne persisted. They tried the Presbyterian church next, and were treated in a friendly manner until they made overtures about seeking membership. Then they tried the Disciples of Christ and the Methodists. Finally they found a relatively comfortable relationship in the Episcopal church, which lasted until Koinonia became a more controversial subject and a target for violence. By then it was clear to the people of Koinonia that they were aliens.)

With the Rehoboth incident and another farming season behind them, the group turned its energies back to the struggle for efficiency and fairness, and a concern for clarity in their relationships to one another. They began to probe for a common definition of what they were about. They were like one large family, and these were sensitive times as they worked through patterns of relationships and sought to deal with their feelings honestly. They were unified around the idea that the koinonia—the fellowship of believers—was the continuation in history of the incarnation, of the life and death and resurrection of Jesus. Their responsibility was to make the fellowship at Koinonia Farm as nearly the body of Christ as they were able. They were sensitive to their shortcomings but excited by their new life.

Clarence stated in one of the meetings: "Something has been set in motion here that I can't stop—something that is eternal. As vaguely as we see it and as dimly as it appears to us, I'm beginning to see that I'm in this thing called koinonia for life. Not at Koinonia Farm for life, but I'm in this thing called koinonia for life and I'm ready now, I think, to commit all to it, and I think my biggest problem has been that I've been thinking in terms of committing myself to principles, when it seems to me that I must commit myself to the people of Koinonia who are making the same struggle as I am. It is a personal commitment. I think I'm just beginning to realize the meaning of the phrase personal salvation or personal commitment to Jesus. I don't think we'll ever love one another or have the spirit of Jesus until it becomes personal."

Apparently it was becoming clear to them that the sharing of possessions was only a part of the concept of sharing they were seeking. The struggles for a group will seemed to be making them recognize how they had withheld themselves from one another in less explicit but equally crucial ways of the spirit. The children somehow became the focus of discussion on this point for a while, and Florence, who was raising the oldest children—Eleanor, 16, Jim, 10, and Jan, 5—was criticized because her children talked about "my house" and did not exhibit a mature attitude toward money. Florence, too, had an independent strain about her that made her seem aloof to many of the group struggles, but while she may have drawn some criticism, her honesty disarmed any lingering hostility. She simply enjoyed being alone, and she preferred that she and Clarence—and not the other adults—take the responsibility for raising their children.

About Florence, Marion Johnson recalled: "She held out against a lot of things over the years, but when it came down to loving and giving herself, Florence did it. She could argue with you until 2 A.M. but the next day it would have made no difference between you."

Clarence was particularly sensitive, however, to the group's feeling that he and Florence were not giving themselves completely to the community. Although it surely would have hurt him to follow through on it, he finally offered to leave Koinonia Farm if the others thought it would unify the community.

Clarence was sensitive then, too, to the fact that many resented his frequent speaking trips. It had begun to be evident to him when he felt he was received "with tremendous coldness" upon his return from a speaking tour in the Northwest hungering deeply for the Koinonia fellowship. (Con Browne was also in frequent demand as a speaker.)

Howard Johnson recalled: "There was nothing Clarence would not have done to put himself down. But we felt that if there were real brotherliness, no one should have to leave." Con said: "Oh, those were painful meetings. We felt, though, that it would be defeating our purpose if we had to have someone like Clarence Jordan leave the experiment."

Eventually they renewed their commitments to one another and culminated their expression in their first written pledge, which was to be the basic statement of commitment for new members from that point on. It read:

We desire to make known our total, unconditional commitment to seek, express, and expand the Kingdom of God as revealed in Jesus the Christ. Being convinced that the community of believers who make a like commitment is the continuing body of Christ on earth, I joyfully enter into a love union with the Koinonia and gladly submit myself to it, looking to it to guide me in the knowledge of God's will and to strengthen me in the pursuit of it.

Ten adults signed the pledge in April of 1951—the Jordans, the Johnsons, the Brownes, the Atkinsons, Norman Long, and Gilbert Butler. By this time Jack Singletary had left the experiment for a farm of his own nearby after he and Clarence had suffered a series of personal disputes. And Millard Hunt had left to marry a girl who was not interested in Koinonia. (The group's persistent analogy of community to marriage—lifetime commitment, for better or worse—was a bit hard on Millard. "I felt like a divorcé," he said, "and had to sort of drum myself out of the community.") Willie Pugh had left, also, after marrying C. Z. Ballard, who lived at Koinonia for a short while.

At this point of renewed commitment, the group also structured a pattern for membership in the community. A potential new member would spend three months to a year as a novice, participating in the community life, but reserving his final commitment and the relinquishing of his possessions. He would spend another three to nine months in provisional membership status, studying the scriptural bases for the commitment he was to make and, in essence, taking one last look before plunging into total commitment. At the time of commitment to full membership, the new member would either dispose of his possessions (give to his family, to the poor, etc.) or turn them into community goods and commit himself to the group, which in turn pledged to care for him and his dependents.

Joseph "Bo" Johnson, the first Negro to share the common life at Koinonia, joined the group as a novice at about this time. He had worked for Koinonia for several years after his father, Candy Johnson, who had sharecropped on the farm, died. Bo left shortly after joining the group to seek work in Florida and rethink his commitments. He returned to the area in 1953 and went to work for Koinonia's neighbor, Rob Hamilton. He restored his friendship with the people at Koinonia, but never again applied for membership.

These struggles for definition and clarity gave birth to an additional commitment, a pledge that marked their renewed vows to one another—that they would "speak to their brothers in love," and deal honestly and openly with the feelings that existed between them. This was no casual addition to their creed. Speaking their minds, expressing resentment or anger or disapproval before the impulse submerged and became part of a secret agenda between them, proved to be a tough pledge to live up to. In fact, in the minds of some, failure on this point prevented Koinonia from experiencing community at its most mature level during those early years.

CHAPTER 6

Elusive Unity

An old black jalopy shuddered into the driveway of Koinonia Farm, coughed to a halt, and delivered a quiet, 40-year-old spinster who asked if she could remain for a visit.

For two or three days she thoughtfully observed and absorbed life at Koinonia, and then she approached Clarence and revealed an interest in joining the group. He encouraged her and explained in detail what Koinonia was striving to be, how one must surrender himself totally to Christ, including all his earthly possessions. At Koinonia, he said, this is achieved by asking everyone to enter the fellowship in a common condition known as "flat broke." Her eyebrows jerked upward a fraction of an inch in alarm, and quite cautiously she began to ask questions.

Clarence was perplexed. "I couldn't understand it," he said. "As poor as she looked, I was really surprised. Jesus said it would be hard for a rich person to enter the kingdom, but we'd never even had one apply at our place. She was really quite agitated."

He asked her what difficulty there would be with relinquishing her possessions. She had a fair-size difficulty, somewhere between $80,000 and $90,000.

Clarence swallowed two or three times and then reasserted that she would have to dispose of the money to become a part of Koinonia. How, she asked? Give it to the poor, he said, give it to your relatives, throw it over a bridge—but you must enter the fellowship without it. What about giving it to Koinonia Farm, she asked?

Clarence grinned, and replied: "No. If you put that money in here several things would happen. First of all, we'd quit growing peanuts and start discussing theology. That wouldn't be a healthy condition for us. And in the next place, unless I miss my guess, you are a very lonely person, and you are lonely because you think every friend you ever had is after your money."

She confirmed that judgment.

"Well," Clarence continued, "if you put that money in here, you would think we courted you for your money, that we loved you for your money. And in the next place, if you put that money in here you would get the idea you were God's guardian angel, that you endowed the rest of us, and that all of us ought to be grateful to you for your beneficence."

She was listening; Clarence pressed his point: "Now for your sake and for our sakes, you get rid of that money and come walk this way with us." Tearfully, the woman replied: "I can't do it." She packed her old car and left.

Clarence took the Sermon on the Mount's admonishment not to put value on earthly possessions as literally as he did its clear advocation of peace and loving response to evil. "Your values and your character are wrapped up together," he said. "What you value and what you really are, is one and the same."

Money and possessions had a way of getting between people, he believed, and that was why he thought the early Christians pooled their possessions and shared, each according to his need. Sharing was one of the major actions that demonstrated the new spirit of life they had discovered; that was why Clarence was attracted to the idea.

Clarence was no student of community. He did not review the history of the Hutterites or visit the Society of Brothers or read about the radical Oneida community, or investigate any other of hundreds of communities in the United States before he started his own experiment. He was moved solely by his immersion in the Scriptures.

The man Jesus was the example, the blood-sweat-and-tears illustration of what God hoped for mankind. Clarence and the others at Koinonia were striving to embody the spirit of Jesus through a life together, much as the early Christian followers had done. Unlike other older community movements, they were not declaring that community was God's ultimate call, the only right and saving way to live. They did not view Jesus as a man who diagrammed a formula for living but as a man who offered a spirit for life, a way that was prompted by the mind and the heart, and not sealed forever by a cultural order.

But at the same time, they believed that the kingdom of God proclaimed by Jesus was to reveal itself in the lives of men and gain expression in their attitudes and life-styles. Community to them was a way to give flesh to an idea they all accepted, a way to incarnate the spirit of Jesus. It was their choice, as a way of making their surrender to Christ a concrete, objective act, to move from a community of spirit to a community of goods, as the Book of Acts records that the early Christians did.

So Clarence did not speak of community as structure. He spoke of community as a family—theologically, the Family of the Father. His vision was a vision of a family made up of children of God who would bear witness to the nature of the Father by sharing their resources according to the principle of love rather than greed, who would defy evil with steadfast goodwill, and who would accept their brothers and sisters of all variations as sons and daughters of the same Father.

Clarence was not one to speak of political solutions to the persisting plagues of poverty, prejudice, and violence. Christians, he felt, should be distinctive whatever the political order, and to him nothing could be more distinctive in the United States than people living in voluntary states of sharing, living, and working together and caring for one another like brothers. That was why the idea of experimenting with the type of sharing exhibited by the early Christians seemed worthwhile to him, and why American society, with its emphasis on competitiveness, seemed like an appropriate place to try it again.

In his earthy, down-home style, Clarence would paraphrase the parable of the rich farmer in the Gospel of Luke, and say: "Let's give him a name, make it more personal. Let's call him Sam— you can call him 'Uncle' if you want to. . . . So, Uncle Sam has an abundant harvest and he has to do something with it. He ignores the starvation in China—'the only good communist is a dead communist'—and in India—'they are just lazy.' He stores it all up, and then just reclines, dines, wines, and shines. But then God says: 'You nitwit, this very night *they* are demanding your soul of you.' Now who is 'they'? It doesn't say, '*your* soul is required of you,' it says, '*they* require your soul.' God didn't kill that man. 'They' means all those barns and all those granaries, and all those fields, and all that stuff he had given himself over the years—*they* are demanding his soul. He didn't die—something more tragic than that occurred. He lived in bondage to the very things he thought would serve him."

It was this workaday relationship with the Scriptures that sustained Clarence's vision. And what his vision lacked in refinement and structure, he and the people who gathered around him more than made up for in sheer exuberance. Many were discovering purpose and integrity in their faith for the first time.

Among those who arrived to stay for several years in the early 1950s were Claud and Billie Nelson, who had heard Clarence speak in 1944 to a Baptist student meeting at the Georgia State

College for Women in Milledgeville, where Billie had been a student. Both Claud and his wife were already deeply committed to pacificism and racial brotherhood and they met with Clarence to express an interest in joining Koinonia. At that time, however, they chose to do volunteer work through the American Friends Service Committee in a slum area of Indianapolis. Later, Claud worked for Hampton Institute in Virginia and, inevitably, Clarence spoke there in 1950 and again prompted the interest of the Nelsons. They visited Koinonia that year and came again to spend the summer in 1952. At the end of that summer they committed themselves to joining Koinonia.

Not long after that, Will Wittkamper and his family arrived with the intention of joining the community. He was 60 years old and had a stormy history as a Disciples of Christ preacher. A midwesterner with a longstanding record of outspokenness against violence and militarism, Wittkamper spent World War I in a conscientious objectors' work camp. When the Great War was over, he went to Butler College under the conviction that he would preach.

"I went to college," he said, "not with the intention of learning to speak, but to at least be able to explain my point of view about the gospel of the kingdom."

Certainly he did not learn how to compromise the message he wanted to proclaim. For the next 30 years, the small, wiry, intense preacher was rejected in church after church because of his devotion to speaking about peace, love, and racial justice as characteristics of the kingdom of God. His unbending testimony against war and militarism most often provoked the churches to ask him to leave, and like an itinerant preacher, Wittkamper took his message across Indiana and progressed from one congregation to another through several states in the West and Southwest.

Tired and disappointed after 30 years of preaching, Wittkamper began searching for a "church" where people lived together and cared for one another and held all things in common, as he felt the early church had done. He corresponded with A. J. Muste, the controversial socialist figure and fiery father of the U.S. labor movements, who referred him to Lawrence Scott, a Quaker who had experimented for a time with a community in Alabama. Scott suggested that he write to Clarence Jordan in Americus, Georgia.

Clarence answered his letter, explaining the nature of Koinonia, and saying at the close that "perhaps you would like to join us." Wittkamper considered the invitation as a call from God. "That made me so happy I sat down and cried," he said. "Here's what I had been looking for." He consulted his wife Margaret, who agreed to go, and his three sons, who asked if the farm had tractors. He said, "Yes"; they said, "Let's go!"

Koinonia's population grew to 19 adults and 22 children (including the Jordan's fourth child, Frank Leonard, born in July 1952), and the experiment had one of its most active summers in 1953. John Eustice, an easygoing midwesterner and experienced outdoorsman, made the most of the fact that Koinonia's land had once been a campsite for Cheehaw Indians, a branch of the Cherokees. Taking the leadership in recreation with neighborhood children, he added Indian lore and forays into the woods for artifacts to the regular summer Bible school for the children. He and Norman Long and Margaret Wittkamper also started boys' club and girls' club weekly activities that summer. Con Browne began developing a religious education program for Koinonia children. And they all combined their talents to plan for a six-weeks' summer camp for 1954 at which they hoped to have 30 underprivileged children.

Then came 1954—the first year since 1947 that no newcomers came to stay. Only Danny, born to the Wittkampers in November, raised the permanent population to 42. Except for Danny's birth, it was not a fruitful year. After a good planting season, and what appeared to be a healthy enough summer, a severe drought set in during the August-September harvest season, and Koinonia, along with every other farm in southwestern Georgia, suffered heavy losses. Only half of the peanut crop could be harvested, and that yielded only one-fourth the nuts per acre expected. The rest was baled for hay. Corn yields did not even cover production costs. Pastures dried up, and the delay in seeding small grain and pasture crops for fall promised a small yield. Feed poisoning threatened the hog enterprise.

Poultry and livestock kept the farm from suffering total disaster, even though the egg market was at its lowest level in five years. Sharing with 1500 friends through a newsletter, Koinonia wrote in December 1954: "A glance in the direction of our sharecropping neighbors makes us uncomfortably conscious of how comfortably well we live and of how relative is the 'simple living' we profess. We are still convinced that our greatest need is not economic but in the realm of the spiritual."

Economic needs, however, were argued over in community meetings. Even though Koinonia was fortunate in having a spring-fed creek running through its property, from which it shared drinking water with its neighbors, the farm still was in trouble. It had good credit going for it, so consideration was given to the idea of purchasing an irrigation system. The cost would be about $30,000, which would require Koinonia to mortgage its paid-for property again. Clarence was uncertain about the wisdom of this, but in one of his vacillating moments, he did not fight it. The community voted to make the purchase. (Clarence confided years later to his friend John Lehman that he had been accused of being dictatorial so often that he kept his mouth shut in this instance just to prove otherwise. It was a costly piece of judgment. The drought broke the next year and the irrigation system never paid its way.)

Since 1950 and Koinonia's spurt of growth, the group had developed a serious interest in the beliefs and life-styles of other community groups, especially the Society of Brothers and the Hutterian Brethren of the Northwest.

The Hutterites are the largest communal sect in the United States, with a heritage that leads back into the sixteenth century and the Anabaptist movement that sprung from the Protestant Reformation. They take their name from one of their first martyred ministers, Jacob Hutter, who, along with founder Jacob Wiedenman, sought to create a communal church based on the life of the early Christians. Persecuted in Austria for their religious beliefs, a remnant of Hutterian Brethren eventually migrated into Russia. When the Russian government revoked exemption from military conscription in the 1870s, they migrated to South Dakota and established their first colony in the United States only 18 miles from the territorial capital of Yankton, bringing over virtually intact a way of life and dress and manner that characterized the sixteenth-century Hutterians. The Great Plains of South Dakota supported their farming interests and absorbed their patterns of living, and other groups followed. Now some 20,000 Hutterites live in about 200 colonies scattered across North and South Dakota, Montana, and western Canada.

The Society of Brothers grew out of similar concerns in Germany after World War I. Under the leadership of a scholar of the privileged class, Eberhard Arnold, who rejected his societal status in a search for justice and meaningful religious faith, a small group of people gathered in the village of Sannerz in 1920 to begin a new life based on love and justice and their study of the New Testament. They, too, adopted the pattern of holding all things in common, believing that this pattern, as recorded in the Acts of the Apostles, was a positive alternative to the destructive war spirit and loyalty to the Fatherland above God that characterized Germany. Their stated aim was to show that under the rulership of God men could live a life of loving harmony and brotherhood.

The Bruderhof (place of the brothers) struggled through its early growth until the Nazi regime's rigid repressions provoked them to migrate to England in 1937. In England, they prospered somewhat, and grew to two communities of several hundred people before World War II broke out and confronted them again with the need to move. If they remained, the German brothers (about half of the Bruderhof population) faced internment. They chose mass migration again, this time to the underdeveloped backwoods of Paraguay.

After World War II, the Bruderhof sent ministers to explore the possibilities of migrating to the United States. At that point, the Hutterites, the Bruderhof, and Koinonia Farm awakened to each other's existence and were drawn into a strange and historical relationship that eventually altered the nature of all three.

Representatives from Paraguay visited Koinonia Farm and a number of the Hutterian colonies, including the Forest River Colony near Inkster, North Dakota, and the Tschetter Colony in South Dakota. Clarence, who was excited to learn from the Bruderhof brethren that the Hutterite colonies existed, visited the Bonhomme Colony while on a western speaking trip. David Decker, the minister at the Tschetter Colony, was prompted to visit Koinonia after he heard the men from the Bruderhof speak of it. He and another Hutterian minister came and they were impressed with Koinonia's youthful enthusiasm and objectives. He even had thoughts about Koinonia becoming a Hutterite colony and urged Clarence to become official "minister" of Koinonia Farm—an essential requirement for any Hutterian colony. Clarence was not responsive to the idea, since the Koinonia experiment was built on a premise of consensus decisionmaking, but he was impressed with Decker, one of the few formally educated Hutterian ministers.

As communication continued between them, Decker encouraged Clarence to visit him at Tschetter. In January 1955, suffering from the drought and in need of help, Koinonia dispatched Clarence and Will Wittkamper to visit Tschetter and several other colonies. Decker had said that the Hutterites would help, and they did. Decker and Joe Maendel, the farm boss at the Hutterites' Forest River Colony in North Dakota, got them a tractor, a cultivator, and a used truck, and raised several thousand dollars in the colonies for a loan.

But as Clarence and Will chugged through Hutterian country that winter in Koinonia's heaterless old Plymouth, their mission of appeals took on the additional dimension of a preaching mission. In a rare break with tradition, the Hutterites permitted this beardless "Englishman" to preach in their meetings.

When they drove into the Forest River Colony just west of Grand Forks, they made a legendary entrance. Clarence's reputation as a preacher and teacher making a stand against racism in the South had preceded him, and when he stepped from the old Plymouth coupe, practically frostbitten and stiff with cold, one of Joe Maendel's daughters ran from a building and said, "You're Clarence Jordan!" Joe was more skeptical. "They had on big overshoes," he said, "and torn-up jeans and they hadn't shaved for a while. I just couldn't believe it was him."

Appalled at how chilled they looked in the near-zero weather, Joe immediately ordered one of his sons to install a heater in their car, and then he started listening to Clarence talk. "I was astounded," he said. "I listened and the man started talking about the Bible so much differently that I didn't know if I had ever read it."

This tough-minded farm boss and his wife and their 14 children became close friends of Clarence over the years. Some of the children who were in elementary school that winter remembered Clarence's Bible stories 15 years later as if they had heard them the day before. They remembered in particular Clarence's lecture on the Prodigal Son parable—and so do most of the Hutterian adults who heard it.

Until that time, it was common practice among the Hutterites to severely punish young men who left the community and then returned repentantly. Looking directly at the ministers and elders when he spoke, Clarence asked where in the Scriptures they took that tradition from, and then he provided the answer: "There is no scriptural basis for this." He spoke about the father who received his son with a glad heart, with love and affection; and about the eldest brother, who was filled with resentment and thoughts of reward rather than the love that characterized the father.

The effect was revolutionary. The Hutterites, who live and breathe by the authority of the Bible, accepted this immediately as scripturally sound, and the word swept through the colonies. Punishment of returning young people was ended.

At one time, public resentment was increasing in the United States and Canada over the Hutterites' prosperous, expanding five- and six-thousand-acre farms. Clarence spoke out for the Hutterites and their way of life in a meeting with a group of lawyers in Winnipeg, and later preached about the Hutterites in a church in Yankton, South Dakota, that counted among its congregation three South Dakota legislators. For a time the legislatures had considered passing laws preventing further land acquisition by the Hutterites. For this concern, and for the fact that he spoke, as one Hutterite minister said, "like an angel," Clarence transcended tradition for a time and was accepted as no other outsider has been among the Hutterites.

In subsequent visits a reaction developed against him, and a number of Hutterites challenged him for remaining cleanshaven. Clarence said: "If you can show me that Christ wants me to have a beard, I'll not only grow it—I'll not even trim it as you fellows do. I'll grow it to my knees."

Early in the summer of 1955, the Forest River Colony appealed to Koinonia for help. Like the other Hutterian colonies, Forest River had its own school through the eighth grade—as far as most Hutterian children were allowed to go—and they needed a schoolteacher. According to Joe Maendel, they had asked the Bruderhof in Paraguay to send them a teacher, but they had been unable to respond.

The group at Koinonia discussed the possibility of freeing someone to spend a year at Forest River. Clarence had requested a leave of absence only a few months before to continue his New Testament work and to experiment with translating the Scriptures. The economic situation had provided the answer at that time—he could not be spared. So when the request came from Forest River, some in the group immediately thought of Clarence. He was willing, but not enthusiastically so. Florence balked. She would not go, primarily because at that time she did not feel the Hutterian way would be good for her children. Also, she did not feel Koinonia would survive in Clarence's absence. When it became clear that if Clarence went, he would be going without his family, the group turned to Claud and Billie Nelson.

In the summer of 1955, Claud and Billie and their four children left for Forest River, instructed by the Koinonia group to "bear witness" for Koinonia but also to be as much a part of the Hutterite community as possible.

Many of the other Hutterite colonies did not approve of Forest River's communication and fellowship with other communities. There was tension in the Hutterite world, aggravated by a few ministers who even thought Forest River should be excommunicated for requesting help from Koinonia and welcoming permanent visitors from the Bruderhof in Paraguay. Forest River, refusing to be threatened, sent John Maendel and his family to Koinonia for several weeks to help with the harvest as a gesture of gratitude for the help of the Nelsons.

Not long after the Nelsons arrived at Forest River and began preparations for the opening of school in September, a stream of families from the Bruderhof began to migrate to Forest River. The Nelsons were impressed with these easygoing Germans and Englishmen and the commitments they seemed to reflect for one another. In particular, their commitment to "admonishment"— to correct one another and to speak frankly—seemed to preempt the kinds of tensions and resentments that they felt plagued the Koinonia experiment.

"In what we experienced together with them," Nelson said, "we came to have a different feeling about life in Christian community than we had had previously. We felt challenged to strive always for complete unity, in a way which we had not seen as possible in our time at Koinonia. We felt challenged to see and feel a common purpose which transcended our needs as individuals, in a newly decisive way."

When they returned to Koinonia in May 1956, the Nelsons sought to share this experience, but they found they were unable to articulate their feelings successfully. Saddened by the fact that they could not seem to express themselves adequately—that something seemed to block the Koinonians from hearing—the

Nelsons requested that they be released from their commitment to Koinonia in order to join the Society's new community in Rifton, New York.

Their thoughts had not fallen completely on deaf ears. Koinonia granted their request, and also agreed to send Howard and Marion Johnson to Forest River for an extended visit. Something in what the Nelsons said had touched the Johnsons, and they wanted to see for themselves.

Howard returned to Koinonia toward the end of July to help with the harvest, and he found himself in a situation similar to that of the Nelsons. He wanted to share this matter of the spirit, this sense of real unity, that he experienced within the Bruderhof. He only got to touch on the matter, however, before violence broke out against Koinonia and attention was turned to the more pressing matters of discussing what the violence might mean for the life of the group. The Sumter County and Americus whites were beginning to exhibit a growing hostility over Koinonia's interracial involvements, and threatening phone calls had begun. In July, shortly before Howard had returned, someone had heaved an explosive at the farm's small roadside stand on the Albany highway, damaging the front of the stand and some of the refrigeration equipment.

After the harvest, Howard went back to Forest River, where Marion and the two children had remained. In October they all returned for a visit. They still felt committed to Koinonia, but they were experiencing a growing feeling of commitment to total community as they had come to know it at Forest River with the visiting Bruderhof families: the total submission of individual desire to group will that had frightened them so at first but that now they felt held the secret of unity in community life.

Like the Nelsons, they sensed an undercurrent of antagonism in the Koinonia group as they sought to explain their experience in the Bruderhof. They tried to promote the idea of further exchanges of families with the Bruderhof, so that others could experience it and Koinonia could learn from it. They recognized what they were up against. They had felt the same reaction when the Brothers visited from Paraguay before; they had balked at the vague talk of unity themselves.

Something in Marion Johnson's experience hints at the mysterious quality of Bruderhof life that attracted them. She had been one of the ones so sensitive to a "lack of unity" at Koinonia, but it had been only in the desperation of her spiritual search that she agreed to go with Howard to visit the Bruderhof at Forest River.

"I went with a sense of frustration and inner need," she recalled. "It was a miserable week. I didn't want to go, really. I knew there was a baby house (a nursery in which all infants were kept during the day to free the women for work) and I had terrific feelings about putting my four-month-old in there. I did eventually, of course, but the first time I went and stayed with him there myself. I'm sure I was more selfish than many. But to experience the power of love in that community—you just can't experience love by so many people and not be changed. That experience of people giving their lives to help each other showed how selfish it was to hold to your own. You can't tend your own babies and give your lives in service. I feel only love could have persuaded me to adopt this way."

The way in which members of the Bruderhof were pledged to admonish one another daily, to correct one another, also impressed Marion as the one step Koinonia seemed unable to take. "We were doing so many good things [at Koinonia], perhaps, that this didn't seem essential," she said. "But I think this last step was the key to what we never could find. You can't live with unresolved barriers standing between you and others. And it is only when you are open yourself to being spoken to that you can speak to your brothers. Here [in the Bruderhof] we are spoken to daily. I don't have to worry if I am efficient or if I am too strict with the children—it's all surrendered to our brothers and sisters. We promise to carry that responsibility for each other."

It was that responsibility for one another in the complexities of daily affairs, the concept that the group—the "church"—knows what is best for the individual, that was absent at Koinonia Farm. The Koinonians had pledged to "speak to one another in love," and so in a sense they were moving toward a concept of "admonishment," or at least a concept of honest confession of feelings. And they were committed to consensus decisions in the life of their community. But the individual was in no way so subjected to a group conscience. For those, such as Marion, who felt Koinonia's stated purpose was to be such a community, Koinonia seemed hypocritical—it was claiming one thing and being another.

Marion felt strongly that what she experienced in the Bruderhof was precisely what Clarence's vision of community had been originally. She was puzzled by the fact that he did not respond more positively to the Bruderhof himself, even to the extent of leading Koinonia into unity with them. She wrote to him during her visit at Forest River:

Clarence, I remember very clearly how thrilled you were when Koinonia had its first contact with the Bruderhof. . . . I remember, too, how soon I came to resent the Bruderhof because I was afraid your enthusiasm might lead us in that direction and I didn't want any part of having to put my babies in a baby house, risk going to Paraguay, etc.

I hardly know what to write to you about my experience here. I do feel that I resisted being drawn into the life because I didn't want any more attachments that would bring me as much pain as the ones I had made at Koinonia. Leaving all of you was by far the hardest thing that I have ever had to do. At the same time . . . I also felt that in Koinonia there was an absence of the living, daily presence of God and the sense of being entirely led by the Spirit. . . .

It seems that Koinonia has somehow two elements—those who really long to follow the guidance of the Spirit and who would want to seek it and wait for it at all costs . . . [and] others [who] are uncomfortable about the very idea, [who think] that God expects us to use our heads and figure out what is best to do in any situation. The mixture of these two elements seems impossible to me. . . .

Gradually, through the months here, I have come to feel a tremendous sadness at the great waste and pity of the two [Koinonia and the Bruderhof] remaining separate. I feel so strongly that the truly committed ones at Koinonia would really find their lives and realize their potentialities under God in this kind of life, and I have particularly felt this about you.

Here I have experienced the coming in to the novitiate of some, and the baptism of others, and there is not one thing involved in either to which we at Koinonia did not also commit ourselves. The question keeps bothering me—then why are we separate? Why? Why?

Clarence, of course, was keenly disappointed at the frustrations and dissatisfactions that seemed to be rocking an experiment dedicated to demonstrating the ways of love and peace to a competitive, violent, troubled world. But he had not given up on the idea of community in general, nor on the idea of Koinonia in particular. The whole group was hurt by those who left. By 1956 it was clear to them how stormy a pilgrimage they were on, and they wanted all the friends they could get.

Clarence answered Marion, in part:

Let me say that you are right about my being thrilled at the first contact with the Bruderhof. Immediately I saw in them a sister community, produced by the same Spirit. I felt the same deep sense of kinship with Forest River when Will and I visited there, and sought to convey that to the group here both by our letters home and in later reports. And this sense of kinship with both Forest River and the Bruderhof has neither left me nor diminished. . . . I have never felt that there was an "either-or" between us, that one was above or below the other, that one was divine and the other human. True, there are differences, in some of which Koinonia excels and in others the Bruderhof excels, but that's all the more reason why we need each other, and why each can help the other to be more Spirit-led.

Marion, you say that the question keeps bothering you: "Why are we separate?" As I said earlier, I have not felt this "separateness" to the extent you feel it, both now and while you were here. While Bob Clement was here from Woodcrest [a new Bruderhof community near Farmington, Pennsylvania], I don't think we ever discussed "unity," yet Koinonia felt an immediate oneness with him. The same was true of Peti. Both seemed to take us for what we were, and simply loved us.

. . . Neither groups nor individuals within groups are wholly and entirely "light" or "darkness." I know how much darkness there is at times in my own heart, yet I know also that the light of God is shining there, sometimes dimly, sometimes brightly. While I cannot speak for the Bruderhof, I can say that this is also true of Koinonia. All of us know how much darkness there is in us at times, yet I have also seen the light of God shining brilliantly in this little group here and I thrill to be a part of it. You simply are not right in saying that "in Koinonia there is an absence of the living, daily presence of God and the sense of being entirely led of the Spirit." Marion, a group just cannot go through what we've been through the past four months [a reference to increasing violence and tension] without some leadership beyond the human. Because to you "the mixture of these two elements seems impossible" you are driven into the position of "either-or," and because Koinonia at times showed evidence of the human you conclude that it therefore could not be spirit-led. . . . Surely we know that the Spirit has not yet led us into the fullness, the maturity, or the stature of Christ, that we have not yet attained or have been made perfect, but forgetting those things which are behind and fastening our eyes on the things before us, we press on toward the mark of the high calling of God in Christ Jesus.

When the Johnsons returned to Koinonia in October, they tried to convince the others that this "unity" that so character-ized the Bruderhof and seemed so elusive at Koinonia was a gift of the Spirit—not something to be earned, but something to be waited on, as the early Christians waited on the power of Pen-tecost. Their message did not get through, however. Koinonia was faced with a frightening upsurge of hostility and the beginnings of an economic boycott. Perhaps the Johnsons did not get the attention they deserved. Or perhaps the Koinonians really were antagonistic to the ideas they were seeking to express. At any rate, in January 1957, the Johnsons withdrew from Koinonia and re-turned to Forest River to seek membership in the Bruderhof, finally winding up in the Bruderhof's new community near Nor-folk, Connecticut.

Koinonia Farm, with its manpower depleted and its spirit wounded, was limping into a new, crucial era that would test the fiber of its fellowship and speed the experiment through a painful metamorphosis.

CHAPTER 7

Persecution

For all his sublimated fighting instinct, Clarence did not look to confrontation as a strategy for exposing hypocrisy. He held firmly to the tactic of persuasion, and regardless of evidence to the contrary, he hoped men's hearts could be changed through grace before their lives had to be changed through law.

He was even known to utter a thought that later characterized desperate segregationists: that forced integration was as bad as forced segregation.

It became increasingly clear, however, that his ideals did not dull his capacity for confrontation. He simply believed in living as normal a course of events as possible, free of fear, without abridging his own freedom or that of anyone else. He would not go out of his way to create an incident, but he would not go out of his way to avoid one, either. Asked in later years if he had ever been on a freedom walk, Clarence replied: "No, but I always walk freely."

When, early in 1956, he was asked to assist two Negro students who wanted to enroll in the previously segregated Georgia State College of Business in Atlanta, he responded affirmatively. The 1954 Supreme Court decision against segregation made it clear that black students were eligible to apply, and so he agreed to help them meet the requirement that applications had to be signed by two alumni of the state system.

Clarence and Harry Atkinson went to Atlanta, interviewed the two students, and suggested that they make an appointment with the president. The students agreed, and Clarence and Harry accompanied them. When the executive secretary of the state board of regents was consulted, he ruled Clarence ineligible as a signatory because he had graduated from a different school in the university system. So Clarence went home without signing the applications.

Reporters had been on the trail of the story, however. The front page of the *Americus Times-Recorder* shouted across Sumter County the next morning that Clarence had signed the applications of two Negro students. Reaction to the Supreme Court ruling had been gathering force for nearly two years, giving rise to white citizens' councils and states'-rights organizations. All the feverish local hostility needed was a target. Those who wanted to take out their emotions violently must have slapped their newspapers that morning and declared to themselves: "That's it. That Koinonia Farm is perfect—it's big, it's defenseless, and it's damn sure suspect!"

The threatening phone calls started that night. The egg market in town closed like a trap, signaling what was to become a massive, thorough boycott. Petty vandalism—fences cut, garbage dumped on the land, corn taken from the fields—became routine overnight. Homemade signs along the Albany highway advertising Koinonia's roadside market were torn down repeatedly until the vandals finally hauled them off. Sugar in the gas tank ruined the engine of a Koinonia vehicle. Bullets from a heavy-caliber pistol were fired into the roadside market.

In June the Sumter County commissioners obtained an injunction to temporarily block the opening of Camp Koinonia, the six-weeks' camp that had been so successful the summer before

for about 30 inner-city children from several states. The second
season was scheduled to open on June 18; the hearing was set for
July 2. Suspecting that the court hassle would tie up the summer,
Koinonia moved the camp to the Highlander Folk School in
Monteagle, Tennessee.

Their suspicions were proved out. On July 2, the county attorney asked for a delay until July 19, saying he had not had time
to prepare his case, and the delay was granted. Then, on July 19,
court convened and Koinonia discovered that four Sumter
County farmers had petitioned the court to be a part of the
injunction on new grounds that read, in part: "The defendants
will operate said camp in a manner that will be detrimental to
morals and purposes, and that they had advertised the camp as
a camping program for children from 8 to 12 and that they will
be shown live pigs being born and have suggested that the camp
and facilities shall be nonsegregated on the basis of sexes."

The courtroom was packed with about 75 spectators, including
six Negroes who were told they would have to sit in the balcony.
Koinonia appeared without a lawyer. The judge, in his opening
remarks, assessed the situation as shaping up to be "a wrangle
between the Gospel and the law." The crowd was merely teased
again, however. The judge ordered both sides to argue by brief
and affidavit, and the deadline was set for September 20.

At the September hearing, both petitions were finally ruled
moot and the cases dismissed due to the summer coming to a
close and the possibility of a summer camp at Koinonia along with
it—but not before Clarence and the solicitor general had a remarkable exchange regarding the morality of birth. Clarence admitted that pigs were due to be born in July while the camp was
in session, but he said that he did not see how the process of birth
could be called immoral without accusing God of immorality.

The solicitor general pressed him: "Did you, as a child, ever belong to any group or organization which allowed you to see such a thing?"

Clarence: "Yes, I did."

"What was it?"

Clarence: "The 4-H Club."

"Why would you allow children under your care to witness it?"

Clarence: "We have been unable to guarantee absolute privacy to our 40-odd sows during farrowing season, and because our hogs are rather stupid, we have been unable to teach them to seclude themselves during this act. Furthermore, we have read all the latest developments on hog-raising, but have discovered no other way of getting baby pigs than by the old-fashioned process of birth."

Meanwhile, the violence had intensified. On July 26, shortly after 10 P.M., an explosive was lobbed at the roadside market, damaging the front of the 20-by-30 building, ripping off a section of roof, and wrecking refrigeration equipment and other fixtures. (Koinonia had established the roadside market a year earlier on a four-acre site on Highway 19 to sell ham and peanuts and other produce on the roadside and by mail order.)

A time of persecution, a time of testing, seemed inevitable now, and yet it seemed so utterly senseless to the Koinonians. They had not been aggressive about their beliefs, nor had they attacked the beliefs of anyone else. They had struggled to be faithful witnesses, and now they were discovering just how threatening their witness was to the larger community around them.

Clarence knew how relentless the ghosts of tradition were. But he also believed that the way of the man called Jesus was a persistant invitation to rise above custom to true manhood. He felt southerners were torn between an ideal and a tradition, many of them professing this radical Jesus with their lips but never quite able to break from tradition with their lives. He and the others at Koinonia had ideas they wanted to share urgently, but not to prove themselves right or to rescue anyone from the pits of hell; it was because they had trusted the ideas themselves and found them fruitful and fulfilling.

So they decided to communicate with the county through newspaper advertisements. Shortly after the bombing, they took out an ad, expressing regret that the actions of one or two persons should bring shame to the whole county. The *Americus Times-Recorder* carried an article of its own, deploring the use of force and coercion, "the very things that our Southland is being subjected to by the United States Supreme Court."

Then, on July 31, Koinonians ran an open letter in the *Times-Recorder*, making a public declaration of their principles and purposes. The letter stated that Koinonia had not made a public statement before, "largely due to the fact that we wanted no one to think that we were trying to force our ideas on them. We wanted simply to live our own lives under God." The letter said that Koinonia Farm did not seek controversy, but that in light of the bombing, people of the county were due the truth. Citing a number of scriptural passages, the letter explained Koinonia's basic beliefs in brotherhood and nonviolence and stated that the community was patterned after the lives of early Christ followers. It mentioned their crops of peanuts, corn, cotton, grain, fruit, and vegetables, their cattle, hog, and poultry endeavors; it said Koinonia Farm borrowed from the local bank, had mortgaged land and good credit, and currently supported about 60 people. The letter also stated that Koinonia was incorporated as a nonprofit religious organization and that it had no connection with any outside group.

"Please do us the favor," the letter closed, "of not believing a rumor until you have checked the facts. We welcome visitors, and will be glad to answer any questions about our life." It was signed by the 22 adults at Koinonia Farm.

With the camp suit hanging fire, Koinonia made another attempt to explain themselves through an ad in the *Times-Recorder*. This time the ad spelled Koinonia phonetically and explained the meaning of the word. "The early church was sometimes called a 'koinonia.' That's what Koinonia Farm seeks to be today. Actually, it is a church—a local church. On Sundays, as well as on nearly every weekday, we meet together for worship, Bible study, and prayer."

The ad told of the ministers at Koinonia—Clarence, Will Wittkamper, Con Browne, Harry Atkinson, and a new resident, J. B. Webster—and it referred to Howard Johnson's experience as a student summer worker for Southern Baptists. It closed: "We pledge ourselves to respect the rights of those who differ with us. We believe the citizens of this county will give us the same consideration."

This time they drew a response. Two days later an ad appeared in a local newspaper signed by a citizen, and it said in part:

If the advertisement [about Koinonia] . . . was an attempt to make the good people of Sumter County sway from their way of thinking or bow their heads in shame, then I am sure I speak for the masses when I say the result was not reached. . . . I would welcome Koinonia's moving to a place well above the Mason-Dixon Line. If I knew that I were living in an area where the bulk of the people did not want me you can be sure I would move away.

Koinonia's communication seemed to fall on deaf ears, with the exception of a few guarded words of encouragement from those who slipped out under the cover of night to whisper: "I'm for you." A good number of citizens obviously chose to take their cue from the citizen's ad and devoted their energies to convincing Koinonia it was not wanted in Sumter County.

The boycott began to solidify quickly in August. They found it impossible to get their cotton crop dusted and ginned. They could not obtain fertilizer and their insurance was cancelled. The farm's poultry produce could not be sold. Farmers who had cooperated with Koinonia in the egg-grading and marketing industry turned their backs and would not even buy the hens or the poultry equipment. Eventually, the remainder of the 4,000 laying hens that could not be given away had to be butchered—a bloodily ironic ritual for the farm that introduced the poultry industry to Sumter County. A mechanic who serviced Koinonia vehicles suddenly refused to be available. They found it difficult to obtain hardware supplies. They lost their checking account and were refused loans even though Koinonia had borrowed and repaid more than $200,000 since 1942. A tractor dealer told a reporter that his business dealings with Koinonia were "satisfactory," but that he had a tractor on practically every farm in the county and public sentiment forced him to quit them.

Koinonia's September 1956 newsletter reported that the cotton was being ginned "by airlift at Shangri-la," an obvious communication to Koinonia's supporters that it was no longer safe to divulge names and places. Gas and oil were reportedly obtained by "airlift."

When Clarence confronted one supplier, he replied: "Nothing personal, understand. It's strictly business with me. I can't afford to lose my customers." Clarence asked him how many customers had put the pressure on him, and he replied: "None, so far. But I'm sure they will." Asked if he were a Christian, he said: "Yes, a Baptist. I admit I don't do a very good job of following Him, but that's not the point here. I just can't lose business."

At about this time, Sumter County solicitor general Charles

Burgamy spoke at the Dougherty County chapter of the States Rights Council, stating that he favored a return to the Ku Klux Klan. The *Albany Journal* reported that he said:

Maybe that's what we need now is for the right kind of Klan to start up again and use a buggy whip on some of these race mixers. I believe that would stop them. . . . I don't know how they feel about it down here in Dougherty County, but I had rather see my little boy dead than sit beside a Negro in the public schools.

Commenting on the violence at Koinonia Farm, Burgamy intimated that the people at Koinonia could be doing it themselves.

In the fall a problem surfaced that was perhaps the toughest. Fourteen-year-old Jim Jordan entered the county high school in nearby Plains, and was suddenly engulfed in a cloud of hostility. Bus rides became almost unbearably tense, with each day feeding an anxiety about the next. The violence until this time had been high drama to Jim and the other children. He and Billy and Greg Wittkamper had slipped out of their houses late at night a number of times to snoop "for evidence" along the road. But now Jim faced the ugliness in a personal, terrifying light.

This was a new experience for the community and a little unexpected. Eleanor had completed high school in Americus only two years before without incident. But Jim faced a daily dose of physical and verbal abuse.

"In one class," he recalled, "a boy threw a knife into the floor right beside my foot. If I sat in the back of the class, no telling what would happen. If I sat in the front, I got a barrage of paper clips and spitballs every time the teacher turned her back. I felt like I entered the playground at my own risk."

The solution was obvious. Jim had to be evacuated from his own home. A number of friends and relatives—including the

Johnsons and the Nelsons in the Bruderhof communities—
offered to take him into their homes. Jim opted for the offer from
the Maendels at the Forest River community, however, and spent
the remainder of the school year living with them and attending
a public school in Inkster, North Dakota.

The publicity from the boycott and the bombing of the market
provoked a wave of letters from friends of Koinonia asking ways
they could help. The October newsletter offered several sugges-
tions, including an appeal for others to join Koinonia either permanently or for a short term. (The list of "friends" was close to
2,000 now and growing rapidly with the increased publicity.)
"We can use carpenters, painters, doctors, dentists, bricklayers,
day laborers, and general farm workers," the newsletter stated. It
also suggested loaning money to the farm, which each year borrowed $12,000–$16,000 for seed, fertilizer, feed, and machinery,
usually at 8 percent interest. A number of people responded by
loaning small amounts of money, to be paid back at certain
intervals.

Late in November, the roadside market was attacked again.
This time buckshot ripped through a $250 refrigerated meat case.
The boycott continued to gain participants, too. When a butane
gas dealer refused to sell, Clarence and one of the other men
confronted him. (This was critical, since butane was the source
of most of the heat, hot water, and cooking fire.) The men
detailed the encounter in a newsletter:

We said our major concern was not to get gas for ourselves but for
the welfare of his own soul. We asked if his action was due to any fault
on our part, and he said no, and that was what made it so hard. We asked
why he had done it and he said he was afraid of the pressure. We asked
how many customers he had lost on account of us—he said, "None!"
We asked who was putting the pressure on him—he said, "Nobody

. . . yet." We said we thought he had given up too easily and was not exhibiting much courage, and did he think he had done right. He said it was wrong, and that he had a splitting headache and was running a fever from it. We asked if he were a follower of Jesus and he said that he belonged to the Methodist Church but was not a very good member. We asked if he thought there was any similarity between his position and that of Judas who sold his Lord for a bit of gain. He said, "Yes, but I feel more like Pilate. I just want to wash my hands and my soul."

We said that tradition has it that Pilate is still trying to wash his hands. "I know," he said, "I know, it's all wrong." He said that he would help us make contact with other sources of supply. We asked if it would be morally right for him, our longtime friend, to ask a stranger to do for us what he himself wouldn't do. He said that he thought that it would not be right, so we asked him if it would be right for us, in time of need, to go to strangers with whom we had not traded regularly when our friend with whom we had traded had refused to stand by us. He didn't think this would be right either. So we asked if he didn't want to reconsider his decision. He said, "No." We said that we would be praying for him. He said, you are doing what Jesus taught, for he said to pray for your enemies and I guess I am your enemy. Friend or enemy, we said, you are an object of God's love and our love. We shook hands with him and told him goodbye.

On December 26, the Sumter County night-riders brought the violence closer to home, pausing across the road from the dwellings and firing four steel-jacketed, heavy-caliber bullets into Koinonia's new electric gasoline pump. Then, on January 1, 1957, they turned their weapons toward the dwellings, ripping the sign at the entrance of the farm with bullets, as if to give fair warning that the new year would bring nightly terror down the Dawson Road.

The community could no longer ignore the question: Should they stay in the face of what appeared to be escalating into complete lawlessness, or should they relocate their experiment in more neutral territory? They had to consider the fact that their fellow citizens in Sumter County were not going to provide protection, or even do much to discourage the violence. No suspect had been questioned on any of the incidents up to that time. And it had been implied in the bombing of the market that the Koinonians themselves might have done it just for the publicity.

The full members met all day for 10 days, hashing their way through everyone's feelings. It would be easy to leave; the farm could be sold and the proceeds invested in a new community location. And would not this be best for the children's sake?

Discussions finally centered down on the ultimate subject—their primary purpose in being there in the first place. If community—their life together—were the primary purpose, then should not the community be protected at all cost? Should not they relocate? But if their witness to racial brotherhood and to a way of peace in the face of violence was foremost, should not they stay, even at the cost of failure as a community?

There was strong counsel from many friends, especially in the Bruderhof, to relocate the community elsewhere, on the grounds that the fellowship should be guarded as the primary purpose. This position was discussed at length, but really never gained serious consideration. They affirmed what Clarence said was the original intention of Koinonia Farm: to remain faithful to the ideas of Jesus in scorn of the consequences.

Florence summed it up: "There was never any feeling that we should leave. We knew we wouldn't be the first Christians to die, and we wouldn't be the last."

Young Jim Jordan reflected years later: "The community was not an end in itself in Daddy's mind. It was a means to a witness. Koinonia was a way of witness and a consequent way of life; not a way of life that suggested maybe we'll make a witness too."

The community did decide, however, that some measure of protection should be taken. At first they decided to light the grounds around the houses to discourage anyone from sneaking up to the dwellings. But this was discarded when they realized that lights around the houses would illuminate the targets. Ora Browne offered the strategy they accepted: lights would be put up along the road, where the shooting was coming from, and night watchmen would stay close to the road armed with flashlights. Her theory was that whoever was doing the shooting would not shoot at a person standing in the open, unarmed except for light. The group agreed, but refused to allow Clarence or Florence to stand watch, figuring that they would be considered primary targets.

Clarence had opportunity, in a little different context, to test that theory. He and Florence were taking a lonely county road home from the roadside market at dusk when a pick-up truck passed them at high speed and disappeared around the next curve. When Clarence went around the curve, his headlights focused on the truck, which was then blocking the road, and more specifically on the shotgun in the hands of the man facing him.

Clarence said later: "I recalled that Scripture that says, 'If a man strikes you on the right cheek, turn to him both heels.' " He stopped, slammed the car into reverse, and probably set a world's record for a 180-degree turn on a small dirt road. "He may have shot at us," Clarence said, "but I didn't hear it if he did. I was traveling faster than the speed of sound."

Shortly after midnight on January 14, the sheriff called to report that the roadside market had been bombed again. Clarence and Harry went immediately to the scene and discovered that the little building had been completely demolished this time. The grass around the building was burning, threatening the beehives nearby, but none of the 40 or so spectators, including the law officers, made a move to help Clarence and Harry extinguish the blaze. About 125 smoked hams and quantities of bacon, sausage, and tongue were destroyed. A few of the hams that were charred badly ˉon the outside were retrieved and eaten without further cooking. All of the refrigeration and cold storage equipment was destroyed, and there was no trace of the peanuts, pecans, honey, popcorn, syrup, and eggs. The loss totaled about $7,000. (The roadside market had done about $7,000 worth of business during its first year of operation in 1955–56. At the end of 1956, however, it did $7,000 worth of business in one month, due primarily to a mail-order business suggested by a Peacemakers conference to help overcome the boycott.)

Later, vandals burned down the sign in front of the market, destroyed the beehives, and in one night chopped down nearly 300 of the apple, peach, and pecan trees planted on the four acres.

On January 17, Ora Browne answered a phone call and a voice said: "Tell Clarence to be on watch tonight, and be careful." Ora felt that the call was from someone who was sincerely trying to warn them. The guard was doubled. In the middle of the night, flames lit the sky about a half-mile from Koinonia's dwellings. It was an abandoned shack on the backside of the property. The men decided not to go to the fire because of the warning earlier in the day. They suspected that it was an attempt to draw them, and particularly Clarence, away from the community.

At 4:30 A.M. that same night, Gil and Marguerite Butler and Clarence went to Jack Singletary's house about six miles away near Plains. Jack was to accompany them on a trip to Atlanta. When they drove up into his yard, they noticed a small fire under his barn, where tractors, a combine, feed, fertilizer, and seed were stored. Clarence and Gil checked it out and extinguished a flare. Two others had fizzled out. (Jack had continued his relationship with Koinonia and experienced some pressure and boycott of his own because of it. In fact, his son was in the hospital in Americus fighting a terminal case of leukemia at about this time, when someone put sugar in the gas tank of his car in the hospital parking lot.)

The tension of fear and fatigue, and the anticipation that the worst was yet to come, moved Clarence late in January to write to President Dwight Eisenhower. The letter opened:

"A community of nearly sixty men, women, and children is facing annihilation unless quick, decisive action is taken by someone in authority. I am therefore appealing to you as a last resort, with the hope and prayer that you might find some course of action before it is too late." The letter described the nature of the community and then stated: "We welcome into our fellowship any person of any color or race. At present there are about 15 Negroes and 45 white people in the group. Until the Supreme Court's decision on desegregation of schools, and the subsequent rise of the White Citizens' Councils, we were not molested. Since then our life together has become increasingly difficult and our very existence more precarious."

Clarence described the violence and the boycott in some detail and explained that a district judge and Senator Herman Talmadge had been consulted with no apparent result.

"Nothing has been done," he wrote. "Groups of 10 to 12 cars are forming and riding at night. We have been told that the end is near. We shall not run, for this is America. It is a land where free men have the right—and the duty—to walk erect and without fear in their pursuit of peace and happiness. Should this freedom perish from our land, we would prefer to be dead. We gladly offer our lives for its preservation."

The letter obviously fell short of the President's desk into pneumatic red tape. More than a month later, a letter from the Attorney General's office arrived, addressed to Clarence. In brief, it acknowledged receipt of his letter, said that it had been for-warded to this office, and expressed "a strong aversion to acts of violence." It further stated, however, that the primary responsibil-ity for the maintenance of law and order rested with state and local authorities, that apparently no Federal law had been breached, and that Clarence's letter, consequently, was being forwarded to the governor of the state of Georgia.

This had to be reassuring. Less than a year before, Governor Marvin Griffin reportedly had called the sheriff of Sumter County —after Clarence's visit with the Negro students in Atlanta—to ask who "this Jordan fellow" was.

In fact, only two or three days before Clarence received the disappointing letter, Georgia Attorney General Eugene Cook was quoted in the *Americus Times-Recorder* as saying that the Georgia Bureau of Invesigation had been investigating Koinonia Farm for more than a year for possible "subversive activities." "Communists have been known to visit a number of times," Cook was reported to have said, but the state had been unable to "ascertain whether the Koinonia operation constitutes a con-spiracy to overthrow the government." The article also quoted the Georgia revenue commissioner as saying that Koinonia had in-come tax and tax penalties due since 1949 and that "we are not going to approve a tax exemption for them. We think it neither charitable nor religious. It's simply a move to integrate the races and I think it is a disgrace."

In light of that, Clarence and the others hardly felt relieved when they read their copy of the U.S. Attorney General's letter to Governor Griffin, which said: "I am sure you will agree that the Koinonia community is entitled to full protection of the law against the kind of conduct about which complaint is made. I am sure that you will also agree that if our constitutional distribution of power between the national government and the states is to be effective, the states must act vigorously to deal with such acts of violence."

The attempt to communicate with authorities had been futile. On a state and local level, as the next few months were to reveal, the authorities were looking into the situation, sure enough, but their intention obviously was not to protect Koinonia Farm. Their aim was to prosecute it. Meanwhile, the heavy implications in public statements by chief law enforcement officers, such as the state attorney general and county solicitor general, were not missed by those who were inclined to violence. Obviously the enemy resided at that strange farm on the Dawson Road, and the law was surely not going to prosecute anyone for treating enemies the way patriots knew enemies should be treated.

The worst *was* yet to come.

CHAPTER 8

Night Riders and
Grand Jury Justice

At about 1 A.M. on January 29, 1957, Con Browne shuffled in from the night watch and stretched out on the living room sofa. He had no sooner dozed off when the terrifying clatter of a machine gun jolted him awake. He raced to the window and looked out across the yard. There was no sign of movement in the other houses or outside in the crisp, cold night. Must have been dreaming, he concluded. He fell back on the couch and dropped off to sleep immediately.

He had looked in the wrong direction. In a Koinonia car parked next to the old house across the Dawson Road, Harry Atkinson was struggling to lift his trembling body from the floorboard. A car had just raced around the curve belching high-caliber bullets from a machine gun, raking the dwelling and pumping one bullet at head height through the night watch car, where Harry had just settled in relief of Con. Tracer bullets had streaked out across the open land in nightmare ribbons of terror.

A visitor from Michigan, a truck driver on a return trip from Florida, was outside hopping on one leg, pulling on his pants, and shouting: "This is war, this is war!" A bullet had thundered through a window in his room, ripped through his hat on the bedside stand, and splintered through the door.

Inside the old frame house, another guest, Ross Anderson, was

121

slapping out a burning curtain apparently set afire by a tracer bullet. Four other holes smoked in the wall beside his bed, where bullets had passed just inches above his body. Seven bullets in all had torn through the house.

The Michigan visitor understandably wanted to get an early start to Detroit. He approached Clarence with his hat, showing him the clean bullet hole in the band and asking if Clarence wanted him to leave it behind as evidence. Glancing at the bullet-riddled house, Clarence laughed and suggested instead that he take the hat home and without saying whether or not his head was in it at the time, explain how the hole got there "as evidence of warm southern hospitality."

Con Browne's brother-in-law, a career Army man decorated from campaigns in Korea, visited Koinonia not long after that, driving over from Fort Benning, near Columbus, Georgia. Told about the machine-gun attack, he became enraged, saying that a machine gun would have to have been military issue. Clarence and Con recalled that the attack had come after a National Guard meeting in Americus. The visitor from the U.S. Army paced up and down the Dawson Road and finally told Con: "This place is completely indefensible. The road runs right through the middle of it." He returned a week later with a trunkload of weapons and said he wanted to take a turn standing the night watch. After vigorous persuasion from Con and the others, he finally agreed to stand watch unarmed. But he pulled a chair out under one of the street lights near the road and sat down in full Army dress—decorations and all—as if to dare someone to shoot at him. No one did.

Just two days after the machine-gun attack, shortly after 9 P.M., two cars approached the farm from the direction of Americus, and men in both cars leaned from the windows firing shotguns toward the houses. Shot sprinkled the lighted volleyball court where the children were playing, sending them sprawling and screaming—but unhurt—into the nearby orchard. One bullet, believed to be from a .22 rifle, cracked through a window in the Brownes' house, narrowly missing their 11-year-old daughter Lora Ruth.

Clarence saw the children scattering from the volleyball court and exploded with anger. He remembered only that he was running toward the road and wishing for his old Army rifle. He knew, for the first time, he said, the primordial urge to kill. "The sheriff had been saying he never could find any evidence. I wanted to get him some, even if it were dead when I got it."

As normal an impulse as that may have seemed, Clarence regretted it deeply. He wrestled with his emotions, finally satisfying himself with the understanding that, "but for the grace of God," he might have been doing the shooting himself. A few months later, he was fired on from a passing car while on a tractor. He just kept working.

Koinonians had to work fast between aggravations to cope with their anger and fear. Only nine nights later, just before midnight, several men arrived in a battered pick-up truck, jumped out, erected a wooden cross covered with oil-saturated burlap, and ignited it. The light from an oncoming car chased them back to their truck and into the cover of darkness. There were three other cross-burnings in the next several nights in the Negro community, which caused many black friends to stay away from Koinonia. One cross was burned at the home of the parents of Alma Jackson, a young Negro man who had recently joined Koinonia. The terrorism rushed to a flamboyant climax on Sunday, February 24, when the Knights of the Ku Klux Klan rallied in Americus.

Some 150 men and women from all over southern Georgia, including the Great Titan of the Sixth Province from Macon, gathered in white robes and peaked hoods for the rally at the

Americus fairgrounds on Friendship Road. A Klan spokesman told an *Americus Times-Recorder* reporter that "the KKK represented a new group of the Klan and that it had no connection at all with the 'old Klan.'" Throughout the meeting the leaders emphasized that the KKK did not condone violence. According to the newspaper report, the meeting opened with a prayer that declared the meeting was being held to "uplift mankind and the kingdom of heaven." The presiding officer talked about "20 million people trying to destroy 140 million others," and about how he could not understand why "the white man had to bow down to minority groups." He said the KKK had no real fight against the Negro, but "against the white men on the inside who are fighting the Negro's cause for money."

One speaker, a minister, called for "all red-blooded Americans who are proud of their white race" to uphold the teachings of the Bible, which he said revealed no evidence to support integration. Quoting from the Old Testament, he declared segregation as God's law and that as such, it would withstand court rulings or any other attack. A Klansman called for unity of purpose against integration.

At the close of the rally, the Klan members took off their robes, formed a motorcade of 70 to 80 cars, and struck out down the Dawson Road to Koinonia Farm.

Margaret Wittkamper was pushing her youngest son Danny in a carriage, walking toward the road with the intention of crossing it. When she saw the slow-moving line of cars snake around the curve, she stopped to watch. The lead car halted in front of her, and the others eased to a halt behind it, remaining in single file. The cars stretched from the gate of Koinonia Farm almost out of sight around the curve toward Americus. Margaret, a short wisp of a woman who never expected the worst from anyone, had not gotten the picture. She was awed by the procession. When a man stepped from the lead car in front of her, she asked politely: "Whose funeral is it?" The man replied gruffly: "It might very well be yours."

Norman Long, who was president of Koinonia at the time, John Eustice, and Chris Drescher walked toward the road to greet the men from the lead car, who had gotten out and asked Margaret where the leader was. (The Jordans were visiting their son Jim at Forest River.) *Americus Times-Recorder* newsmen Rudy Hayes was on the scene, and he said that the men were not from Sumter County. He reported that the meeting was congenial, and that each party addressed the other as "gentlemen."

One of the Klansmen asked the Koinonia group if they were Communist. Norman Long answered: "No, unless Jesus Christ was a Communist. We follow his teachings." A Klansman remarked that the reason for the motorcade was to protest the interracial living at the farm. Asked who they represented, the Klansmen answered: "A group of interested citizens." The Klansmen then proposed that the people of Koinonia move on out of southern Georgia, saying that the Klan would see to it that they received full value for their property and equipment. Long replied: "If anyone makes us an offer, we'll consider it, but we're making no commitments."

The encounter lasted only about eight minutes. (Hayes reported in his news article: "Prior to the meeting it was not generally known that Americus has a [Klan] unit, but it was described as 'Unit 10.' ")

Young Billy Wittkamper remembered: "That was the first time we could really see fear in the faces of the adults."

The pressure began to build after the Klan visit. The lights along the road were shot out. The fence was cut repeatedly, allowing the hogs out on the highway at night and creating a driving hazard. John Eustice was fired on at near point-blank range when he rushed to investigate a car that had stopped at night alongside Koinonia's hog fence. Bullets ripped the flashlight from his hand and smashed the outside rear-view mirror of the night watch car.

Anger in the county was compounded when a light-skinned Negro girl walked down the streets of Americus with two Negro boys, sharing popcorn from a single bag. She was mistaken for a white, and startled onlookers apparently made immediate association with Koinonia Farm.

The Associated Press reported Sheriff Fred Chappell as saying: "The people have had it up to here. We get reports of whites and Negroes strolling down the streets together in Americus. One report said a white girl and two Negro boys walked down the street all eating popcorn out of the same bag." The same news service quoted Charles Crisp, president of the Americus Bank of Commerce: ". . . when they deliberately tried to upset our equilibrium by having a white girl and a Negro man walk down the street side by side, eating peanuts out of the same bag, it was a calculated affront."

Rufus Angry, a tall, lanky Negro who had sharecropped in Sumter County before bringing his family to Koinonia Farm in 1955, finally broke under the strain. The shots, the scurrying in the night, the hushed voices, the piercing drawl of the sheriff in the darkness—all of the nightmare routine that accompanied the violence—began to haunt him. "I really liked Koinonia," he said, "and I'd be there yet if I hadn't got so upset. All that shooting really got next to me and I just couldn't get over it."

Tension weighed heavy on all of them. The community decided the Angrys should be moved and that another family should accompany them for a time. Friends in Pennsylvania, John and Mary Thomas, told Clarence of the Hidden Springs community

in central New Jersey, an outgrowth of an experiment in cooperative gardening begun by five families in 1940. The families at
Hidden Springs agreed that the Angrys could move into the one
available residence. Koinonia decided the Atkinsons should accompany them. The two families left immediately, the Angrys
taking the house at Hidden Springs, the Atkinsons staying temporarily with the Thomases. (The evacuation developed into a full-
scale attempt at establishing a second Koinonia, but the next year
revealed that New Jersey townships were no sanctuary from resentment and discrimination.)

Meanwhile, the boycott continued to suffocate Koinonia Farm
economically and the pace of the violence continued to gain
momentum. With the last of the insurance policies canceled, the
farm faced a crisis. The land was mortgaged and the mortgage
called for a minimum of $10,000 insurance. A friend of Koinonia,
Louis Smith of the College of the Bible in Lexington, Kentucky,
organized the Christian Brotherhood Insurance Plan, and Koinonia's mailing list got another chance to participate in this embattled experiment. The plan called for friends to sign a promissory
note of up to $50 in the event of major damage to property. Two
thousand pledges would amount to $100,000 worth of insurance.
If a $10,000 loss occurred, each person would put up $5.00, or 10
percent of his pledge. The idea worked. Within a few weeks
nearly 2,000 friends around the country had signed such a pledge.

Others came to share the experiences of Koinonia in these
times. Ross Anderson, undaunted by the machine-gun attack on
one of his first nights at the farm, joined the community as a
novice. He was a slim, bearded Californian, soft-spoken and legally blind, although he could see well enough to get around
unassisted. He was a good cook and took charge of much of the
kitchen activity. Wally and Juanita Nelson of Philadelphia, who

had met Ross and others from Koinonia through an organization known as Peacemakers, volunteered to live at Koinonia for four months, beginning in March 1957.

The Nelsons were a soberly activist Negro couple who made a career of opposing militarism, working only at menial jobs and earning as little salary as possible in order to carry on their resolve not to pay taxes because of rising military expenditures. Wally served 33 months in prison for walking out of a conscientious objectors' camp during World War II. His meaningful work was through Peacemakers, Juanita's as a free-lance writer.

Norman Long had invited the Nelsons, writing to Wally that local Negroes were being intimidated and that Wally could be of help. Norman wrote: "Being a Yankee, an outsider, a Negro, and an agitator all rolled into one, you would be quite loathesome. So if you feel you should not come, you should not hesitate to say so."

Wally, who was short, quiet, and poker-faced, spent a good bit of his time running the boycott. Traveling with crisp new dollar bills, he would go to neighboring towns for peanut seed, feed, and other necessities. "Nobody knew me," he said. "I never spent so much money in my life. On my first trip to Albany [Georgia], I had thirteen $100 bills. Really, I think most of the people could have guessed where I was from, but when I pulled out that roll of bills each time, they were ready to take it." (Later, this got on the conscience of the community, and they agreed not to use visitors to trick the boycotters.)

On Easter Sunday 1957, an unusual number of cars drove by the farm, and from one a sadly symbolic scrap of paper fluttered to the side of the road. One of the children retrieved it. The small piece of paper had been torn from the bottom of a church bulletin. On one side were mimeographed the words: "Blessed is the man whose words and deeds are day by day and every day a witness to the living and loving Lord." On the other side, crudely penciled in large letters, was written: "Get out, You Mongrels!"

Later that week, John Gabor rushed out to the road when he saw a car stop at night near where the hog wire had been cut time and again. The car raced off after someone inside fired a gun in Gabor's direction. Seventy-year-old Chris Drescher was fired on while sitting his night-watch shift in the car. Not long after that, Eleanor Jordan came home for a weekend from the University of Georgia. At about 10:30 P.M. she entered her room, pulled down the shade, and turned on the light. At that second a bullet from a high-powered rifle pounded through the wall, splattered through the mirror in front of her, and crashed through two other rooms before thumping into a hall closet, scattering tinker-toys and coming to rest in a jigsaw puzzle.

The same week a load of buckshot was pumped into the home of the Top Wilsons, an elderly Negro couple who were not members of Koinonia but who were provided with a house on the farm and worked for wages. On another night, six shots were heard again at the farm, awakening everyone but causing no apparent damage.

When the Nelsons insisted on taking their turns on the night watch, the community balked. First of all, the Nelsons did not profess to be Christians and were not members of the community. Should they be allowed to risk their lives? And secondly, they were black, and everyone felt that those doing the shooting would have no compunction against shooting a black person. But Wally and Juanita insisted on taking their turns, and so, with great trepidation, the community consented.

All those who stood watch had to deal with fear. As Con Browne said: "I knew if I didn't walk toward the road when a car came by, I would forever be running from it." (One elderly woman who paid an extended visit to the farm had the opposite sort of problem. During the day, working in the garden near the road, she would look up and stick out her tongue at every car that passed, compelling the others to explain to her what they meant by "loving one's enemies.")

Fear had to be dealt with and so did the increasingly critical economic situation. It was beginning to be questionable whether or not the farming program could continue. No feed or seed or fertilizer was available locally, nor was gasoline or oil or any of the other hundreds of items normally considered routine for operation.

Adding aggravation to aggravation was the miraculously persistent presence of a vile-talking, eccentric, knuckle-cracking man who at one time had enjoyed a friendly relationship with Koinonia. He was unstable and eager to please, however, and some in the town obviously used him to taunt Koinonia. He dogged Con on the egg route and cursed him openly and loudly in every store, and he spooked the children when he saw them in town. He would call the farm in the middle of the night and start off a discussion with Clarence saying something like: "Hello you goddamn Communist, you crazy old bastard. I hear your daughter. . . ." Wherever people from Koinonia went in the county, he was there. It was as if someone paid his carfare to keep up with them. Once he spotted Florence in a neighboring town with a distinguished visitor—tough, intellectual Dorothy Day, one of the founders of the Catholic Worker movement and editor of the Catholic Worker periodical. They were trying to buy peanut seed when he verbally assaulted them, calling Miss Day "a g-g-goddamn northern Communist whore."

Dorothy suffered a worse fright when she took a turn on the night watch with North Carolina visitor Elizabeth Morgan. A car sped by and an occupant fired a rifle at the night watch car. The bullet entered the hood of the car, spent itself ripping through metal, and fell flat at Dorothy's feet. Ora Browne, who always was the first to come running to see if anyone was hurt, ran up to Dorothy, noticed that her elderly friend was trembling, and offered her coat. Stern, fiery Dorothy turned to her and refused the coat, saying: "That ain't cold, baby, that's scared."

One would have thought that the people at Koinonia were suffering the most from tension, battle fatigue, and fear. But one night that spring, when Con Browne and a visitor from Virginia, Cliff Hoffman, were standing watch together, a pick-up truck rolled into the driveway and a man stumbled from it with a pistol in his hand. Stone drunk, he weaved his way toward the two watchmen, muttering that he was coming to kill Clarence Jordan because Clarence's very presence in the county was about "to give his father a heart attack." His father was a merchant in town and among those boycotting Koinonia. Con and Cliff managed to calm him down, and after a few more incoherent remarks, the man stumbled back to his truck and drove off.

In the spring, the pressure on Koinonia took a more official tack. Clarence, Con, Wally Nelson, and Alma Jackson were summoned before the Sumter County Grand Jury. Koinonia Farm was to be investigated.

Clarence did most of the testifying, and the mailing list and financial records that he carried with him were taken by the court over his protest. "I tried to explain to them the difference between Christ and Marx," he said, "but it soon became clear that they didn't know anything about either one of them."

After seven days of investigation, on April 5, 1957, the jury returned a no-bill. No indictments were brought, but the grand jury's 16-page report catalogued a number of charges against Koinonia, including the implication that Koinonia was Communist-supported. The statement was published in the *Americus Times-Recorder* and mailed to congressmen, senators, the gover-

nor, and the U.S. Attorney General. The charges (or implications) were, briefly:

—That the weight of evidence indicated Koinonia Farm not
only profited from the violence; the community committed the
violence on itself.

—That Koinonia's claim to Christianity "is sheer window
dressing and its practice of Christianity has no precedent in the
religious annals of the United States."

—That Koinonia's charter as a nonprofit religious corporation
is "misleading, false, and fraudulent and, under the shelter of a
charter designating it as a nonprofit corporation, certain individuals are amassing to themselves enormous profits."

—That Koinonia profited from the destruction of the roadside
market by collecting insurance.

—That Koinonia owed tax and penalties since 1949.

—That Koinonia's claim to interracial brotherhood was untrue
and that Negroes at the farm have "relegated themselves into a
status of brainwashed peonage, while those few members of the
white race higher up in official personnel enrich themselves at the
expense of the Negro's toil."

—That "any known Communist in the United States is a
welcome guest."

—That Clarence L. Jordan's integrity was in such question that
"we have had to discard as untrue some testimony he gave to this
grand jury under oath, as we could not believe it."

The report presented charges of perjury, fraud, disturbing the
peace, and suspicion of conspiracy, was published countywide,
and was sent to authorities all over the state and in Washington,
D.C.—all that, but no formal indictments were returned.

Quoting from Koinonia's financial records, the jury showed
how the farm had received $27,500 in donations since the out-
break of violence 10 months earlier, and then implied that the

$7,000 loss of the roadside market was the only loss Koinonia had during those months. The roadside market's sales, the jury stated, also had jumped from $7,000 a year to $7,000 a month since publicity of the violence.

The report said that Koinonia, after the incidents of violence, consistently called the Associated Press "and other news agencies" before notifying local law enforcement officials. Two examples were cited: the report of the shooting at John Eustice about midnight on March 5, 1957, and the report of the shooting out of three floodlights on February 15, 1957.

The jury charged that the "physical facts" did not "coincide with the story as to how the incidents occurred as given by members of Koinonia Farm, Inc." The jury claimed that the alleged shooting involving night watchman Eustice "was a framed and fixed act of violence on the part of Koinonia Farm, Inc." The report said it was impossible for buckshot to have been fired at Eustice and knock the flashlight from his hand without hitting him. Then it said that Eustice reported that only two shots were fired and yet evidence showed that three bullets from a pistol had pierced the outside mirror of the car and two had hit the flashlight. The jury concluded that the angle at which the bullets entered the flashlight proved that Eustice could not have been holding the flashlight as he testified. The state crime laboratory report showed powder burns on the flashlight, indicating that the shots were fired at close range. Eustice had said about 15 feet, but that would not have been close enough to cause powder burns, the jury reasoned.

The jury stated further: "There was glass in the flashlight, and in the car mirror immediately before the shooting took place and John Eustice and the investigating law enforcement officials were unable to find any glass or fragments thereof at the scene where it was alleged to have happened."

According to the jury report, officers could find no evidence of shattered glass from the floodlights, either. In the bombing incidents, it was a Koinonia spokesman, not a law officer, who described the explosive as "dynamite." And a Koinonia car was reported to have been near the scene minutes before the bombing. Also, the jury said, "we find that many residents who sleep at Koinonia Farm, Inc., at night were never awakened during any of these so called acts of violence. . . ."

The jury declared the Koinonia newsletters "are in effect propaganda sheets and used for the purpose of soliciting donations and creating sympathy by the statements contained therein which were not true and, by innuendo and implication, to present a false picture as to these reported incidents of violence to the people of the United States. On the mailing list of Koinonia Farm, Inc., consisting of so called friends and sympathizers, are the names of known Communists and Communistic organizations."

(Clarence later recalled being questioned about "untruths." He said he asked for an example and the following statement from a Koinonia newsletter describing the frequent cutting of the hog wire was quoted: "Lest some passing motorist, traveling fast at night, be seriously hurt, it might be necessary to equip each of our pigs' tails with a reflector button." This was read aloud and followed by: "There! You know you can't put a taillight on a pig!"

(The attorney also referred to the newsletter that claimed the sheriff never investigated the burning of the abandoned house on Koinonia property. The sheriff told the jury he did investigate it, and Clarence apologized to him.)

The jury charged that the Koinonia testimony revealed that "they would welcome Communists into their community and corporation. They further testified under oath it was their policy to accept or do business with any individual without any inquiry into the character of the individual or any concern as to his loyalty to the Government of the United States." Pursuing this line, the report said Jordan was on the board of directors of the Southern Conference Educational Fund, Inc., the predecessor of which was a known Communist organization on the U.S. Attorney General's subversive list. The list of directors, the jury claimed, contained the names of known Communists. Jordan, the jury said, denied knowing any of the other directors or officers of the corporation but admitted being a director.

Then the report turned to the Highlander Folk School at Monteagle, Tennessee, where Koinonia had moved its summer camp the year before. Highlander was another known nest of Communists, the jury stated, and the director, Myles Horton, was "known to be a member of the Communist party. He has visited at Koinonia Farm, Inc., where his views must have been favorably received. Otherwise, the children would not have been transferred to an establishment under his supervision and control."

The jury concluded: "We have received expert advice to the effect that this evidence is insufficient to convict of communism in a court of law. However, we are pleased to leave to the good judgment and understanding of the people who read these presentments the question of whether there exists extremely close kinship between the Communist party and Koinonia Farm, Inc."

The jury report claimed that many Koinonia residents were living "in abject poverty"; that Koinonia was not affiliated with any religious group, and that, in fact, "its only claimed religious gatherings are held on its own premises"; that prospective members are subjected to "severe mental strain and punishment" to convince them to deed all of their material possessions to the corporation; that no Negro had ever progressed beyond the first stage of membership and thus had no word in policy decisions; that one of the Negroes interviewed before the jury said that he received no compensation for his labor; that Koinonia had become a haven for conscientious objectors, many of whom had served terms in the Federal penitentiary for their refusal to register for the draft; and that "the reported violence at Koinonia Farm, Inc., can and will be stopped when Koinonia Farm, Inc., sees fit to stop such violence."

The grand jury's presentments also included an admonishment of the Americus and Sumter County Ministerial Association for approving a resolution deploring the violence directed at Koinonia Farm. The jury stated: "We feel that the Americus and Sumter County Ministerial Association should be mildly rebuked for taking ill-considered action which did reflect discredit upon our county and its people without making sufficient effort to ascertain the facts and without bringing more deliberation to bear upon the results of such hasty action. We believe it fair to state that neither the pastor of the First Methodist Church of Americus, the pastor of the First Baptist Church of Americus, nor the pastor of the Central Baptist Church of Americus participated in this action, and that many ministers throughout the county were not present; and certainly they are expressly excluded from any criticism herein. This grand jury believes that the people of this county are entitled to expect the sincere cooperation and helpfulness of those gentlemen who constitute the personnel of the ministerial association. If they are going to live with us they should work with us and, if they can't do us good, they should strive not to do us harm."

Koinonia prepared a detailed response to the presentments and tried to buy advertising space in the Americus newspaper in order to publish it. The newspaper refused. Koinonia then printed the response in pamphlet form and mailed a copy to everyone in the Americus-Sumter County phone book.

To the charge that Koinonia was responsible for the violence, Koinonia replied: "This is absolutely untrue. . . . Law enforcement officers have had full access to the grounds of Koinonia Farm at all times and the Farm is open to any kind of investigation that they may wish to make."

Referring to the shooting out of the floodlights, Koinonia said there may not have been glass around the floodlights when the sheriff investigated, but that the marks of buckshot were still clearly visible in the reflectors. Then, in reference to the incident involving John Eustice, Koinonia stated: "The presentments state that the evidence makes it impossible for John Eustice to have been fired upon in the manner indicated in his testimony. One of the main reasons given is that the damage to the flashlight he was holding could not have been caused by a shotgun blast without striking him as well. Neither John Eustice nor any other resident of Koinonia Farm testified to the Grand Jury or said at any other time that this was the result of a shotgun blast. On the contrary, all indications are that the shots in question were fired by pistol or rifle. The Grand Jury nowhere explains why it concluded that a shotgun must have been involved, but it proceeds to build up a mass of contradictions based on this conclusion. The fact that bullets struck the flashlight from different angles is also alleged to present 'impossible' contradictions in John Eustice's testimony. While we are not ballistics experts, we offer the common sense explanation that John Eustice would most likely have moved in the course of the shooting and that the position of the flashlight in his hand would logically have changed."

Koinonia said that a member of Koinonia Farm was able to find pieces of shattered glass at the scene, even though the jury reported that law officers could not find any. The farm's statement said that the matter of powder burns could not be explained, but added: "All of the evidence was turned over to a representative of the Georgia Bureau of Investigation. We were disturbed to learn that immediately after returning from his investigation at

Koinonia, and before the flashlight was submitted to the state laboratory, this GBI agent expressed himself to Lee Griggs, reporter for *Time*, as convinced that the whole incident was staged by Koinonia persons and falsified by them. The agent said it was his idea that the Koinonia people knew the reporter was coming and wanted to create some news for him. An account of this exchange was given to us in writing by the reporter involved and is on file at Koinonia Farm."

The jury also had attached some significance to the fact that Koinonia people used the word "dynamite" in referring to the bombing of the roadside market. Koinonia said the dynamite was referred to only because it is "the explosive most commonly available and most commonly used to cause an explosion." Koinonia also stated, in answer to the jury's reference to residents sleeping through the violence, that the violence had been frequent and the night watchmen were instructed not to awaken everyone when it occurred.

Koinonia also denied that it had gained any economic advantage from the violence, stating that the community was willing to have a professionally qualified certified public accountant examine the books and make an audit. Koinonia confirmed that about $20,000 had been received as gifts and donations since the violence, not $27,500. The other $7,500 reflected the amounts turned over to the common funds of the farm by new members.

"There is nothing insidious about the fact that the very real violence against Koinonia should have prompted persons of good will to offer such assistance," the statement read, adding that the jury had made no mention of the $13,000 worth of property damage, the productive energies of members dissipated in meeting legal harassment, boycotts, the moving of two families out of the area, the greatly reduced farm income, or of the fact that a number of notes had become due because of Koinonia's inability to maintain insurance.

Koinonia also revealed that the roadside market had done $7,-000 worth of business for only one month and that gross sales since the violence had averaged only $1,809.62 per month.

"Even if the Grand Jury's account were accepted," Koinonia said, "who could believe that Koinonia itself would destroy a property that was yielding so much revenue?" Koinonia also reported that insurance had recovered only slightly more than $1,-000 of the $13,000 damage.

Little needed to be said in response to the jury's claim that Koinonia Farm was racist and discriminated against Negro residents "for the gain of a few." In recent years, only three Negroes had applied for the first stage of membership and this was granted, Koinonia's statement said. No Negro had applied for the final stage of membership and "none has been denied or would be denied because of race." As to a few whites getting rich, Koinonia simply stated that it was "completely and legally impossible for any individual to profit personally from the proceeds of Koinonia Farm." Koinonia also pointed out that novices, provisional members, and full members participated with equal voice in decisions affecting business matters and that full members had exclusive authority only in spiritual matters.

(The jury had questioned Alma Jackson who, when asked, said he had received a pair of shoes, a pair of pants, and pocket change since living at Koinonia. "I got what I needed," he said. "That's all I needed." The attorneys mentioned in front of Alma that they suspected Con Browne of the market bombing.)

Responding to the allegation that it was profit-making, Koinonia referred to its Federal classification as a nonprofit corporation and the fact that no members of the corporation received wages, salary, dividends, or bonuses, and that the corporation met living expenses and personal needs. The grand jury's report that Koinonia had a net worth of $150,000 was declared "utterly false" by the Koinonians, who pointed out that the jury did not mention nearly $60,000 of indebtedness, the inflation of values in the past 14 years, nor the assets new members had put into the community. Koinonia also clarified that Clarence Jordan had filed an income tax return every year, even though he could claim no income, adding: "We further state that Koinonia Farm pays all state and county taxes on its property, claiming no homestead or other exemptions."

The farm's statement denied that Koinonians had made a practice of calling the press before notifying the sheriff of the violence, and·pointed out that the first publicity of violence was in the *Americus Times-Recorder*. Koinonia confirmed that reporters had requested that the farm notify them of the incidents, but that the policy always had been to notify the sheriff first.

Koinonians also denied that they had lied under oath before the jury, and said that if they had done so they would have been guilty of perjury and subject to indictment by the jury.

To the implication of Communist affiliation, Koinonia replied that its sustained witness to nonviolence was in direct conflict with the Communist philosophy, and that the jury itself had stated that members of Koinonia had served in prison rather than take up arms against their fellow men.

Regarding visitors, Koinonia said that the jury distorted a letter to Georgia's Attorney General Cook, which said:

Should a Communist party member visit us here he would be welcomed in Christian concern, just as would a member of the Methodist church, the Republican party, the Americus Chamber of Commerce or the White Citizens' Council. But such welcome would not signify any affiliation with or ideological agreement with any of these, just as our recent receiving of the Ku Klux Klan did not signify agreement or affiliation with them.

As to Clarence's appointment as a director of the Southern Conference Educational Fund, Koinonia stated that shortly before the grand jury investigation, he was notified that he had been elected as a director. His intention was to turn down the opportunity—which he later did—because of the pressing circumstances at Koinonia. Clarence did not know the other directors mentioned to him by the attorney and answered accordingly.

"We wish to make it clear that we have no reason to believe that the SCEF is a Communist organization," the statement said, "and we note that the Grand Jury presents no specific evidence to support such a conclusion."

Regarding the Highlander Folk School affiliation, Koinonia said it still directed and controlled the children's camp at that site (the camp was given up a year later) and that there was "no evidence to our knowledge that Myles Horton 'has for long years been known to be a member of the Communist Party.' Again, the Grand Jury has produced no evidence to support such a charge."

Finally, Koinonians deplored the fact "that the Grand Jury sees fit to sit in judgment on the sincerity of the Christian conviction of members of Koinonia Farm and others."

Then they concluded: "We wish to reaffirm our faith in God and in the essential goodness of every human being which He has created. We are convinced that as His Spirit broods over us we shall be less inclined toward strife and more inclined toward peace. It is our belief that the solution to the problem of the South—and the Nation—does not lie in violence, force and coercion. It lies in the redemptive love of God as revealed in Jesus Christ."

Events yet to come were to indicate that the powerful people of Americus and Sumter County could be an influence for ending the violence. All that had to happen, apparently, was for that violence to reach town.

CHAPTER 9

In Scorn
of the Consequences

With hostility smoking and blazing around Koinonia Farm and the embattled community experiment reeling under one assault after another, Clarence received a letter from the pastor of an affluent suburban congregation assuring him of sympathy and "our daily prayers." Clarence impatiently fired off a response by return mail: "Don't you sympathize with me. . . . I sympathize with you, in all your wealth and with men speaking highly of you. . . ."

The "bath of fire" should be taken for granted by the serious Christian, Clarence believed, and he was quick to repudiate the association of "God's work" with absence of tension. "The dove doesn't roost on a person who is scared to get hurt," he often stated. "If you want to share the life of Christ, you should be prepared for the suffering of Christ."

Speaking of Koinonia's persecution, Clarence declared before one audience: "I would rather face the frantic, childish mob, even with their shotguns and buggy whips, than the silent, insidious mob of good church people who give assent to boycott and subtle psychological warfare. What can I say for those who know the word of God and will not speak it?"

Faith, to Clarence's way of thinking, was "a life in scorn of the consequences." Why was faith so scarce? "The answer is fear,"

Clarence would bellow to his audiences around the nation. "Faith and fear, like light and darkness, are incompatible. Fear is the polio of the soul, which prevents our walking by faith."

In a sermon usually remembered by hearers under the assumed label "Giants in the Land," Clarence would deliver a riotous account of the children of Israel on the brink of the Promised Land. A committee, he said, was elected to cross over and scout this land; they returned talking of "land flowing with milk and honey" and giants, next to which the committee members were but grasshoppers. "Their eyes were distorted by the material aspects of the country," Clarence said. "Those giants were probably not more than five or six inches taller than they were."

"So the children of Israel gave as their excuse giants in the land. Fear blinded them to the express command of God. No doubt these people justified themselves by planning study courses on giants. I can see them looking up the information: Giants, species of; Giants, life histories of; Giants, emotional habits of; Effects of giants' heels on grasshoppers. As a result of the study they determined they would have to be practical, have to map out a strategy. They appointed a social action committee that decided to invade the land with leaflets and promote a 'Be Kind to Grasshoppers Week.' Then the finance committee would raise funds for 'Be Kind to Grasshoppers Week' and for relief of the widows of squashed grasshoppers.

"But all their study, all their enlightenment, all their activity was nothing because it was not coupled with faith in the God who had told them, 'Go on in—it's yours.'

"Fear will be overactive in us as long as it sees the specter of death. If we are going to be triumphant over fear, we must have an assurance of triumph over death. The clue, then, to the triumphant faith of the early Christians lies in the power of the resurrection. They did not go everywhere preaching the ethics of Jesus. They went everywhere preaching that 'this Jesus whom you slew, God has raised him from the dead.' Death had lost its sting and the grave its victory. Fear no longer was overactive in them, and they could go everywhere and say: 'We must obey God rather than men.'"

In May, a brief, bright-burning cinder of hope—a fleeting expectation that the siege was faltering—literally exploded into disappointment.

Herbert Birdsey of Macon, Georgia, who owned the Birdsey Flour and Feed Store chain, wrote Koinonia Farm to apologize for the boycott and to declare his Americus store open to the community. Enclosed was a carbon copy of a letter to the manager of the Americus store ordering him to sell to Koinonia. Relieved and grateful, Koinonia dispatched a truck and purchased a load of feed for the cattle. Perhaps this was the first softening in the rigid boycott. After all, Koinonia spent $150,000 a year to maintain its operation, and other local businessmen might be eager to regain their share of trade.

But the boycott responded with a shudder felt around the county. At about 1 A.M. on Sunday morning, May 19, an explosion ripped the front of the feed store at Lee & Forsyth Streets, shattering glass in four adjacent stores on the square and in the Citizens Bank Building, chipping the face of the courthouse clock, and tearing a hole 10 inches long, 7 inches wide, and 3 inches deep in the sidewalk.

"No one, with the possible exception of those guilty of the crime, could believe that such a thing could happen in Americus, a city of peace-loving, church-going, cultured people," said an *Americus Times-Recorder* editorial. "Violence is foreign to our way of life and thinking. Regardless of how we feel toward Koinonia, this violence, from whatever source it comes, must be stopped."

The police theorized that the blast was directed at the Birdsey store because of its transaction with Koinonia Farm. The *Times-Recorder* report said: "A voluntary and unorganized boycott of the communal farm has existed for some time among some Americus and Sumter merchants."

Herbert Birdsey came to Americus, looked over the damage, and decided to close his Americus franchise. In that regard, the explosion was a backfire for the boycott. But in another sense, the incident was significant to Koinonia. The president of the Americus and Sumter County Chamber of Commerce contacted Koinonia and arranged for a meeting the next Sunday afternoon. The leading citizens, it seems, were now concerned enough about the violence to at least communicate with Koinonia Farm.

The meeting was held in the Jordans' living room at Koinonia Farm at 2:30 P.M. on May 26. Representing the Koinonians were the Jordans, Ora Brown, Will and Margaret Wittkamper, Iola Eustice, Norman Long, and Jeanette Drescher. There were ten in the citizens group: attorney Frank Myers, president of the Chamber of Commerce; Charles Crisp, president of the Bank of Commerce; Fred Bowen, mayor of Americus; Jimmie Lott, Standard Oil distributor; Dr. J. H. Robinson, a physician; J. R. Blair, editor of the *Americus Times-Recorder;* George Matthews, chairman of the Sumter County Board of Commissioners; J. P. Luther, secretary of the Chamber of Commerce; Tom Clark, an attorney in the firm of Dykes, Dykes, Marshall and Clark; and one unidentified citizen.

The atmosphere was thin with apprehension and strained with small talk and nervous cordialities as everyone found a chair. The Koinonians, perhaps, held the edge, sitting in one of their own houses, dressed casually. The citizens were dressed in suits and ties, and they were understandably tense as they waited for the right moment to start the proceedings. It is warm in southern Georgia in the month of May.

Myers opened the meeting, easing the tension some with a wordy explanation about how the Chamber of Commerce had requested this meeting, and saying: "... we have a problem which we've got to recognize; we can't be like an ostrich with its head in the sand."* He turned to Charles Crisp, the eldest in the group and the official spokesman.

After an icebreaking attempt at a joke about his balding head and his age earning him official spokesmanship, he stated in a deep and steady voice: "Now your experiment has provoked the sensibilities of a vast majority of our people. Some of our people feel that you are out here to create trouble and chaos or to make money. ... If that's true, why, there would be no use for us to come out here. We come out here on the basis that you are serving what you believe to be Christian principles and are dedicated Christians. You say you are and we accept that. Now our philosophy is that the first duty of a Christian would be to—well, peace on earth, goodwill to men—to make brotherly love in the community. Unfortunately, your experiment has not done that. It has set brother against brother; it has created bitterness; it has created hatred; it has created every emotion that is contrary to my concept of Christianity."

Saying that the citizens of the city and county were distressed by the explosion and unhappy over the other acts of violence and anxious that no one be hurt, Crisp then stated the group's major appeal: "It is our belief that unless this experiment is moved to

---

*This encounter was recorded on tape. The following quotations are lifted directly from the transcript.

other fields that tempers will get to such a point that somebody is going to be hurt. We deplore it; we don't want it. We want to appeal to your good judgment to pray over it and think over it and see if you don't think you'll be serving the best interests of the community and certainly the best interests of your Lord to move and leave us in peace."

Crisp said the group realized the investment Koinonia had in land and equipment and that the people of the county would "try to help you realize all you could if you elected to go somewhere else where you could do more good."

In the discussion that followed, Clarence softly questioned whether or not Koinonia's leaving would not be an admission that the county could not maintain law and order and that people really were not free to worship God as they saw fit.

Crisp answered: "We would have to accept that responsibility. I think you will agree that our country is a peace-loving country. I think our people love peace. Yet four times in my lifetime we've been engaged in a great war, and shed gallons and gallons of blood. We've created great destruction. While our nation wants peace, still there are forces outside that have goaded us and pushed us until eventually we have turned to acts of violence. Now how long these things can be held in check, I don't know. . . . If you continue to goad people so far, acts of violence are going to occur."

George Matthews, chairman of the County Board of Commissioners, added: "There's no way in the world for us to furnish you police protection out here and we don't have any control over these folks slipping around at night and throwing a stick of dynamite, not only on your place but up there on the streets of Americus. We just don't have that kind of protection."

When the discussion got around to racial tensions and riots in Indiana—an obvious attempt to illustrate that the North was as bad as the South—Clarence said: "That confronts us with a problem. Where would you suggest *we* go?"

Crisp replied: "I understand you have a farm in New Jersey. Perhaps the climate there is more favorable. I simply don't know. But I know that the line of battle, if we can use that word, has been so drawn here that I don't know anything that we can do or you can do except for you to move. . . . My preacher told me the other day that St. Paul—and I certainly wouldn't want to get into any Bible quotes with you, because I know that your knowledge is infinitely greater than mine—but he just made the statement that St. Paul said, 'If eating meat offends my neighbor, I'll quit eating it.' "

Clarence responded: "That was one thing that Paul said but never practiced."

"Well, as I said, I certainly wouldn't get into any discussion with you about those things," Crisp said. "That was just the point that he made to me. It might be relevant here. If your practices are offending us, then quit your practices."

Clarence countered: "This is why our forefathers were driven from Europe—on these same grounds—because their practices did offend the people over there and they wanted a measure of freedom where they would be free to worship as they saw fit. Now to us our way of life is a very, very important part of worship. Obedience to Christ comes first with us, even before prayer. It is difficult for us to convey to you the fact that what we actually have here is a church which is seeking to be true to Christ. I think you have it in your power to drive us out. Religious people have many times been driven out. I would want to make it quite clear and to be quite frank with you, I think Sumter County has a very great responsibility in this too."

Clarence admitted that the ways of Koinonia were not agreeable to many if not most people in the county, but he said the county itself had provoked trouble, particularly with the camp injunction initiated by the county commissioners. Matthews started defending the county's action, but Myers brought the discussion back to the immediate problem at hand, as he saw it —the appeal for Koinonia to leave—stating that the county just was not prepared to deal with the violence attracted by Koinonia. "You people might have some friends in business in Americus that would like to do business with you, but I believe all of you realize that they are absolutely scared to do it for the simple reason that that thing happened up there the other night," Myers said.

Clarence asked if there were not a solution other than Koinonia leaving, and Dr. Robinson answered: "I don't [think so], and believe me, it's so serious I can hardly talk. You've hurt me. I'd do nothing to hurt you. You don't intend to hurt me. You've hurt me and my family, unintentionally, but truly have hurt me."

Ora Browne asked what element in Americus and Sumter County had everyone so frightened. One of the citizens' group answered that it was not an "element—it's the mass of the people. When the mass of the people in the United States want something, they get it, if they have to resort to armed forces to do it."

Myers stated that the city and county law enforcement officials were doing their best and would try to protect Koinonia's property "as well as protect our own property," but he added that "we're not prepared to cope with that kind of thing." Then this exchange took place:

Clarence: "You don't think that bringing a detective in here to really find out who is back of it would help in any way?"

Myers: "Well, I don't know how far to go, but I just tell you that I know that a lot of measures have been taken. There have been two special agents in here all week, so far as that goes, and I understand there have been others in here before. An attempt was [made] to get qualified help and it can't be gotten. But that wouldn't solve the problem, I don't think, even if we did." (Myers had appealed to the FBI himself, but the FBI rejected his appeal on the grounds that no Federal laws were broken.)

Clarence: "Finding out actually who is behind all this wouldn't help?"

Myers: "Oh, I think it would be a help, and I think we want to know, but I don't think it will solve future problems. It may create more."

Matthews: "We certainly wouldn't have put the rewards we've put up if we weren't trying to do it. Money usually brings out some evidence, but it hasn't so far. . . . I believe they're doing everything they can to find out who it was who did that bombing in Americus. It's bad, folks going along slipping dynamite. They could have killed a dozen innocent children just happened to be passing there. And that's what we're afraid of. Somebody asked me the other day who that was threw that dynamite up on the sidewalk, and I told him if I knew I wasn't going to tell anybody, because I don't want any of it in my automobile, 'specially with me in it."

Luther: "Have you been led to think there's any sympathy in the county for your program?"

Clarence: "It's hard to tell, Mr. Luther, how much peoples' feelings are hidden by fear. Before all this terrorism started, I had a feeling of friendship with all of you in here, Jimmie Lott here, Mr. Bowen, Frank Myers. We've done business with Mr. Bowen here for years and years and I don't know of any unpleasant feelings we've ever had. So it is difficult to tell how much is genuine feeling and how much is out of fear. Now Mr. Matthews just said he would be glad to tell who it was but he didn't want any dynamite in his car; he wouldn't want to do it. I think there's a large percent of it [fear] here. If you weren't afraid of losing business, you'd still be doing business with us, for we've done nothing to offend you. This would probably be true of all the rest of the people."

Matthews: "Mr. Jordan, you came from a county that has had just about as much lawlessness as any county in the state of Georgia—Talbot County. You can remember a lot of lynchings that took place in Talbot County."

Clarence: "I don't remember."

Matthews: "Well, it happened right here. And nobody has ever been convicted, so far as I know they never had a hearing on it. I know, because I came from that county too, and I knew about a lot of it. White and colored been lynched in that county, yet there's nobody been convicted of any crime for that. You can't tell about these people going around here at night."

Clarence: "The point I was trying to make was that for many years we enjoyed good fellowship with you here, and now all of a sudden something has blown up. We have gone right on doing what we've been doing all these years, and now people who have been our lifetime friends tell us that they are against us. I don't believe as many people are against us as appears on the surface."

Myers: "You missed a great point, Mr. Jordan. Some of my best friends are my severest critics. I come as that kind of friend. I'm not mad at you at all. You and Mrs. Jordan I know and I know your family, have known you for years up here in the church, but when it reaches a point of an impasse, I think it is my duty as your friend to go to you and tell you the way I feel and maybe you can't see it. . . . Maybe you can't see all the facets of it. That's my purpose in coming. I'm not angry with any of you."

Lott: "Not a man here is, Mr. Jordan. We've come for a true and fair and impartial presentation of the facts. This thing has just come to a head here and it's gotten out of hand. For your safety and for the safety of this fine people you've got around out here, it's dangerous. We don't know what's going to happen, and we wanted to come out here and let you know the facts of the case."

Myers: "We're interested in your welfare as well as our own. There would be no point to come otherwise."

Clarence: "In our physical or spiritual welfare?"

Myers: "Well, I hope that we're big enough to be interested in your spiritual welfare, but we're particularly, right now, interested in your physical welfare."

The meeting broke up at this point, with Crisp saying one more time: "I hope the Lord will tell you that maybe you can do him more good . . . in some other place than you can here."

In the brief exchanges that took place as the citizens' group stood to leave, Clarence pressed the point that there was an alternative to Koinonia leaving the county. "If strong men, men of Christian courage, can stand up and say: 'We're going to believe in religious freedom——' "

Someone interrupted him, stating flatly: "It has gone too far."

Clarence persisted: "We haven't planted any dynamite. The grand jury, I think, knew that. And when they said that Koinonia was doing all this violence, they took in their hands the responsibility for that thing which happened last Saturday night. They knew better than that. They knew that we are not that kind of people. If that grand jury had gone into this thing and said: 'We're going to preserve law and order; Koinonia might be doing what we hate and we'd like to spit on them, but America is that kind of nation, where we can live together, where we can tolerate those kinds of people,' some of the businessmen could have stood up and said: 'We'll not boycott; blow up our business, but we're going to be free men in a free society.' Sumter County then could have gone down as the most glorious little county in all the world. It could have stood out as a shining light to the rest of the nation —for freedom, for truth, for justice."

Refusing to allow either religious or patriotic rhetoric to deflect them from their original intention, one of the citizens' group commented: "That might be true. If you didn't have the racial equality issue in it, then I think you would find this to be true." Another said: "We don't want any dynamite in our cars." And they moved on out of the house, to their cars, and down the Dawson Road to Americus, probably not as content as they had hoped to be for doing what they had convinced themselves was right to do.

In just a few weeks, Koinonia responded to their visit by issuing an invitation of their own. No violence had occurred during this intervening period. It was all quiet on the Dawson Road and hopefully a stable truce could be pursued through a second meeting. The citizens' group came to hear Koinonia out. It was a much more relaxed encounter than before. Clarence opened the session by stating that Koinonia did not believe that moving out was the only alternative. He then proposed that some impartial third party be called in "to help all of us see clearly and to determine the whole matter on the principles of fairness, justice, and democracy."

He suggested that Koinonia ask some national organization such as the National Council of Churches to name a representative and that the citizens ask some other organization such as the National Chamber of Commerce to name a representative, and the two appointees together would name a third party to comprise a board of arbiters. The three arbiters could come to Americus, set up public hearings, and conduct a thorough investigation before issuing a recommendation of their own.

"If they decided that the best interest of the state and nation would be served by our leaving Georgia, then we would do so," Clarence said. "If on the other hand, they felt that as citizens we had a right to live here and that we should be given protection of the law and that the boycott should be lifted, we would expect this to be done."

The citizens promptly rejected the proposition on the grounds that no one outside of Georgia could understand the situation in the South. Clarence restated the proposal suggesting that Georgia organizations be called on rather than national bodies. This was rejected.

"They emphatically repeated that there was but one solution, and that was for us to move away," Clarence said. "We then emphatically reaffirmed our intention to remain. Thus the conference ended."

Throughout the summer and early fall, the citizens made no other attempts at official communication. The violence subsided but the boycott absorbed the Sears and Roebuck store. Even as the violence abated, it became increasingly clear that Koinonia Farm was in for a long, intense, and desperate economic struggle.

Direct-mail marketing of the farm's country hams had been profitable for a short time before the market was destroyed. With any sort of livestock operation definitely ruled out by the boycott and field crops becoming increasingly difficult, the Koinonians investigated the possibility of a direct-mail shelled pecan business. Four good reasons supported the idea: (1) the market for shelled pecan products was almost entirely outside of Georgia; (2) pecans could be obtained through state-operated auction markets where Koinonia could not be boycotted; (3) pecan-shelling equipment was powered by electricity from Rural Electric Association lines, a source of power safe from boycott; and (4) the busy season for pecans was the fall, the slack season for farming. On the negative side: it would take some $50,000 capital to get established in such a business, even with used equipment.

They decided to raise the money through the same plan they had successfully employed to gain insurance. Through their newsletter, they invited supporters to loan $25.00 on notes bearing 4 percent interest. Koinonia offered a plan through which the notes would be paid over a period of 10 years, with 200 notes becoming due each year. Possibly they could have borrowed the money from a bank, but as they wrote in the newsletter: "This becomes a cold business transaction, and gives us no sense of partnership with those who wish to stand with us in this struggle."

People wanted to stand with them. A group of supporters in Washington, D.C., raised money that summer to provide Koinonia with a good used car. A group in Cincinnati printed and distributed the newsletter requesting the loans. A group in Pennsylvania helped raise money for a down payment on the farm in New Jersey where the Atkinsons and the Angrys had gone. And friends in Chicago commissioned several individuals to come to Koinonia and help stand the night watch.

With a promising response flowing in to the request for loans, Koinonia purchased an old pecan-cracking unit and converted one of the abandoned chicken sheds to house it. Buying the pecans wholesale at the auctions, they began shelling and advertising: "Help us get the nuts out of Georgia."

Orders started arriving in the fall, and morale picked up at the farm. Another adjacent chicken house was cleaned up and converted into a storage and order-processing plant, and the Koinonians began packaging orders. Con Browne, free at last from the egg route, drove the mail orders into town in the station wagon.

On one occasion, he pulled the car in alongside the railway express office, near the town square, and unloaded the back of the station wagon. It was about noon. When he came out and leaned into the front seat to grab an armful, someone behind him asked what he was doing. He stood with a handful of packages, turned to face the man, and answered. He was a large, heavy-set man, and when Con spoke, the man exploded with heavy fists, smashing Con in the face with three or four blows that sent him sprawling back into the car between the dashboard and the seat. The man leaned in on him, continuing to pummel him, shouting all the time. And then, just as suddenly as he had appeared, he vanished. Con groped his way from the car, bleeding profusely from the nose and from deep cuts on his face, and limping from bruises on his thighs.

Mr. Smith, the railway express agent, had not seen the incident, and he gasped audibly when Con appeared in the doorway. He helped Con to a clinic, where a doctor stuffed his nose with gauze, treated the cuts, and advised him to spend the next 24 hours in bed.

Meanwhile, Mr. Smith had called the farm. Clarence and Ora called Episcopal rector Paul Ritch and asked him to meet them at the clinic, and then sped into Americus. Ora was furious and kept insisting that they all go to the police station immediately to report the incident. Although the suggestion about bed seemed best to Con, he acquiesced and he and Ora walked to the police station nearby and reported it. Paul Ritch then drove Con home and Clarence and Ora went to the express office to deal with the station wagon and the packages.

Clarence left Ora for a few minutes at the express office to take care of some other errand, and in that interval a resident of Americus who had been seen by Koinonians in a car from which a gun was fired at the farm, came storming up to confront her. At the police station, Ora had angrily suggested that the man may have been the assailant, and he had been told about it. He was furious, but probably did little to intimidate Ora, who could have chewed nails at that moment. He went stomping off after a brief exchange and apparently returned to the police station with a suggestion of his own.

By the time Clarence returned a police officer was there to

charge him with driving a car with improper license plates. The station wagon, which had just been returned from the New Jersey Koinonia, still displayed the New Jersey tags. Clarence, of course, had not driven the car, and he argued that it was registered in both Georgia and New Jersey. The city police did not press charges, but someone apparently referred the situation to Sumter County officials. By the time Con had arrived home and settled in bed, the sheriff was at the door of the Brownes' house. He charged Con with driving a car with improper license plates and told him to get dressed—he was going to jail.

Paul Ritch was still present and he protested to the sheriff that Con was in no shape to be jailed. But the sheriff was insensitive to that fact. He drove Con into the county jail and locked him in a cell with a convict in transit who had accumulated 999 years for murder and attempted escapes and assorted other brutalities.

If putting Con in a cell with a convicted murderer was meant to intimidate him, the scheme could not have backfired more favorably. "The guy was concerned as he could be," Con said. "He did everything he could possibly do to make it easy for me. I was groggy and he sort of tucked me in. Whenever I moved in the night, he was right there."

The authorities set bond at $500, and then refused to take either cash or property bond from Koinonia on grounds that the law required a real estate bond and Koinonia real estate did not qualify because it was not held privately. Jack Singletary volunteered but the sheriff said his land did not qualify because it was mortgaged. Koinonia finally sidestepped the issue and posted a cash bond with the nearby Talbot County sheriff.

Con was not pleased when he discovered after the fact that bond had been put up for him. He had assumed that one night in jail had been sufficient before trial on such a heinous charge as driving with an out-of-state tag. "I think if you get arrested you should stay in there, not put up bond right away," he argued. "Keep them embarrassed."

In January 1958, Con appeared in county court without benefit of counsel. A lawyer friend from Atlanta had come down to represent him, but by the time Con's case was called, the lawyer had grown so fretful that he deserted him.

"We sat in the hall while they called all the white people [to face the judge]," Con said. "Then they called all the black people who had white people there to help them. Then they called all the black people. We got called last. Clarence and I went in without the lawyer to face the judge. When he found out we had had the Georgia license plates at the time of the arrest, he changed the charge to improper display and beating myself up with the attempt of getting sympathy from passers-by. He charged us almost $90 in fine and court costs, and then said that whenever we brought that car across state lines, we were to stop immediately and put the Georgia tags on."

In the spring, violence flashed again briefly. A five-gallon jug of gasoline was ignited on the porch of the home of Alma Jackson's parents, near Plains, and probably would have burned the house down had not someone in the family heard footsteps on the porch and gone to look. The same night shots were fired into the house of another person who had worked at Koinonia.

On a Saturday evening in April, when several of the men and boys were unloading a truck at Koinonia Farm, a car cruised around the curve and four shots rang out. The Koinonians, by now seasoned to the smell and feel of violence, just kept working. Minutes later, the car drove past again and one shot cracked across the open area. Still no response from the workers.

Added to the eruption of violence again and the ever-tightening choke-hold of the boycott, Representative Murr of Sumter County introduced a bill in the Georgia House of Representatives that called for it to investigate Koinonia Farm. The bill rang with familiar rhetoric and charged Koinonians with the redundant assertions of defrauding the state with its profits, holding people in involuntary servitude, shooting at themselves, bombing themselves, beating themselves, etc., etc., etc. The bill said all these crimes were "reliably substantiated by findings of the Sumter County Grand Jury" and the general assembly better have its own look into the matter.

The bill finally passed the Georgia legislature, but it obviously was an embarrassment. The legislators axed out the power of subpoena and refused to grant funds for implementation. It was a dead resolution and hopefully could be forgotten. Obviously, any such investigation would have to look not only at Koinonia Farm but at the law enforcement officers in Sumter County and Americus, the intimidated merchants, the pressured professional men, and the Negroes who had been terrorized. Apparently, Murr's action carried the threat of revealing too much. He was soundly defeated in his bid for reelection that year.

Koinonia experienced another case of Sumter County justice before the year was out. Lee Peery and Paul Goodman, two young men who were living at Koinonia and considering full membership, were sent into town in a truck to pick up a railroad car of lime purchased direct from a Georgia quarry. Koinonia could not get lime locally, but Perry and Goodman had to pick up the lime at the local dealer's, where the rail cars arrived. A trestle arrangement was used for unloading commodities such as lime, but trash consisting mainly of lime and sand and coal had built up under the trestle, and Koinonia's truck could not make it up under the rail car. Peery and Goodman shoveled several hundred pounds of the debris into the Koinonia truck to gain clearance and then proceeded to unload the rail car of lime. The dealer stepped from his office and accused the two men of stealing lime. He called the sheriff. The two were promptly put in jail and formal charges were filed.

Clarence went to talk to the accuser and asked him to withdraw the charges. He refused, saying he would not be doing his Christian duty if he did not prosecute. Clarence said Christians should settle their differences out of court, but the lime dealer said he was sure Jesus did not want him associating with thieves.

After a brief trial and 15 minutes of deliberation by the jury, the two men were found guilty. They were given one-year suspended sentences in the state penitentiary and fined $250 apiece.

In the fall of 1960, Koinonia for the first time took a court action of its own. Jan Jordan, Lora Ruth Browne, and Billy Wittkamper were refused admission to the Americus High School, even though 27 other students from the county system were admitted under an agreement between the city and county school boards. No reason was offered other than that it was "to the best interests of all concerned." But as far as the Wittkampers, the Brownes, and the Jordans were concerned, their children were being discriminated against on account of their religious and social beliefs. They filed suit in the Federal district court in Macon, asking that the school board be enjoined from refusing admission to children whose parents were members of Koinonia Farm.

They could have sent the children on to the county high school in Plains, but they felt the Americus school was superior as a college preparatory school and they felt the method by which the students were rejected made the case a matter of conscience.

The school board contended in court that it was not obligated to accept any student from outside the city limits and that legally it could decide arbitrarily on the applications of such students. In this particular case, the school board said the Koinonia children would be an invitation to trouble and dissent in the school.

In the proceedings, Clarence was asked if Koinonia believed racial integration was morally right. He answered: "I wouldn't put it in those terms. We simply have advocated that we believe in the kind of God as revealed in Jesus Christ . . . that He looks not on the outward part but upon the heart. . . . Being followers of Jesus . . . we accept as our brother anyone who is a son of God, whether he is white or black or what. . . . We do not call that integration. We simply call it a practice of our Christian beliefs."

One of the school board members, an attorney who had voted with the others to reject the Koinonia applicants, was moved by Clarence's testimony. He came to the farm and apologized for his participation in the rejection of the children, and later tried to be a moderate force for reconciliation when the civil rights movement surfaced in Sumter County. His law practice was boycotted, however, and he soon was forced to leave town.

The judge was persuaded, too. He ruled that equal protection of the law was due all applying students from the county system when the city decided to accept any of them, and that fear of trouble was no grounds to deny the rights of the Koinonia children.

Jan and Lora and Billy entered the Americus school and discovered that the school board had correctly anticipated the reaction of its students. The Koinonia students faced several years of relentless hostility. (Clarence refused the offer of an escort of Federal marshals for the children on their first day, saying if he did not believe in violence, he was not going to do something that required the threat of violence from somebody else.)

Adding to all these harassments was the inevitable collapse of the New Jersey project, an effort that had begun as a simple evacuation and then had escalated into the hope of a second Koinonia.

CHAPTER 10

Friends

The violence subsided and the wounds of the community lay exposed. Where danger had drawn some closer in common determination, it had also intensified the personal struggles of others and made their cry for a solution to their individual needs all the more urgent. Some who had weathered the hostility from without had been withered from within during the years of attack.

Something had eluded them, something that seemed to defy articulation and yet was certain in the yearning of them all, something of the spirit they called unity—the undefinable factor that would exterminate resentment and mistrust and make the group all they wanted it to be. And so they were moving on—some to other communities and some out on their own.

Frustration had dogged every hope, it seemed. The New Jersey Koinonia, where the Atkinsons and the Angrys were, had loomed with promise in the minds of the battle-weary souls in Georgia. Perhaps it would become a retreat where the veterans could gain a break in the tension without deserting the cause.

The intention, of course, had simply been to find the Angrys a place to live and work. But when the Hidden Springs group offered to sell their 140 acres of rolling crop and pasture land near Neshanic Station, New Jersey, for a fair price, Koinonia accepted. The idea of a second community seemed promising. Lee Pagano, a leather craftsman and artist, met the Atkinsons, visited Koinonia Farm, and expressed an interest in being a part of a new Koinonia. Chris and Jeanette Drescher came up to stay, and Jim Jordan decided to attend high school there.

They began working on arrangements for selling Koinonia Farm's pecans and peanuts from Hidden Springs, for farming the land, and for establishing a leather crafts shop for Pagano. But then the old dark force of suspicion and prejudice revealed its Yankee face.

Neighbors obtained an injunction to block the leather shop, and Koinonia was in court again. The New Jersey township's zoning regulations were used to define the leather shop as an "industry." And while the officials consented to farming, they said the selling of pecans and peanuts would be forbidden as industry also. A number of citizens at the hearing questioned Harry unmercifully about tax exemption, the presence of the township's "first Negroes," and Koinonia's intentions.

"This was heartbreaking," Harry said. "We found that discrimination was just as real there as it was in Georgia. It just about knocked me out."

One evening carloads of people gathered in front of the Atkinsons' home and started toward the door. "I didn't know whether the Ku Klux Klan had found us again, or what," Harry said. He stepped to the porch and heard them out. "They did not want the Negro family there," he said. "They were nice but firm. They said they wanted us to leave."

With the possibility of self-support and community acceptance denied them, the New Jersey Koinonia began a slow fade. Rufus got a job with a contractor and later worked on a farm near Malvern, Pennsylvania. Harry began the proceedings for selling the Hidden Springs property. But more than that was weighing on him. He was beginning to resist the idea of returning to Koinonia Farm.

"The question was what to do," he recalled. "I came to where I felt I had to face just what my commitment was. I had been back to Georgia the summer before and they were still having night watches, still having the lights shot out, and so on. And it just became a question of what our real commitment was. Allene and I felt more of a commitment to community than to an interracial struggle.

"We went to Woodcrest [the Society of Brothers community in Rifton] for an extended visit. Inwardly we didn't have the strength to carry on. We really needed the rest we had hoped for at Hidden Springs—not just from the violence but from the struggle Koinonia was going through—the constant turmoil over differences. We had hardly settled at Woodcrest before we felt that this is where we wanted to be."

Harry and Allene's experience was not unlike that of the Nelsons and the Johnsons a few years earlier. Coming from Koinonia, where community life boiled along through trial and error, where structure was at a minimum, and where hostility always impinged from without, they immediately experienced within the cloistered, authoritarian structure of the Bruderhof what they despaired of discovering at Koinonia—unity, peace, security.

Without question, Koinonia Farm was an insecure place to be much of the time. But holding on there in the South through hell had given Koinonia a quality of its own. It had a lean toughness that came from being out where the light hit the darkness, and it had friends that supported it even when death seemed imminent.

Joe Maendel and his family were faithful supporters of Koinonia even while they were suffering setbacks of their own. By this time, Forest River was neither a Hutterian nor a Bruderhof community, and Joe was captaining an economically crippled, independent community in North Dakota's flat Red River valley. A severe split had developed between the Society of Brothers and the Hutterites by 1957, partly over biblical interpretation, partly over economic decisions, and partly over community politics. Joe had found himself in little accord with either group. To simplify a complex story, the Hutterite families had returned to their Canadian communities, the Society had moved its families to a new Bruderhof in Rifton, New York, and Joe Maendel and his family and the Alan Baers had remained at the 6,000-acre Forest River location and assumed a huge debt.

Covering every possibility for working cash, Joe had written to Clarence and asked for a $1,000 loan. Koinonia itself was on the ropes economically from the heavy blow of the boycott, but Clarence and Florence had contacted friends and raised the money themselves to meet Joe's request. As he achieved some measure of stability at Forest River, he returned Koinonia's favor many times over.

Like most Hutterian men, Joe was a precision mechanic and an excellent farmer. To those who knew him well at Koinonia, he was all that and more—a sort of legendary figure, in fact, whose name evoked smiles and funny, lovable memories. A traditional-looking Hutterite with baggy black pants, suspenders, a straw hat pulled hard down on his head, a greying beard, a childlike humility, and a heavy German accent that sparkled with good humor, he was a disarming combination of gentle curiosity and savage decisiveness. Where Clarence would be ambivalent and reluctant to order anyone to do things his way, Joe would consider no argument for what he knew to be right. He did not deliver orders with a question mark.

During one of Joe's extended visits to Koinonia, he walked out in a field and decided the corn was being set an inch too deep. He questioned the Koinonia man on the planter, who replied that he knew what he was doing, and besides, Clarence had told him to do it his own way. Joe responded: "No, I say you don't plant it one inch deeper unless you want to lose 10 bushels an acre." He reset the planter to seed an inch shallower and left the man to his work.

"That was the trouble with Clarence," Joe said. "Clarence could never explain something to a man who didn't want to hear it. As far as I am concerned, Clarence could never manage that farm to make real money. If a man wanted to hear, Clarence could tell him real good. But Clarence was no good to manage people—he was too soft-hearted."

Perhaps for this reason, Joe was not easily convinced himself when Clarence cautioned him on one visit not to try to buy parts in Americus or Albany. Joe was working on one of the tractors that was out of commission, and without saying anything to Clarence, he took a Koinonia truck and headed for Albany.

He located the local dealer for the manufacturer of the tractor, walked in, and matter-of-factly ordered the part he wanted. The man behind the counter retrieved the part and began filling out an invoice. The office manager appeared, glanced suspiciously over Joe's appearance, and asked where he was from. "From North Dakota," Joe replied. "What are you doing down here?" "Helping a friend work on some equipment." Then the manager narrowed his eyes and said: "What friend?" Joe recalled: "Well, Clarence said don't tell no lie, so I said: 'My friends at Koinonia Farm.'" The manager stiffened with rage, tore the invoice from the attendant's hand, and shouted at Joe incoherently.

Joe's humility may or may have not been present that day, but his stern German intransigence certainly had been provoked. "I have to use your phone," he stated with authority, and neither of the men stopped him. In fact, the manager stopped raving and listened with his mouth open as Joe pulled a small notebook from his shirt pocket, patiently looked up a number, and then called long distance to Grand Forks, North Dakota.

When he got the dealer for the same manufacturer in Grand Forks on the line, he explained his predicament, saying: "I'm down here working for the same interests that I do up there and I need this part. This man here won't sell it to me. I want you to call headquarters [of the manufacturers] and tell them to call this man and order him to sell this part to me." He told the Grand Forks dealer that the part could be charged to the Forest River account there, and then he hung up and stood there, his hat jammed down over his eyes, his hands in his baggy pockets, and waited. He knew what he was doing. Forest River had about $300,000 in that brand of equipment.

Time ticked off slowly. The manager and the clerk shuffled papers and mumbled to one another, subdued by this bearded German's unflinching posture and stern countenance. He had to look stranger than strange to them, and they probably wished for the courage to laugh at him or to go over and pop his suspenders, but they just shuffled papers and mumbled.

When 25 minutes had passed, the telephone rang. The manager answered, Joe thought with a rather high-strung "Hello!" It was the home office calling. They wanted to know if a "Joe Men-dale" was there. Smelling defeat, confused by such aggression, the manager handed Joe the phone. Joe accepted it with one broad hand gently—he always handled equipment appreciatively—and said, "Hallo." He repeated his side of the story and then it was the manager's turn again. The manager obviously was told to give the man the part—it was already paid for. As the clerk handed it to him, Joe permitted himself one triumphant glance in the manager's direction. Then he shook the dust from his feet and headed for Koinonia Farm.

On another occasion, Joe was asked to enact the charade

through which Koinonia obtained gasoline. Dutifully, he followed his instructions to the letter. He drove a truck carrying two 1000-gallon tanks into Albany and followed a set of complex directions that took him to a service station. He passed slowly through the station's ramp, back out onto the street, parked the truck, and left the keys in the ignition. He walked one block to a coffee shop, ordered a cup of coffee and a roll, and sat there, skeptically waiting to see if the facts bore out what he had been told would happen.

Sure enough, in half an hour the truck passed slowly by the coffee shop. He waited a few minutes and then, on pure faith, went into the restroom. The man was there, just as Clarence had said he would be, waiting to be paid. Speechlessly, Joe paid the man, took the keys from him, and walked behind the coffee shop. The truck was there, loaded. "Amazing," he muttered.

Clarence Jordan and Joe Maendel together constituted a potent combination of personalities. Both were emotional, dramatic, expansive storytellers who could send nightmare shudders through their eager audiences as they told of some hair-raising experience, and then choke them with laughter as they added their own peculiar brand of embellishment. They both provoked extreme feelings in the people they encountered, either winning their undying devotion or eliciting their eternal curse. They both were tough-minded, tender-hearted, frank-talking spirits who were unafraid to engage their detractors in intellectual and spiritual combat. They were both close to the earth and they worked for a faith that expressed itself as the soil expresses itself —in rich, fruitful, seminal, life-feeding growth and metamorphosis. They both grew out of dark religious tradition and then sought to claim the best of it while they rejected the worst. They were prophets, in their own contexts, who stood between the past and the future and tried to speak of life in new ways that would connect the present with the lifeblood of history and the vision of tomorrow.

Even their contrasting traits seemed to complement one another. Joe was short, stocky, and dark, with a slightly bent, shuffling presence that carried the gentle look and heavy strength of a bear. Clarence was much taller and leaner, with a high-hipped, long-striding gait of a race horse and a bright, open countenance that gave him an optimistic air when he was not brooding. Clarence was given to brooding on occasion; Joe vented his emotions as they came. Joe was the tougher, more decisive manager, but Clarence was the more patient, understanding leader.

Once, when Joe accompanied Clarence to a civil rights meeting in Albany, a white policeman confronted them as they moved through a crowd to a black church, and spit at them. Joe stopped cold as if he were about to spring on the man, but Clarence took him gently by the arm and said: "C'mon, Joe." "I wanted to give that man some mouthful," Joe said later, "but Clarence wouldn't let me."

Clarence was the man of letters, the scholar-farmer, who, when he sat with his long legs crossed and an open book on his thigh, looked as if God had made him that way. He could look at a peanut plant that was slightly off color and say that nitrogen or phosphate or some other chemical was lacking. Joe was a man of earthy instinct who had never completed grammar school but who had worked on every sort of machinery and grown every sort of crop the Northwest had to offer. Clarence looked to Joe for information about bees and honey, not because he could spout scientific laboratory knowledge, but because he had studied his bees, slept out in the grove with them, traced their every activity —and got double the honey per hive that anyone at the University of Manitoba could produce.

When Koinonia seeded pine trees in crop land, Clarence produced expert statistics to show how many trees could be planted in so much time in so much space. Joe shrugged off the expert advice and told Clarence that his son-in-law Paul Waldner and Joe, Jr., who were visiting Koinonia with him, could plant four times that many trees in the time. And they did.

Joe took Clarence aside and told him he did not know how to run a farm; he was too soft and yielding just when tough decisions were called for. Clarence took Joe aside and told him he did not know how to read the Bible; he read it all the time but he read blindly.

Clarence conceded his weaknesses as a manager (although he only "managed" what was assigned to him), and permitted Joe to make decisions while visiting the farm. And although it must have been hard for a Hutterite who read his German testament daily, Joe heard Clarence out on the charge that he did not know how to read the Bible.

"I had been trained to think that Jesus' words were in the Bible from one end to the other, that the whole book from the first page to the last contained God's words on law and order," Joe said. "Clarence just put his arm around me and said, 'Joe, you don't know how to read the Bible.' And then he took me home and showed me.

"He showed me where some of the Bible is just history, where some of it is just telling how so-and-so applied what Jesus said, and how some of it just sets the stage for what Jesus did or said. He told me there is only one place where Jesus starts giving you orders and that was in Matthew five, six, and seven. He showed me how Jesus didn't talk about community or how to be a Christian—he talked about love, and mercy, and humbleness—and Clarence said if you have these, you have community automatically. Clarence said you can argue about the rest of the Bible if you want to, but there is no argument about Matthew five, six, and seven.

I tell you, that man had some gift for saying what Jesus meant."

Clarence would laugh at Joe's bluntness, and then he some-times seemed to envy it. Joe would be moved to tears by Claren-ce's expressiveness and he learned from him.

Joe challenged Clarence sternly when Clarence confessed he just could not accept the idea of hell. "How do you explain Lazarus?" he bellowed. And Clarence, softly, said: "But Joe, if I loved a man so much I gave my life for him, I couldn't turn around and condemn him."

In the summer of 1959, Alan Baer decided to leave Forest River and move to Koinonia Farm. He was spiritually restless and hoped Koinonia would be the place to gain a new perspective. He and his wife and children left for Georgia by train, and Joe Maendel, Jr., Paul Waldner, and Sammy Maendel left Forest River with a truckload of the Baer's possessions.

The young men drove all night and all the next day, approach-ing Americus an hour or so before nightfall on the second day. Joe, Jr., a taller slimmer likeness of his father, was driving. Unsure of directions, he pulled into a small grocery and service station just a few miles short of Americus to call Koinonia Farm. When the attendant asked who he was calling, Joe told him. The man got angry and ordered him out of the office, shouting at him to back his truck out of the driveway.

Joe had turned off the road and into the station, driving over a narrow dirt bridge that covered a culvert. The man ordered him to back straight out onto the highway, not allowing him to pass through the station and out the other side. Joe tried to comply with these instructions, but when he stopped on the culvert to check traffic before backing on out, the culvert began collapsing under the weight of the truck.

A Georgia highway patrolman appeared and motioned for Joe

to get into his car. "I thought if anyone was going to help me, he would," Joe recalled. "But he started quizzing me about where I was from, where I was going, and so on. I asked him to turn on his light and help me flag down a truck for help, but he just sat there."

Joe finally got out of the patrol car and flagged down a truck himself. But as it rolled to a stop, the patrolman motioned for the driver to move on. Tired, exasperated, and justifiably afraid, Joe and Sammy started walking down the road to find a phone, leaving Paul with the truck. They walked about a mile until they saw a farmhouse with a Negro couple sitting on the porch. Joe asked if they could use the phone. The man said: "It's in the bedroom—go on in." But as they mounted the porch, the man nervously started asking questions. This time, Joe mentioned no names, but the man somehow sensed what the situation was and he stood and asked them to leave. He was afraid, he said, for his wife and children, and he picked up a large stick to prove how serious he was.

By this time, it was sunset. They walked only a few hundred yards before a car stopped by them. A woman's voice said: "Get in the back." Joe was ready to take any risk at this point, and the two men crawled in the back of the automobile. There were two women in the car who said they had passed the station. They had correctly perceived what was happening, so they drove the men into town and dropped them by a public telephone booth, saying that was all they could do. Joe called Clarence, who came for them immediately.

By the time they got back to the truck, it was past sunset, and a crowd of teenagers and men had gathered at that station. Paul was sitting quietly in the truck, ignoring the jeers and taunts. Some of the men were carrying rifles and acting as if they wanted to use them. Someone noticed a can of gasoline near the truck and said loudly: "That gas could spill and that would be some kind of accident, wouldn't it?" Clarence had asked someone else at the farm to drive a tractor to the station, but when it arrived, it was of no use. The patrolman, who made no move to control the crowd, said he could not allow them to pull the truck out onto the highway with the tractor. And the service station attendant said they could not pull the truck forward onto his property.

With the crowd still hungry for action, Clarence and Paul stayed with the truck while Joe and Sammy drove back to the farm to get a set of jacks. By two o'clock that morning, they succeeded in getting the truck's back wheels up on the shoulder of the road where they could back out onto the highway. And they succeeded in outlasting the mob, which finally tired and quit the scene.

The Reba Place fellowship in Evanston, Illinois, was another group that shared its life with Koinonia Farm as Koinonia struggled in the grips of the boycott and suffered the anemia of numerical decline.

Reba Place was an urban expression of the same spirit Koinonia sought to manifest. Established in 1957 by a group of Goshen College graduates and a professor who had studied and discussed the idea of community for years, Reba Place sought to evolve a new church form, a common, shared life for members who pooled their possessions but worked "in the world" at the tasks they had been trained to perform.

They had established themselves in large, two-family houses on or near Reba Place in a transitional section of Evanston. Their homes and automobiles were held by the corporation, to which they submitted their paychecks and from which they drew modest but comfortable living allowances. In this way, the nine or so families and dozen single members had committed themselves to a common standard of living. The teacher, the psychiatrist, the businessman, the social worker, the student—all exercised their special gifts in their functional capacities "in the world," and then shared their experiences in common worship and close relationships.

Clarence visited this group and felt an immediate kinship. John Lehman, Don Mast, David Gale, and others visited Koinonia and added their weight of work at crucial times of need. John, a social worker who was among the founders of Reba Place, was free for a time in 1960 after completing two years of alternative service as a conscientious objector. He spent two months that winter at Koinonia Farm at the same time Joe Maendel, Jr., was sent from Forest River to help out. Koinonia was expanding its nut business to include pecan candies and fruit cakes, and John and Joe helped construct the freezer space and the candy kitchen.

By this time field crops and cattle operations had been suspended. The expanded pecan business was the mainstay of support as Koinonia continued to struggle against the boycott.

But economics was only one factor in Koinonia's troubles at this juncture of its turbulent history. Only the Brownes, the Wittkampers, the Dreschers, and the Jordans remained of the "old-timers," whose days at Koinonia dated back before the violence. Ross Anderson and Dorothy Swisshelm, a former psychiatric counselor from Cincinnati, were still committed to staying at Koinonia. But others were coming and going, failing to discover whatever they were searching for in the frantic work pace and unending tension that plagued Koinonia in the last half of the 1950s.

Dorothy Swisshelm suspected that many of those who came and went in those years were disillusioned after being won to the cause when they heard Clarence on a speaking tour somewhere. Clarence was a powerful, forceful communicator and exhibited the sort of personality that made people want to confide in him. When people came to Koinonia, they wanted to spend time with this giant of a man whose compassion seemed large enough to encompass a multitude's problems and whose gift of the tongue seemed to flow from a limitless spring. But Clarence at Koinonia Farm was a man with problems and frustrations of his own, and he was one of a group who got assigned work to do just like everyone else. At Koinonia, in short, he was not in the role of the powerful exegete of Scriptures nor did he seek to be.

A pastor friend who invited Clarence for a week of meetings in his church asked Clarence if his trips did not spoil him, since he ate well and rested during the day between meetings and was so enthusiastically received by his audiences. Clarence laughed and said: "No. When I get home, they'll put me on the manure spreader and that will bring me back down to earth."

The fact that he experienced glory on the road was bound to create adjustment problems when he was off the rostrum and among his loved ones. But Clarence was a gifted teacher with few peers, and the fact that his most powerful offering was subdued when he was at home was perhaps the primary flaw in Koinonia Farm's make-up. The group floundered from lack of spiritual leadership much of the time, and in their midst was one of the nation's extraordinary New Testament teachers.

Clarence back-pedaled from this role partially out of sheer humility and partially out of frustration over how to guide those closest to him in the intimacy of their spiritual lives while at the same time dealing with his own personal relationship needs. It was a tricky, fragile sort of problem, and Koinonia never really worked out a comfortable solution.

"Part of the failure of Koinonia [as a community] was not to provide a context for using Clarence's gift," John Lehman suggested. "He should have been allowed somehow to be the teacher.

I know there was a reluctance on Clarence's part. We had the same problem with John Miller [the Old Testament scholar who helped found the Reba Place Fellowship]—we had to constantly reassure him that we wanted his scholarship. Otherwise we wouldn't get it."

So, in many ways, Koinonia Farm's purpose was losing definition. Conversation in community meetings focused for a time on the possibility of some other group—Reba Place, perhaps, or Joe Maendel and his family, or one of the peace churches—assuming control of the farm to stabilize it economically and spiritually. Discouraging group talk eventually splintered into individual decisions—more people began to leave.

Seventy-five-year-old Chris Drescher, who spent a career as a plumber and his later years as a self-educated explorer for the kingdom of God, felt his abilities were not appreciated, and he left with his wife Jeanette for a community in Alabama, and then finally back to home territory in Des Moines, Iowa.

Ross Anderson, the soft-spoken, tender idealist who burned with the desire for involvement in the major issues of the day, left the community to join a vigil protesting chemical and biological warfare preparations at Fort Dietrich, Maryland, and later joined the Albany Movement in Albany, Georgia.

Dorothy Swisshelm, who had resigned social service work in Cincinnati to join Koinonia, left after five years with the feeling that she needed to go where she could use her skills. She went to Biloxi, Mississippi, where she worked in family services for the United Church of Christ.

Con and Ora Browne, too, the real long-termers besides the Jordans, left in 1963 when Con was offered a position with the Highlander Folk School in Tennessee.

While many of these decisions were being thought through and acted upon, Clarence initiated one of the first major shifts from the original format of the experiment—he suggested eliminating much of the burden of group decisionmaking by shifting to a family allowance concept. Each family or individual would simply state how much cash was necessary for its personal and family needs and the community would provide it. There was little discussion; it was agreed upon. During this time, too, although perhaps none of them were aware of it, the membership structure simply evaporated. No one was coming, anyway; they were leaving.

An era was obviously making its silent close. Koinonia Farm was not yet at an end, but it seemed only a matter of time. The Jordans and the Wittkampers remained, but Clarence and Florence were tired—and disappointed—and hungry for a change, for something that would restore their spirit. The two families agreed that the experiment in community was finished, and they agreed to pray and search for some new direction.

It was at this low point in the corporate history of Koinonia Farm, and perhaps in the individual pilgrimage of its founder, too, that the great force of Clarence's unique gift rumbled to the surface and refused to be denied any longer. Something that later came to be known as the Cotton Patch Version of the New Testament Scriptures entered the breach and began pushing and shoving its way to delivery.

CHAPTER 11

According to Clarence

Koinonia Farm seemed to have sputtered to a standstill just as the civil rights movement was beginning to roll, just when people were beginning to move for what was right, in scorn of the consequences—marching, pleading, fighting, and dying for justice. What a time for Koinonia, which had seen so much action in its day, to be dissipated and too weak to respond.

Clarence longed for some new, more aggressive expression of what was within him. But he was tired and for the moment without vision. He knew only that the old community idea alone was too isolated and immobile to be effective in an age of events flashing past with increasing velocity.

He returned to his source of inspiration, the New Testament, and again began to work closely with the Greek texts, deciding he would no longer subordinate an urge that had been with him since the early 1950s—the urge to attempt a translation.

A number of good modern English translations were already available, but he felt something more could be done, something bolder. He felt he was equipped to make the Scriptures come alive in a unique fashion, and that if he began writing his interpretations down, he might prompt others to a more radical way—and discover a new container for his own fermenting faith.

Most translations, no matter how contemporary in language, still read like ancient history, peering back over hundreds of centuries to recount a tale so detached from current affairs that it seemed to be viewed through a dusty stained-glass window. Clarence wanted to put the "Good News" not only in his own tongue but in his own time. He wanted to rescue the New Testament drama from the sanctuary and classroom and see it "put out under God's skies where people are toiling and crying and wondering, where the mighty events of the Good News first happened and where alone they feel at home." He wanted to recapture the ideas of the New Testament in a contemporary context that would make people feel like participants, not spectators.

He wanted "to help cotton-picking Christians understand what their pea-picking preachers had been saying." And so he began writing down his "cotton patch version" of the New Testament.

Much of his groundwork had already been accomplished. Clarence had been speaking steadily over the years before American Baptists, National Baptists, United Churches of Christ, Churches of the Brethren, the Mennonites, and the Lutherans, and "cotton-patching" had been his natural style. Often he would stand in a pulpit or at a conference rostrum with a tiny Greek testament in his hands, reading the Scriptures, and come out with something like this: "But the Sunday School teacher, trying to save face, asked, 'But . . . er . . . but . . . just who is my neighbor?'

"Then Jesus laid into him and said, 'A man was going from Atlanta to Albany and some gangsters held him up. When they had robbed him of his wallet and brand-new suit, they beat him up and drove off in his car, leaving him unconscious on the shoulder of the highway.'"

" 'Now it just so happened that a white preacher was going down that same highway. When he saw the fellow, he stepped on the gas and went scooting by.'"

(Clarence would add: "His homiletical mind probably made the following outline: (1) I do not know the man; (2) I do not wish to get involved in any court proceedings; (3) I don't want to get blood on my new upholstery; (4) the man's lack of proper clothing would embarrass me upon my arrival in town; and (5) finally, brethren, a minister must never be late for worship services.")

" 'Shortly afterwards a white Gospel song leader came down the road, and when he saw what had happened, he too stepped on the gas.' "

("What his thoughts were, we'll never know," Clarence would say, "but as he whizzed past, he may have been whistling 'Brighten the corner where you are.' ").

" 'Then a black man traveling that way came upon the fellow, and what he saw moved him to tears. He stopped and bound up his wounds as best he could, drew some water from his water jug to wipe away the blood and then laid him on the back seat. He drove on into Albany and took him to the hospital.' "

("All the while," Clarence would say, "his thoughts may have been along this line: 'Somebody's robbed you; yeah, I know about that, I been robbed, too. And they done beat you up bad; I know, I been beat up, too. And everybody just go right on by and leave you laying here hurting. Yeah, I know. They pass me by, too.' ")*

Clarence drew heavily from his own experience in the cotton patches and peanut rows of Koinonia Farm. A simple but classic example of his fertile relationship with the soil was his discussion of faith the size of a mustard seed. He talked instead about the peanut seed and how he walked out in the field one day after a hard-packing rain had covered the recently planted peanut seed with a tough, thick crust.

"I thought those tiny little seeds would never make it," he said. "But I went out in the field a few days later and there was a little

*This discourse and subsequent quotations from the New Testament are taken from the Cotton Patch versions, published by Association Press, New York.

old seed pushing up a chunk of dirt 15 or 20 times as heavy as it was, as if to say: 'Get out of the way, clod, I'm moving on to God.' "

So in his versions of the New Testament, Jesus was born and raised in the red dust of Georgia. The angel Gabriel came to Mary in Valdosta, and Joseph and Mary went up to Gainesville in northern Georgia to register during a time when Augustus was president and Quirinius was secretary of war. Luke, chapter three, which tells of the beginning of John the Baptist's ministry, became a contemporized version of what Clarence believed to be the Gospel writer's own wry presentation:

"Now during the fifteenth year of Tiberius as President, while Pontius Pilate was governor of Georgia, and Herod was governor of Alabama, his brother Philip being governor of Mississippi, and Lysanias still holding out over Arkansas; while Annas and Caiaphas were co-presidents of the Southern Baptist Convention, the word of God came to Zack's boy, John, down on the farm."

Clarence would add: "Now, Luke was saying something by mentioning all these dignitaries. He was implying that God passed over all these likely candidates to go to this little old guy down on the farm. This is an account of the first New Testament 'pass-over.' "

In one lecture, Clarence read the passage that relates the message of John the Baptist: "Here's what he was saying to the crowds who were coming out to get dipped by him: 'You sons of snakes, who put the heat on you to run from the fury about to break over your heads? You must give some proof that you've had a change of heart. And don't start patting one another on the back with that 'we-good-white-people' stuff, because I'm telling you that if God wants to, he can make white-folks out of this pile of rocks.' "

He commented: "Now this is a pretty rough way to start out if you are a candidate for the pulpit. I tell you, I can't understand how John could have so much power with so little positive think-ing, and still be 'a-Peale-ing.' "

Wherever possible, Clarence translated, rather than tran-sliterated, the names of New Testament characters. His most obvious success was with the apostle Peter, who was in fact Simon Bar Jonah. Translated, Clarence said, it is Simon, son of John; or John's son; or "Johnson." Jesus nicknamed him Petros, which means "rock," making his name "Rock Johnson." So Clarence talked about Rock and Andy, the original Johnson brothers—"I can just see it on the side of their new fiberglass boat."

Clarence enjoyed weaving a few laughs into the Scriptures. As he said about Paul's Epistles: "We want Paul's letters to have the simplicity, the humbleness, the earthiness which they had before Christians erected temples of mortar and stone." The Cotton Patch versions were not meant for people who cherished a strict reverence for the most elegant King James rendering. When the Cotton Patch Version of Paul's Epistles was published, slangy phrases such as "hell no" and "if God is rooting for us" and "the damned bastard" created in many readers a ready acceptance of Clarence's joking but modest reference to his own work as "sub-standard."

A woman challenged him once, asking if he couldn't translate a little more politely. Clarence replied: "I'm sure I could, but unfortunately the Scriptures were written before the days of Klee-nex Christians."

One reader in Illinois was not so polite himself. After reading portions of the Cotton Patch Version of Paul's Epistles, he wrote: "The author should be shot for making such a mockery of the Scriptures. If I were you I'd burn all copies—that way you might get a small idea what it will be like in hell. For anyone who is such an infidel to write such trash will end up in hell."

This sort of reaction was little threat to Clarence, who believed

Cotton Patch Paul was still a more discreet and genteel version than the original. He did agree, after several exchanges of correspondence, to allow the publisher to substitute "genitals" for "penis" in the first book of Thessalonians. But he wrote: " 'Penis' . . . has no vulgar connotations and would hardly cause most people these days to bat an eye, except perhaps those dainty souls who think of Jesus as a eunuch and that when the Word became flesh it was angelic flesh, not plain, sweaty, down-to-earth flesh."

Clarence believed modern Christianity was a victim of second-century docetism. Most believers could not accept the idea that Jesus was, in fact, "plain, sweaty, down-to-earth flesh," especially if that flesh were a different color than they were—God only seemed to have taken on a physical body. Thus, Christians spent so much energy trying to assure themselves of the deity of Jesus that they in fact denied the humanity of God in the process. This constant deification of Jesus, which Clarence felt was supported by the more polished but less earthy translations, explained the grievous error of so many churches that dodged responsibility in human affairs by substituting worship for obedience, liturgy for service, contemplation for action, programs for people, piety for compassion, and a futuristic orientation for the reality of the present.

Hammering home this point, he often told about a church in Georgia that spent $25,000 to install a large, circulating fountain on its lawn, when in the same town hundreds of homes did not even have running water. "I was thirsty, and ye built me a fountain." As long as God is God and not man, he said, we know how to handle him—we can build him a fountain on the lawn. "But as soon as we see God as man, then we have to give him a cup of water."

To justify elaborate facilities and to give witness to an earthly Jesus, Clarence said churches should spend at least as much "trying to house their brothers whom they have seen as they do trying to house God, whom they have never seen."

"People reject the incarnation by the deification of Jesus," he preached. "We create in our minds an image of him as a super-being, and thus safely remove him from our present experience and his insistent demands on us. We manage to keep him in this elevated and removed position by not allowing any familiarity with him or the Scriptures. Any attempt to make him human and embarrassingly present is angrily denounced as sacrilegious. By carefully preserving our image of him as God, we no longer have to deal with him as the Son of Man. That is, by protecting his deity we can escape his humanity. Preachers by the dozens who vehemently affirm his deity shamelessly deny his humanity if he is black and poor."

The essence of the incarnation and the resurrection, Clarence said, was that man has to deal with God in the flesh. He saw crosses on steeples not as glorious testimony to the humanity of God but as offensive reflection of the church's persistent deification of Jesus. He once said to a pastor who had just proudly pointed out the modern $10,000 cross atop a new church that he had been cheated on that price. "Time was," Clarence said, "when Christians could get those crosses for free."

Clarence viewed the resurrection as God's refusal to stay on the other side of the grave. "He raised Jesus, not as an invitation to us to come to heaven when we die, but as a declaration that He himself has now established permanent residence on earth," Clarence said. "The resurrection places Jesus on this side of the grave, here and now, in the midst of this life. The Good News of the resurrection is not that we shall die and go home with him, but that he is risen and comes home with us, bringing all his hungry, naked, thirsty, sick, prisoner brothers with him."

Cotton Patch was an extension of Clarence's proclamation on this point. He believed the "prettifying" of the Bible texts lifted the Gospel ideas out of this world and kept them hidden away behind "artificial piety and the barriers of time and distance." His drive in preaching and teaching, his purpose in experimenting with community, and his intent in "cotton-patching" the Good News was to put contemporary flesh once again on the radical ideas of the God Movement as he saw them spelled out in Scripture.

His efforts received their formal debut in 1963 when he lectured on the Book of Ephesians at the American Baptist Convention in Detroit. The demand for copies of his version of Ephesians escalated into a project that resulted in the publication of the Cotton Patch Version of Paul's Epistles, the Cotton Patch Version of Luke-Acts, and the Cotton Patch Version of Matthew and John (the first eight chapters only).

With the civil rights movement baring the bitter racism of the nation, he chose Ephesians as a contemporary, practical epistle that dealt with both social and personal crises. Most important, he felt it dealt directly with the tensions beleaguering Birmingham, where only a few months later four Negro children in a Sunday School class were ripped and torn by a racist's bomb. He titled his version: "The Letter to the Christians in Birmingham."

Clarence read with force and humor about the leaders with varying abilities who were "to help us quit being babies, so easily swayed and carried away by every windbag that comes along with some clever gimmick, with some big show to snare the gullible." "Become God's mimics. Make love a habit." But what probably captured the imaginations of his listeners the most, created the demand for copies, and made the Version so uniquely "cotton patch," was his translation of the second chapter of Ephesians:

In days gone by you all were living in your sin and filth like a bunch of stinking corpses, giving your allegiance to material things and ruled by the power of custom. . . . But even though we were a bunch of corpses rotting in our mess, God in his overflowing sympathy and great love breathed the same new life into us as into Christ. . . .

So, then, always remember that previously you Negroes, who sometimes are even called "niggers" by thoughtless white church members, were at one time outside the Christian fellowship, denied your rights as fellow believers, and treated as though the Gospel didn't apply to you, hopeless and God-forsaken in the eyes of the world. Now, however, because of Christ's supreme sacrifice, you who once were so segregated are warmly welcomed into the Christian fellowship. He himself is our peace. It was he who integrated us and abolished the segregation patterns which caused so much hostility. He allowed no silly traditions and customs in his fellowship, so that in it he might integrate the two into one new body. In this way he healed the hurt, and by his sacrifice on the cross he joined together both sides into one body for God. In it the hostility no longer exists.

His rendering of "gentiles" (sometimes called "uncircumcised") as Negroes (sometimes called "niggers") symbolized exactly what the Cotton Patch Version was all about. It placed the idea of reconciliation in Christ squarely in the context of the South's angry struggle against equality. The Gospel idea of brotherhood was where it belonged—in the discomforting here and now, not in the distant and unthreatening then and there.

He was taking liberty with the text, but as he explained it, the Greek word commonly translated "gentiles" had two meanings, one racial and the other spiritual or ethical. To the Jews, "gentile" referred to all non-Jews. So from this vantage point, the white man would think of all nonwhites as "gentiles," or more specifically in a southern context, as Negroes. From a spiritual viewpoint, the Jews used "gentile" to designate those who did not walk in the ways of Abraham. In this context, it would be about the equivalent of non-church member or non-Christian.

"So," Clarence said, "when the racial aspect of the word seems uppermost we have translated it 'Negroes,' assuming the viewpoint of the 'superior' white man of today to correspond to that of the 'proud' Hebrew of New Testament times. When the spiritual and ethical meaning is paramount, we translate it with phrases like 'the rest of society' or 'the people of the world.' " (Clarence always emphasized that he was translating the ideas of the New Testament, not the words.)

As always, his exegesis was laced with witty and biting commentary that made the passages jump with contemporary meaning:

Paul didn't say, "Well, the Supreme Court has said to integrate—it's coming sooner or later, dad-gum it; we might as well start integrating. Poor us!"

No. That isn't the Christian approach at all. Paul was saying, "You are like a bunch of stinking corpses and God smelled you when he passed over and he decided to do something about it. Rather than bulldoze you into a common grave, he decided to raise you from the dead and give you a new life." Instead of accepting this begrudgingly, we ought to thank God we are alive instead of stinking corpses, that we've been freed from these old prejudices and old hates that blight our lives, and that there has been new life breathed into us by the Almighty God.*

Clarence was a blunt and confronting preacher, a dogged debater, and he drew firm conclusions from the Scripture, as his further comments on this section of Ephesians illustrate:

*Although many scholars doubt that Paul authored Ephesians because of the difference in vocabulary, style, and doctrine, Jordan held to Pauline authorship on the grounds that it could have been written at the close of Paul's life and thus reflect a changed perspective and knowledge.

I never had a southerner to beat me in the argument that Christ
teaches that in his family, men are brothers. This is why I studied Greek
—not to impress anybody with a little bit of learning. I knew I would
be going into the southland to give my life to the Lord and that I would
not be pastoring a church. I could not pastor one in the Deep South.
But I knew I would be coming into contact with a lot of people—both
clergy and laity—who claimed to be followers of Jesus Christ and I
wanted to know what the man was saying. I didn't want some little
jackleg preacher tying me up in knots because I didn't know what the
Lord said. I rooted myself in the Greek language that I might understand. And I think by His grace I do understand, at least this little part
in Ephesians here.

As an emotional, dramatic speaker, Clarence made no attempt
to hold his commentary in rein and to restrain himself from
breaking into a little country Baptist preaching.

The thing that just burns my heart out is that the Supreme Court is
making pagans be more Christian than the Bible is making Christians
be Christians. I can hardly stand it sometimes when the whole integration struggle is being fought not in the household of God but in the
buses, the depots, and around the Woolworth tables in arguments about
whether or not we can sit down and eat hamburgers and drink cokes
together. We ought to be sitting around Jesus' table drinking wine and
eating bread together.

It just burns me up that we Christians with the Word of God in our
hearts have to be forced to sit around Woolworth's tables and still
segregate Christ's table. The sit-ins never would have been necessary if
Christians had been sitting down together in church and at Christ's
table all these many years. If anybody has to bear the blame and the guilt
for all the sit-ins and all the demonstrations and all the disorders in the
South, it's the white-washed Christians who have had the Word of God
locked up in their hearts and have refused to do battle with it.

Clarence was beginning to express a growing impatience with religion that pecked people silly with talk of salvation but produced no incarnational activity. "Desperate, lost, hungry people are being offered 'faith, hope, and salvation' (instead of 'love' as in I Corinthians 13)," he would say mockingly, "and the greatest of these is salvation."

Christianity started out as a revolution, he believed, and he preached a return to that revolutionary fire. In his exegesis of the crucifixion passages, he often contrasted the fate of two revolutionary leaders, Barrabas and Jesus—one the leader of a violent revolution bent on destroying Rome, the other the leader of a love revolution insistent in calling on his followers to love their enemies. According to some biblical sources, he said, Barabbas' name also was Jesus. Since "Barabbas" meant "son of the father," the Romans had two revolutionaries on their hands, both of whom were known as Jesus, son of the father.

"When Pilate said, which will you have, this Jesus of the love revolution or this Jesus of the violent revolution," Clarence said, "it was the religious people who cried, 'Give us this man of violence; crucify this man of love.'

"I've heard too many preachers get up in front of pagans and preach on 'what will you do with Jesus.' But this wasn't a preacher standing in front of pagans saying what will you do with Jesus. This was a pagan standing in front of preachers saying, 'What are *you* going to do with him?' "

Clarence's version of the Gospels, then, did not speak of the kingdom of heaven. Instead, it spoke of the God Movement as if it were a revolutionary new order that Jesus was initiating and inviting people to join now. Chapters five, six, and seven of the Gospel of Matthew—the Sermon on the Mount—was not a sermon at all, Clarence taught; it was the platform of the God Movement.

"It was a lesson," he said, "which Jesus may have required his students to memorize. Its purpose was not to evoke inspiration but perspiration. Jesus was the leader of a revolution, of people alive with these ideas, not static with doctrine."

Lecturing on the Sermon on the Mount, Clarence usually began in the fourth chapter of Matthew and explained the purpose of Jesus' forty days in the wilderness and the temptation experiences. The story was simply a dramatic way of saying that Jesus spent an intensive period analyzing the major ideas that currently were competing for the minds of men. Clarence referred to the devil as "the Confuser."

The first temptation, to turn the stones into "pones of bread," Clarence said, was the proposition of materialism. It was not the temptation for Jesus to break a fast and feed himself; rather, it was the reminder that people were hungry, and that by exercising his power to make bread, or to provide material needs alone, he could establish a powerful earthly kingdom. Men with their bellies full would make him their king.

He labels the second temptation, in which the Confuser tried to bait Jesus into leaping from the top of the temple to demonstrate his power, as the proposition of pure ecclesiasticism, the temptation to establish a great ecclesiastical empire. As Clarence told it:

The Confuser took Jesus into the holy city, up to the holy temple that was on the holy hill, up to the top of the steeple—the very jumping off place of holiness. You can't get any holier than that. Then he told him: "Now, it doesn't matter if you jump off with some fuzzy theology. You can jump off with any theological bull . . . the college of cardinals will catch you. If you don't want to be Stalin, how about pope? Go ahead, you will be un-fallable. . . ."

After refusing the possibilities of either a purely materialistic or a purely ecclesiastical kingdom, Jesus faced a hybrid proposition in the Confuser's offer for power over the nations: to use the might of militarism to establish a political kingdom.

Rejecting these three propositions, Clarence said: "Jesus was making it perfectly clear that certain ideas were not to be a part of his movement."

Jesus then came out of the temptation experiences preaching: "Reshape your lives, for God's new order of the Spirit is confronting you," and began putting flesh on his ideas by choosing a small band of followers to demonstrate them.

Jesus was choosing his followers, building a microcosm of the world as an experimentation plot for the ideas of the Kingdom. He knew if he could take a fanatical zealot like Simon and a collaborating tax collector like Matthew and cause them to have the love of God in their hearts so that they could walk down Main Street in Jerusalem calling each other "brother," then the kingdom of God was here. It would be absolute proof that the power of God had changed these people from little old caterpillars of hate and prejudice and greed and had made them into the butterflies of his new order. So if someone asked him where is this kingdom you speak of, he could say, "Right there—there is Simon, there is Matthew. These are the people in whom I have planted my ideas and this is how they are expressing themselves."

Jesus was seeking to experiment with these ideas, trying to demonstrate that the new order of the spirit was dawning. I think this is what God is always trying to do. The incarnation is not a point in history, it is a process. The ideas of God are constantly struggling for expression in the experiences of man. Before this new order can ever become a reality it's got to take root in our own lives. Somewhere we've got to build a fellowship where men are transformed from the old things, where the old things pass away and all things become new. We cannot enter this new order with the old trappings.

With his experimental band together, and the crowds beginning to respond to his preaching, Jesus delivered the Sermon on the Mount, the manifesto of his movement.

The cotton Patch Version presents Matthew 5:1–12 this way:

The Spiritually humble are God's people, for they are citizens of His new order.

They who are deeply concerned are God's people, for they will see their ideas become reality.

They who are gentle are His people, for they will be his partners across the land.

They who have an unsatisfied appetite for the right are God's people, for they will be given plenty to chew on.

The generous are God's people, for they will be treated generously.

They whose motives are pure are God's people, for they will have spiritual insight.

Men of peace and goodwill are God's people, for they will be known throughout the land as His children.

They who have endured much for what's right are God's people; they are the citizens of His new order.

You all are God's people when others call you names, and harass you and tell all kinds of false tales on you just because you follow me. Be cheerful and good-humored, because your spiritual advantage is great. For that's the way they treated men of conscience in the past.

These were the great ideas that were to govern the development of the movement, Clarence taught, so Jesus presented them stairstep fashion, as the process of conversion, "as stages of the metamorphosis Jesus was talking about in changing one's philosophy of life." The first step, to be spiritually humble, is to recognize one's self as a spiritual pauper, to acknowledge that God alone empowers the movement. Secondly, what normally is translated "blessed are those who mourn" Clarence interpreted as "concerned," meaning "to the point of action."

Then comes the beatitude most familiar as "blessed are the meek. . . ." Clarence translated it: "They who are gentle are His people . . . ," but even Clarence must have been a little dissatisfied. He usually paused at this idea and went into detail about the Greek word translated as meek or gentle.

It is used only twice again in the Bible to describe people, for one Old Testament character—Moses—and for one New Testament character —Jesus. It does not mean a Mr. Milquetoast, a spiritual doormat for humanity. Can you see Moses coming in, saying: "Good morning, Mr. Pharoah, how are you this morning? Would you mind, please sir, letting my people go out on a little two-hour picnic?" No. Moses walked in and said: "Thus sayeth the Lord, let my people go!" That's being meek.

In classical Greek, the word is used almost totally in reference to horses, those trained to wear the bridle. When Peter and John were threatened by the Sanhedrin saying, don't you preach in the name of this Jesus character anymore, Peter said to that austere body: "Whether it be right for us to obey God or man, you judge, but we cannot but speak those things which we have seen and heard." That's one of the meekest statements in the Bible.

The meek man is the man who obeys the pull of God, who isn't afraid to lose his influence or his head. The meek man has got no better sense than to be a fool for God. They're the martyrs. They aren't weak, insipid, inane little two-by-four Christians who never stir up anybody. These meek folks are the folks who turn the world upside down. And God said they will be his partners across the land.

The ultimate level of maturity reflected in the conversion process was the ability to suffer all manner of harassment and persecution. Clarence often remarked: "I don't think a Christian is worth his salt who has not been called a Communist today. Trying to refute that epithet is about like running for your birth certificate when someone calls you an s.o.b."

Moving through the Sermon on the Mount, with lengthy emphasis on the admonishments against violence and materialism, Clarence often ended his lectures by reading portions of the final verses: "The man who hears these words of mine and acts on them shall be like a wise man. . . . The man who hears these words of mine and fails to act on them shall be like an idiot. . . ."

"Let's go forth," Clarence would say, "and classify ourselves."

Something new was rising close to the surface in Clarence, but he was not yet aware of it. The ideas he had claimed had only begun to gain expression, and the man who would help unchain his mind and set it roaming again in a far-ranging vision, and join him in shaping a new, aggressive endeavor at Koinonia Farm, was on his way.

CHAPTER 12

New Vision:
Koinonia Partners

Millard Fuller was a tall, skinny Alabama lawyer with a trainload of audacity stoked up in a thrusting countenance and a capacity for making money by the carload underlying his deceptive country-boy simplicity. He was dark and brooding and preoccupied, always plunging to and fro in an angular, hurried stride, elbows flying, his mind focused on what counted the most—money. In fact, he had steamed up to a near-explosion point not long before he stumbled into Clarence Jordan and heard so simply articulated what he had been groping for under the magic spell of profit.

The spell that came over him as a youngster when he first dreamed of a million dollars seemed to have cast him into a permanent headlong rush. As a boy near Lanett, Alabama, he raised pigs, rabbits, and cows, practically took over junior achievement; later he pitched semi-pro baseball in central Alabama with thoughts of lucrative professional contracts in his mind until he threw out his promising left arm. He sold hose and underwear door-to-door for the Real Silk Hosiery Company—"Hello, I'm Millard Fuller, your Real Silk representative."—worked on a truck in Chicago, and served as a waiter while attending the University of Alabama. As law students, he and his partner, Morris Dees, sold Christmas trees, mistletoe, and "oriental berries"— chinaberries dipped in silver paint. And later they escalated the project of selling imported Italian holly wreaths to the Tuscaloosa boy scouts into a $3-million, nationwide, direct-mail business that included tractor cushions, doormats, toothbrushes, and cookbooks.

Millard seemed to have a stream of energy flowing through him that, if it could be photographed, would resemble Niagara Falls.

And yet, when he generated up to $1 million in 1964—four years out of law school—and reset his objective at $10 million, some little irritant in the back of his mind, some lingering question of past commitment, spoiled any sense of fulfillment, gave him severe neck pains, and made it hard for him to breathe. His tall, soft-blond wife Linda gave final definition to the matter—she left him for a few days to think about whether or not she wanted to be a part of all that anymore. And she left him with the two children. When he tucked his five-year-old son into bed one lonely night and the boy said, "Daddy, I'm glad you're home," Millard started wondering where he had been. And when he thought about it, the spell broke, and he shook the mist from his mind, and set out to regain his wife and his two children, and a commitment he had almost forgotten—a commitment he had made during his intense involvement in the United Church of Christ, back before he had started making money—a commitment that he was giving his life to God.

He took off for New York City and found Linda, and after much talk they stood in a dark storefront entrance somewhere in Manhattan and cried one night until they were exhausted, and then they laughed and held each other and agreed to dump their money and their business. With their way of thinking completely changed, but with Millard's little Niagara still flooding his system with energy, they fairly lunged back into Montgomery, started selling houses and horses and farms and boats and cars, and arranging for Dees to buy their half of the business and for ways to give the money away. And then they packed the car and went wandering down into Florida with Chris and Kim, relaxing for a change, living at an easy pace for a change, enjoying the feast of it, rediscovering each other, and praying and talking themselves into a whole new way of life.

When he turned the station wagon northward, Millard thought about an old friend, Al Henry, who had been pastor of the Pilgrim Congregational Church in Birmingham, and he remembered he had moved temporarily to some strange community place called Koinonia Farm near Albany, Georgia. He called the information operator in Albany, and she said the place was near Americus. And so they made their way over there to see Al and his wife Carol for a couple of hours or so, maybe to stay for lunch. And they stayed a month.

They entered the Koinonia property just before noon, visited with Al and Carol for a few minutes, and then sat down to lunch in the community dining room. They were already into their meal when Millard looked up and saw this large man step in, a guy in blue jeans and work boots—obviously a farmer. The man took a seat at the same long table where the Henrys and the Fullers were, and so did a young man who was apparently a reporter, who was firing questions at this farmer. Millard found himself leaning and craning to catch the answers. The reporter was asking him about war and peace and racial concerns and religion, and his answers were quiet and deep.

"I knew this wasn't any ordinary farmer," Millard said, "and I asked Al who it was. He said it was Clarence Jordan. I knew I wanted to talk to that man."

When Millard got to him and started talking and listening, he knew the Fullers were going to stay around a while. He and Clarence worked together and talked, walked together and talked, ate together and talked. Clarence unfolded much of what had passed at Koinonia Farm and his desire for new direction, and Millard revealed the nature of his own struggle. The Henrys and the Wittkampers were sensitive to the tumultuous period of change that the Fullers were in the midst of, and the fellowship proved supportive.

"At noon meals and at night we talked in groups," Millard said. "Our subjects ranged from civil rights marches to the crucifixion to fruit cakes, to the war in Vietnam. But the common elements running through all that was said and done at Koinonia were love and an abiding concern for us as we prepared ourselves, emotionally and spiritually, for a new life. Clarence pounded home to me time and again that God calls us to faithfulness rather than 'successfulness.'"

Early in December, while the Fullers were visiting, an association of local churches scheduled a mass meeting at which Walter Moore, Carol Henry's father, was to speak. The association published an ad in the paper announcing the meeting and declaring that the public was invited. The Henrys, quite naturally, were going, and they invited the others to go with them. Collins McGee, a young Negro living at Koinonia temporarily, accepted and so did Clarence, thinking that perhaps this was the time to enter a white Baptist church, if it was ever to be accomplished; perhaps events were working together to finally make it possible for a black man to sit comfortably among white Christians. And so Clarence, Collins, Greg Wittkamper, the Fullers, and the Henrys drove into town for the 7:30 meeting at the church. They were apprehensive; Clarence cautioned everyone to be as polite as possible no matter what happened.

It was about 7:25 when they arrived and crowds of people were funneling into the entrance. The Koinonia group kept close and walked up the steps and in the door past an usher, who was handing out little cards.

Realizing that a black man had walked past him, the usher flushed with anger, looked at Greg and, nodding in the direction of Collins, asked sharply: "Who is that?"

Greg said: "Why, that's Collins McGee," and kept going.

Clarence led the way in as the congregation started singing "Gloria in Excelsis Deo," and they filled one pew about eight rows from the back. Before the song ended, the people in the pew directly in front of them had moved to the other side of the aisle, but everything seemed calm. They breathed a little easier as they turned to "It Came Upon a Midnight Clear" in their hymnals —until they saw the head usher bolting up the aisle looking as if he had just dashed out of a breath-holding contest.

He motioned to Collins, who was in the middle of the pew, to come out, at the same time saying to Al: "He can't come in here." When Collins failed to respond, he started into the empty pew in front of the Koinonia group, saying loudly: "You have to leave." He grabbed Collins by the wrist, and Clarence leaned over and asked: "Do you have the authority to do this?"

When the usher said yes, Clarence asked to see the pastor. The man replied: "I'm in charge here; you don't have to see the pastor." And then he turned to Collins again: "Am I going to have to drag you out?" They ceased any resistance at that point, and shuffled out into the aisle to leave voluntarily.

On the step of the church, one man said to them: "This is our church. We control it. We paid for it. The Federal government didn't put one dime into this building."

Millard asked him if he did not think that he and the others in the church should consider the will of God in their policy.

He answered: "That's neither here nor there."

The pastor appeared and sought to ease the tension, saying to the deacon that the meeting was an associational gathering and that the policy of the church pertained to the worship services of the church. But the deacon insisted that the congregation was responsible for whatever went on in the building.

The Koinonians began to walk away then, as Clarence put in a parting shot: "Well, everything in Americus is integrated now except the churches and the jails. And I have hope for the jails."

Millard and Linda and the two children stayed at Koinonia through Christmas, and helped Al and Carol with a project called "Bikes and Trikes for Tikes." They delivered 60 bicycles and tricycles on Christmas Day to children in the area.

These experiences were meaningful to Millard, who had rejected one way of life for another, but who still was working through deep struggles of adjustment. Turning his back on a $1 million financial statement appeared to be something like the plunge of a runaway elevator—he was unsure about what would happen at the bottom. He was considering attending the seminary, or possibly accepting an offer from the United Church of Christ to travel in Africa visiting mission stations and then speaking in the United States about what he had seen. He had also been offered a position as an attorney for the United Church Board for Homeland Ministries. The Board for World Ministries also had suggested the possibility of managing a mission hospital in Africa.

The race problem in the United States, however, was burning in him as the greatest moral, ethical, and religious crisis facing the nation, and he wanted somehow to be part of a solution. The offer that appealed to him most was to become development secretary for Tougaloo College, a predominantely Negro school north of Jackson, Mississippi, which was supported by the United Church.

At the beginning of a new year, 1966, he and Linda moved to New York City, where he established a development office for Tougaloo. For two years, Millard traveled and spoke on behalf of the school and the United Church mission board, and maintained an erratic but meaningful correspondence with Clarence.

In February 1968, Millard received a note from Clarence that said he was going to be in New York and wanted to spend some time with Millard. Koinonia had published a pecan cookbook at Millard's suggestion and needed help promoting it. Over lunch at the Fullers' house, they discussed first the cookbook project and then Clarence's growing despair over a lack of direction for his own life.

The Koinonia community was without question at an end. Only the Jordans and the Wittkampers remained. The Henrys had left in 1967 when Al had accepted a job in Atlanta. The 1100-acre farm and the pecan business was an enormous burden on Clarence, who was feeling an increasing sense of urgency to get on with something new. He had tried to give the farm to the Reba Place Fellowship, but they had turned down the offer. No vision seemed alive in Clarence; just a restlessness.

A month later, Millard resigned from his position at Tougaloo, still groping for meaningful expression of the cataclysmic change in his own life. On a plane from New York to Chicago, en route to a speaking engagement, he thought of Clarence and immediately asked the stewardess for pen and paper. He scrawled a three-line letter and mailed it from Chicago. It said simply: "I have resigned my position at Tougaloo. What have you got up your sleeve?"

Clarence received the letter at a time of personal despondency. He had nothing up his sleeve; in fact, he had not felt as adrift in his entire life. But the note from Millard sparked a hope in him that he could not articulate. He called Millard and said: "Look, I haven't got anything up my sleeve, but maybe God has something up his sleeve for both of us."

Millard said later: "There was a commitment in Clarence that

God was in control and had plans. He wanted to work in partnership with God. He believed absolutely that if you are obedient, then God will use you."

The two men agreed to meet in May in Atlanta, where Clarence was to deliver a series of messages at the Oakhurst Baptist Church. Millard came for the last night of the three-day meeting, and the next day, he and Clarence met in the pastor's study for an intensive day-long session.

With each man admiring and feeding the boldness of the other, something was bound to spring from the encounter. Early in their meeting, they knew they wanted to be together, to be partners in whatever took shape in their minds. From that point, they began to volley ideas around. Clearly, Clarence had a gift for writing and teaching that needed to gain fuller expression than had previously been possible. Koinonia Farm would have to be sold to relieve the economic pressure. They both might need to live in Atlanta, close to a major airport. Clarence had been flooded with speaking invitations for 20 years, so perhaps now he could turn to them as the major opportunity before him and spend the rest of his years writing and speaking. Millard, too, had a powerful presence as a speaker and a dramatic life to tell about. They began to think about having a school—a discipleship school, they would call it. They could conduct weekend and week-long sessions in some simple building—perhaps a barracks of some sort—and invite people from around the country to come to Atlanta for one- and two-week seminars.

Clarence described what was firing their imaginations: "The thing that kept pushing in on us was this idea of man's estrangement from God. He's really afraid to say that word, afraid to even think of that dimension of his life. Man is alienating himself, or like the elder brother in the parable of the prodigal son, just refusing to come into God's feast. We kept feeling that man needs to be restored to a sense that God has a job for him to do, that we can be, by God's grace, partners with Him. We discussed all the alienation and isolation and loneliness and anonymity of man, his competitiveness, his wars, his racial pride, and all this fragmentation of man. It kept coming back—we need to learn to be partners. This word partners, partners, just kept hitting us time and time again because it speaks of an upward reach and an outward reach."

These discussions filled a day, with only one conclusion: that the Fullers would join Clarence and Florence as soon as Millard could clear away all his other commitments. Both men felt that Koinonia Farm would have to be sold and Clarence wanted Millard to handle the sale. So in July 1968, the Fullers moved back to Koinonia, expecting to get things in order for sale of the land and be on their way to Atlanta by the time school opened in September.

During the first few days after their arrival, however, the feeling began to grow in both men that it might take them a year to get to Atlanta. And so with Florence and Linda in agreement, they relaxed, decided to give their ideas a year to take shape, and began to ask others to contribute to their thinking.

They had already planned for a meeting at the farm in August, and had invited men whose lives indicated that they struggled for faithfulness to the same ideas: Ned Coll, a Catholic layman from Hartford, Connecticut, who founded the Revitalization Corps; Bob Miller, alumni secretary for Union Theological Seminary and mayor of Englewood, New Jersey; Bob Wood, a salesman for the Waterbury Tag Company in Westport, Connecticut; Ted Braun, of the department of interpretation of the United Church Board for World Ministries, from New York; Leroy Ellis, a black businessman from Westport, Connecticut; Richard Jones, a black Baptist pastor from Brooklyn who had recently become chaplain at Tougaloo College; Bob Swann, an itinerant but persistent protester of war and an active member of the Committee for Nonviolent Action, from Connecticut; John Miller from the Reba Place fellowship; Sam Emerick, director of the Yokefellow Institute at Earlham College in Richmond, Indiana; Ladon Sheats, a young IBM executive from New York, active in Faith at Work, and in Young Life's unusual activity on the lower east side of Manhattan; Slater King, a black businessman from Albany, Georgia; and Doc Champion, a local black Baptist pastor.

By the time these men arrived for a three-day session in August, Clarence and Millard were talking about their still-nebulous vision as the Partnership Movement. They knew basically that they were struggling for a context—a container—in which the ideas of peace and love and sharing could ferment and gain expression. The Koinonia community had been a good container in its day, but Clarence was looking for something new, something of a broader scope, something more aggressive and confronting that people could be involved in wherever they were. So the spirit of partnership had become their key concern, with a school of some sort as the most immediate interest and a revolutionary concept of land reform as the most far-reaching aspect of their idea.

The war on poverty was getting headlines in Washington, but Clarence and Millard wanted to wage a war on wealth. They wanted to create a way of sharing that would make the rich man a partner of the poor, the educated a partner of the uneducated, the skilled a partner of the unskilled, the laborer the partner of the thinker. They had not nailed it all down with specifics, but they were thinking big. They wanted to see muscle and brain, strength and powerlessness, fat wallets and thin come together somehow.

They wanted to make some introductions, to say: solid mansion and fine front lawn, meet drafty leaky shanty and red dirt dust;

steak-three-times-a-week-with-linen-napkin, meet fried-chicken-sometimes and boiled-greens-all-the-time; hot and cold running water and sparkling porcelain and bright-colored toilet seat, meet see-through breeze-through frozen-damp clapboard outhouse rot; antiseptic, perfumed manicure above shiny wing-tips, meet 100-varieties-of-stink fly-rat-maggot on chicken bone and runny sores on bare feet; privacy of leisure love taken upon silken sheet, meet hurry-lust lurched out upon mattress mat hoping children asleep; warm family around the hearth, meet cold dull-eyed-life-lost family on the dump, hope-gone; protective law—"yes sir, we'll check right into it"—meet oppressive law—"I kicked your ass, boy, let me hear a thank you sir." They wanted to say world, meet the world, and offer a chance at a fulfilling partnership to anyone who would take the time to see and hear. They even wanted to make so bold as to say: "Here is land for you to work, brother, just as God intended. It's yours as long as you can use it, and when you can't, why, someone else will." They wanted to say to hell with competition and urge men to embrace the more mature relationships of cooperation.

The men came together and, although they had been given little warning as to what to expect, they sensed the excitement and the expectancy that gripped Clarence and Millard.

Clarence hitched up his jeans and pushed the group immediately into his own persistent need to think as far out as possible. "We got to think big," he said time and again. "This is not a time for spiritual pygmies. We're living in a land of giants, and pygmies seldom have influence on giants. We're going to have to think in gigantic terms. I know the extremities man without God can be driven to. But this is God's world and we've got to think about it and reorder it along those lines.

"Millard and I share a deep sense of rightness that God is agonizing trying to bring something into existence. We have a deep feeling that we want to be His partners in this. And by partners we don't mean it like the businessman who says he'll take God as his partner, and if He blesses him, give Him back 10 percent. We mean a sense that God himself has work to do in this world and that He needs some junior associates.

"One of the things we feel is that man has got to quit this competing. The era of competition, each man like a snarling wolf trying to get his little bit of carcass, must pass away and a new era of partnership with each other must be allowed to break through. White must quit being 'White,' black must quit being 'Black,' rich must quit being 'Rich,' poor must quit being 'Poor,' nation must quit being 'Nation'—and we must be people together, partners under God."

Then he took the lead in stating what he and Millard wanted to do and to call others to do with them.

First of all, by preaching and writing and singing and whatever else offered itself, they wanted to communicate ideas to people. Referring to the New Testament, he said: "We've got a body of ideas here that the Marxists can't hold a candle to; no one can."

Secondly, he said, after spreading ideas expectantly, they wanted to take the ideas and drill them into people who responded initially until they became incarnate ideas. "We haven't gotten anywhere until we see the word become flesh," he said. "We want to make fanatics out of the people who respond to the spreading of the ideas."

And thirdly, they wanted concrete ways to be involved in implementing the ideas themselves, and to have specific ways to call people into partnership.

"Now on this," Clarence said, "we've got to take a hold somewhere, to get a beachhead. We're convinced that the present structure of capitalism is wrong, especially in the matter of land tenure. We need to return to the Old Testament idea that the earth is the Lord's; it's still His property—no man can give you a clear title. If you trace the title back far enough, somebody stole it."

Clarence proposed the establishment of a Fund for Humanity through which land could be purchased and made available to people by virtue of usership rather than by virtue of ability to pay. The Fund for Humanity, in effect, would be a legal means of restoring land to humanity, as well as a dignified channel through which the more affluent could share with the less fortunate. A poor man cannot afford to farm anymore due to exorbitant interest rates, Clarence stated. But if some way could be provided to make it possible for the poor rural folks to stay on the land, they could find dignified life and the stream of impoverished people heading for last-stop urban ghettos would dry up.

There is no more right to take the land and hold onto it for profit than there is to take the air, Clarence said, adding: "If you don't have a right to take the air, why would you have a right to take the land? Just because the strong are able to exploit the weak, does that justify the exploitation?" Something new—a new attitude—is needed, he said.

The Fund for Humanity, then, was Clarence's proposal for a legal way of buying and holding land in trust for families to farm in partnership, and he believed it could be done. "We want to begin by buying one million acres of land—now that isn't much. At $300 an acre that's only $300 million—that's only five days of the Vietnamese war."

The minds in the meeting were reeling under Clarence's far-ranging speculations. What he was talking about sounded nothing short of revolutionary. To Clarence, however, it was the way he believed Christ followers were supposed to think—"Reshape your lives (change your whole way of thinking), for God's new Order of the Spirit is upon you." He pressed on.

"Now, you can engage in a bloody revolution to appropriate land," he said. "Or, you can shed your own blood and sweat for it." And that is what he was proposing: a revolution built around *buying* the land back for humanity, a revolution applying peaceful economic means in order to reassert that the land is God's gift to *all* men, and that it should be used justly.

It may have sounded far out and in fact highly impractical, but somehow Clarence made it sound more sensible than a system through which a United States senator could make thousands of dollars a month for growing absolutely nothing on his land, while some black son-of-a-sharecropper could work from sunrise to sundown year round providing the populace with corn and peanuts and only go deeper in debt. Such way-out ideas sounded sensible when Clarence told about Charlie, Jr., in Atlanta, whose land just up the Dawson Road was in the soil bank bringing probably $20,000 a year, while old Zack, the last tenant farmer on the place, was preparing to move his wife and 10 children to Hartford to join his relatives on the welfare rolls because he just did not have anything more to make it on.

Justice was not an ideal promised by a kingdom yet to come, Clarence insisted, but a manifestation now of God ruling in the hearts of men. When Jesus stood and delivered his inaugural address in the synagogue, he was proclaiming a new order, a new spirit *now* (in Luke 4). In that situation, Clarence declared, Jesus was announcing the permanent arrival of the spirit of the Year of Jubilee—in Jewish tradition the 50th year, set aside as a year-long "sabbath of sabbaths," a time when the spirit of God was to rule the hearts and minds of men. Slaves were freed, captives released, debts forgiven, and land returned to original owners.

"The Jews," Clarence said, "had a built-in check against exploitation. Jesus felt that if you could live like that one year out of 50, you could live like that permanently."

The Fund for Humanity would be a way, a method, a structure through which people living comfortably could help provide an inheritance to the disinherited, a way to say to someone like Zack: "Look, man, you are growing corn for us to eat and we appreciate it. We're not going to make you furnish the land; we're going to furnish it for you."

"If we could get millions of acres with land tenure based on usage rather than on property deeds, these people whose earthly fathers can't leave them any inheritance would be counted in for the inheritance from the heavenly Father," Clarence said. "If He's concerned about the sparrows and the crows, then somewhere His people ought to be dealt in on the divine inheritance."

Two, three, or four families could group together on one or two thousand acres and farm the land in partnership. Or, if a man did not want to work in partnership, he could be assigned a plot to handle alone. Since the land would be paid for, and the farmers would only be responsible for paying taxes, good profits would virtually be assured. And it was a major part of Clarence's dream that such "partners" could be taught to share, and thus voluntarily give back to the Fund for Humanity a portion of their profits so that more land could be purchased elsewhere for others. In other words, Clarence said, if it is truly more blessed to give than to receive, then it ought to be made possible for the poor to have something to share and a way to share. A poor man then would become a man with a mission.

The Fund for Humanity also could finance housing with no–interest loans and make it possible for some of the large, low-skilled rural families who could not qualify for commercial loans to live in a decent house, and have a home to pass on to their children.

Where would the money come from? "Our first step is to beg," Clarence said. "We are boldly going to become monumental beggars." Churches should be a major target, since they have so much money to spend on buildings and cushioned comforts. "If they spend that kind of money on their own spiritual pride, then they should be able to spend at least as much on others. If they can invest that much for a God they hope will put in an appearance, they ought to be able to spend an equal amount for people whom they can see have need. All those churches that are agonizing about what they can do—we want to give them an opportunity to do something. I think we ought to ask them to put into the Fund for Humanity an amount equal to the cost of their own sanctuary."

Questions broke from the throats of the men in the room and roiled the hot August air over their heads. Isn't it asking too much to expect a family raised in deprivation to share the first time they have something? Do you really think several families could govern themselves on a common portion of land, especially families so ill-equipped for managership? Do you really know what you are saying when you talk about it being wrong to buy and sell land for a profit? Aren't you pruning the Gospel down a little narrowly to simply reduce it to a welfare program? And so on.

Clarence and Millard did a great deal of listening for the better part of two days after the initial introduction of their plans. But to the questions of impracticality, Clarence, characteristically, would not give an inch: "We're not just trying to solve economic problems. We're trying to think of man in all his dimensions. Man is more than a belly in search of bread. 'Man shall not live by bread alone'—this is not just a pious statement from Jesus; it is a deep insight into the nature of man. We're not going to put 10 greedy people out here on the land and expect them to become altruistic angels. There will have to be spiritual and psychological approaches. But just as we envision people who can give technical advice—men with training and experience—linking up in partnership, we also envision spiritual shepherds—people with gifts along the line of helping people be altruistic—joining in.

"The real minister of the future may not be a man behind a pulpit who gives off with a lot of ministerial rumblings. The real minister of the future will be a shepherd out there keeping his eye peeled for wolves. There will need to be good shepherds to live with the people and to love them. Unless the spirit of man can be reached, I see little hope. A greedy, selfish spirit can destroy any system. But we want to meet human need in all its grossness and all its dimensions, and not set something up for a few elect, a spiritual elite.

"We've got to start with people where they are, with the resources we have. I don't see any guarantee in this Partnership Movement that it won't be a fiasco. But we sure can't make things any worse. Granted, there will be problems. A man is a problem, and when you take on a man, you take on a problem."

The discussions on the use of land led the group to the conclusion that Koinonia Farm again offered the best starting place. Where before, Clarence and Millard had thought in terms of shedding the heavy responsibility of the farm in order to be free to start over, it now became clear that the 1100 acres along the Dawson Road, with its cluster of houses, its nucleus of a job-producing industry (pecan plant), and its long-fallow land, was *the* place to begin. It could continue to be a demonstration plot for what others could do elsewhere. Also, Clarence already had sold about a dozen half-acre lots for housing in the pine grove along the northern boundary, selling them for $75 to $200, depending on what he thought the families could pay. The site was perfect for a housing village.

The group rejected the name Partnership Movement, basically for the reason that a movement is something that gets underway spontaneously. You can hope for a movement, but you cannot plan one, they said. So it became simply Partners, later Koinonia Partners, and then Koinonia Partners, Inc.

Clarence and Millard invited another group of men to the farm two months later, but by then they were rolling with the momentum of increasing certainty about what they wanted to do: "We want to throw every ounce of our weight into helping men to radically restructure their lives so as to be in partnership with God."

Koinonia Partners would consist of three major thrusts: communication, instruction, and application.

By communication, they meant the spreading of the radical ideas of the Gospel message, the proclamation of the new Order of God's Spirit, the call for men to restructure their lives under the rule of God. They planned tapes, records, films, and books, as well as speaking engagements already in abundance.

By instruction, they meant more intensive encounters with smaller groups of people who sought to join into the spirit of partnership with God and man, people who hungered for a more expressive and active faith—people who were searching to put working clothes on their faiths. The possibilities ranged from weekend to two-week sessions of intensive biblical study and an exchange of ideas about what God is doing in the world and how man can participate. Clarence and Millard, and later others, would go anywhere to conduct these "discipleship schools," as well as invite groups to Koinonia Farm.

By application, they meant the Fund for Humanity, through which they planned to provide partnership industries, partnership farming, and partnership housing. The fund would provide an inheritance for the disinherited and offer a means through which the possessed could share with and invest in the dispossessed. "What the poor need is not charity, but capital, not caseworkers but coworkers," they said. "And what the rich need is a wise, honorable, and just way of divesting themselves of their overabundance."

The fund would accept gifts and donations as well as non-interest-bearing loans. (Hopefully, communication efforts would also encourage other groups to organize their own funds for humanity. Koinonia Partners would be in the idea-sharing business.)

For jobs, Koinonia Partners would immediately make plans for Koinonia land to be farmed in partnership. The pecan, candy, and fruit cake direct-mail business would be expanded under Millard's leadership to provide jobs and help beef up the fund to create capital for other low-overhead industries.

Taking on the acute housing need as a priority, Clarence and Millard laid off 42 half-acre homesites along the northern boundary of the farm, with a four-acre plot marked for playground and family recreation area. On the "street" where Clarence already had sold a few lots when he thought Koinonia Farm was to be sold, they would continue to sell the sites. Another street would run parallel to the first, and the lots would be leased from the Fund for Humanity at a nominal fee. Through the fund, three–bedroom houses with furnished kitchens would be built for about $6,500 and sold for that amount. The money would be loaned to purchasers interest-free, reducing by more than half the monthly payment that a poor man would face if he ever did qualify for a regular commercial loan. The money would be loaned for a period of 20 years, making monthly payments about $25. And the recipients would be the folks who needed such opportunities the most —the people in the old tenant shacks with no water or any of the other "conveniences" that are considered absolute necessities by most people.

Hopefully, those who received loans or jobs or land to farm would join in the spirit of partnership and share with others through the Fund for Humanity. But no such expectation was to become a requirement, nor was allegiance to any particular set of beliefs to be required. Need would be the sole criteria.

It still all smacked of pipe dreams and unrealistic speculation. And yet something in the power of Clarence's past experiences and in the force of his current faith—something in the stream of history that brought him to this point in his life—mixed with the boldness of Millard's mind and the action of his faith made it seem possible. In general, the group of men who gathered in October to react to the idea of Koinonia Partners cheered and gawked and said: "Go get 'em." They were impressed, and their imaginations were kindled and their hope revived. And even if they did not think they could get away with something as far out as all that themselves, something in the way Clarence and Millard presented it made them think: "Wow, just maybe. . . ."

And so it began to be. In a "personal letter from Clarence Jordan to friends of Koinonia," mailed out toward the end of October 1968 to Koinonia's mailing list of about 12,000, Clarence announced Koinonia Partners and invited participation. He and Millard were overwhelmed by the enthusiastic response as hundreds of people responded immediately with cash donations. The Fund for Humanity became a reality almost overnight.

Al and Ann Zook and their four children, who were among the founding families of the Reba Place Fellowship, moved to Koinonia to enter into a farming partnership with Bo Johnson and his family. Koinonia was going to be farmed for the first time since the boycott had forced the community to give up field crops in 1959. And the fund immediately added 300 acres by purchasing Rob Hamilton's place adjoining.

Arrangements were made with a contractor to begin work on the houses in the 21-acre tract so designated. Bo and Emma Johnson's house was the first built. Before another year would end, two contractors would be working full time on houses as a waiting list of families grew.

In the area of communication, Ladon Sheats, the young IBM executive who had played such a major role in facilitating discussion and clarifying direction in the August meeting, arranged a series of discipleship schools in the New York City area, providing Clarence with several small, committed, intensely interested audiences for two- and three-day sessions. Lori DeGilio, an executive secretary at *Guideposts* magazine, attended one of these sessions and a few months later arrived at Koinonia Farm to be a secretary. Ladon attended each of these sessions, too, and began to feel himself stuffed full of content that would scramble an inhuman computer. Somewhere along the way his mind left the tracks, and while he continued to pole vault through the IBM brain trust, the next year exposed his old ambition as a futile effort. Within the following 12 months, he would drop his $40,000-a-year job and drive his Firebird down south to Koinonia Farm—to stay. (Others were coming, too. In fact, by mid-1970 the traffic was to be thick again at Koinonia, especially with young people coming as long- and short-term volunteers and as permanent participants in Koinonia Partners.)

One clear intention of Clarence and Millard never saw a hint of fulfillment—that was the move to Atlanta. When they decided to keep Koinonia Farm, Millard was going to manage it until another manager could be recruited, and Clarence was going to move on to Atlanta with his family and concentrate on the communication ministry. But things began to happen and the momentum generated by the birth of Koinonia Partners swept them up in such an involvement that any thoughts of moving to the city were obscured.

Millard began to nose around the pecan plant and the direct-mail operation to see what could be done to build up the business.

He discovered that Clarence had ordered 20,000 pecan cookbooks but had sold only 2,000. It took only a small calculation in Millard's impulsive head to know what to do—he decided to give half of them away. In the next few months, Koinonia Partners sent $2.95 pecan cookbooks absolutely free to 10,000 people on the mailing list. Sales accelerated upward immediately, and before long, pecan cookbooks were being reprinted and were putting dollars into the Fund for Humanity.

Millard thought that there ought to be more adequate office space, instead of one of the little houses. He also thought that a tractor shop would be needed for the coming farm year, and that the yellow house that had been the office should be remodeled for a dwelling again, so he checked with Clarence. Clarence hesitated and seemed indecisive—and Millard began to sense just how he could supplement the powerful talents of his scholarly friend. He withdrew the questions and told Clarence just to forget it. And then he moved into action. A large Butler building was installed for the office, shipping room, and pecan storage. The hay barn was converted into a tractor shop, and the little house was remodeled for residence. Then he set about financing the new farming venture and seeing how he could double the income from the pecan plant in a year and expand the mailing list to 30,000.

Clarence still served as a consultant on pecan candy and fruit cake production and farming, but mostly he settled into the dusty, cobweb-draped little study shack he had built out in the field about 300 yards from the houses and worked on his Cotton Patch translation of the New Testament epistles of Peter and John. The farm's diverse activities were clearly moving beyond his control, and he was pleased and more relaxed than he had been in years.

In the spring Millard arranged a trip to Africa for Clarence and Florence through the mission boards of the American Baptist Convention and the United Church of Christ. In a Ghana village, they talked to a man who had saved money from his meager earnings for years in hopes of buying a mill for grinding grain in the village—there was no mill for hundreds of miles and grain was ground by hand. The man had saved faithfully, and in fact had accumulated the amount of money that had been his original goal. But inflation had outpaced him. Clarence and Florence consulted on the spot, advanced the man $500 from the Fund for Humanity, and became his partners.

Clarence kept speaking, of course. In May he spoke in Atlanta before a combined meeting of the Associated Church Press and Catholic Press Association. And when all the handclapping and handshaking and backslapping and "that-was-fine-thank-yous" were over and the banquet hall had emptied of all but a few of the 600 delegates, a lone young woman stood with Clarence and Millard and expressed her interest in becoming an active part of Koinonia. A month later, Carol Brink resigned her position as an assistant editor on *Colloquy* magazine and joined the office staff of Koinonia Partners.

Koinonia Partners was incorporated as a nonprofit corporation, and a board of directors, consisting of three to seven people most of whom were not residents at Koinonia, was selected to implement its objectives. Clarence and Millard both chose to be only consultants to the board, rather than directors. Millard received authority for managing the organization on a day-to-day basis.

As people began to gather, a community of spirit began to rise again from the fertile soil at Koinonia Farm. The old community of goods idea was out; houses and cars and utilities were provided, but individuals and families received living allowances that they designated in order to take care of personal and family needs. The spirit of a shared life and a common commitment began to rebuild a "spirit-filled fellowship" at that still-suspect spot along the Dawson Road.

Clarence had said it nearly 20 years before, when the Koinonia community was fresh on its way, and he was feeling it again now: "Something's been set in motion here that I can't stop—something that is eternal. I'm beginning to see that I'm in this thing called koinonia for life."

CHAPTER 13

The Enduring Spirit

The southern sky was chilled clear by autumn winds on Wednesday, October 29, 1969. Clarence had been ill for several days, aching with a low fever, but after lunch on this brisk day he was impatient to work. He had recently finished translating the epistles of Peter, John, and Jude, calling them *Letters from Partners*, and he was now eight chapters into the Gospel of John.

He came downstairs from the apartment above the community kitchen, caught Florence's eye at the clothesline, and sent her the quick little flick of the hand that had come to communicate not only his affection, but his direction. She knew he was headed for the study shack, and so did Toby, the big red English shepherd, who rolled up from his lazy sprawl in the sun and trotted after him.

Clarence was seldom seriously ill. His heart had throbbed light warnings to him in 1955 and 1965, but he had lost weight and remained physically strong and active. He looked tired, however. He had aged considerably over the last decade, appearing to have gone from one extreme to another. For years he had looked younger than Florence even though he was a year her senior. Now he looked much older, seeming closer to 60 than 57.

Friends who had known Clarence in the earlier days of his ministry thought he had changed in some other more subtle ways. The changes in his body were no particular surprise, but some-

221

thing in the mood of the man seemed to jar with their memory of him. He had hardened, it seemed to them, become less compromising in attitude, seemed more on the attack than ever before. Where, as a younger man, he had exercised the charm of youthfulness to persuade reluctant minds of the wisdom of his path, he now seemed unbending in his demands for the great masses of Christians to share their wealth, to clearly and unequivocally step forward on the side of peace and brotherhood. He was saying to church people, without reservation: "You ought to spend at least as much trying to help house your poor brothers whom you have seen as you do trying to house God whom you have never seen."

It may have been confusing to old acquaintances. If anything, could they not have expected Clarence to have softened and mellowed along with the rest of the old reformers of the pre–World War II days? Could they not have looked for him to have found his place and made his peace with the world, to have eased up and to be reflecting on the gains of his earlier causes rather than to be striking forth on some new vision? The man seemed to be rushing ahead with more momentum than ever instead of tailing off reflectively and fading away like a true campaigner. Far from having come to terms with the realities of slow change and unwieldy bureaucracy, any patience he ever had with the slow, deadening weight of ecclesiastical bulk seemed to have died in him. Was he not slugging away with a prophet's abandon and scorn of excuse when he should have been winding down toward the autumn of his years, looking forward to a well-deserved rest and maybe even an honorary degree or two?

His old friends were right. Clarence had changed. It could be said fairly of Clarence that in the early days of his ministry, in spite of a few beliefs that seemed out of place, he had been well on his way to becoming one of the denomination's finest. He had approached his education at the seminary with humility, marveled at the wisdom of his professors, and stood speechless in the wake of the evangelistic zeal of the student preachers who had preceded him in his little country pastorates. He had been popular and loved and accepted, and like most everyone else, that was what he had wanted. He had not been rebellious and antagonistic. Quite the contrary, he had sought to be a part of the mainstream, and had not attempted to trouble the waters unduly.

But he had taken a peculiar approach to the Scriptures. He in fact had taken his fundamentalist heritage literally—he had plunged into the Scriptures as if he were expected to respond to what he learned. When he had grasped Jesus' teaching about violence and responding to evil with good-will, he had tried to exercise that idea. When he had grasped the essence of the reconciling spirit that breaks down the barriers between men, he had tried to embody that spirit. When he had understood something of what Jesus was driving at in speaking of the spiritual dimension of men's lives, he had claimed its value, and had sought to put his store not in possessions and praise from others but in a spirit of sharing and brotherhood.

And step by step he had found himself alienated, despite the fact that he had felt respect and gratitude for the denomination that had raised and educated him. He in fact had sought to be a loyal servant of a Baptist body long after he had known how painfully different his own understanding of the Christian life was from the denomination's mainstream of understanding. Despite his patience and loyalty, and the agreeable, go-slow manner in which he had begun to share his own ideas, that body had cut him out as a cancer, branding him as a sneak who sold himself to the people only to release the germ of brotherhood in their guarded midst.

Violence had exploded, the churches had turned away, and the people at Koinonia Farm had been forced to accept the heartbreak of estrangement. Increasingly, Clarence had hung these experiences on the New Testament passages that assured him honor and praise were not among the gifts of the spirit. And increasingly he had clung to faithfulness as the one and only responsibility of the follower of Jesus—not to save the world, not to save the church, not to usher in the kingdom, but to be faithful, as Jesus himself had been in the face of what seemed to be absolute failure. To any argument that a man should hedge on the truth in order to maintain a position of influence, Clarence would reply: "I don't see how faithfulness to Christ can hurt the cause of Christ."

It was true. Where Clarence had begun his ministry with an almost pleading persuasiveness, he was now thundering penetratingly and without quarter, trying more urgently than ever to introduce a spirit of partnership into the land. He was deeply disappointed that a generation had passed, and Christians had still failed to respond significantly to the social upheavals around them. Most of his life he had not believed in creating confrontation outside of natural circumstance, but now he was wondering aloud if the faithful should not stand up in the congregations in the land and openly challenge them, perhaps even commandeer the pulpits to shock people from their spiritual stupor. He had accompanied an integrated group from Koinonia to the First Methodist Church of Americus in August. They were blocked from entering the service, and for once Clarence was virtually mute with disappointment and anger.

Members of Christian churches professed Jesus as Lord, and Clarence believed that the test of lordship was obedience. He had recently asked a pastors' conference what percentage of their congregations would choose to follow Jesus if they were confronted with a clear-cut instance of choice between Jesus Christ and custom, money, and law. He had repeated the question and reiterated that the assumption was that the matter was a clear-cut choice. (This had come at the end of his sixth lecture in a series on the Sermon on the Mount.)

Someone said "two percent," another "perhaps one percent." One man said ".02 percent," and another ".00 percent." Clarence interrupted to restate the question and to ask them to be as generous and optimistic as possible. But the answers were the same, with no estimate over three percent.

Clarence concluded: "Then the biggest lie being told in America today is, 'Jesus Christ is Lord.' What you have just told me is that roughly 98 percent of those who profess Jesus Christ as Lord are liars."

He could surely have guessed the outcome of his questioning, and most certainly he had been prepared with his answer. He had set them up for it. But it was not in delight that he had delivered the punch line. It was, in fact, the great disappointment of his life. He had started out his own ministry in earnest, and then he had discovered that the church which had raised him on the Scriptures could not tolerate what he considered to be his faithful response to those Scriptures.

Addressing the American Baptist Convention in Seattle in May, Clarence had spoken on the idea of the church as the mother of the children of God, and he had alluded to his own experience. Developing a comparison between Mary as the mother of Jesus in one body and the corporate Church as the mother of Jesus in many bodies, he had declared that the Church was confused by her sons and reluctant to free them to get about the Father's business, as Mary had been by Jesus.

The Church gives birth to the sons of God in a very real sense. She is the womb in which they are conceived. The little Baptist church in which I grew up nurtured me; in its womb I learned the Scriptures; I suckled at its breasts. But the little church thought it was not only my mother but also my Father. And when I got to go about my Father's business, the church said no, son, you're piercing our hearts and we don't want to give you up. And when I persisted in going about my Father's business, my mother the church renounced me. It's hard for a mother whose womb conceives a child of God to quit being a mother and let that son get about his Father's business.

But at last Mary learned to be the mother of Jesus by giving him to mankind to do his Father's business. I hope and pray before I pass on to glory that little church that expelled me from its fellowship will realize that I really am its son, that I really do love it, and that it will gather with me, perhaps even after the crucifixion, along with the rest of the brethren, and realize that you only become a true mother of a child of God when you relinquish your motherhood and give him to all mankind. For God did not give his son to the Church, he did not give his son to Mary. She was the mere instrument through which he came. God gave his son to the world.

When our sons and daughters give themselves in abandon to following their Father in the lowly paths of the world, let not the Church hold back and say: "Come children, be your mother's children." Let us grasp their hands, seeing in them the image of their Father and say to them: Sons, though it leads you to a cross, be a good son of your Daddy.

Clarence did not end it there, however. He had not come to reflect on his own experience, nor to dress his thoughts on the role of the Church in sentimentality. He had come to deliver his message with all the force he could muster, with a sense of urgency, almost as if every opportunity might be his last.

"The job of the Church," he had thundered in his second lecture, "is to be the womb through which God can bring his children into this world. Now the early Church was willing to become pregnant. But I think the trouble with God's bride today is that she either has passed the menopause or she is on the pill."

Laughter roared forth from the audience, indicating from many a delightful acceptance of his earthy analogy. But as the laughter died down, he followed with a less humorous assertion: "Or perhaps even worse, the Church has gone awhoring."

The audience fell silent. "It could be she has sought other husbands to impregnate her, and generally when a woman goes awhoring and gets pregnant she hopes the offspring will favor her rather than the father. It's not that we are failing to beget children—we are. But they are not bearing the image of the Almighty. They are bearing the image of false gods! Mammon is one of those gods the Church is awhoring with. We are begetting children, but I wonder if they are not bearing the image of their true father, Mammon."

He may have sounded pessimistic and frustrated, but he wanted to jolt somebody into action. He felt great opportunities were at hand and too many people refused to see them. He likened the situation to the passing of a chuckwagon amidst hungry people who failed to see it. Revolutionary change for the good was not just a dream, but a live possibility, if people only had eyes to see and the will to act. He was beginning to evidence a mystical fascination with potential spiritual power.

"There are forces close to us that God can make known to us," he said. "Matthew five, six, and seven is a mighty gushing stream from which we've only taken one or two drops.

"I just have the feeling we are standing on the brink of discovery of gigantic forces, and we are afraid of them. We are at a banquet table laden with bounties and we are doodlebugging around trying to decide if we want cream of wheat or cold cereal."

It was not pessimism but a plea to reclaim a liberating truth that Clarence sought to communicate when he closed his second message before the American Baptist Convention: "It's when the

Word of God becomes powerful among us, when His Spirit becomes energizing in us, creating us into the image of his son, it is then that the world is faced with the presence of God Almighty on this earth. God is not in his heaven and all's well on the earth. He is on this earth and all hell's broke loose!"

So, on that brisk October Wednesday, as Clarence strode slowly toward the shack down the grassy road that separated a field of young pecan trees on his left from acres of corn stubble lying spent from harvest on his right, guarded from the chill by an old green sweater and a bright orange cap, he could know that if his body felt worn and weary, his spirit was on the ascent even yet, still warmed and muscled for new encounter.

Lena Hofer, a young Hutterite woman and a niece of Joe Maendel, had arrived at Koinonia Farm in July to stay indefinitely. She had left her home in the Deerboine colony in western Manitoba a year before, after a longstanding disagreement with the elders, and eventually, through the Reba Place fellowship in Evanston, had made her way to Koinonia. At 22, she had enrolled that fall in the Sumter County High School as a freshman, intent on continuing the education denied her in the colony and on becoming a nurse. She was slim and strong and curious, and hungry for the growing fellowship that enveloped her during the early days of Koinonia Partners. And in turn, those in the fellowship were amazed by her shy wisdom, perceptive contribution, and tough, determined faith.

Clarence in particular admired her, especially after she had unfolded her tale of struggle for faithfulness within the Hutterite colony, and her willingness on faith to break from the security of family and tradition to seek a new life of expressive discipleship. They had talked for hours on end, Clarence listening and counseling Lena into the sureness of a new fellowship, and Lena in turn listening and perceptively responding to the flow of history and reflection her story evoked from Clarence. They developed a unique friendship within only a few months.

On this Wednesday, Lena had taken records of Clarence's lectures on the parables to school, and, having previously cleared the way with her teachers, she had played them in each class for discussion. That morning, Lenny Jordan, who was a senior at Sumter High, had passed Lena's English class. And although the records were made under studio conditions and lacked the force and spontaneity that Clarence had when responding to a live audience, Lenny came up short.

"I heard his voice and it sounded so real," he said, "that I thought Lena had gotten Daddy to come to the class to speak. But then I went back and looked in and it was only a record."

When Lena arrived home with Lenny and Danny Wittkamper and Thomas Woods, she wanted to run down to the shack and tell Clarence about how well her day with the records had gone, how attentively she thought the students had listened, and how meaningful she thought the discussions had been. She also found a disturbing letter from home awaiting her, which put her mind onto a matter that she wanted to speak to Clarence about. And, too, she knew that Clarence must have her autographed copy of his Luke-Acts book, which was just off the press.

But she checked all these impulses, knowing that Clarence had been feeling an urgency about his work and that he had missed several days due to illness. She knew if she interrupted him he would stop everything and give her his full attention, as he did everyone who sought him out, and she knew she would linger too long. As Lenny and Thomas hitched a wagon full of pecan shells to a tractor and set out to spread them around the trees, Lena turned to her own work—for the moment, studying biology.

The night before, though he had still felt weak and feverish, Clarence had responded to the excitement of the young people returning from a Sumter High party and had made popcorn. This was a special treat from Clarence, part of his style, an expression of the simplicity and profound ways of his life—like the Muscadine wine he made every year from Koinonia's four-acre vineyard, or his remarkable storytelling, or his readings from *Winnie the Pooh*, or his treatises on the constellations delivered flat on his back in the early autumn grass, with the whole community snuggled together under the blue-black southern Georgia night. Someone had gone for fruit cake from the candy kitchen. And Clarence had broken out some of the '68 wine and had teased Florence as if she had not wanted any, when in fact she had breathed the suggestion of it into his ear. Someone had laughingly mentioned communion, and Clarence had responded thoughtfully that the substance of communion was present.

When Lena realized that her mind had drifted back to that special evening, and she remembered the other reasons she had for seeing her friend, she walked from the house toward the shack, her biology book in hand, hopeful she would be able to study out in the field. She decided to step into the shack and make as brief a visit as possible, asking him only one question of advice about the letter from home, giving only a brief account of her day at school with the records, and asking quickly if he had her special copy of the new book. It was between 4:30 and 5:00 P.M. She knocked, and, as could be expected of Clarence, he quit his notes, welcomed her enthusiastically, and offered her a cup of coffee. She refused the coffee, and even refused to sit down, insisting that she had only come for a minute.

Before she even asked, he told her he had a copy of Luke-Acts for her at the house, but that he had wanted to give it to her personally. Lena smiled her gratitude, and then related to him the nature of the problem revealed in the letter from home. Clarence made a helpful comment, and she moved immediately to the day at school and made such a hurried report that Clarence laughed and told her to sit down and quit rushing. But Lena stood her ground, protesting that she knew he had to study, and so did she. She was leaving.

He laughed and said: "C'mon then, and give me a hug," and stretched out his arms for the embrace that had come to characterize the expression of love among everyone in the community. She leaned over his chair and hugged his neck. His hands started to reach around her, but then his body jerked suddenly. His head fell back and his arms dropped to the sides of the chair. Lena straightened quickly, seized his head in her hands, and yelled his name. He seemed to look at her but not to see; his body was failing him. She tried to prop his head up, and then she turned to the door, looked back desperately, and ran for help.

By the time she reached the gate into the community yard, she was flailing the air in exhaustion. Lenny and Thomas were approaching her with the tractor and wagon. Lenny was in the back of the wagon and he called out to her. But Lena was unable to say what she knew to be true. She yelled back: "Something is wrong with your dad," and kept running.

Thomas stopped the tractor and Lenny rushed to the station wagon parked nearby. He drove down to the shack, leaped from the car, and rushed up to the door. When he opened the door Toby bounded out with a whine. Lenny stepped in, stared briefly at his father, and then started giving him mouth-to-mouth resuscitation. He stopped after a minute or so and ran back to the car.

Lena had run on to the new office building, dashed across the shipping room and into the office area. She stopped outside Florence's office and said: "Florence." Florence responded without looking up: "Just a minute, hon."

But when Lena interrupted a second time—"Florence!"—
Florence leaped up and grabbed her coat instinctively. Millard
and Al Zook rushed to Lena, who again uttered only: "Something
is wrong with Clarence." They dashed to the nearest car and
drove toward the shack. At the gate to the field they drew alongside Lenny, who was driving up from the shack. He gazed at his
mother and said: "It's too late. He's dead."

They drove on down. Florence entered the little shack and
adjusted her husband's body to a more comfortable posture. Millard put his ear to his friend's chest, felt his pulse, and satisfied
all doubt that life had left the body.

There was a suspended, incommunicable moment when each
person on the scene turned to another, and held on.

Millard and Florence decided that the body should be moved
to the house and laid on a bed. Then Millard called the officials
to report the death and, in order to comply with the law, to ask
one to come out and officially pronounce Clarence dead. No one
would come, and after several awkward moments, the official
finally offered as a reason: "You moved the body. That's against
the law."

Millard asked if he thought they should have left the body
slumped in the chair. The man said no. And after fumbling for
words again, he finally said he would come out if Millard could
convince another official to come with him.

So Millard called the other man, who also begged off, saying
he had been up since early that morning. He told Millard to call
an ambulance and have the body brought to the hospital. Millard
hung up in disgust, knowing he could not spend money on an
ambulance for a man who had believed that no money or other
resources should be used on a lifeless body. He got help to move
the body into the station wagon and drove it into town himself,

shrugging away his irritation and smiling as he drove through Americus, thinking that Clarence was being treated in death as he had been in life, and how appropriate that was.

Attendants brought the body inside the hospital, but Millard waited an hour before the medical examiner appeared to declare Clarence dead. Then the coroner put in an appearance and concurred in the decision. Both of them withdrew for consultation, and then they told Millard they wanted to do an autopsy. He called Florence, who did not object, and the body was kept for another three hours. Millard finally got away from the hospital at midnight. The autopsy had revealed heart failure and the onset of pneumonia.

The men in the community, with the help of Jack Singletary and another neighbor, Plezy Nelson, worked through the night and the next morning digging a grave in the sloping pasture known to the Koinonians as Picnic Hill.

At 3:30 P.M., after the Jordan children and their families and other relatives had arrived, six men lifted the mattress bearing Clarence's body, brought it down the stairs, and laid it into a cedar box—a crate of the kind used to ship coffins. As the men lifted the lid to be placed over the body, one of the young women knelt and laid a rose on Clarence's chest. The lid was nailed shut and the box was placed in the back of the battered old green Chevy van.

The six men walked behind as it moved slowly down the grassy road, under clear skies, past the shack, past the old Camp Koinonia site, on beyond the 30-acre corn field, down through a field of pecan trees to pine-covered Picnic Hill, where about 75 people stood waiting. There were a few affluent faces in the crowd, but mostly there were the dusty, calloused bodies and soft spirits of those known as common folk. A few were in suits, Sunday hats, and high heels; others were barefoot and in working clothes.

When the van stopped near the grave, the men lifted the cedar box from the back and set it in the grass and pine needles.

Millard Fuller read portions of Scripture from Clarence's translation of I Rock and I Jack, called *Letters from Partners* (I Peter and I John in more polite versions): "In order that you all too might be our partners, we're plainly telling you about something that's real, something that we ourselves have heard, that we have seen with our own two eyes. It's about the idea of life which we looked at and even felt of with our own hands. Now the life took shape and we saw it, and we are giving you our word and plainly telling you about the spiritual life which was with the Father and which took shape in front of us. Our partnership, then, is with the Father and with his son Jesus Christ. And we are recording this so that the joy of us all may be completely full.

"Loved ones, I'm not introducing a *new* instruction to you, but an old one which you've had all along. The old instruction is the message you listened to. And yet, it is a new instruction that I'm writing about, and it's true both in his experience and yours, that the darkness is lifting and the true light is already dawning. Now a man who claims to be in the light but still hates his brother is in the darkness right on. The man who loves his brother lives in the light and has no trick up his sleeve. But he who hates his brother is in the dark, lives in the dark and has no idea what direction he's going, because the darkness has blind-folded him.

"Don't love the old order or the things which keep it going. If anyone loves the old order it is not the Father's love that's in him. For everything that's in the old order—the hankering for physical comforts, the hankering for material things, the emphasis on status—is not from the Father but from the old order itself. And the old order, with its hankerings, is collapsing, but he who lives by the will of God moves into the New Age.

"So don't be surprised, brothers, if the old order hates your guts. We ourselves are convinced that we have switched from death to life because we love the brothers. The man with no love still lives in death country. The brother-hater is a man-killer, and you know that no man-killer has spiritual life residing in him.

"Loved ones, let's love each other, because love springs from God, and every lover has been fathered by God and is sensitive to God. The non-lover is not sensitive to God because God *is* love. And God's love took shape in our midst when he sent his one and only son into the world so we might start living. And *that's real love*—not that we loved God, but that he loved us and sent his son to answer for our wrongs. Loved ones, if God loves *us* that much, then *we* ought to love one another. Nobody has ever once caught a glimpse of God. Yet if we love everybody, God is present among us and his love is brought to maturity in us.

"Now that by your response to the truth you have dedicated your inner lives to genuine brother-love, go ahead and love one another straight from the heart with all you've got. For you all have been refathered, not by a mortal man, but by the immortal word of a living and abiding God.

> Every human being is like a blade of grass,
> And his appearance is like a blossom.
> The grass dries up, the blossom falls off;
> But the Word of the Lord lives on and on."

The six men lifted the box with ropes, lowered it into the deep red grave, and started shoveling. As the clods of Georgia soil plunked down onto the old cedar crate, and the grief lurched from within those gathered around, some vital substance of what Clarence had been trying to say in his life suddenly appeared with unspeakable simplicity in his death. There was an awareness of just how present the man's spirit was, of how authentic his investment in spiritual values had been. The people there had seen his body locked into a cedar box and stuffed into the soil. And yet in an instant, registering silently within them like a shift of the wind, they knew how much Clarence had given. The best of the man had passed from him to them. The evidence of it was alive in them. This understanding swept over the little gathering and breathed into their grief a surge of joy at having glimpsed what it is in a man that transcends the restriction of a single human body, and even the finality of death. It was like saying goodbye to the old Clarence and greeting the new.

Two-year-old Faith Fuller seemed to sense the essence of the celebration, to perceive that it marked a beginning and not an end. She stepped up by the men who were working out their emotions with shovels and softly sang one verse of her favorite song: "Happy birthday to you, happy birthday to you, happy birthday dear Clarence, happy birthday to you."

Epilogue

Koinonia Farm entered the "post-Clarence" era quietly. The fall rush of pecan product orders kept the plant bristling with activity —otherwise the dozen Koinonians seemed to move at a slower, more thoughtful pace. But there was a vague aroma of anticipation on the breeze that created the sensation that these people were not moving quietly because the end had come, but instead were readying themselves for the beginning of something. Something was imminent. You could feel it in the cooling air.

It began after a quiet Christmas holiday at the end of 1969, a mere trickle at first.

Two students from Defiance College arrived for a month-long work visit as part of their school program. A sociology student from Beloit College came for a semester, and later a young Quaker man from Washington D.C. arrived, curious to experience what he had heard about this Christian community. A Young Life area director in Philadelphia took a leave of absence and brought his family down for five months. A quiet, blond Rod Steiger-type pulled in on his Triumph from Connecticut (in January!), and another guy arrived by bus from California. A stocky wrestler from Princeton University appeared for a work semester, and so did a shapely blonde from Pittsburgh. Ladon Sheats, the IBM executive, moved from New York in February, following a rent-truck down in his car. He stepped out shaking his head, still

237

awestruck as he watched the 6'8½", long-haired guitar-playing philosophy major from Gordon College—who had just appeared at Ladon's apartment in New York looking for a ride south—rise up from the truck cab and give the place the once over—a smiling giant with a spirit that brought music to the soul.

Millard Fuller opened the farm house at Sunny Acres, the newly acquired property adjoining Koinonia Farm, and pointed the flow of male volunteers in that direction. By spring the dusty, green-rambling old place was jumping and creaking with new life, and a stereo drummed relentless reveille to the aged brick foundation.

Something was happening. There was an invigorating, fresh quality about the encounter between old communitarians like Will Wittkamper and the on-the-road spirits of young people who were careening through experiences of self-discovery searching for authentic purpose. There was no gap—these people found each other. They worked together, and studied together, and they sang, as if they were experiencing something and not just singing about something: ". . . they will know we are Christians, by our love, by our love. . . ."

By summer, the trickle had become an estuary extending into a sea of searching people, and the visitors and volunteers rolled in by the waves. A permanent volunteer program was formed that made it possible for a certain number of people to work varying lengths as volunteers, receiving bed and board and participating fully in the fellowship of the community. Several conscientious objectors, including Joe Maendel's youngest son George, managed to get assigned to Koinonia for their two years of alternate service. A great common experience began linking these people together, and many of the long and short term volunteers committed themselves to becoming permanent "Koinonia partners."

A tie-dyeing and sewing industry sprang from the activity of the volunteers and grew quickly into a stable industry that offered jobs to women in the neighborhood. A potter from Connecticut came down, took on a young black woman as her partner, and established a pottery in a garage at Sunny Acres. The farming partnership expanded to include George Maendel, Ed Young—the singing, smiling giant—and Bo Johnson. Al Zook consulted the farmers but increasingly devoted more time to the pecan business, which had boomed under Millard's magic touch. Donations continued to pour into the Fund for Humanity and most of the money was channeled into the priority item of building and selling low-cost houses to local low-income families. By mid-1971, a dozen families were in their own new homes and a second contractor had been hired to step up the building pace in the Koinonia Village.

In the area of communications, the discipleship school idea caught on quickly, with Ladon and Millard providing leadership. And new books, records, and tapes were added to the products list to communicate the applied ideas of peace, love, and sharing.

Several other people were making plans to join the Koinonia Partners endeavor in 1971, including a young couple experienced in the fashion industry who wanted to guide the sewing business into a large, job-producing activity; and a man with a doctorate in agriculture who wanted to add his expertise to Koinonia's goal of providing land to the rural disinherited.

The Sumter County and Americus community ignored these developments for the most part. When Clarence died, the *Americus Times-Recorder* ran only a few paragraphs of a wire service story, cutting the story in the middle of a quote of Clarence's that read: "An integrated, Christian community was a very practical vehicle through which to bear witness to a segregated society a decade ago, but now it is too slow, too weak, not aggressive enough."

The obvious intent was to leave the impression that the whole Koinonia thing was at last buried with that man. But obviously, the citizens were only seeing the beginning.

71 72 73 10 9 8 7 6 5 4 3 2 1

The Constitution and Race

DONALD E. LIVELY

PRAEGER

New York
Westport, Connecticut
London

Library of Congress Cataloging-in-Publication Data

Lively, Donald E.
   The Constitution and race / Donald E. Lively.
      p.   cm.
   Includes bibliographical references and index.
   ISBN 0–275–93914–6 (alk. paper).—ISBN 0–275–94228–7 (pbk.)
   1. Race discrimination—Law and legislation—United States—
History.   2. Slavery—Law and legislation—United States—History.
3. Afro-Americans—Civil rights—History.   I.   Title.
   KF4755.L57   1992
   342.73′087—dc20
   [347.30287]   91–30280

British Library Cataloguing in Publication Data is available.

Library of Congress Catalog Card Number: 91–30280
ISBN: 0–275–93914–6
        0–275–94228–7 (pbk.)

First published in 1992

Praeger Publishers, One Madison Avenue, New York, NY   10010
An imprint of Greenwood Publishing Group, Inc.

Printed in the United States of America

The paper used in this book complies with the
Permanent Paper Standard issued by the National
Information Standards Organization (Z39.48–1984).

10 9 8 7 6 5 4 3 2 1

To Donald and Dorothy Lively
for their values
and
Pamela and Rico Lively
for the opportunity to
share them

Contents

Preface

Law is the means by which society governs itself. As the function of cultural priorities and ideals, law also affords insight into a society's nature and character. American constitutional law comprises the nation's charter document and two centuries of developmental jurisprudence. Because it iterates and amplifies principles that are basic and overarching, constitutional decision-making affords an especially apt reference point for gleaning societal truths and realities.

This book examines two centuries of accumulated constitutional jurisprudence pertaining to race. Accommodation of slavery in 1787 to facilitate the Union's actualization represented an original exercise in ordering priorities. The framers' interest in establishing a viable republic resulted in deferral rather than resolution of significant race-based issues. What was avoided then would be confronted later in the constitutional context of slavery, official segregation, and remediation.

Racial justice or injustice is a reflection of the values and ideals that define a society's moral character and inspire its laws. Over two centuries, race-dependent considerations of personhood, citizenship, liberty, and equality have presented the nation with significant moral and legal choices. Modern constitutional law case books—lacking attention to racially significant decisions influencing the Constitution's framing, making little if any reference to the Supreme Court's endorsement of slavery, and rushing through the separate but equal era, which has defined most of the Fourteenth Amendment's existence—suggest a discontinuity between past and present. Contemporary racial jurisprudence, which is quick to assert its distance and dissociate itself from embarrassing antecedents, reinforces an impression that reflects more illusion than reality.

Modern investment in constitutional color blindness, when race-conscious remediation is a paramount issue, denotes further how societal priorities are ordered and what dominant imperatives will countenance. Cultural norms and preferences similarly preordained the repudiation of color blindness a century ago when official segregation was the eminent question, and avoidance of the question two centuries ago when slavery and a viable union were competing interests. Much of the constitutional record pertaining to race, as modern jurisprudence acknowledges, is "sorry." Recognizing rather than disclaiming the ties between doctrinal past and present is essential not only for the purpose of affording meaningful context but also as a prerequisite for reckoning fully and finally with the Constitutional Convention's unfinished business.

ACKNOWLEDGMENTS

Several persons deserve special mention for their help in preparing this book. The original manuscript was facilitated by the processing efforts of Carmen Gonzalez, Fran Molnar, and Marie Liliane Wilks. Research assistance was provided by Patrick Casey, Sandra Czaykowsky, Joanne Guy, Lisa Lesperance, Neal Lechtner, Barbara McCalla, and Ellisa Taylor. Reverends Theodore Roddy, Charles Scott, and John White, of the African Methodist Episcopal Church, provided and facilitated access to information concerning racially significant events in Philadelphia during the year of the Constitutional Convention. Dr. Dennis Dickerson, A.M.E. Church historiographer, generously shared his insights into the framing process. Especially helpful were the comments of professors Henry Bourguignon and Stephen Plass, who reviewed an early manuscript. The author also is indebted to John Harney who as acquisitions editor has been a much appreciated source of encouragement, support, and patience.

Introduction

The Original Ordering of Constitutional Priorities

Philadelphia in 1787 was a city of two tales that disclosed significant truths with respect to the culture and the law it inspired. The time and place are well known as when and where the Constitutional Convention transpired. What eventually emerged from the deliberation and ratification processes was a blueprint of governmental power and an enumeration of basic rights and liberties. The resultant document also attended, albeit in rather furtive terms, to the institution of slavery. Although forthrightly charting federal powers and explicating fundamental guarantees previously reposing in the amorphous realm of natural law, the Constitution's architects avoided any overt mention of slavery. To secure the Deep South's support and thus ratification, however, the institution was accommodated in calculated if not direct terms.

Relevant passages in the nation's charter were striking for their failure either to use the term "slavery" or to identify the race that it victimized. The provision prohibiting congressional interference with the slave trade until 1808, for instance, was framed in terms of "[t]he Migration or Importation of such Persons as any of the States now existing shall think proper to admit."[1] Apportionment formulas for political representation and taxation in similarly cryptic fashion referred to "the whole Number of free Persons ... and ... three fifths of all other Persons."[2] Even the fugitive slave clause was crafted in facially race-neutral terms: "[n]o Person held to Service or Labour in one State, under the Laws thereof, escaping into another, shall, in Consequence of any Law or Regulation therein, be discharged from such Service or Labour, but shall be delivered up on Claim of the Party to whom such Service or Labour may be due."[3]

Such terminology may have reflected the tension between the ideals of liberty and equality enshrined in the Declaration of Independence and the pragmatic aims of forming a union and consequent accommodation of slavery. Although well established in five southern states, slavery already had been or was being abolished in the North and was regarded by many as a terminal institution.[4] In the same year that the framers met in Philadelphia, Congress prohibited slavery in the Northwest Territory.[5] Such results did not obscure the reality of racism and prejudice, which animated law and custom without regard to geography. Racial truths were disclosed less by lofty rhetoric than by contemporary deed. At Old St. George's Methodist Church, not far from where the republic's founders had assembled, black members were assigned segregated seating and advised they no longer could kneel in prayer with the rest of the congregation.[6] Threatened with expulsion, Richard Allen led a walk-out and subsequently founded what endures as the African Methodist Episcopal Church.[7]

Allen, who as a child was the slave of the future Chief Justice of the Pennsylvania Supreme Court,[8] became the nation's first ordained black minister.[9] Records do not reveal whether any of the framers were present at Old St. George's Methodist Church when Allen and others were singled out on the basis of their race. Nor, except for the sake of an effective historical anecdote, is their presence or absence critical to comprehending the cultural forces that inspired the Constitution. Moral sentiment against slavery at the time of the document's framing may have been developed enough that, absent any significant competing consideration, the institution would not have been tolerated, much less accommodated.[10]

Elimination of slavery, however, was not a strong enough priority that it would be allowed to jeopardize other aims. Rather, the institution's continuing existence and consequences were considered acceptable costs of effecting a union. Dominant attitudes not only accommodated slavery but also defined the existence of nominally free blacks who, North and South, were bound by a panoply of laws governing their employment opportunities, restricting their movement, and forbidding their presence. Terminological hedging in the nation's charter may disclose moral and legal tension, but the equivocation illuminates rather than obscures the reality that founding principles of liberty for practical purposes were selectively afforded.

Chief Justice Taney, in rendering the Supreme Court's opinion in *Scott v. Sandford* seven decades later, noted that when the Constitution was drafted, blacks "for more than a century [had been] regarded as beings of an inferior order, and altogether unfit to associate with the white race, either in social or political relations; and so far inferior, that they had no rights which the white man was bound to respect."[11] The *Scott* decision has been characterized as a "derelict[] of constitutional law"[12] and "the most frequently overturned decision in history."[13] Taney's depiction of racist ways and attitudes, however, was an accurate reflection of dominant conventions that endured long after the Constitution was ratified. Not until 1954 did the Court, in *Brown v. Board of Education*, meaningfully confront the consequences of official racism. Reality is that Taney's characterization is more rather than less apt with respect to most racially significant jurisprudence over the nation's history.

Ratification of the document proved to be a departure rather than a termination point for establishing the Constitution's meaning. Barely more than a decade later, the Supreme Court in *Marbury v. Madison* defined its own function in broad terms that included being the final authority on "what the law is."[14] Having defined the power of judicial review in expansive fashion, the Court was positioned to resolve questions that invariably would arise concerning open-ended constitutional terms and conditions. The Marshall Court over the next few decades fashioned a legacy of constitutional interpretation that facilitated a strong central government in the Federalist image. Given the economic tension and disorder among the several states, prompting reexamination of the Articles of Confederation and influencing the Constitution, early judicial attention to structural and material interests was expectable. Indeterminate and impressionable as the commerce, contracts and necessary and proper clauses may have been, their meanings were jurisprudentially amplified within the Court's first few decades.[15] The constitutional business of slavery, in contrast, was not directly reckoned with by the Court until the mid-Nineteenth Century.

Even as the republic was being chartered, slavery had proved itself to be potentially disruptive to a workable and durable political order. Although not the only obstacles to framing and ratifying the Constitution, the competing agendas of northern and southern states imperiled a new political system even more profoundly than the conflict over representation of large and small states. As James Madison observed, sectional divisions were not a function

of size, but...other circumstances; the most material of which resulted partly from climate, but principally from the effects of their having or not having slaves. These two causes concur in forming the great division of interests in the U[nited] States. It did not lie between the large [and] small states; it lay, between the Northern [and] Southern.[16]

Disagreement between North and South in 1787 was less suffused with the friction and acrimony that the slavery issue engendered in subsequent decades. Original stakes in the union's formation were considered significant enough, however, that concessions to slave interests were negotiated without significant resistance or misgiving. The Georgia and South Carolina delegations, representing interests most dependent on slave labor, warned that they would not join a union that separated them from their crucial economic resource. For many framers, including some southerners, slavery presented a moral issue and a practice that were difficult to square with the republic's founding principles of liberty and equality. Even if anti-slavery sentiment was broad, it was not profound enough to vie with the imperative of forming a republic. Historians have attributed the accommodation of slavery, despite significant hostility toward it, to

a small but vociferous proslavery group [which] fought tenaciously to protect and strengthen slavery. Whenever this group apprehended a danger to slavery, its members raised a protest, made a deal or threatened to start packing. Through bluster, compromise, and political blackmail over the question of union itself, they secured power and protection for slavery.[17]

Thus were obtained concessions on taxation, representation, the slave trade, and fugitive slaves.[18] Critics of the institution such as George Mason argued that "the general government should have power to prevent the increase of slavery,"[19] but eventually conceded that it would "involve us in great difficulties and infelicity to be now deprived" of slavery.[20] Thomas Dawes of Massachusetts observed that "[i]t would not do to abolish slavery, . . . [but] it . . . will die of a consumption."[21] The antislavery position in the framing process thus was reduced to precatory terms anticipating the institution's eventual and natural demise. Such contemplations, even if sincere rather than rationalized, may have been misplaced if premised upon the notion that slavery could not survive once cut off from its overseas source of replenishment. It has been noted that the South understood from its Revolutionary War experience that the institution could endure even when imports ceased, but pro-slavery delegates indulged northern assumptions to the contrary.[22] As Winthrop Jordan observed, in any event, "the Convention could not consider even the eventual termination of domestic slavery; propositions on this head would have sent half the delegates packing."[23]

The original ordering of constitutional priorities resulted in a charter that neither directly endorsed nor prohibited but nonetheless accommodated slavery. William Wiecek has identified at least ten charter provisions devoted entirely or partly to slavery.

1. Art. I, § 2, which apportioned representation in the House on the basis of population count, and considered slaves as three-fifths of a person.

2. Art. I, §§ 2 & 9, which required apportionment of direct taxes among the states pursuant to the same fractional formula.

3. Art. I, § 8, which vested Congress with power to suppress insurrections including those by slaves.

4. Art. I, § 9, which immunized the slave trade from congressional restriction until 1808.

5. Art. I, §§ 9 & 10, which exempted exports, including the output of slave labor, from federal and state taxation.

6. Art. IV, § 2, which precluded states from liberating fugitive slaves and required their return upon demand.

7. Art. IV, § 4, which obligated the federal government to protect states from domestic violence, including slave insurrections.

8. Art. V, which insulated constitutional provisions concerning the slave trade and direct taxes.[24]

Debate has persisted over the actual nature and extent of original attention to slavery. Provisions that some have identified as friendly to slavery, such as clauses empowering the federal government to quell violence or insurrection, have been explained by others as merely coincidental.[25] Arguments that allowance for the slave trade until 1808 denotes a pro-slavery constitution from the inception have elicited the counterpoint that a finite time limit effectively identified federal power to regulate and prohibit the institution over the long run.[26] Notwithstanding any uncertainty over the actual nature of original contemplations, the decision to delay proscription of the slave trade for twenty years allowed in James Madison's words "all the mischief that can be apprehended from the liberty to import slaves."[27] Despite eventual formal renunciation of such commerce, federal policy in practice consisted of lax enforcement and disinterest in British proposals for joint efforts at effective policing.[28] The exact shading of original expectations may be indeterminate but does not obscure significant and discernible realities. Accommodation of slavery, in greater or lesser terms, resulted from what were perceived as overarching societal interests. Concessions were made to a focused and fixed southern faction in the cause of establishing a union; what was considered as less significant was traded off for what was perceived as more important.

The norms of 1787 responsible for the calculated slighting of virtually an entire class of persons subsequently were deviated from, but the process of ordering priorities then has remained pertinent since. A century later, in *Plessy v. Ferguson*, the Supreme Court legitimized the dominant "customs, usages and traditions of the people" that supported official segregation and repudiated constitutional color blindness.[29] The passage of another century has found the Court, in *City of Richmond v.*

J. A. Croson Co., rejecting color-conscious remediation in part because such policies engender racial politics.[30] As in 1787, racial justice competes with concern for the viability of and perils to the political system.

The original compromise on slavery enabled the framers to bypass an otherwise inconvenient and confounding issue. Initial understanding reflected the sense that individual states possessed the power to permit or prohibit slavery and the federal government was to be neutral. A scheme dependent on mutual tolerance and noninterference was feasible to the extent North and South could sequester themselves from the effects of each other's preferences and interests. Territorial expansion and the problem of fugitive slaves, however, soon disclosed that mutual immunity was an impossibility.

The ultimate fate of slavery was an issue that the framers left to posterity. Territorial expansion from 1787 until the Civil War provided serial opportunities for revisiting the issue. During that period, the original premise of a disinterested federal government was transformed into a debate upon whether it had a constitutional duty to support or prohibit slavery. The decision in *Scott v. Sandford* represented an effort to end the debate in conclusive fashion, but it instead exacerbated sectional divisions. Despite the extensive criticism it elicited, the decision's inspiring racist ideology was not an immediate source of significant objection.

The institution of slavery ultimately was defeated by the Thirteenth Amendment. The ideology that supported it in 1787 and denied the humanity of all blacks in 1857, however, survived. Considerations of racial equality did not enter the mainstream of political debate until the Reconstruction period. Even then, black rights in a constitutional sense were introduced as a qualified notion. The Fourteenth Amendment, ratified in 1868, secured the Civil Rights Act of 1866 and established racial parity in contract and property rights and equality before the law. The Fifteenth Amendment, ratified in 1871, prohibited race-dependent impairment of the right to vote. Nevertheless, constitutional jurisprudence continued to accommodate preexisting attitudes and priorities. Racial segregation was characterized as a "[m]ere discrimination[]"[31] and tolerated to the extent separate could be regarded as equal.[32] Abrogation of voting rights was disregarded pursuant to Justice Holmes' sense that judicial intervention against racial prejudice would be "pointless."[33]

Notwithstanding the Fourteenth Amendment's repudiation of *Scott v. Sandford*, the Supreme Court did not meaningfully confront the racist ideology of the decision until the passage of another century. By declaring that racially separate education was "inherently unequal,"[34] the Court commenced the constitutionally mandated foreclosure of officially prescribed race-based distinctions. To the extent it postponed relief for a term, in hopes of overcoming resistance and eliciting cooperation, and required eradication of segregation with "all deliberate speed," the Court still factored in and at least accommodated the realities of racism. The strategy did not prevent widespread evasion, delay, and disregard of the new constitutional mandate. Within a couple of decades, moreover, equal protection demands were blunted, pursuant to a sense that the Court had "gone far enough in enforcing the Constitution's guarantee of equal justice."[35]

Constitutional jurisprudence concerning remediation of a two-century legacy of racism covers barely more than a decade. Within that time frame, however, the Court has moved from limited approval of minority preferences[36] to a general prohibition of race as a remedial factor.[37] Color-blindness, which was rejected when official segregation was the dominant racial issue a century ago, now operates when remediation is the prominent concern. The result is jurisprudence that acknowledges the nation's "sorry history of . . . racial discrimination"[38] but still attends to competing priorities. Pending analytical methodology that more effectively reckons with the interests of racial justice, within the purview of democratic consent, the business of 1787 will remain unfinished.

The original purpose of the Fourteenth Amendment has been the subject of extensive scholarly attention and debate. Some commentators have argued that it incorporated the Bill of Rights, fundamental liberties and guarantees derived from natural law, and equality in the broadest sense.[39] Others have expounded a more restrictive understanding of the amendment as the function of a narrow vision focused on basic opportunity for material self-development and equal standing before the law, rather than a broad spectrum of rights or comprehensive equality.[40] A thesis of this book, expressed in the final chapter, is that the minimalist view, glossed with indisputable anti-discrimination precepts that displaced official segregation, affords more potential than expansive concepts as a predicate for actuating the Fourteenth Amendment. Grander theories invariably engender resistance and dispute, which, among other things, render them academic. Some may interpret the Fourteenth Amendment in broader fashion, but all would agree that it at least covers what is described by the modified minimalist position. Such common ground, if fully mined, affords a promising basis of accounting for what is at least the amendment's core concern.

NOTES

1. U.S. Const. art. I, § 9, cl. 1.
2. *Id.* art. I, § 2, cl. 3.
3. *Id.* art. IV, § 2, cl. 3.
4. The pre-constitutional history of slavery, from the early colonial period forward, is accounted for comprehensively in A. Higginbotham, Jr., In the

Matter of Color (1978). The legal realities of slavery through the antebellum era are detailed in M. Tushnet, The American Law of Slavery (1981).

5. The nature and ambivalence of formative anti-slavery sentiment during and after the drafting process are detailed in D. Fehrenbacher, The Dred Scott Case 11–27 (1978); W. Wiecek, The Sources of Antislavery Constitutionalism in America, 1760–1848, at 62–105 (1977).

6. See R. Allen, The Life and Experience and Gospel Labors of the Rt. Rev. Richard Allen 6–7, 25 (1960).

7. See id. at 7, 25.

8. See id. at 5.

9. See id.

10. Delegates from as far south as North Carolina, including many of the convention's most notable figures, expressed their disapproval of or discomfort with slavery. Their objections were not collectively profound enough, however, to prevent compromise with the focused and insistent Deep South delegation. James Madison, in the course of the convention proceedings, observed that it would be "wrong to admit in the Constitution the idea that there could be property in men." 2 M. Farrand, The Records of the Federal Convention of 1787, 417 (1937). In the North Carolina ratification debates, future Supreme Court Justice James Iredell observed that the end of slavery would "be an event most pleasing to every generous mind, and every friend of human nature; but we often wish for things which are not attainable." II J. Elliot, The Debates in the Several State Conventions of the Adoption of the Federal Constitution, v. 4, at 100 (1941). Even so, objections to slavery often were equivocal and coupled with sympathy for the interests of slaveowners. See id. at 101 (Galloway).

11. Scott v. Sandford, 60 U.S. (19 How.) 393, 407 (1857).

12. Meese, The Law of the Constitution, 61 Tul. L. Rev. 979, 989 (1987). (quoting P. Kurland, Politics, the Constitution and the Warren Court 186 (1970)).

13. D. Bell, Race, Racism and American Law 21–22 (1973).

14. Marbury v. Madison, 5 U.S. (1 Cranch), 137, 177 (1803).

15. See Gibbons v. Ogden, 22 U.S. (9 Wheat.) 1 (1824) (commerce clause); Trustees of Dartmouth College v. Woodward, 17 U.S. (4 Wheat.) 518 (1819) (contracts clause); McCulloch v. Maryland, 17 U.S. (4 Wheat.) 316 (1819) (necessary and proper clause).

16. 1 M. Farrand, supra note 10, at 486.

17. P. Finkelman, An Imperfect Union 23 (1981).

18. Id.

19. II J. Elliott, supra note 10, v.5, at 458.

20. I J. Elliott, supra note 10, v.3, at 270.

21. Id., v.2, at 41.

22. See P. Finkelman, supra note 17; W.E.B. Du Bois, The Suppression of the African Slave-Trade to the United States of America, 1638–1870 61–62 (1896).

23. W. Jordan, White over Black: American Attitudes Toward the Negro 323 (1968).

24. W. Wiecek, supra note 5, at 62–63.

25. The federal government used its authority to suppress insurrection to defeat the Whiskey Rebellion in 1794 and to respond to the South in 1861. Fehrenbacher, Slavery, the Framers, and the Living Constitution, in Slavery and Its

Consequences: The Constitution, Equality and Race (R. Goldwin & A. Kaufman eds. 1988).

26. *Id.* at 10–11.

27. 2 M. Farrand, *supra* note 10, at 415.

28. P. Finkelman, *supra* note 17, at 26.

29. Plessy v. Ferguson, 163 U.S. 537, 550 (1896).

30. City of Richmond v. J. A. Croson Co., 109 S. Ct. 706, 721 (1989).

31. The Civil Rights Cases, 109 U.S. 3, 25 (1883).

32. Plessy v. Ferguson, 163 U.S. at 550.

33. Giles v. Harris, 189 U.S. 475, 488 (1903).

34. Brown v. Board of Education, 347 U.S. 483, 495 (1954).

35. Milliken v. Bradley, 418 U.S. 717, 814 (1974) (Marshall, J., dissenting).

36. Regents of the University of California v. Bakke, 438 U.S. 265, 311–15 (1978) (Powell, J.).

37. City of Richmond v. J. A. Croson Co., 109 S. Ct. at 721. Race-conscious remedies are allowable to the extent they are narrowly tailored to fix a specific constitutional violation. *Id.* at 729–30. Race-dependent measures also have been upheld to the extent "they serve important governmental objectives within the power of Congress and are substantially related to achievement of those objectives." Metro Broadcasting, Inc. v. Federal Communications Commission, 110 S. Ct. 2997, 3008–09 (1990).

38. City of Richmond v. J.A. Croson Co., 109 S. Ct. at 724.

39. *E.g.*, J. Baer, Equality under the Constitution: Reclaiming the Fourteenth Amendment (1983); J. ten Broek, Equal under Law (1965).

40. *E.g.*, R. Berger, Government by Judiciary (1977).

Chapter 1

Constitutional Law and Slavery

The finessing of slavery at the republic's inception effectively accommodated the institution, albeit in terms that obscured the Constitution's connection to it. The calculated bypass, however, deferred rath r than avoided eventual reckoning. Despite Congress's explicit power to terminate the import of slaves beginning in 1808, the decision to allow or prohibit the institution itself was left to each state. Even before the ink had dried in Philadelphia, problematic questions pertaining to slavery had materialized. As the nation evolved over the next several decades, effective answers would be increasingly scarce. Original expectations that slavery would die of its own accord, or be satisfactorily reckoned with by the political process, were miscalculated or misplaced. Society instead became ever more deeply immersed in and confounded by the slavery issue.

In 1787, the Congress under the Articles of Confederation passed the Northwest Ordinance, which precluded "slavery . . . in the said territory, otherwise than in the punishment of crimes, whereof the party shall have been duly convicted."[1] Competing sentiment exists as to whether the enactment represented "a symbol of the [American] Revolution's liberalism" or was "part of a larger, and insidious bargain" constituting "the first and last antislavery achievement by the central government."[2] On its face, and despite inclusion of a fugitive slave clause, the Northwest Ordinance may seem consonant with a sense that slavery was a terminal institution. Some historians, noting that the ordinance was enacted by a southern dominated Congress one day after the three-fifths compromise on apportionment, suggest that the prohibition was an exercise in calculated cynicism. They propose that support for the territorial proscription was offered in exchange for constitutional concessions on slavery, to secure political debts that would translate into support of the South's agenda in Congress, and to establish a tacit understanding that slavery was permissible in the Southwest.[3]

Two years after the Northwest Ordinance was passed, the Southwest Territory, comprising the future states of Kentucky and Tennessee, was created in almost identical terms. The key difference in the new enactment was a provision to the effect that the federal government would not interfere with or prohibit slavery. A like restriction conditioned establishment of the Mississippi Territory. As the Nineteenth Century began to unfold, the Louisiana and Missouri territories elicited more extensive debate over slavery, and anti-slavery amendments to the respective enactments were defeated. Pertinent legislation eventually was structured without any explicit provisions for or against slavery. Congress, however, did prohibit slavery in Illinois, Indiana, and Michigan territories. By the early nineteenth century, slavery had become an increasingly complicating factor in the process of establishing new territories and expanding the union. Over the next few decades, what commenced as a thorny issue hardened into an intractable problem and national crisis.

An especially portentous confrontation between North and South on the issue of slavery occurred in 1819, as Congress considered proposals to grant Missouri statehood and to create an Arkansas territory. An initial House bill that would have banned slavery in Missouri, where it already was well established, provoked a profoundly negative southern response. Arkansas's territorial candidacy was advanced without restrictions on slavery, and southern representatives coalesced to block Maine's simultaneous application for admission to the union. With Maine's statehood held hostage by the South, the House eventually approved a Senate amendment that allowed Missouri to become a state without slavery restrictions and admitted Maine as a free state. The resultant Missouri Compromise provided that slavery would be forever forbidden in the remaining Louisiana Territory north of a line etched at 36° 30' North. The Maine and Missouri controversy, although eventually settled, disclosed that the slavery debate was ratcheting in the direction of increasing sectional rancor. Despite persisting expressions that slavery was a dying institution and individual decisions by such luminaries as Jefferson, Madison, Taney, and others to liberate their slaves, the issue was enlarging rather than vanishing.

Early decades of territorial expansion indicate a general assumption that Congress possessed the power to determine slavery's permissibility in the territories and to condition statehood accordingly. That sense originally was disclosed by the South's endorsement of the Northwest Ordinance in anti-slavery terms. It persisted, despite sectional antagonisms manifested by the Missouri and Maine controversy. Evolving political thought, increasingly acrimonious debates over new territories and states, northern recognition of slavery's actual reach, and southern perceptions of vulnerability, however, eventually destabilized initial assumptions. Further challenging the basic premise of federal neutrality and the models of compromise and accommodation was the emergence of radical abolitionism.

During the 1830s, abolitionism burst into American thinking with new arguments about what the Constitution required or prohibited. The South's intolerant response to the promulgation of abolitionist views evidenced not only the region's heightened sense of imperilment but also its evolving sense that the issue was no longer debatable. Southern prohibition of anti-slavery literature would have presented in later times a First Amendment crisis.[4] Asserting that Congress had no power over slavery, southern representatives maintained also that abolitionists had no freedom to petition for anti-slavery legislation.[5] Southern political assumptions, previously consonant with the exercise of federal power on questions of slavery, began to challenge the legitimacy of such authority. Debates concerning slavery in the District of Columbia and Texas further evidenced the hardening of pro-slavery sentiment. Although Congress possessed authority "[t]o exercise exclusive Legislation in all Cases whatsoever" in the District of Columbia,[6] southern influence assured the vitality of slavery there.

As perceived threats to slavery had magnified and the stakes accordingly had increased, southern strategists searched for more secure doctrinal footing. A key reference was the Constitution itself, which, although originally avoiding outright endorsement or repudiation of slavery, was increasingly the object of revisionist interpretive notions. Abolitionist thinking would divide over whether the Constitution was an anti-slavery document that should be so animated or a pro-slavery charter that should be structurally overhauled. The South, meanwhile, turned toward doctrinal formulations that would not just accommodate but support slavery. In championing slavery in the District of Columbia, southern legislators asserted that the federal government was an agent of the several states with the affirmative obligation of supporting their various institutions, including slavery. Presaging a significant premise in *Scott v. Sandford*, they also argued that slaves were property protected by the Fifth Amendment.[7]

The issue of Texas annexation, which Congress faced in the 1840s, disclosed further how constitutional thought was coursing beyond premises of a neutral federal role to competition over whether the document required an affirmative position for or against slavery. The Wilmot Proviso, which would have prohibited slavery in all territory acquired from Mexico, ultimately failed but not without sharpening sectional divisions. The proviso was significant, even if not enacted, insofar as it contemplated a deviation from the lines drawn and the sectional balance struck by the Missouri Compromise. Its mere proposal suggested a movement in the North and South away from accommodation and toward confrontation.

Such events were the backdrop against which consensus was fragmenting. Pro-slavery sentiment, as noted previously, progressed toward an assertive interpretation of the Constitution as prohibiting interference with the institution. Anti-slavery thinking, which never merged into a unified front, presented a variety of sometimes conflicting positions. The perspective of William Lloyd Garrison was that the Constitution endorsed slavery. For him, the deficiency could be accounted for only by dissolving the union. Competing with Garrison's analysis was the notion that the federal government had no power over slavery in the states and must dissociate itself from any support for the institution.[8] Other theorists, described as "constitutional utopians," considered the due process and privileges and immunities clauses, notwithstanding their operation against federal power, as potential reference points for an anti-slavery charter or at least a theory of review favoring liberation.[9]

Multiplying perspectives of what the Constitution did or did not require were consistent with the expanding contours of debate beyond the original question of whether Congress had the authority to ban slavery in territories. Congress's territorial powers, if analyzed without the distorting frictions of the time, may not have presented such difficult questions or have been so susceptible to competing interpretation. The exercise of such power during and after the Constitution's drafting, with southern participation and support, suggests that the federal interest and role were apt and initially uncontroversial. This impression is reinforced by review of congressional power in circumstances unrelated to slavery. In *American Insurance Co. v. Canter*, the Supreme Court had determined that "[i]n legislating for the territories, Congress exercises the combined powers of the general, and of a state government."[10] Despite recognition of broad federal power over the territories, reflected by jurisprudence and by actual practice, arguments for slavery sought to redefine congressional authority. The debate thus reflected movement beyond original considerations of state determination and federal neutrality and toward an eventual constitutional showdown.

Attention to the Constitution's meaning for slavery was renewed and revised as a function not merely of the nation's expansion but of other realities and perceptions as well. Like territorial governance, the question of fugitive slaves originally presented no significant controversy. The fugitive slave clause of the Constitution was not a subject of significant attention or debate when framed. Soon after ratification, Congress enacted a fugitive slave law which also was notable for its immediate uncontroversiality. As the nation's attention became more focused on slavery in subsequent decades, however, the fugitive slave clause would move from the margins to the center of debate. Even if the actual number of slave renditions was relatively few, fugitive slave legislation, more discernibly than territorial compromise, manifested congressional aiding and abetting of the institution. The fugitive slave controversy effectively heightened northern awareness of the reality that slavery implicated the entire nation rather than just a region. Even if a slave was apprehended and returned, his or her economic value was diminished by the act of running away and the consequently disclosed risk of future escape. The fugitive slave issue nonetheless acquired significant political meaning. For the South, it represented a test of the federal government's willingness to accommodate and later support slavery. For the North, it clarified how entangled the entire society was in the institution.

Fugitive slave legislation, more visibly than its constitutional predicate, directly implicated the federal government in the cause of slavery. The Constitution's fugitive slave clause provided that

[n]o person held to Service or Labour in one State, under the Laws thereof, escaping into another, shall, in Consequence of any Law or Regulation therein, be discharged from such Service or Labour, but shall be delivered up on Claim of the Party to whom such Service or Labour may be due.[11]

The provision was housed in Article IV, which concerns interstate relations, rather than in Article I, which delineates the powers of Congress. Because it also did not have an explicit implementation provision, like the Full Faith and Credit clause in the same article, a credible argument existed that it provided no authority for a congressional enactment.[12] Although the clause eventually elicited intense constitutional controversy, its original purpose is uncertain. The provision was drafted and adopted without debate or formal vote as the convention was winding down. Not surprisingly, given its vagueness and relative inattention afforded it, the fugitive slave clause was a source of diverging interpretations ranging from the sense that it established a right of recovery anywhere in the nation to the perception that it simply precluded another state's emancipation of runaway slaves.[13] The observation has been made that, during the framing process, no one "could foresee a federally regulated Fugitive Slave Law with marshals and special commissioners."[14] Soon after ratification, however, Congress enacted legislation that enshrined the clause as a predicate for affirmative federal support of slavery.

Congress initially accounted for the fugitive slave problem by passing the Fugitive Slave Act of 1793. The act (1) imposed on a state the duty to return fugitives upon official demand, and (2) enabled a slave owner to cross state lines, apprehend the alleged fugitive, and, upon proof of ownership to a judicial officer, reclaim and remove the person.[15] Although the act itself provided no incidents of due process, such as the right to a hearing, several states enacted laws prohibiting the kidnapping of blacks or at least providing opportunities to contest the claims of slave owners or their agents.[16]

Fugitive slave legislation represented an early paradox in the federal system. Slavery had been constitutionally accommodated pursuant to the premise of federal neutrality and individual state determination. Imposition of universal obligations to account for fugitive slaves constituted an early exercise in the expansion of federal power. The constitutional predicate for the policy, as previously noted, was dubious but originally uncontroverted. Reaction to and debate over the fugitive slave clause and federal legislation, therefore, was effective in illuminating sectional incompatibility and enhancing mutual disaffection.

The fugitive slave controversy also revealed some significant truths with respect to the North. The variance between the status of slaves in the South and nominally free blacks in the North was reducible essentially to a difference between full and partial disability. As Chief Justice Taney accurately noted in *Scott v. Sandford*, presumptions of racial inferiority were pervasive and unqualified by geography.[17] Reality was that Taney's racist premises were reflected as much by northern customs and attitudes as by southern priorities. Freedom for blacks was more common in the North than in the South, where it became an increasingly rare phenomenon. Blacks in the South were denied virtually any incident of citizenship and most basic constitutional protections. By their mere presence, or as a consequence of violating the law, they risked reverting into slavery.

Even if the danger of enslavement in the North was limited to possibilities created by fugitive slave legislation, legal burdens and social exclusion there nonetheless were profound. Most free blacks were not allowed to vote, and at least two states, Indiana and Illinois, enacted laws prohibiting their immigration. Congress excluded blacks from military service and certain federal jobs. In Washington, D.C., where slavery flourished until the middle of the nineteenth century, blacks were denied voting rights and prohibited from engaging in various types of businesses.

Particularly indicative of northern racial attitudes were official policies of segregation. The Massachusetts Supreme Court, for instance, articulated the principle of separate but equal nearly half a century before the U.S. Supreme Court subscribed to it in *Plessy v. Ferguson*. In *Roberts v. City of Boston*, the state supreme court upheld a racial segregation requirement at variance with state law, which generally provided for student placement at the nearest school. Assignment of a black student to a school across town was upheld on grounds she was afforded an equal education.[18] Not until 1954, when the Court in *Brown v. Board of Education* declared separate to be "inherently unequal,"[19] would the racially separatist doctrine introduced in *Roberts* and reiterated in *Plessy* be defeated. Even then, transportation burdens, which did not impress the *Roberts* court when carriage was less efficient, would be reintroduced as a premise for limiting desegregation remedies.

Despite their common linkage to racial animus, inconsistent state policies toward blacks, even apart from slavery, engendered constitutionally awkward circumstances. Before the Constitution was amended after the Civil War to secure liberty and equality notwithstanding race, as discussed in the next chapter, questions concerning possible citizenship and rights of free blacks directed attention to the constitutional possibilities. Early attention focused on the provision that "[t]he Citizens of each State shall be entitled to all Privileges and Immunities of Citizens in the several States."[20] The privileges and immunities clause essentially provided that a state could not differentiate between its citizens and those of other states with respect to the rights and protections it afforded. Although not prompted by any preconception or contemplation of black citizenship, Article IV, Section 2 would have had profound implications if glossed in such terms. Southern states in particular would have been required to afford black citizens of other states equality of legal status. The issue was not directly addressed but at least was implicated in a lower court decision in 1823 and an attorney general's opinion in 1824. Both rulings determined that a South Carolina law, prohibiting entry of black sailors into the state's ports, was precluded by exclusive federal power over interstate and foreign commerce and foreign relations.[21] Confrontation of the question in terms of citizenship or freedom, however, was avoided.

Several years later, following adoption of similar restrictions by other southern states, another attorney general's opinion depicted race-dependent exclusions as a legitimate exercise of state power under the Tenth Amendment.[22] It also did not attend specifically to the status or rights of free blacks. That issue was directly confronted in yet another attorney general's opinion authored by Roger Taney in 1832. Consistent with his opinion in *Scott v. Sandford* a quarter of a century later, Taney's affirmance of state power disclosed an official sense of a class properly reduced to slavery. He thus observed that

[t]he African race in the United States even when free, are everywhere a degraded class, and exercise no political influence. The privileges they are allowed to enjoy, are accorded to them as a matter of kindness and benevolence rather

than of right. They are the only class of persons who can be held as mere property, as slaves. . . . They were never regarded as a constituent portion of the sovereignty of any state. . . . They were not looked upon as citizens by the contracting parties who formed the Constitution. They were evidently not supposed to be included by the term *citizens*. And were not intended to be embraced in any of the provisions of that Constitution but those which point to them in terms not to be mistaken.[23]

Although not officially published, Taney's opinion succinctly previewed the sentiments he would express in upholding slavery twenty-five years later.

The exclusion of black sailors from southern ports surfaced as a congressional issue during the early 1840s. A House report asserted that such state action was contrary to the supremacy clause and the privileges and immunities clause.[24] The report, although suggesting the potential of the privileges and immunities clause, had no impact on policy. Congress enacted no legislation that would have enforced or effectuated the terms of Article IV, Section 2 in a racially significant way. Such inaction was consistent with dominant northern sentiment, which, even if opposed to slavery and supportive of broad federal power in the field of commerce, assumed the legitimacy of race-dependent burdens and distinctions.

Northern blacks, existing in a twilight zone between slavery and full citizenship, presented a special challenge to the legal system. With racial questions having been largely avoided since the republic's origination, it is not surprising that standards for possible citizenship or standing to sue were underdeveloped or nonexistent. The status of blacks, however, was not without possibilities for contemporaneous analogy. Corporations were entities whose identity also did not fit into any preexisting legal categories.

In 1809, the Supreme Court had found that a corporation was an "artificial, invisible body, existing only in contemplation of law" and thus was without the standing of citizenship.[25] By 1844, the Court had determined that a corporation qualified as a citizen for purposes of suing and being sued.[26] Although corporations eventually would be regarded as citizens for general purposes, their split or uncertain legal personality was akin to the contemporary status of free black persons in the North. Just as corporations had fewer rights and privileges than did actual persons, the list of guarantees and liberties for blacks was shorter than that for whites. The similarities eventually would prove academic, however, when the Court in 1857 denied any notion of black citizenship and reduced the affected class to a status beneath even fictional persons.

Although it never directly or meaningfully addressed the possibility of black citizenship during the first half of the nineteenth century, the

Supreme Court rendered several racially significant decisions. In *The Josefa Segunda*, for instance, the Court upheld a federal law which prohibited importation of slaves and took effect when the constitutional moratorium on such enactments expired.[27] The opinion of the Court referred to the slave trade as an "inhuman traffic, for the abolition of which the United States have rendered an early and honorable anxiety."[28] Such a characterization may have reflected a jurisprudential sense of the slave trade as "contrary to the laws of nature."[29] The Court, however, declined opportunities to explore the possibilities of personal liberty under law and limited its focus to relatively narrow or technical considerations.[30] Despite invitations to restrict slavery further, the Court's decisions prior to the 1840s evinced no interest in broadly reviewing the institution or its incidents.

Constitutional jurisprudence at least until the *Scott* decision was calculated largely to avoid disrupting the premises of federal neutrality and state determination. Cases concerning the moratorium clause and the commerce power thus were relatively simple and uncontroversial compared to the issues that surfaced in an increasingly venomous and divisive political context. As noted previously, the fugitive slave problem was congressionally tended to by legislation that accommodated the interests of the South. Consistent with that slant, the Court invariably decided fugitive slave issues in terms favorable to slavery. Choice of law questions presented when freedom was claimed in the North were resolved in favor of southern law. Such rulings, although determining relatively technical legal issues, had profound decisional consequences. Because liberty could not be effected by the state of refuge, it was an exclusive function of the slave jurisdiction. So long as slavery endured, therefore, legal freedom could be secured only in rare and discretionary instances of manumission.

Fugitive slave jurisprudence reflected an ordering of priorities akin to what influenced the Constitution itself. The original emphasis on the imperatives of establishing a union was reiterated in terms of maintaining intramural cooperation and thus the union's continuing viability. Despite its formalistic appeal, such reasoning necessitated denial of practical realities. In *Commonwealth v. Aves*, the Supreme Judicial Court of Massachusetts thus related how it was

well known that when this Constitution was formed, some of the States permitted slavery and the slave-trade, and considered them highly essential to their interest, and that some other States had abolished slavery within their own limits, and from the principles deduced and policy evolved by them, might be presumed to desire to extend such abolition further. It was therefore manifestly the interest and the object of one party to this compact to enlarge, extend and secure, as far as possible, the rights and powers of the owners of slaves, within their own limits, as well as in other States, and of the other party to limit and restrain them. Under these circumstances the clause in question was agreed on and introduced into the constitution; . . . was intended to secure future peace and harmony . . . [and should be interpreted] to afford effectual security to the owners of slaves. The States have a plenary power to make all laws necessary for the regulation of slavery and the rights of the slave owners, while the slaves remain within their territorial limits; and it is only when they escape, without the consent of their owners, into other States, that they require the aid of other States, to enable them to regain their dominion over the fugitives.[31]

The *Aves* decision diminished a free state's legal interest in slaves, whether sojourning or seeking refuge, and indicated a constitutional duty to accommodate slavery. It thus acknowledged but soft-pedaled the reality of how federal law drew the entire nation into the service of slavery.

The implications of fugitive slave arrangements could not be permanently avoided or downplayed, however, given a system in which sectional competition over slavery in general was enlarging and deepening. Many northern states, responding to Congress's failure to afford basic legal process or to deter disregard of even pro forma legal procedure, enacted personal liberty laws. Legislation in some instances provided for writs of habeas corpus or like devices and prohibited the kidnapping of blacks. During the 1820s, Pennsylvania authorized detention of alleged fugitives only by judicial officers, required more extensive proof of ownership, and criminalized private seizure of a black person. The legislation endeavored to balance the state's obligation under the 1793 act with due process concerns, especially for free blacks who otherwise were vulnerable to mistaken identification or exploitation. It also resulted in comprehensive judicial review of the fugitive slave law. The consequent decision, in *Prigg v. Pennsylvania*, has been described as "rival[ing] *Dred Scott v. Sandford* in historical importance."[32]

The circumstances of the *Prigg* decision illuminated precisely the concerns that prompted enactment of the Pennsylvania law. At issue was the status of a Maryland slave couple's daughter, never herself previously claimed as a slave, and her children. The woman had married a free man and moved to Pennsylvania where some of her children were born. After she had resided in Pennsylvania for five years, descendants of her parents' owner sought to have her and the children returned to Maryland. Although the offsprings' agent Edward Prigg obtained a warrant for arrest, the Pennsylvania court refused to provide a certificate for removal. Prigg nonetheless took the woman and her children in violation of the state law. Maryland initially refused to extradite Prigg, but the Pennsylvania legislature enacted a law providing him with special procedural consideration and safeguards so that the constitutionality of the state law could be assessed. Prigg was convicted and, within a year, had appealed to the U.S. Supreme Court.[33]

The *Prigg* decision was authored by Justice Story who had been a long-time critic of slavery. Story nonetheless rendered a decision that invalidated the Pennsylvania law on the grounds it conflicted with the Fugitive Slave Act of 1793 and the Constitution. In sum, he determined that the federal law was constitutional, a state law at odds with the statute was impermissible, and slave owners could recapture fugitive slaves on their own initiative and by their own devices.

Determination that the federal law of 1793 was constitutional, although perhaps unsettling to Story's moral precepts, was consistent with a jurisprudential style characterized by a nationalist ideology and a commitment to judicial restraint.[34] He discerned that congressional power to enact the Fugitive Slave Act of 1793 was reasonably inferred from the fugitive slave clause of the Constitution.[35] Simple as the premise was, the Court's analysis was not airtight. Because the fugitive slave clause is set forth in Article IV, as noted previously, a credible argument existed that it spoke to relations among the states instead of providing a basis for congressional action. The Court itself avoided meaningful inquiry into whether the act was at odds with specific constitutional guarantees. The federal law denied even the rudimentary incidents of due process to free blacks who might be wrongly or mistakenly apprehended. As a consequence, Congress and the Court permitted a deprivation of fundamental liberty that they almost certainly would have repaired if white persons had been similarly slighted. The enactment and Story's response to it suggest that Taney's subsequent blurring of legal distinctions between free blacks and slaves was neither aberrational nor unique.

A critical aspect of the Court's decision was the determination that fugitive slaves were within the federal government's exclusive jurisdiction.[36] This finding was consistent with jurisprudence that, in the time between *Marbury v. Madison* and *Scott v. Sandford*, had invalidated no federal statute. The grounding of the Fugitive Slave Act in Article IV at least offered an eminent point for distinguishing *Prigg* from otherwise expansive readings of national power. The Court, however, bypassed any such analysis.

The *Prigg* decision warned against state legislation that would "interfere with or . . . obstruct the just rights of the owner to reclaim his slave."[37] Favorable as the ruling was to the immediate interests of slavery, it nonetheless communicated a mixed message to the South. Although resolving the fugitive slave question in terms favorable to southern interests, the decision introduced the unsettling prospect that slavery itself was a federal rather than a state concern. Chief Justice Taney sensed the possibility that if the federal government could provide for slavery, it also could operate against it. He thus wrote separately to make the point that states were not only prohibited from interfering with a slave owner's rights but also obligated to protect them.[38]

The Court's decision, if examined solely within the context of its four corners, would seem to have an undeniably pro-slavery cast. Endorsement of a virtually unqualified right to recapture a slave, pursuant to a slave owner's own methodology, effectively extended the law of southern states into the North. Despite constitutional and statutory intimations of at least minimal procedural protection,[39] the only limitation on recapturing a slave or kidnapping a free black was that it be effected "without any breach of the peace, or illegal violence."[40] Demands of the South, at least for fugitive slave purposes, thus became requirements of the nation.

The *Prigg* ruling, however, enhanced rather than terminated the controversy. By illustrating how inextricably the whole nation was bound up in slavery, it compounded anti-slavery sentiment and destabilized rather than secured the institution. For radical abolitionists, the *Prigg* ruling further validated their view of the Constitution as a pro-slavery document. The manifest implication of the entire nation in slavery defeated imagery of a wall between northern and southern custom and enhanced the conviction that the Constitution should be resisted even at the cost of disunion. In his abolitionist publication *The Liberator*, William Lloyd Garrison observed that allowing a slave owner to claim his property in any state "establish[ed] the constitutionality of slavery in every State in the Union."[41]

Despite the criticism it engendered, the decision soon became a source for undermining the interests it supposedly had secured. Story had determined that Congress could authorize state courts to enforce the law but could not, without abridging state powers, require them to do so.[42] He further ventured that "it might well be deemed an unconstitutional exercise of power of interpretation, to insist that the states are bound to carry into effect the duties of the national government, nowhere delegated or instructed to them by the Constitution."[43] Story also noted that state judges, although not obligated to enforce federal law, nonetheless could do so "unless prohibited by state legislation."[44] Such observations restated common understandings of the imperatives and incidents of federalism. Offered in the context of a profoundly divisive ideological conflict, however, effect proved disproportionate to purpose. As Chief Justice Taney accurately forecast, these statements, although not part of the Court's holding and thus not binding, became a departure point for neutralizing the otherwise pro-slavery cast of the *Prigg* decision. Noting the scarcity of federal judges in many states, he warned that "if the state authorities are absolved from all obligation to protect this right, and may stand by and see it violated without an effort to defend it, the act of Congress of 1793 scarcely deserves the name of a remedy."[45]

Taney's worst fears promptly were confirmed, as many northern legislatures and courts, respectively, enacted laws and rendered decisions transforming a principle favorable to slavery into one antagonistic to the institution. Several states prohibited their judges from enforcing the federal law. Even without legislation, courts cited to *Prigg* itself for purposes of disclaiming authority to hear fugitive slave actions. Five years after the decision, Pennsylvania enacted a law precluding jurisdiction in all fugitive slave cases. Instead of settling an account in favor of slavery, therefore, the ruling actually advanced the anti-slavery cause. Having been sensitized to their nexus with the institution they condemned, northern states responded in terms and deeds calculated to sever their linkage. Ambivalence that could accommodate slavery thus became increasingly susceptible to displacement by cognition of the institution's real and broad demands.

By enhancing northern awareness of slavery's national significance, the *Prigg* decision quickened and deepened societal antagonisms. Prior to *Prigg*, the law had accommodated slavery while largely avoiding the imagery of real involvement with the institution. Evidencing how effectively that illusion was pierced, northern participation in rendering fugitive slaves actually diminished after *Prigg*. Despite pervasive racism in the North, conversion of an essentially pro-slavery decision into an anti-slavery principle disclosed an enhanced sense of how slavery infected the entire nation and consequent effort to minimize its reach.

So extensively and effectively was *Prigg* repudiated and offset in the following decade that Congress enacted a new fugitive slave law. Central to the legislation was neutralization of the dicta that had become the basis for northern resistance to rather than cooperation in recaption and rendition. To compensate for state reluctance to effectuate the law, a federal bureau was established and vested with enforcement power. Fortification of the fugitive slave law was part of a broad congressional effort to resolve several thorny problems associated with the general question of slavery. Not only did the resultant Compromise of 1850 codify new fugitive slave legislation. It also provided for California's admission to the union as a free state, organized the Utah and New Mexico territories as slave jurisdictions, and prohibited the slave trade in the District of Columbia. Architects and supporters of the compromise envisioned it as a final resolution of the slavery issue. The legislative premises, however, were grounded in the problem-solving model of the past when the South perceived less peril to slavery and the North was less conscious of its connection to the institution. Given the significantly altered operational circumstances, it is not surprising that the Compromise of 1850 proved to be a temporary rather than a permanent melioration.

Just how unsettled pertinent norms and practices had become was evinced shortly after the Compromise of 1850 was enacted. Southern opposition to the creation of Nebraska as a free territory challenged the long-established dividing line etched by the Missouri Compromise. Instead of maintaining a geographical bright line, Congress considered more complex premises for determining how territories were to be established and states admitted to the union. Competing for acceptance were Democratic Party concepts of popular sovereignty and competing notions of free soil.[46] Experience in Kansas and Nebraska was defined by the Democratic principle of allowing a territory's populace to determine its institutions. The result was unbridled turmoil, chicanery, and violence. The Democratic consensus itself would soon subdivide into competing northern and southern positions respectively staked to readings of the Constitution as neutral but accommodating slavery and actually supporting and protecting it.

Having wrestled with slavery for more than half a century, and having crafted policy yielding ever-diminishing returns, Congress appeared increasingly incapable of formulating a durable solution. Hardened differences between northern and southern legislators of different parties, compounded by the split between northern and southern Democrats, augured unfavorably for a consensus on federal policy. In its representative capacity, Congress was a microcosm of the profound sectional antagonism and mutual distrust that had come to define the nation. Increasing attention to constitutional imperatives, although a competitive exercise among slavery's supporters and detractors, pointed toward the judiciary as a possible forum for resolving the issue. What the framers had avoided and Congress could not successfully compromise thus eventually was reckoned with by means of litigation.

Constitutional jurisprudence by the midpoint of the century already had established a favorable disposition toward the South at least in terms of accommodating slavery. Dominated by southern jurists, the Court in the 1850s enhanced that tradition. Decisions preceding *Scott v. Sandford* revealed an enthusiasm for the southern position that at times was excessive. In *Strader v. Graham*, the Court dismissed a case on procedural grounds but proceeded to decide substantive questions anyway.[47] The action originated in Kentucky, where a slaveowner sued a party who helped his slaves escape to Canada. The defense was premised on the argument that upon setting foot in Ohio the slaves were free. The Kentucky court rejected the proposition, and the Supreme Court dismissed the case for lack of jurisdiction.[48] Normative principle of review precluded the Court from resolving issues unnecessary for disposition of a case. Despite that basic premise, the Court gratuitously observed that the law of a slave state applied in determining the issue of freedom.[49] Although the principle was not essential to the action's resolution, the Court in 1852 asserted the primacy of the slave state's interest.

A decade after *Prigg*, the Court revisited fugitive slave questions. In

Moore v. Illinois, it upheld a state law punishing individuals who aided fugitive slaves.[50] The decision was an extension of *Prigg* insofar as the Court earlier had suggested that state police power could be used to promote and aid but not interfere with the interest of slave owners.[51] Unlike *Prigg*, the ruling was an unequivocal reminder of the North's unwanted obligations to the South. Northern understanding of slavery as a national rather than a regional phenomenon accordingly was further enhanced.

By 1850, the debate between North and South was notable for how it had been redefined. With respect to slavery, original thinking had contemplated a neutral federal role and individual state determination. Over the course of several decades, that premise was unsettled by fugitive slave experience and territorial expansion. Congress effectively extended the reach of slavery nationwide in 1793 when it enacted legislation protecting slaveowner interests in runaways. Despite jurisprudential efforts to effectuate the act and legislative attempts to enhance it, southern attitudes increasingly and accurately assumed that the North wished to distance itself from and minimize the operation of slavery. The refusal of free states to turn over fugitive slaves, contrary to the Supreme Court's delineation of duty, represented an exercise in detachment. Refusal to respect the claims and interests of slave owners, which the South had secured through the legislative and judicial processes, revealed that a final and comprehensive decision on the institution itself could not be avoided forever.

Intense competition between North and South already was manifesting itself in efforts to define policy in the remaining territories. The admission of California as a free state denoted the South's failure to extend the Missouri Compromise line to the Pacific. Southern legislators responded by defeating a bill for the Nebraska Territory, which was introduced on the premise that slavery was prohibited north of the latitude of compromise. The Kansas-Nebraska Act, passed the following year, divided what originally was one territory into two and provided that eventual admission of each as a free or a slave state would depend on what their respective constitutions resolved. Implicit in the act was the possibility that the proposition of slavery might be resolved according to the concept of popular sovereignty. Subsequent political events and violence in Kansas over the content of the state's constitution indicated the high stakes involved for North and South.[52]

Dispute over the status of Kansas and Nebraska revealed compounding fractures in the body politic and a further diminished congressional capacity. The Republican party emerged from the Kansas-Nebraska episode as a national force and primary exponent of free soil principles. The Democratic party split into northern and southern wings, divided by subtle but significant distinctions over the meaning of popular sovereignty. At issue was not the general question of territorial or state status but when and by whom the decision would be made. For southern Democrats, popular sovereignty enabled the people of a territory to permit or prohibit slavery when framing the constitution for statehood. Northern Democrats maintained that territorial legislatures could determine whether slavery should be permitted or prohibited. Both shared the view that the Constitution's territory clause did not vest the federal government with power to provide for or against slavery. The northern position, expounded most notably by Senator Stephen A. Douglas of Illinois, differed from the southern view in that territories were regarded as incipient states with full sovereignty. Such a perspective was inimical to southerners, concerned that if Congress could delegate power to prohibit slavery in the territories, it could pass judgment on the institution in general. The Douglas formula, which has been referred to as territorial rather than popular sovereignty,[53] represented an effort to bridge the widening gap between North and South. Its failure demonstrated the profundity and insurmountability of sectional differences.

The Kansas-Nebraska controversy and contemporary political developments disclosed how vexing and convoluted the slavery problem had become for representative governance. The Kansas-Nebraska Act advanced a notion of popular sovereignty that, although subject to varying interpretations, added a new wrinkle to the traditional federal policy of neutrality. Self-determination in the new jurisdictions was made "subject only to the Constitution."[54] Given the manifest division over constitutional meaning and requirements, such direction was at least imprecise. It also was superfluous because judicial review is appropriate for any legislative action alleged to be unconstitutional. Even if unintended, passage of the act symbolized a timely invitation for judicial attention to an otherwise intractable problem. The Court, although having rendered several decisions concerning slavery, had yet to confront the territorial question. Judicial review thus loomed as an option for an effectively stalemated legislative process and the nation's interest in a final constitutional resolution of a seemingly interminable problem.

In 1857, the Supreme Court attempted to resolve the slavery controversy as a function of constitutional imperative. Its effort, however, exacerbated rather than muted sectional differences. The case of *Scott v. Sandford* resulted when the slave of a military doctor, who had lived on extended assignments in Illinois and the Minnesota Territory, claimed his liberty as a consequence of lengthy residence in free jurisdictions. The case could have been decided without reaching the general issue of slavery or its constitutionality. A judgment against Scott could have been premised on choice of law principles requiring disposition pursuant to Missouri rather than Illinois law. The Court also might have followed the precedent of *Strader*; it could have determined that the parties were not citizens of different states and thus federal jurisdiction did not exist. Instead, Chief Justice Taney attended comprehensively to questions of black citizenship, congressional and territorial power, and the rights of slave owners. The result was a decision that enhanced the controversy and diminished the Court's prestige.[55]

The *Scott* decision comprised nine separate opinions, including six concurrences and two dissents. Chief Justice Taney's rendering was presented as the opinion of the Court, and because its status was not contested by the other justices, it may be considered authoritative. Immediately evident in Taney's opinion was an inclination to avoid a narrowly premised decision and instead to reckon with slavery in sweeping terms.

Scott's complaint in the Missouri trial court had elicited a plea in abatement which, under common law pleading, challenged the time, place, or manner in which an action was brought. The pleading asserted that the defendant had assaulted and falsely imprisoned the plaintiff, his wife, and two children. Sandford's plea in abatement challenged the court's jurisdiction on the grounds the plaintiff, as a black man, was not a citizen and thus could not sue. The trial court, although not determining citizenship in broad terms, found that at least for purposes of suing in federal court Scott qualified as a citizen under the Constitution's diversity clause.[56] The Supreme Court rejected Scott's argument that the defendant waived the jurisdictional issue by eventually pleading to the substantive merits of the case.[57] As Chief Justice Taney properly noted, jurisdiction if contested at the trial court level remains a proper issue upon appeal.[58]

Analysis of whether any black person qualified as a citizen, although not essential to a decision that could have rested on choice of law or diversity principles or that could have been narrowed to whether slaves were citizens, constituted nearly half of Taney's opinion. For the chief justice,

[t]he question is simply this: can a negro, whose ancestors were imported into this country and sold as slaves, become a member of the political community formed and brought into existence by the Constitution of the United States, and as such become entitled to all the rights, and privileges, and immunities, guaranteed by that instrument to the citizen.[59]

To sue in federal court as a citizen of the United States, Taney determined that a person would have to possess full citizenship under the Constitution. Because blacks were considered "a subordinate and inferior class of beings" at the time the document was framed, he concluded that any "rights or privileges" accruing to them were a function not of the Constitution but of governmental discretion.[60] The constitutional status of blacks, or more precisely the lack thereof, thus was fixed by a sense that the entire race originally was regarded as a slave class.

By focusing on national citizenship, Taney did not disturb the power of any state to confer rights and privileges on black persons. Refusal to acknowledge that they were "citizen[s] in the sense in which that word is used in the Constitution of the United States," however, not only disabled blacks from suing in federal court but also limited any rights "to the State which gave them."[61] The privileges and immunities clause, which required states to accord a "perfect equality to its citizens and those of other states as to rights of persons and rights of property," was construed to protect only the incidents of national rather than state citizenship.[62] It thus was not pertinent to black persons, whether emancipated or not, who had been afforded no national citizenship and were state citizens only to the extent so provided.

Taney noted that persons recognized by the states as citizens when the Constitution was adopted also were citizens of the nation.[63] To offset the reality that some blacks were recognized as state citizens and thus qualified as national citizens, the chief justice offered his understanding of the society's founding values and attitudes. Taney related that for more than a century before the Declaration of Independence and the Constitution were framed, black persons had

been regarded as beings of an inferior order, and altogether unfit to associate with the white race, either in social or political relations; and so far inferior, that they had no rights which the white man was bound to respect and that the negro might justly and lawfully be reduced to slavery for his benefit.[64]

The conclusion that black persons "had no rights which the white man was bound to respect" represented a perversion of the historical record. Reality was that blacks in several states at the time of the republic's founding possessed rights to sue in court, to contract, and to acquire, own, and sell property.[65] Although anti-miscegenation laws were common and discrimination pervasive, the notion that blacks were entirely bereft of rights represented an exaggeration.

The chief justice also suggested that neither the Declaration of Independence nor the Constitution contemplated black citizenship. Taney dismissed facial indications in the Declaration that its self-evident truths comprehended all of humanity by referring to contemporaneous political exclusions of and attitudes toward blacks. In spite of the document's unqualified terms, he opined that it was "too clear for dispute, that the enslaved African race were not intended to be included" within its purview.[66] To fortify his premise, Taney found the slave trade and fugitive slave clauses to be evidence that blacks were not "a portion of the people or citizens of the Government then formed."[67] Glossed over were the

Constitution's own distinctions referenced toward slavery rather than color.

Resolving the question of general black citizenship was not essential to the disposition of the *Scott* case. As noted previously, the question was reducible to whether a slave could sue in federal court. Insofar as the Court had determined that corporations were state citizens for purposes of diversity, if not under all circumstances, a legitimate precedent existed for at least allowing a right to sue.[68] By converting a dispositive jurisdictional issue into a question of whether all blacks were entitled to national citizenship and its incidental rights and protections, Taney deviated from the principle that courts should avoid unnecessary issues.

Having determined that blacks were not citizens, Taney then depicted them for constitutional purposes as property. Referring to provisions for ending the slave trade and accounting for fugitive slaves, the chief justice concluded that the Constitution identified a property right entitled to federal protection.[69] Acknowledging only an authority "coupled with the duty of guarding and protecting the [slave] owner in his rights," Taney found Congress powerless to compromise the property rights of slave owners.[70] The depiction of slaves as property was crucial for purposes of identifying an interest that a citizen could not be deprived of "without due process of law."[71] It translated the Constitution, which by its original terms had evaded and at best accommodated slavery, into a prohibition of federal interference with and an endorsement of the institution.

Although having pursued the citizenship question further than necessary, the Court had reached a logical termination point for its decision. Determined to resolve the slavery question in conclusive and comprehensive terms, however, Taney proceeded to confront the dominant and divisive political question of the time. He thus concluded that Congress had no power to prohibit slavery in territories and that the Missouri Compromise itself was unconstitutional. Over the course of the nineteenth century, the Supreme Court consistently had interpreted federal powers expansively, and the *Scott* decision represented the first time since *Marbury v. Madison*[72] that it had struck down a federal law. The result reflected a narrow reading of the territory clause, which, by its terms, authorized Congress "to dispose of and make all needful Rules and Regulations respecting the territory...belonging to the United States...."[73] Taney maintained that this provision related only to land claimed by the United States in 1789[74] and was not a basis for exercising power over subsequently acquired territories.[75]

The interpretation was problematic for several reasons. It rationalized congressional action, contemporaneous with the Constitution's framing, providing for governance of the Northwest Territory in terms that prohibited slavery. Taney's view conflicted, however, with the established principle that, under the necessary and proper clause,[76] Congress may enact laws reasonably related to an enumerated power, provided they do not conflict with a specific constitutional prohibition.[77] His reading also departed from precedent to the effect that a territory was "governed by virtue of that clause in the Constitution which empowers Congress 'to dispose of and make all needful rules and regulations, respecting the Territory, or other Property belonging to the United States.' "[78] Finally, the chief justice's analysis was contrary to the actual exercise of congressional power for seven decades.

Taney nevertheless introduced the notion that persons in federal territories and existing states were on a constitutional par. He maintained that

an act of Congress which deprives a citizen of the United States of his liberty or property, merely because he came himself or brought his property into a particular Territory of the United States, and who had committed no offense against the laws, could hardly be dignified with the name of due process of law.[79]

Contrary to the argument he had made successfully a quarter of a century earlier, in *Barron v. Mayor and City Council of Baltimore*,[80] Taney then identified the Fifth Amendment as a specific check on Congress's territorial power.[81] He thereby planted in constitutional jurisprudence the seeds of substantive due process. By the end of the century, as discussed in Chapter 4, the premise would become a significant source of unenumerated but nonetheless fundamental rights and liberties.

Given his earlier disposition against substantive due process notions, Taney may have seemed an unlikely exponent of such an activist principle. Identification of a fundamental, albeit constitutionally unspecified right, however, was a useful premise in foreclosing federal territorial governance. Consistent with the views of southern Democrats, Taney further concluded that if Congress could not set the terms of territorial rule, it "could not authorize a Territorial Government to exercise them ... [or] confer [any] power on any local government, established by its authority, to violate the provisions of the Constitution."[82]

As the chief justice related it, delimitation of congressional power was the function not of constitutional implication or radiation but rather of "a right of property in a slave [that] is distinctly and expressly affirmed in the Constitution."[83] Even if such a guarantee was not manifest pursuant to an objective reading of the document, Taney found it expressed by the slave trade clause, allowing "a right to traffic in it ... for twenty years."[84] From the fugitive slave clause, he also deduced an affirmative federal duty to protect the institution at least to the extent of accounting for runaway slaves.[85] The conclusion that a right of slavery was "expressly affirmed" at minimum turned any notion of literalism on its ear. Identification of a property right in slavery also was at variance with the original sense of a neutral federal role and state determination. The slave trade clause itself was a dubious source of a durable right insofar as the provision connoted eventual prohibitive power. To the extent slavery was under comprehensive review, the fugitive slave clause was a logical candidate for reevaluation rather than reiteration and extension. The reasonable possibility that the clause defined imperatives of inter-state cooperation, instead of furnishing a basis for federal action, none-theless received no attention.

Having identified multiple predicates for its holding, the Court con-cluded that "[u]pon these considerations it is the opinion of the court that the act of Congress which prohibited a citizen from holding and owning property of this kind in the territory of the United States north of the line therein mentioned, is not warranted by the Constitution, and is therefore void."[86] The immediate consequence of the decision was that "neither Dred Scott nor his family were made free by virtue of their transit to free territory even if their owner had intended to be a per-manent resident."[87] Its broader significance was a translation of the Con-stitution into terms not only recognizing the right of slavery but also denying the personhood of an entire race.

The Court thus resolved the issue of slavery by clothing its ideology in constitutional fabric of its own weave. Because its underlying philos-ophy and consequent doctrine remained in dispute, the decision fueled rather than dampened the controversy. It accordingly has been observed that "[a]s a bid to settle political issues, the Dred Scott venture was a ghastly failure. Instead of pacifying, it created worse turbulence. It forced politicians and the public into more intense and agonizing reap-praisals of constitution and priorities."[88] Rather than ameliorating sec-tional frictions, the Court hardened the split between northern and southern Democrats, Democrats and Republicans, and North and South. Its judgment and opinion facilitated the southern agenda and predict-ably prompted northern outrage. Criticism except in radical abolitionist circles, however, was selective and qualified. The Court was condemned primarily for its invalidation of the Missouri Compromise.[89] Objection to the constitutional reduction of blacks was muted and disclosed that, despite their differences on the general question of slavery and federal power, the North and the South shared significant common ground with respect to racial ideology.

Notwithstanding the northern outcry in response to the Scott decision, racism and racial phobias were widespread phenomena. Although the Court's endorsement of slavery became a dominant issue for congres-sional elections in 1858 and the presidential election in 1860, political marketing responded to racial reality. While advocating free soil and criticizing the Scott decision, Republicans avoided identification with the plight of slaves or blacks. Even if opposed to fugitive slave legislation and territorial expansion of slavery, they still acknowledged a constitutional obligation to abide by fugitive laws and accommodate the institution at least where established. Concern with the civil circumstances of black persons was considered so risky that even opponents of slavery were moved to emphasize their racial disdain. Lincoln thus emphasized a "natural disgust in the minds of nearly all white people to the idea of an indiscriminate amalgamation of the white and black races."[90] His pronouncement differed from Taney's insofar as it suggested a subclass rather than non-class of persons. Critical focus and caution were revealing not only with respect to the candidates but also the society toward which their message was pitched.

Even if selective, objections to the *Scott* decision were trenchant. The Court had deviated from the traditional premise that slavery was allowable pursuant only to positive state law and not when specifically prohibited. Although some critics anticipated the possibility that the decision eventually would be overruled, Lincoln presented a significant challenge to the principle of judicial review. Essentially he argued that the Court's judgment, although controlling with respect to the actual parties, did not bind government or become general law until it became "fully settled."[91] Barring indisputable coextension of legal principle and public belief, Lincoln asserted that Congress should not consider itself bound by the decision.[92]

The possibility of northern defiance manifested itself when a Wisconsin court freed two persons, convicted in federal court for facilitating the escape of runaway slaves in violation of federal law, pursuant to a writ of habeas corpus.[93] The state court effectively assumed the responsibility of filling "the procedural gap Congress left in the Fugitive Slave Law when it omitted jury trials for alleged runaways and prohibited testimony by them."[94] In *Ableman v. Booth*, the Supreme Court upheld the national law and emphasized the imperatives of federal court immunity from state challenge.[95] The decision, authored by Chief Justice Taney, ironically urged respect for the conditions of a national union which the *Scott* ruling helped imperil.

The 1860 presidential election devolved into a three-way campaign among southern Democrats, northern Democrats, and Republicans. Southern Democrats maintained that the *Scott* decision had settled the territorial issue conclusively and established affirmative constitutional support for slavery. Northern Democrats asserted that the territorial question remained open but could be resolved by a future ruling. Republicans continued to challenge the decision's legitimacy and maintained that Congress still could exclude slavery from new territories. Even after Lincoln was elected, Congress made a final effort to mediate sectional differences and forestall the union's unraveling. A Senate committee proposed several constitutional amendments designed to resolve the slavery issue permanently. The amendments among other things allowed and required protection of property including slaves in territories south of the Missouri Compromise line, prohibited abolition of or interference with slavery in states where it existed and made unamendable all constitutional provisions directly pertinent to the institution.[96] The proposal was defeated as Republicans held fast to principles of slavery's containment.

The *Scott* ruling itself was nullified for practical purposes by the Lincoln administration's calculated neglect of it. Failure of the political (legislative and executive) and judicial branches to resolve the issues of societal division led inevitably to civil war. The conflict commenced over the scope of congressional power but terminated with the abolition of slavery, repudiation of *Scott*, and a commitment to secure black citizenship. In the years immediately following civil war, the Thirteenth Amendment prohibited slavery, the Fourteenth Amendment established black citizenship and at least limited equality, and the Fifteenth Amendment prohibited racial discrimination in voting rights.

Despite its constitutional renouncement, the *Scott* decision remained a fair reflection of geographically unqualified values and attitudes. The opinion and judgment were rendered at a time when racism was rampant in the North, racial disadvantage was effectuated and maintained nationwide, and racial phobias were accentuated by the concern that emancipated slaves would migrate North and compete in a largely if not exclusively white job market.[97] Although mainstream abolitionism promoted liberation, it did not contemplate racial equality in a comprehensive legal or normative sense. Even when eventually ordering emancipation, Lincoln continued to disclaim notions of racial parity, observing that

[t]here is an unwillingness on the part of our people, harsh as it may be, for you freed colored people to remain with us.... [Even] when you cease to be slaves, you are far removed from being placed on an equality with the white man.... I cannot alter it if I could. It is a fact.[98]

When read against such a moral and ideological backdrop, Taney's opinion offers more than an idiosyncratic reflection of southern values. The sense of a racial group as "beings of an inferior order, ... altogether unfit to associate with the white race"[99] comports not only with the imperatives of slavery but also with the priorities of general society which by law had pervasively and overtly expressed its racism. Notwithstanding context, the *Scott* opinion's infamy has been seen as radiating from "its smug assumption of racial superiority; ... its shameful equation of citizenship with whiteness; ... its sweeping exclusion of black people from belonging to America;...its bland acceptance of their relegation to an inferior caste."[100]

To the extent the *Scott* decision was an extension of dominant values, it does not fit retrospective characterization as a "derelict[] of constitutional law."[101] Modern understanding of it as an aberration may reflect functional if not real exorcism from the nation's jurisprudence. A sense that the decision is relatively insignificant for modern purposes may be intimated by its virtual disappearance from most contemporary constitutional law case books.[102] Dismissal of *Scott* as irrelevant, however, is misconceived.

Original accommodation of slavery, even if merely anticipating deferral of a final decision, at least assumed the risk that the institution would ultimately be endorsed rather than disavowed. Although the Thirteenth and Fourteenth Amendments eventually repudiated *Scott*, its spirit endured in subsequent jurisprudence. By the late nineteenth century, the Supreme Court had ratified the separate but equal doctrine in a ruling criticized at the time for being "quite as pernicious as...the *Dred Scott Case*."[103] Parallels also can be argued with respect to curtailment of the desegregation mandate and foreclosure of affirmative action in the latter half of the twentieth century. The influences and considerations that defined antebellum law and culture did not vanish with the abolition of slavery. Subsequent history has disclosed that although the *Scott* decision was formally disowned within a decade, its ordering of racial priorities and underlying spirit would prove more durable.

NOTES

1. Ordinance of 1787: The Northwest Territorial Government, art. VI.
2. P. Finkelman, An Imperfect Union 83 (1981) (*quoting* S. Lynd, Class Conflict, Slavery, and the United States Constitution 186 (1967)); U. Phillips, American Negro Slavery 128 (1918).
3. *See* S. Lynd, *supra* note 2, at 185–213.
4. *See* W. Wiecek, The Sources of Antislavery Constitutionalism in America, 1760–1848, at 172–82 (1977). Not until the next century would the First Amendment be applied to the states through the Fourteenth Amendment. *See* Near v. Minnesota, 283 U.S. 697, 707 (1931); Gitlow v. New York, 268 U.S. 652 (1925).
5. *See* W. Wiecek, supra note 4, at 183–89.
6. U.S. Const. art. I, § 8, cl. 17.
7. D. Fehrenbacher, The Dred Scott Case 122 (1978).
8. *See id.* at 236–48.
9. *See* R. Cover, Justice Accused 154–56 (1975). Some analysts regard the utopian vision as apprehending a constitution that was affirmatively anti-slavery. *See* J. ten Broek, Antislavery Origins of the Fourteenth Amendment (1951); Graham, *The Early Antislavery Backgrounds of the Fourteenth Amendment*, 1950 Wis. L.Rev. 610 (1950). The perception has elicited criticism to the effect that the

utopians merely looked to principles of superseding natural law. *See* R. Cover at 156.

10. American Insurance Co. v. Canter, 26 U.S. (1 Pet.) 511, 546 (1828).

11. U.S. Const. art. IV, § 2, cl. 3.

12. *See* D. Fehrenbacher, *supra* note 7, at 25; R. Cover *supra* note 9, at 163.

13. *See* P. Finkelman, *supra* note 2, at 27.

14. *Id.*

15. 1 Stat. 302 (1793).

16. *See* D. Fehrenbacher, *supra* note 7, at 61–64.

17. 163 U.S. 537 (1896), discussed in Chapter 4.

18. Roberts v. City of Boston, 59 Mass. (5 Cush.) 198 (1850).

19. Brown v. Board of Education, 347 U.S. 383, 393 (1954).

20. U.S. Const. art. IV, § 2, cl. 1.

21. *See* D. Fehrenbacher, *supra* note 7, at 69; W. Wiecek, *supra* note 4, at 137–38.

22. *See* D. Fehrenbacher, *supra* note 7, at 70.

23. The Taney opinion is excerpted in Mr. Justice 43–45 (A. Dunham & P. Kurland eds. 1964).

24. W. Wiecek, *supra* note 4, at 138.

25. Bank of the United States v. DeVeaux, 9 U.S. (5 Cranch) 61, 73 (1809) (emphasis in original).

26. Louisville, Cincinnati & Charleston Railroad Co. v. Letson, 43 U.S. (2 How.) 497, 559 (1844).

27. The Josefa Segunda, 18 U.S. (5 Wheat.) 338, 356–57 (1820).

28. *Id.* at 357.

29. The Antelope, 23 U.S. (10 Wheat.) 66, 120 (1825).

30. *See supra* notes 27–29 and accompanying text. *See also* Queen v. Hepburn, 11 U.S. (7 Cranch) 290 (1813); Scott v. Negro Ben, 10 U.S. (6 Cranch) 3 (1810).

31. Commonwealth v. Aves, 35 Mass. (18 Pick.) 191, 220–21 (1836).

32. D. Fehrenbacher, *supra* note 7, at 43.

33. Background of the case is detailed in Finkelman, *Prigg v. Pennsylvania and Northern State Courts*, in The Law of American Slavery 160 (K. Hall ed. 1987).

34. Story regarded the Court's function as nondisruptive and viewed the Constitution as "practical [in] nature . . . designed for common use and fitted for common understanding." J. Story, Commentaries on the Constitution of the United States 345 (1905).

35. Prigg v. Pennsylvania, 41 U.S. (16 Pet.) 539, 613 (1842).

36. *Id.* at 616–17.

37. *Id.* at 625.

38. *Id.* at 627–28 (Taney, C. J., concurring).

39. Fugitive slave provisions, for instance, spoke in terms of "be[ing] delivered up on Claim of the Party. . . ." U.S. Const. art. IV, § 2, cl. 3; 1 Stat. 302.

40. Prigg v. Pennsylvania, 41 U.S. (16 Pet.) at 613.

41. Liberator, Mar. 11, 1842, *quoted in* Finkelman, *supra* note 33, at 172.

42. Prigg v. Pennsylvania, 41 U.S. (16 Pet.) at 614.

43. *Id.* at 625.

44. *Id.* at 615–16.

45. *Id.* at 628–29 (Taney, C. J., concurring).

46. *See* D. Fehrenbacher, *supra* note 7, at 172–87.

47. Strader v. Graham, 51 U.S. (10 How.) 82 (1850).

48. *Id.* at 97.

49. *Id.* at 93–94.

50. Moore v. Illinois, 55 U.S. (14 How.) 13, 17 (1853).

51. Prigg v. Pennsylvania, 41 U.S. (16 Pet.) at 625.

52. An account of the violent and convoluted efforts to define Kansas as a slave or a free state is provided by D. Fehrenbacher, *supra* note 7, at 193–201.

53. *See id.* at 196.

54. *Id.* at 184.

55. A. Mason, The Supreme Court from Taft to Warren 37–38 (1958).

56. *See* Scott v. Sandford, 60 U.S. (19 How.) 393, 400 (1857); U.S. Const., art. III, § 2, cl. 1.

57. Scott v. Sandford, 60 U.S. (19 How.) at 402–03.

58. *Id.*

59. *Id.* at 403.

60. *Id.* at 404–05.

61. *Id.* at 405.

62. *Id.* at 406–07.

63. *Id.* at 406.

64. *Id.* at 407.

65. *See* D. Fehrenbacher, *supra* note 7, at 349–50.

66. Scott v. Sandford, 60 U.S. (19 How.) at 410.

67. *Id.* at 411.

68. *See* Louisville, Cincinnati & Charleston Railroad v. Letson, 43 U.S. (2 How.) at 559.

69. Scott v. Sandford, 60 U.S. (19 How.) at 451–52.

70. *See id.* at 452.

71. *Id.*

72. 5 U.S. (1 Cranch) 137 (1803).

73. U.S. Const. art. IV, § 3, cl. 2.

74. Scott v. Sandford, 60 U.S. (19 How.) at 432.

75. *Id.* at 442.

76. U.S. Const. art. I, § 8, cl. 18.

77. McCulloch v. Maryland, 17 U.S. (4 Wheat.) 316, 421 (1819).

78. American Insurance Co. v. Canter, 26 U.S. (1 Pet.) at 542 (quoting U.S. Const. art. IV, § 3 [2]).

79. Scott v. Sandford, 60 U.S. (19 How.) at 450.

80. As attorney general of Maryland, Taney had argued against adding substantive meaning to the Fifth Amendment's due process clause. *See* Barron v. Mayor and City Council of Baltimore, 32 U.S. (7 Pet.) 243 (1833).

81. *See* Scott v. Sandford, 60 U.S. (19 How.) at 450.

82. *Id.* at 451.

83. *Id.*

84. *Id.*

85. *Id.* at 451–52.

86. *Id.* at 452.

87. *Id.*

88. H. Hyman, A More Perfect Union 22 (1973).

89. See *id.*

90. D. Fehrenbacher, *supra* note 7, at 436.

91. *Id.* at 442.

92. *Id.* at 442–43.

93. *See* H. Hyman, *supra* note 88, at 25.

94. *Id.*

95. Ableman v. Booth, 62 U.S. (21 How.) 506 (1859).

96. *See* D. Fehrenbacher, *supra* note 7, at 546.

97. *See* R. Berger, Government by Judiciary 12 (1977).

98. C. Woodward, The Burden of Southern History 81 (1960).

99. Scott v. Sandford, 60 U.S. (19 How.) at 407.

100. K. Karst, Belonging to America 44 (1989).

101. Meese, *The Law of the Constitution*, 61 Tul. L.Rev. 979, 989 (1987) (*quoting* P. Kurland, Politics, the Constitution, and the Warren Court 186 (1870).

102. *See* Lively & Plass, *Equal Protection: The Jurisprudence of Denial and Evasion*, 40 Am. U.L. Rev. 1307 (1991).

103. Plessy v. Ferguson, 163 U.S. 537, 559 (1896) (Harlan, J., dissenting).

Chapter 2

Toward a More Perfect Union

Civil war and its aftermath presented the opportunity to redefine the union and tend especially to the deficiencies that had compromised its viability. Armed conflict was calculated to determine whether the republic as created would endure or divide. Northern objectives originally consisted of saving the union but by war's end had broadened to include the elimination of slavery. Actual abolition required not only disregard of the *Scott* decision but also formal proscription of slavery. Insofar as blacks as a class generally had been denied recognition as persons, much less citizens, laws also proved necessary to define the incidents of their new status.

In the years immediately following the Civil War, the Constitution was amended so as to repudiate *Scott*, prohibit slavery, and establish the citizenship and basic liberties and equality of black persons. Such change was exceptional for a society that, barely a decade before, largely was unresponsive to criticism of Taney's racist ideology. Evidencing how profoundly political direction and opportunity had been redefined was the fact that, in early 1861, Congress with Republican support had approved a constitutional amendment "in the direction of a perpetual commitment to the sanctity of slave property in *states* where it then existed."[1] The amendment quickly became "a casualty of the war it was designed to prevent."[2] Constitutional change, albeit with significant qualification, was a logical extension of societal experience and developments during the war years.

Even before the post-war amendments, the *Scott* decision was undermined by legislative and executive action. Congress in 1862 repealed the Fugitive Slave Act and eliminated slavery in the District of Columbia. It also enacted confiscation laws, which were to operate against disloyal southerners. Insofar as they contemplated deprivation of slaves, the statutes actually perpetuated the premise of persons as property. The irony, however, did not persist long. Effective the first day of 1863, the Emancipation Proclamation liberated slaves in any state still engaged in rebellion. Given the realities of secession, the proclamation's significance largely was symbolic. Presidential and congressional action evidenced, however, that federal power no longer would be exercised to facilitate or accommodate slavery. The emancipation order itself was premised on the president's authority as commander-in-chief and did not pertain to slave states that were either loyal or occupied. Its basis thus was almost as narrow as its reach was limited.

The war experience influenced public opinion, so as to make attention to the status of blacks a politically feasible rather than risky proposition. Attitudes still were characterized by a sense of white superiority and phobias concerning racial mixing. The participation and performance of blacks in combat contributed to a sense that it was illogical to deny their personhood and citizenship. Given the basis and scope of the Emancipation Proclamation, it was evident that freedom would have to be fastened to a more secure predicate. With the war having been fought eventually to defeat slavery, it became both sensible and possible to account politically for the consequences of victory and the incidents of incipient citizenship.

Early notions of reconstruction included a sense that rebel states not only would have to renounce secession but repudiate slavery.[3] As noted before, emancipation's limited basis and ambit as a function of presidential war power militated toward identification of an indisputable and durable predicate to eliminate slavery. Turning initially to the Constitution as it existed, the Republicans in 1864 maintained that slavery was inconsonant with Article IV, Section 4's provision that "[t]he United States shall guarantee to every State in this Union a Republican Form of Government . . . ."[4] The construction reflected a novel reading of the article that was never argued in *Scott* and was unlikely to have been contemplated by the framers. Such interpretive creativity nonetheless demonstrated the reality of moral development, which for the first time was supporting political efforts to reckon with racial injustice. The Republican party, which in 1860 had avoided the slave issue as a race issue, by 1864 was defining a Constitution that not only repudiated slavery but also afforded civil equality.[5]

The possibility of reconstructing the nation without altering the Constitution soon proved unrealistic. Congress in 1864 enacted Reconstruction legislation that, among other things, prohibited slavery, guaranteed the freedom of all persons within the states, and extended "the laws for the trial and punishment of white persons...to all persons."[6] Lincoln pocket-vetoed the law for reasons that included doubt over whether Congress could emancipate merely by legislation.[7]

Defeat of the Reconstruction proposal delayed formal effectuation of black freedom. Lincoln's concern that congressional authority was inadequate to emancipate left liberty dependent, for the time being, on the even narrower authority of executive decree. The vulnerability of presidentially declared emancipation to constitutional challenge was noted by legislative critics. As they observed, "the right of a slave to freedom is an open question before the State courts [and]...[w]hat the Supreme Court would say, who can tell?"[8] Such commentary reflected not only distrust of the high court, whose reputation still was diminished by the *Scott* decision,[9] but also a growing sense that existing authority was deficient for the task at hand. Rather than stretch the Constitution in a way that evoked uncertainty and doubt, logic favored changing it to account directly for new reality.

Reconstruction eventually was defined after the war and without Lincoln's participation. The question of slavery, however, was resolved in conclusive constitutional fashion early in his second term. Shortly before Lincoln's assassination, Congress framed and the president endorsed the Thirteenth Amendment. The amendment as ratified reads as follows:

Section 1. Neither slavery nor involuntary servitude, except as a punishment for crime whereof the party shall have been duly convicted, shall exist within the United States, or any place subject to their jurisdiction.
Section 2. Congress shall have power to enforce this article by appropriate legislation.[10]

The Thirteenth Amendment unequivocally extinguished the institution of slavery in the United States. It also introduced more possibilities and concerns than it resolved. Until the amendment's ratification, provision and protection of civil rights and liberties were a function of state responsibility. The Thirteenth Amendment made freedom a national interest and vested Congress with power to enforce it against the states. Federal policies that might define that national interest, as well as state actions that might offend it, remain subjects of constitutional debate. For Lincoln, the amendment effectively incorporated the essence of the Declaration of Independence into the Constitution.[11] Viewed from his perspective, the Thirteenth Amendment not only foreclosed slavery but also established civil rights as an incident of freedom. The notion that such rights flowed from the constitutionally secured status of freedom was not an illogical inference. It was not a premise, however, that would inspire the meaning of the Thirteenth Amendment then or later.

Even if civil guarantees were not manifestly incidental to the Thirteenth Amendment, Section 2 provided a credible basis for Congress to identify and secure basic rights attendant to freedom. Prior to the Civil War, concepts of citizenship and personal allegiance were associated with the states. The war, defined and pursued in terms of saving the union and the consequent emergence of the Thirteenth Amendment, helped engender a transcendent sense of citizenship and loyalty. The experience accelerated evolution of a national identity and established a departure point for fastening the rights and freedoms of federal citizenship.[12] Explication and vitalization of those interests were hastened by post-war developments in the South. Despite the North's battlefield triumph and the constitutional eradication of slavery, it was soon evident that the South was committed to undermining and evading the new political and social order.

Although the Thirteenth Amendment eliminated slavery, it did not uproot the ideology on which it had been premised. Notwithstanding the expectations of Lincoln and many of the Thirteenth Amendment's architects, civil rights and equality were not to flow naturally from the provision's ratification. Much like the desegregation mandate a century later, which would be responded to with widespread evasion and resistance,[13] abolition was circumvented and frustrated by methodologies that sought to establish slavery's functional equivalence.

Racially calibrated law and established custom effectively reduced blacks in the post-war South to a status not meaningfully distinguishable from slavery. The Black Codes in particular imposed special legal disabilities that mocked concepts of civil freedom and equality. State constitutions were rewritten in terms that prohibited slavery but effectively denied any meaning to liberation.

The Black Codes, adopted immediately after the Civil War, represented a slave society's effort to change as little as possible, if at all. Although itemizing the legal rights of blacks, the codes were notable primarily as devices for maintaining the traditional social status of and distance between whites and blacks. Their introduction communicated a swift and powerful message that civil rights would not be self-actuating as a result of the Thirteenth Amendment's ratification. Although southern laws had been revised to acknowledge contractual, property, marital, and litigative rights and liberty to travel, such guarantees effectively were vitiated by provisions that

defined racial status, forbade blacks from pursuing certain occupations or professions (e.g., skilled artisans, merchants, physicians, preaching without a license); forbade owning firearms or weapons; controlled the movement of blacks by systems of passes, required proof of residence; prohibited the congregation of groups of blacks; restricted blacks from residing in certain areas; . . . specified an etiquette of deference to whites;... forbade racial intermarriage and provided the death penalty for blacks raping white women, while omitting special provisions for whites raping black women ... [and] excluded blacks from jury duty, public office, and voting. Some Codes required racial segregation in public transportation. Most Codes authorized whipping and the pillory as punishment for freedmen's offenses.[14]

The codes accounted for the interests of a free labor system vitiated by slavery's prohibition. Laws concerning vagrancy and paupers, regulations for apprenticeship, and punishment for impoverished criminal offenders effectively redirected emancipated blacks into a master-servant relationship. In sum, the codes preserved slavery in fact after it had been abolished in theory. Their introduction and operation disclosed that efforts to secure racial justice, instead of culminating in the Thirteenth Amendment, had barely commenced. The codes also were evidence that the conflict between federal and regional interests had reverted from the battlefield to the political process where it would be pursued throughout the next century and beyond.

In 1865, the Joint Committee on Reconstruction was established and charged with formulating and coordinating reconstruction policy. The committee, created by the Thirty-Ninth Congress, consisted of six senators and nine representatives. Also established, several months earlier, was the Bureau of Freedmen, Refugees, and Abandoned Land. Functioning within the War Department, the Freedmen's Bureau was vested with "control of all subjects relating to refugees and freedmen in the rebel states."[15] Its responsibilities included providing legal protection for recently freed blacks and for white unionists who were subject to retributive harassment and disability.

The bureau's experience and performance previewed the difficult task confronting the reconstruction committee. As a consequence of presidential policy, inadequate funding, and indefeasible racial prejudice and custom, the Freedmen's Bureau failed to realize its potential. Plans for land redistribution were frustrated when President Johnson ceased confiscation proceedings and granted pardons to many former Confederates. Funding of the bureau was dependent largely on private donations. Efforts to effectuate new legal relationships between blacks and whites were confounded by inadequately trained or insensitive personnel and southern intransigence. To the extent bureau agents actually attempted to ensure the rights of newly freed blacks, southern officials and courts used the Black Codes to resist, evade, and confound their efforts.

The reconstruction committee assumed its responsibilities in 1865, therefore, with a clear sense that civil rights and equality would not be self-fulfilling incidents of freedom. As Reconstruction commenced, it also was evident that, despite improvements in the legal condition of northern blacks, prejudice and discrimination still were pervasive. Actual policy was to be a function not only of what was necessary to effectuate meaningful freedom in the South but also of what was politically acceptable in the North. At minimum, the war had demonstrated that federal power was not the only source of official peril to civil rights and liberties. As originally focused, constitutional attention to official imperilment of rights and liberties was directed toward the national government. Prior to the Civil War, the Court had resisted efforts to translate the Fifth Amendment into a check on state power.[16] Post-war use of state authority to deny basic freedoms, however, prompted a reexamination and eventuated a profound restructuring of the constitutional system.

The Thirteenth Amendment, as noted previously, made freedom a national policy and empowered Congress to enforce it. What the amendment accomplished by its own terms beyond eradication of slavery became an immediate subject of debate. President Johnson, consistent more with the Democratic position than the drift of his own party, expounded the minimalist position. He maintained that the amendment only abolished the institution of slavery and did not alter the preexisting relationship between nation and states.[17] Congressional action and subsequent constitutional retooling, however, soon dated the notion that federal and state powers and the union itself were not being substantially redefined. The South's response to the Thirteenth Amendment, characterized by the harassment of unionists, impedance of black freedom, and negation of the Freedmen's Bureau, convinced Congress that the elimination of slavery was not enough to guarantee in every state the incidents of a republican form of government.

The plight of southern blacks, a consideration freshly removed from the political closet, had become by 1866 a prime focus for further constitutional and statutory attention. Action was prompted by recognition that the war's objectives and achievements, as eventually defined and attained, were in danger of being compromised if not altogether vitiated by southern recalcitrance. Despite the racial phobias and ideologies that persisted in and pervaded the North, the South's response to the Thirteenth Amendment thus made possible a national accounting for civil rights.

Federal attention to civil rights was inspired by post-war realities but was nonetheless constrained by two significant factors. Concepts of black liberty and equality were limited by societal moral development, which was still rooted in white supremacy. Racial considerations aside, disagreement existed with respect to the nature and extent of civil rights. The very concept of such guarantees defied consensus insofar as civil freedoms had descended from innately amorphous natural rights. Defining civil rights thus was to be a competitive process influenced by the perimeters of racial tolerance and agreement on what the essential incidents of citizenship were. Radical Republicans, for instance, asserted that civil rights at minimum were defined by the Declaration of Independence and the Bill of Rights. Although most of the Bill of Rights has been incorporated jurisprudentially into the Fourteenth Amendment, the radicals' position of comprehensive effectuation was a minority position then and now.

Even if civil rights could not be readily and neatly itemized, it generally was agreed that they represented the privileges and immunities appurtenant to status as a free person. Such rights traditionally had been defined by the state, as noted previously, and had been perceived largely in economic terms. Incipient federal interest in securing them, although introducing a new basis, evinced no consensus for altering their linkage to material considerations. At minimum, civil rights as then conceived included the rights to contract, own and transfer property, sue and be sued, travel, and enjoy personal security.

Southern interference with those incidents, considered crucial to full and equal participation in civil society, prompted a reformulation of basic law, which recontoured the relationship between federal and state government. Political power was redefined and redistributed, as Congress further repudiated the *Scott* decision and negated another antebellum ruling that had regarded constitutionally furnished guarantees as a check only on the federal government.[18] Statutory and constitutional reckoning was a function of the freshly demonstrated abusive potentiality and actuality of state power. Congress responded to the circumstances with legislation calculated to advance Thirteenth Amendment aims and to fortify the Constitution itself and thereby better secure the civil rights of all citizens.

Accounting for the incidents of freedom required policy that, unlike the prohibition of slavery, was affirmative in nature. The Civil Rights Act of 1866, as an extension of the Thirteenth Amendment and a preface to the Fourteenth Amendment, represented a seminal effort to secure what neither the war nor the Thirteenth Amendment itself had attained. Like its constitutional predicate, the civil rights bill was rooted in the relatively new concept of national citizenship and concomitant federal obligation to protect its incidents. Neither the 1866 act nor the Fourteenth Amendment catalogued civil rights. The lack of itemization, as previously mentioned, is consistent with the imprecise nature and extent of civil rights. It also has been suggested "that the framers found it natural to adopt the mode of generality already used elsewhere in the Constitution to express limitations on the states and on the national government."[19] Although failure to specify these rights presents problems in understanding their actual scope and coverage, perceptual difficulties would not be avoided entirely even in the event of particularization. Disagreement over the ambit of contractual rights, indisputably secured in 1866, manifests itself even in modern times.[20]

Prior to 1866, the closest approximation to a comprehensive judicial definition of civil rights was related by a federal court in *Corfield v. Coryell*.[21] The decision, authored by Justice Washington as circuit justice, alluded to those rights "which are, in their nature, fundamental; which belong, of right, to the citizens of all free governments; and which have, at all times, been enjoyed by the citizens of the several states which compose this Union."[22] Included among the fundamental privileges of citizenship were

Protection by the government; the enjoyment of life and liberty, with the right to acquire and possess property of every kind, and to pursue and obtain happiness and safety; ... [t]he right of a citizen of one state to pass through, or to reside in any other state, for purposes of trade, agriculture, professional pursuits, or otherwise; to claim the benefit of the writ of habeas corpus; to institute and maintain actions of any kind in the courts of the state; to take, hold and dispose of property, either real or personal; and an exemption from higher taxes than are paid by other citizens of the state; ... [and] the elective franchise, as regulated and established by the law or constitution of the state in which it is to be exercised.[23]

The *Corfield* decision arose out of circumstances that, in comparison to those inspiring the Civil Rights Act of 1866 and the Fourteenth Amendment, seemed relatively trifling. At issue were the rights of another state's citizens to harvest oysters in the waters of New Jersey.[24] From that context emerged principles of equal respect for citizens of all states.[25]

While precedent established that a state must be even-handed toward the citizens of other states, to the extent it afforded any rights to its own citizens, the 1866 act and the Fourteenth Amendment sought to secure incidents of national citizenship as a matter of constitutional imperative rather than comity—the principle of respect for the law of other jurisdictions. Instead of merely forbidding discrimination against citizens of another state, the Thirty-Ninth Congress prohibited discrimination by states against their own citizens. It did so by means of legislation that sketched basic rights in general terms, akin to the articulations of *Corfield*, and prohibited qualification of these rights on the basis of race.

The civil rights enactment thus provided that

there shall be no discrimination in civil rights or immunities ... on account of race ... but the inhabitants of every race ... shall have the same rights to make and enforce contracts, to sue, be parties, and give evidence, to inherit, purchase, lease, sell, hold and convey real and personal property, and to full and equal benefit of all laws and proceedings for the security of persons and property, and shall be subject to like punishment.[26]

The enumeration, described by one legislator as "the fundamental rights of citizenship,"[27] was consonant with *Corfield*'s characterization of the basic incidents of citizenship. What was revolutionary about the civil rights bill was the regard of fundamental freedom as a federal interest.

Civil rights legislation in its seminal form responded to the introduction and operation of the Black Codes. Given Congress's use of language broader than necessary to invalidate the codes, and aims characterized as otherwise "too inconsiderable," the Civil Rights Act of 1866 has been styled as a "statute of permanent and universal applicability" calibrated toward establishing "a federal principle of racial equality in the enjoyment of state-created rights."[28]

The newly established federal interest, however, reflected neither a congressional nor a public mandate for an expansive definition of civil rights. Despite Justice Washington's inclusion of suffrage as a civil right a few decades earlier in *Corfield*, his perception was not consensually subscribed to even after the war. The congressional record itself is suffused with commentary disclaiming any intention to secure voting rights, depicting the franchise as a political right, and distinguishing suffrage from civil rights.[29] Nor was an integrated education system or other modern accoutrements of the Fourteenth Amendment, such as the rights of privacy and personal autonomy, on the mind of Congress in 1866. Public education, which eventually would be regarded as so crucial to citizenship that desegregation would be judicially mandated,[30] was a marginal and underdeveloped institution and not a primary object of legislative attention. The general sense at the time, consistent with established custom, was that racial separation in schools and other contexts presented no constitutional affront. Contemporaneous with the adoption of the Civil Rights Act of 1866 and the Fourteenth Amendment, in fact, Congress provided for segregated education in the District of Columbia.

Consistent with a congressional aim that was qualified rather than comprehensive, the House chair of the Joint Committee on Reconstruction repudiated the notion

that in all things, civil, social, political, all citizens, without distinction of race or color, shall be equal [. . .] By no means can [civil rights and immunities] be so construed. . . . Nor do they mean that all citizens shall sit on juries, or that their children shall attend the same schools. . . . I understand civil rights to be simply the absolute rights of individuals, such as "The right to personal security, the right of personal liberty, and the right to acquire and enjoy property." [Nor should anyone] be subjected to obligations, duties, pains and penalties from which other citizens are exempted.... This is the spirit and scope of the bill and does not go one step beyond.[31]

Understanding the basic and limited aims of the Civil Rights Act of 1866 is essential for appreciating the contemplated ambit of the Fourteenth Amendment as ratified in 1868. Like its legislative precursor, the Fourteenth Amendment was the function of a qualified civil rights agenda. It reflected, however, further experience with the post-war South and a mounting apprehension that hard-won achievements might be at risk when Reconstruction was finished and the South regained its political influence. The possibility that a reemergent South might dominate the federal government and repudiate the aims of war and reconstruction was a real concern. Given a response to the Thirteenth Amendment, resulting in the vitiation of black freedom, it was not hard to imagine how the South actually might function in the new political structure. With congressional representation no longer bound by the "three-fifths of a person" formula applied to slaves, the South might deny blacks the right to vote and still expand its representative basis. Concern with the prospect of a renascent but effectively unreconstructed South was accentuated by a sense among some legislators, compounded by President Johnson's unsuccessful veto of the civil rights bill, that the enactment might be vulnerable to constitutional challenge.[32] Constitutionalization of the 1866 act by means of the Fourteenth Amendment thus removed any doubt about the existence and basis of federally secured civil rights.

The Fourteenth Amendment as originally conceived represented an effort to enshrine the incidents of citizenship "beyond normal politics ... [and] fix [them] in the serene sky, in the eternal firmament of the Constitution, where no storm of passion can shake ... and no cloud can obscure."[33] It did so in the following terms:

Section 1. All persons born or naturalized in the United States and subject to the jurisdiction thereof, are citizens of the United States and of the State wherein they reside. No State shall make or enforce any law which shall abridge the privileges or immunities of citizens of the United States; nor shall any State deprive any person of life, liberty, or property, without due process of law; nor deny to any person within its jurisdiction the equal protection of the laws.

Section 2. Representatives shall be apportioned among the several States according to their respective numbers, counting the whole number of persons in each State, excluding Indians not taxed. But when the right to vote at any election for the choice of electors for President and Vice President of the United States, Representatives in Congress, the Executive and Judicial officers of a State, or the members of the Legislature thereof, is denied to any of the male inhabitants of such State, being twenty-one years of age, and citizens of the United States, or in any way abridged, except for participation in rebellion, or other crime, the basis of representation therein shall be reduced in the proportion which the number of such male citizens shall bear to the whole number of male citizens twenty-one years of age in such State.

Section 3. No person shall be a Senator or Representative in Congress, or elector of President and Vice President, or hold any office, civil or military, under the United States, or under any State, who, having previously taken an oath, as a member of Congress, or as an officer of the United States, or as a member of any State legislature, or as an executive or judicial officer of any State, to support the Constitution of the United States, shall have engaged in insurrection or rebellion against the same, or given aid or comfort to the enemies thereof. But Congress may by a vote of two-thirds of each House, remove such disability.

Section 4. The validity of the public debt of the United States, authorized by law, including debts incurred for payment of pensions and bounties for services in suppressing insurrection or rebellion, shall not be questioned. But neither the United States nor any State shall assume or pay any debt or obligation incurred in aid of insurrection or rebellion against the United States, or any claim for the loss or emancipation of any slave; but all such debts, obligations and claims shall be held illegal and void.

Section 5. The Congress shall have power to enforce, by appropriate legislation, the provisions of this article.[34]

Discerning the original understanding of the Fourteenth Amendment is complicated by more than a century of jurisprudence that has extended its meaning far beyond its relatively simple beginnings. The amendment was designed to secure civil rights against future tampering by a post-Reconstruction Congress. Support for the Fourteenth Amendment, as with most enactments, represented a mixture of justifications and motives. Some of its champions urged a broad meaning that would have transcended the Civil Rights Act of 1866. During the framing process itself, they advocated the Fourteenth Amendment as a means for implementing broad concepts of rights and equality reposing in the Declaration of Independence and the Bill of Rights.[35] Such expansive incorporation, however, was not subscribed to by a congressional majority still cautious with the novelty of national citizenship and protective of traditional state powers and functions. Even supporters of a broadly encompassing guarantee eventually acknowledged that "(v)irtually every speaker in the debates on the Fourteenth Amendments—Republicans and Democrats alike—said or agreed that [it] was designed to embody or incorporate the Civil Rights Act."[36] As originally conceived, therefore, Section 1 of the Amendment provided the necessary framework for the rights incidental to citizenship.

The significance of Section 1's structure has proved a durable subject of debate. Some scholars maintain that each clause had a well-defined and particularized function. From Raoul Berger's perspective, for instance, the privileges and immunities clause accounted for the substantive rights secured by the Civil Rights Act of 1866; the equal protection clause prohibited legislative discrimination with respect to those rights; and the due process clause ensured recourse to an impartial judiciary.[37] Competing with that formalistic understanding of Section 1 is the sense that "[t]here was no serious effort to differentiate the function of the various clauses . . . [and] the section in its entirety was taken to guarantee equality in the enjoyment of the rights of citizenship."[38] Consistent with the latter premise is the notion that whatever was or might be accomplished pursuant to a particular clause is achievable by extrapolation from Section 1's conferral of national citizenship.[39]

What the Fourteenth Amendment did not clearly account for, at least originally, were rights that many considered political rather than civil in nature. Although theoretically useful to the Republican party's vitality, black suffrage was not well established in the North and was strongly resisted by most whites. A constitutional demand on the South, which would have required northern states to extend rights they were not prepared to offer themselves, did not translate into a politically viable option. As a Kentucky senator observed, "Negro suffrage is political arsenic. If it is not, why do not the free States open wide their throats and gulp down the graceful and invigorating drought."[40]

Even if black suffrage was not immediately feasible, the linkage between voting and the meaningful operation of civil rights was not entirely unappreciated. A prominent architect of Reconstruction policy characterized the franchise as "the Great Guarantee; and the only sufficient Guarantee."[41] Ratification, however, required endorsement by three-fourths of the states and thus concession to political reality. As members of the Reconstruction committee concluded, "it was our opinion that [such support] . . . could not be induced to grant the right of suffrage, even in any degree or under any restriction, to the colored race."[42] Reiterating the basic point, the Senate chair identified not "the slightest probability that [black suffrage] will be adopted by the States . . . [or] would commend itself to anybody."[43]

The framers of the Fourteenth Amendment thus confronted a dilemma in accounting satisfactorily for citizenship and its incidents. Black freedom and equality were to be secured in a society still rooted in tenets of white superiority and still resistant to the notion of fully sharing political and economic power and opportunity. The more precise and immediate challenge was to preclude the emergence of a fortified white southern bloc in Congress without offending northern constituents generally opposed to black suffrage. Section 2 of the Fourteenth Amendment thus provided an incentive but did not require southern states to extend the franchise to blacks. Its key provision reduced the basis of representation if the right to vote was denied or abridged. Even if an indirect or convoluted methodology, the section was clear in its purpose "to deprive the lately rebellious states of the unfair advantage of a large representation in this House, based on their colored population, so long as that people shall be denied political rights."[44]

The Fourteenth Amendment effectively left determination of voting rights to the individual states. Even the forthcoming introduction of a constitutional proscription proved inadequate, for nearly a century, in defeating racially motivated deprivations of voting rights in the South. As subsequent events demonstrated, southern states were bent on maintaining an exclusively white political process without regard to constitutional risk. Such intransigence, as discussed later, eventually would help engender the Fifteenth Amendment.

Meanwhile, experience with the South was demonstrating that respect even for the limited range of rights and liberties contemplated by the Fourteenth Amendment would not be easily established. The Black Codes were effective not only as an instrumentality of oppression but in radiating the South's determination to define the contours of civil rights and liberties pursuant to the criteria it saw fit. Despite introduction of the Thirteenth Amendment, most southern blacks remained the functional equivalent of slaves.[45] It was toward the Black Codes in particular that the equal protection clause responded as a guarantor of "equality of protection in those enumerated civil rights which the States may deem proper to confer upon any race."[46] As another emanation of the Civil Rights Act of 1866, it required "each State [to] provide for equality before the law, equal protection to life, liberty, and property, equal right to sue and be sued."[47]

Modern equal protection analysis, which concerns itself with suspect classifications—those based on race, gender, alienage, and parental marital status—and impairment of fundamental rights, represents a substantial jump from the original sense that "[w]hatever law protects the white man shall afford *equal protection* to the black man."[48] Consistent with the Fourteenth Amendment's initial concern with a discrete set of rights and liberties, equal protection as initially calibrated did not comprehend perfect equality. Advocates of a broader guarantee, like proponents of sweeping rights and freedoms, were compelled to defer their aims to the reality of a society not yet prepared for such a cultural overhaul.[49] Although itself not a source of rights, the equal protection guarantee prohibits race-dependent denial or qualification of any state-created rights or immunities.[50]

From the Fourteenth Amendment's due process clause, over the course of its existence, has emerged a panoply of fundamental rights and liberties. Although such guarantees are not specified by the amendment or otherwise enumerated in the Constitution, the Supreme Court in less than a century cultivated the due process clause in substantive terms that accounted for economic liberty, privacy rights, and personal autonomy. Such jurisprudence has been the source of extensive controversy and criticism of the Court's function. Investment in substantive due process coupled with cramped readings of the commerce power eventually prompted a serious political challenge to the judiciary when, in response to persistent invalidation of New Deal legislation, President Roosevelt introduced a plan for packing the Court and redefining its ideology.[51] Even in disclaiming jurisprudentially glossed economic rights doctrine, the Court has continued to identify unenumerated interests as fundamental.[52]

Such developments diverge from strict notions of due process as "only applicable to the process and proceedings of the courts or justice; they can never be referred to an act of the legislature."[53] The characterization, related by Alexander Hamilton, pertained to the meaning of due process afforded by the Fifth Amendment. Raoul Berger maintained that the absence of extensive attention to due process or evidence of a profoundly different meaning, in debates concerning the Fourteenth Amendment, indicates that due process was not reinvented or substantially redefined.[54] His understanding is not universally shared. Thomas Cooley, within a decade of the Fourteenth Amendment's ratification, observed that nothing "necessarily implies that due process of law must be judicial process."[55] Justice Field contemporaneously advanced the sense "that the Amendment and related legislation reflected Congress' intent to place a dynamic, broad body of common rights, including economic interests, under national judicial protection."[56] Specifics of the due process clause itself are further diminished in significance if substantive protection is inferred from Section 1's creation of national citizenship.[57] What the Fourteenth Amendment at least changed, if not the meaning of due process, was its scope and beneficiaries. As one legislator put it, "[t]he Constitution already declares generally that no person shall be deprived of life, liberty, or property without due process of law . . . ; [the Fourteenth Amendment] declares particularly that no State shall do it."[58] The due process clause, even if merely enabling all citizens to enforce civil rights and equality by means of access to a fair and impartial judicial system,[59] further denoted a redistribution of federal and state interests.

Included in the Fourteenth Amendment are sections that, at least for modern purposes, are vestigial. Section 2, as noted previously, reduced the political strength of states that denied or limited the franchise.[60] Section 3 precluded officials who had supported rebellion from holding federal or state office.[61] Section 4 reaffirmed the validity of the nation's war debt and disclaimed liability for Confederate borrowings or claims for the loss of slaves.[62] Each of those provisions has been rendered obsolete by altered political realities and the passage of time. Of more enduring significance is Section 5, which conferred on Congress "power to enforce . . . the provision of this article."[63]

The assignment of enforcement power to Congress rather than the judiciary may have reflected abiding distrust of an institution that had validated slavery a mere decade before.[64] One of the legacies of the *Scott* decision was the Supreme Court's self-inflicted loss of credibility and prestige. The Court's reputation had been diminished by the perception that it was "the citadel of Slaveocracy."[65] Section 5 imposed "upon Congress the responsibility of seeing to it, for the future, that all the sections of the amendment are carried out in good faith, and that no State infringes the rights of person and property."[66] The assignment of enforcement power was further evidence of how profoundly the relationship between federal and state government had been recontoured. Section 1 provided a benchmark against which state action could be measured. Section 5 suggested that the federal legislature might enact laws on matters previously reserved to the states. Although not charged with plenary authority for purposes of establishing a body of comprehensive municipal law, Congress at least might supersede state enactments implicating Section 1. A central meaning of the Fourteenth Amendment, therefore, was that civil rights were a national interest that might be effectuated by national policy.

Even in redistributing power between federal and state government, the Fourteenth Amendment generally and Section 5 specifically were influenced by traditional considerations of federalism. Although fashioning and endorsing the Fourteenth Amendment, many Republicans second-guessed whether "the nation . . . could, or should police every Southern hamlet."[67] The amendment was recognized as a cutting edge with the potential for paring traditional state powers and concerns. The law of contracts, for instance, reflected a generally local interest qualified by a newly and constitutionally established federal policy of nondiscrimination. The new mix of federal and state concerns not only challenged traditional political perceptions and thought but, as discussed in the next chapter, also resulted in tension with evolving principles of laissez-faire economics.

As the 1860s drew to a close, southern resistance to new statutory and constitutional demands hardened rather than abated. Persisting intransigence doused northern hopes, even if unrealistic, for a cooperative, harmonious, and efficient Reconstruction. Feeding the South's intractability were the words and deeds of President Johnson in opposition to forceful Reconstruction policies. Congressional attention and energy during the post-war period thus were spread between two adversaries— the chief executive and the remnants of the Confederacy. Mixed signals radiated from congressional passage and presidential veto of civil rights legislation and from contrary legislative and executive rhetoric. Not surprisingly, the South tuned in to the message of its liking.

Despite the political risks attached to the cause of black suffrage, which

previously had limited and foreclosed its championing, unvarying southern attitudes and diminishing patience with Reconstruction resulted in
serious attention to the subject. For advocates of comprehensive liberty
and equality, the right to vote was the missing constitutional link for
meaningful citizenship. They assumed that no state would tamper with
civil rights if it faced accountability at the ballot box. Black suffrage, for
those who may have resisted or avoided it before, presented an opportunity to end the post-war era and its seemingly intractable problems. For
a nation becoming increasingly weary of Reconstruction, extending the
franchise offered a final solution that would clear race from the political
agenda and enable society to move beyond Reconstruction.

The Fifteenth Amendment thus was proposed by Congress in 1869
and ratified in 1870. More like the Thirteenth than the Fourteenth
Amendment in its length and detail, the Fifteenth Amendment provides
that

Section 1. The right of citizens of the United States to vote shall not be denied
or abridged by the United States or by any State on account of race, color, or
previous condition of servitude.

Section 2. The Congress shall have power to enforce this article by appropriate
legislation.[68]

Pursuant to its enforcement power, Congress promptly enacted implementing legislation. The Enforcement Act of 1870 made public or
private interference with the right to vote a criminal offense.[69] The
voting process itself was subjected to oversight, as legislation passed the
following year provided for federal supervision of registration and certification of election results.[70] Contemporaneous with its effort to secure
voting rights pursuant to the Fifteenth Amendment, Congress also
sought to reckon with racially motivated violence and intimidation that
jeopardized civil rights in the South. Fourteenth Amendment enforcement power was the basis for the Ku Klux Klan Act adopted in 1871.[71]
That legislation directed itself not only to deprivation of civil rights under
color of state law but also to private action denying equal protection.

Debate over the Ku Klux Klan Act reignited the controversy as to
whether the Thirteenth Amendment could support legislation that was
not directly and proximately concerned with eradicating slavery. In spite
of arguments that Section 2 of the amendment enabled Congress to
enforce by positive enactment the prohibition provision of Section 1,[72]
doubt persisted with respect to whether it afforded an adequate legislative departure point. Similar concern prompted reenactment of the
Civil Rights Act of 1866 pursuant to the Fourteenth Amendment. Such
action, coupled with passage of the Ku Klux Klan Act and voting rights
legislation, represented the post-war apex in federal accounting for civil

rights. The outburst of initiative, however, would prove to be only a preface to subsequent court decisions delimiting the Fourteenth Amendment's potential as a source of racial justice and transforming it into a platform for new rights and liberties of a general nature.

The Reconstruction amendments and implementing legislation nonetheless had effected profound change in the blueprint of governmental power and personal freedom. Reality was that "as the years passed and fervor for racial equality waned, enforcement of [voting rights] laws became spotty and ineffective, and most of their provisions were repealed in 1894."[73] Pursuant to the Fourteenth Amendment, Congress in 1875 passed further civil rights legislation prohibiting discrimination in public accommodations.[74] Concern with the reach of federal power into the private sector and impatience with still intractable problems of race soon prompted a trimming of Congress's enforcement power. Depicting the racial classifications proscribed by the Civil Rights Act of 1875 as "[m]ere discriminations"[75] and a function of private rather than official action, the Court in the *Civil Rights Cases* invalidated the law.[76] Within a decade of Reconstruction, therefore, doctrine repudiated the special constitutional or legislative attention to the interest of the nation's new citizens.[77]

Jurisprudential cramping of congressional power disclosed an immediate irony that remained significant in the framing of modern civil rights legislation. By reenacting the Civil Rights Act of 1866 pursuant to the Fourteenth Amendment, Congress had sought to clarify and fortify the law's constitutional premises. Although the enactment may have been secured against challenges to legislative authority, redirection traded away the potential utility of an amendment not subject to a state action requirement. Given the temper of society as it coursed through and past Reconstruction, legislation directed toward private discrimination and premised on the Thirteenth Amendment probably would have been invalidated anyway. Congress in recent times has been allowed to account for "the badges and incidents of slavery"[78] in a broader sense, but early Thirteenth Amendment analysis favored a restrictive reading of those terms. As the Court noted in 1883, "[m]ere discriminations" that denied certain privileges afforded white citizens or limited access to public accommodations, reflected settled custom rather than badges of slavery.[79] Although the Court eventually comprehended that discrimination in public venues merited congressional attention,[80] initial restrictions on legislative authority survived as constitutional impediments to modern reckoning with discrimination. The Civil Rights Act of 1964, which prohibits discrimination not only in public accommodations but in education, employment and other contexts, thus was predicated alternatively on the Fourteenth Amendment and the commerce power.

Collectively, the reconstruction amendments established a national interest in the incidents of national citizenship and enabled Congress to secure them against racially discriminatory action by the states. The amendments have been described as "equating the rights of United States citizenship to the natural rights of free men.... In short, the legal theory of national civil rights enforcement authority under the Thirteenth and Fourteenth Amendments posited a virtually unlimited national authority over civil rights."[81] Despite such grand descriptions, the process of charting respective perimeters of federal and state interests and powers has been central especially to the Fourteenth Amendment's evolution and meaning. The amendment may not have established a consensus for eliminating all racial prejudice and discrimination. Broad support existed, however, for the limited aim of ensuring that racism did not deny basic opportunities for material development and equal standing before the law.

Although voting rights were tended to by the Fifteenth Amendment, initial reluctance to constitutionalize the franchise reinforces the sense that the Fourteenth Amendment originally was intended to account for a narrow band of rights and equality. Reality is that the framers, as agents of the society they represented, did not enact a broad anti-discrimination principle. Nor did they intend to eradicate racial distinctions that did not implicate basic interests of life, liberty, person, and property. Subsequent jurisprudence has construed expansively the provision's racially nonspecific text. Principles evolving from the amendment's core concern, however, have been mostly circumspect or circumscribed. Within a few years of its ratification, the provision was subject to review that permanently would distort its original concern and meaning. The Fourteenth Amendment's legacy, at least until the middle of the twentieth century, would prove notable primarily for doctrines that responded to interests unrelated to race or solidified race-dependent impairment of citizenship and its incidents.

NOTES

1. H. Hyman, A More Perfect Union 46 (1973) (emphasis in original). Pertinent terms of the provision were that "no amendment shall be made to the Constitution which will authorize or give to Congress the power to abolish or interfere, within any state, with the domestic institutions thereof, including that of persons held to labor or service by the laws of said state." Cong. Globe, 36th Cong. 2d Sess. 1284–85 (1861). President Lincoln's position was that the measure comported with what constitutional law already implied and thus he would not object to its explication and irrevocability. See H. Hyman, supra, at 47.
2. See H. Hyman, supra note 1, at 47.
3. See H. Hyman & W. Wiecek, Equal Justice Under the Law 269 (1982).
4. U.S. Const. art. IV, § 4.
5. See H. Hyman & W. Wiecek, supra note 3.

6. *Id.* at 272–73.

7. *See id.* at 274.

8. *Id.* at 275.

9. A. Mason, The Supreme Court from Taft to Warren 38 (1958).

10. U.S. Const. amend. XIII.

11. *See* H. Hyman & W. Wiecek, *supra* note 3, at 278.

12. *See* R. Kaczorowski, The Politics of Judicial Interpretation: The Federal Courts, Department of Justice and Civil Rights, 1866–1876 108 (1985).

13. *See* Chapter 5.

14. H. Hyman & W. Wiecek, *supra* note 3, at 319. The experience of the Freedmen's Bureau is examined in R. Koczorowski, *supra* note 12, at 27–48.

15. H. Hyman & W. Wiecek, *supra* note 3, at 315.

16. *See* Barron v. Mayor and City Council of Baltimore, 32 U.S. (7 Pet.) 243, 250–51 (1833).

17. H. Hyman & W. Wiecek, *supra* note 3, at 389.

18. Barron v. Mayor and City Council of Baltimore, 32 U.S. (7 Pet.) at 250–51.

19. K. Karst, Belonging to America 55 (1989). It also has been noted that, given the need to accommodate competing purposes as in any multi-sided political debate, "one time-honored way to achieve compromise ... is to enact broad language that is capable of bearing more than one meaning." *Id.* at 55–56. *See* Sandalow, *Constitutional Interpretation*, 79 Mich. L.Rev. 1033, 1046 (1981).

20. The Court determined that 42 U.S.C. § 1981, a direct statutory descendant of the 1866 act, prohibits discrimination in the making of contracts but does not concern itself with post-information harassment. *See* Patterson v. McLean Credit Union, 109 S. Ct. 2363, 2373 (1989). The distinction was criticized as an unjustified exercise by the Court in "snatch[ing] away with one hand [what] it gives with the other." *Id.* at 2379 (Brennan, J. dissenting).

21. 6 F. Cas. 546 (C.C.D. Pa. 1823). Evolution of the concept and meaning of citizenship in American society, from the early colonial period to the Civil War's immediate aftermath, is examined in J. Kettner, The Development of American Citizenship, 1608–1870 (1978).

22. Corfield v. Coryell, 6 F. Cas. at 551.

23. *Id.* at 551–52.

24. *Id.* at 547.

25. Disagreement is discernible before and after *Corfield* with respect to whether privileges and immunities were a function of state determination or fundamental incidents deriving from national citizenship. *See* J. Kettner, *supra* note 21, at 258–61.

26. Cong. Globe, 39th Cong., 1st Sess. 474 (1866).

27. *Id.* at 1151 (Rep. Thayer).

28. C. Fairman, VI History of the Supreme Court of the United States, Reconstruction and Reunion, pt. 1, at 1228 (1971). R. Berger, Government by Judiciary 26 (1977). For an account of how civil rights evolved from concepts of national citizenship, including initial concerns for whites and blacks in the South, *see* H. Hyman, *supra* note 1, at 414–32.

29. *See, e.g.,* Cong. Globe, *supra* note 26, at 599 (Rep. Trumbull); *id.* at 606 (Sen. Saulsbury); *id.* at 632 (Rep. Moulton); *id.* at 704 (Sen. Fessender); *id.* at

744 (Sen. Sherman); *id.* at 1124 (Rep. Cook); *id.* at 1151 (Rep. Thayer); *id.* at 1159 (Rep. Windom); *id.* at 3034–35 (Sen. Henderson).

30. *See* Chapter 5.

31. Cong. Globe, *supra* note 26, at 1117 (Rep. Wilson).

32. K. Karst, *supra* note 19, at 51; R. Berger, *supra* note 28, at 23 n.12.

33. Cong. Globe, *supra* note 26, at 2462 (Rep. Garfield).

34. U.S. Const. amend. XIV.

35. *See* W. Nelson, The Fourteenth Amendment: From Political Principle to Judicial Doctrine 71–77, 117–19 (1988).

36. H. Graham, Everyman's Constitution 291 n.73 (1968).

37. *See* R. Berger, *supra* note 28, at 18.

38. *See* K. Karst, *supra* note 19, at 18.

39. *See* C. Black, Jr., Structure and Relationship in Constitutional Law 51–66 (1969).

40. Cong. Globe, *supra* note 26, at 246 (Sen. Davis).

41. *Id.* at 685 (Sen. Sumner).

42. *Id.* at 2766 (Sen. Howard).

43. *Id.* at 704 (Sen. Fessenden).

44. *Id.* at 141 (Rep. Blaine).

45. *See* C. Fairman, VII History of the Supreme Court of the United States, Reconstruction and Reunion, pt. 1, at 134 (1987); R. Berger, *supra* note 28, at 169.

46. Cong. Globe, *supra* note 26, at 1293 (Rep. Shellabarger). *See* C. Fairman, *supra* note 45, at 134 (equal protection reckoned with the "gross injustice and hardship" of the Black Codes).

47. *Id.* at 1622 (Rep. Moulton).

48. *Id.* at 2459 (Rep. Stevens) (emphasis in original).

49. Even champions of comprehensive equality conceded that prerequisite societal remolding was unrealistic, and thus "we shall be obliged to be content with patching up the worst portions of the ancient edifice." *Id.* at 3148 (Rep. Stevens).

50. As noted in Chapters 5 and 6 the equal protection clause eventually became the basis for challenging official racial discrimination.

51. For a discussion of the operation and criticism of substantive due process and the political friction it caused earlier in this century, *see* L. Tribe, American Constitutional Law (567–58 2d ed. 1988).

52. *See, e.g.,* Zablocki v. Redhail, 434 U.S. 374 (1978) (right to marry); Moore v. City of East Cleveland, 431 U.S. 494 (1977) (sanctity of family); Roe v. Wade, 410 U.S. 113 (1973) (liberty to elect abortion); Griswold v. Connecticut, 381 U.S. 479 (1965) (right of privacy).

53. R. Berger, *supra* note 28, at 196 n.11 (*quoting* Alexander Hamilton).

54. *See id.* at 193–200.

55. Weimar v. Bunbury, 36 Mich. 203 (1874), in H. Hyman, *supra* note 1, at 169.

56. H. Hyman, *supra* note 1, at 536 (*quoting* Slaughter-House Cases, 83 U.S. (16 Wall.) 36 (1873) (Field, J., dissenting)). Support for an expansive reading of due process also exists in J. ten Broek, The Antislavery Origins of the Fourteenth Amendment 222–23 (1951).

57. *See supra* note 39 and accompanying text.

58. Cong. Globe, *supra* note 26, at 256 (Rep. Baker).

59. *See id.* at 1117–18 (Rep. Wilson).

60. U.S. Const. amend. XIV, § 2.

61. *Id.* § 3.

62. *Id.* § 4.

63. *Id.* § 5.

64. *See* R. Berger, *supra* note 28, at 222–23.

65. A. Mason, *supra* note 9, at 16.

66. Cong. Globe, *supra* note 26, at 2766 (Sen. Howard).

67. H. Hyman & W. Wiecek, *supra* note 1, at 404.

68. U.S. Const. amend. XV.

69. 16 Stat. 170 (1870).

70. 16 Stat. 433 (1871).

71. 17 Stat. 13, now codified as 42 U.S.C. §§ 1983, 1985(3).

72. Cong. Globe 42d Cong., 1st Sess. 85 (1871) (Rep. Stevens). *See* H. Hyman & W. Wiecek, *supra* note 3, at 470–71.

73. South Carolina v. Katzenbach, 383 U.S. 301, 310 (1966).

74. Civil Rights Act of 1875, 18 Stat. 335 (1875).

75. Civil Rights Cases, 109 U.S. 3, 25 (1883).

76. *Id.* at 20.

77. *Id.* at 25.

78. Jones v. Alfred H. Mayer Co., 392 U.S. 409, 439–41 (1968).

79. Civil Rights Cases, 109 U.S. at 25.

80. The Civil Rights Act of 1964, 42 U.S.C. §§ 2000a to 2000a–6, insofar as it prohibits discrimination in public accommodations, was upheld as a proper exercise of Congress's commerce power. Katzenbach v. McClung, 379 U.S. 294 (1964); Heart of Atlanta Motel v. United States, 379 U.S. 241 (1964).

81. R. Kaczorowski, *supra* note 12, at 1.

Chapter 3

Constitutional Amendment and Doctrinal Development

The Reconstruction amendments resolved some fundamental issues that had been bypassed or deferred when the Constitution originally was drafted. The Thirteenth, Fourteenth, and Fifteenth Amendments, individually and collectively, demanded profound political and social change. Eventual meaning would be defined by jurisprudential glossing, with the Fourteenth Amendment eventually becoming an especially prolific source of constitutional jurisprudence and eminent departure point for congressional action. The provision with the most immediate and obvious impact, however, was the Thirteenth Amendment which permanently foreclosed slavery.

Early readings of the Reconstruction amendments reflect an abiding discomfort with and even resistance to enhancement of the federal government's interest and power. Although quick in acknowledging the amendments' primary concern with the nation's new citizens, the Supreme Court soon fashioned doctrine that limited their utility with respect to core interests but increased their potential for facilitating other aims. Early jurisprudence thus reflected the nation's drifting interest from racial affairs to other priorities such as economic growth and development. Early case law and practical constitutional meaning thus developed as a function of superseding considerations and racial fatigue.

The scope of the Thirteenth Amendment had been a source of controversy and uncertainty almost since its ratification. As noted in the preceding chapter, many framers considered it a dubious predicate for establishing or securing civil rights. To alleviate precisely that doubt,

Congress had reenacted the Civil Rights Act of 1866 pursuant to the Fourteenth Amendment. Whether the Thirteenth Amendment prohibited more than personal bondage or could be a basis for civil rights legislation ultimately was to be resolved by the Supreme Court. Congress's final significant Reconstruction enactment, the Civil Rights Act of 1875, was based on the Thirteenth and Fourteenth Amendments. The act prohibited discrimination in public accommodations, much like the Civil Rights Act of 1964. In 1883, however, the Court in the *Civil Rights Cases* determined that such discrimination did not constitute a badge of slavery or servitude.[1] The Thirteenth Amendment[2] was found inadequate as a basis for the 1875 act, and Congress's enforcement powers were accordingly trimmed.

For several decades, the Thirteenth Amendment was considered pertinent only to the extent a nexus was discerned between a challenged practice and the institution of slavery itself.[3] Not until the middle of the twentieth century, after having vitalized the Fourteenth Amendment with anti-discrimination principles, did the Court finally revisit the question of whether the Thirteenth Amendment affords a sufficient basis for civil rights legislation. Specifically at issue, in *Jones v. Alfred H. Mayer Co.*, was whether Congress could ban private racial discrimination in the sale of real estate on the grounds it constituted a badge or incident of slavery.[4] The statute under review, 42 U.S.C. § 1982, descended directly from the Civil Rights Act of 1866. Contrary to its restrictive approach and displacement of legislation nearly a century earlier, the Court afforded Congress broad latitude in determining what constituted "badges and incidents of slavery" and enacting legislation rationally related to eliminating them.[5]

In *Griffin v. Breckenridge*, the Court emphasized that unlike the other Reconstruction amendments the Thirteenth Amendment did not impose a state action requirement.[6] Victims of a racially motivated attack on a public road in Mississippi during the height of the civil rights movement thus were allowed to sue under federal law.[7] The pertinent statute, 42 U.S.C. § 1985(3), afforded relief from private racially inspired efforts to interfere with equal protection or privileges and immunities and was construed specifically to secure the right of interstate travel.[8] Although previous interpretations of the law had required state action,[9] the Court found no such qualification to the extent the enactment was rooted in the Thirteenth Amendment.[10]

The aims of the Civil Rights Act of 1866 were further invigorated and ties to the Thirteenth Amendment renewed when the Court, in *Runyon v. McCrary*, upheld a provision prohibiting racial discrimination in making and enforcing private contracts.[11] It thus found that a private school could not deny black students the right to contract for an education.[12] Pursuant to 42 U.S.C. § 1981, the Court determined that the "right 'to make and enforce contracts' is violated if a private offeror refuses to extend to a Negro, solely because he is a Negro, the same opportunity to enter into contracts as he extends to white offerees."[13]

The validity and scope of the law were revisited more than a decade later in *Patterson v. McLean Credit Union*.[14] The consequent decision reaffirmed that Section 1981 prohibited racial discrimination in the making and enforcement of contracts.[15] Although the law was found applicable to employment contracts, the Court qualified its reach in finding that the provision did not extend to post-formation racial harassment by an employer.[16]

Despite enhanced congressional latitude for legislation pursuant to the Thirteenth Amendment, litigation has been less extensive and doctrine more circumscribed than under the Fourteenth Amendment. The narrower perimeters may reflect the Thirteenth Amendment's more obviously discrete focus, the early curtailment of its operation, and the absence of an inherent limiting principle equivalent to a state action requirement. Recent Supreme Court decisions demonstrate a continuing disinclination to animate the amendment forcefully.

In *City of Memphis v. Greene*, the Court was unmoved by arguments that erection of a street barrier, routing black traffic around a white neighborhood, constituted a "restraint on the liberty of black citizens that is in any sense comparable to the odious practice the Thirteenth Amendment was designed to eradicate."[17] Despite the city's long and not too distant history of formal segregation and the evident racial impact, the Court was satisfied that racially neutral safety considerations justified the traffic diversion measure.[18]

The Court also has indicated that legislation enacted pursuant to the Thirteenth Amendment is subject to significant limiting principles. In *General Building Contractors Association, Inc. v. Pennsylvania*, the Court determined that a Section 1981 offense did not exist without proof of discriminatory intent.[19] Given the identical origins of Sections 1981 and 1982, it would follow that the discriminatory motive requirement would apply to both. Such a standard is consistent with criteria that define modern equal protection review. As discussed in Chapter 6, however, discerning motive is a vexing exercise to the extent intent may be hidden, mixed, or impossible to identify. It thus represents a qualifying standard of major proportion.

The Thirteenth Amendment was introduced in response to an institution that characterized and defined a discrete region. By contrast, the Fifteenth Amendment operated against general inclinations and methodologies for excluding blacks from voting. In 1869, when the Fifteenth Amendment was introduced, only twenty states gave blacks the right to vote. Half of those were southern states obligated to provide such rights in exchange for readmission to the union. Proposals for extending the franchise to blacks consistently had been defeated in northern states, where opposition remained so intense that Republicans in 1868 advocated black suffrage as a function of federal law in the South but state determination in the North. Supporters fought hard for the amendment, and its ratification was narrowly secured. Significant support for the amendment was prompted by the sense that, with voting rights assured, the nation could dispatch the problem of race. The Fifteenth Amendment thus confronted a culture that had extended the franchise as a function of convenience rather than enthusiasm.

Within a year of the amendment's ratification, Congress enacted enforcement legislation. The Force Acts criminalized public or private impairment of the right to vote and provided for federal supervision of registration processes and certification of election results.[20] Although reflecting genuine enforcement commitment, the laws were soon victimized by southern resistance, the nation's shifting attention and priorities, and the eventual repeal of statutory conspiracy provisions in 1894.

Judicial review of Fifteenth Amendment claims, until the middle of the twentieth century, was largely unproductive. The Supreme Court refused, for instance, to read the provision as prohibiting private interference with voting rights.[21] The distinction between private and public action seemed largely immaterial. In *Giles v. Harris*, the Court concluded that it would be "pointless" to intervene, even if a state refused to register black voters.[22] Confronted in 1903 with a constitutional mandate and state disrespect for it, the Court declined to order what it sensed would be ignored.[23] The Court thus reckoned with manifest racism by accommodating it and advising, in Justice Holmes' words, that "relief from a great political wrong, if done, as alleged by the people of a State and the State itself, must be given by them or by the legislature and the political department of the government of the United States."[24]

For the better part of the twentieth century, the Court remained mostly unresponsive to racially inspired interference with voting rights. Consistent with its endorsement of official segregation, the Court allowed the operation of devices calculated to exclude blacks from meaningful civil and political participation. Methods of disfranchisement—such as poll taxes, literacy and general knowledge tests, property requirements, and character qualifications—effectively served their racially exclusionary purpose and were generally upheld by the Court.[25] Impediments, unless overtly race-dependent, withstood constitutional challenge even into the desegregation era. In *Guinn v. United States*, the Court invalidated a literacy test that applied by law only to persons qualified to vote in 1867 and thus manifestly excluded blacks.[26] The existence of state action and overt purpose also were critical to decisions, based on the Fourteenth Amendment, invalidating Texas laws that resulted in exclusion of blacks from primary elections. The Court struck down enactments establishing all-white primaries[27] and enabling political parties to exclude blacks.[28] By the middle of the century, the Court had emphasized the linkage of party-run primaries to general elections and found racially based exclusions and restrictions offensive also to the Fifteenth Amendment.[29]

Pursuant to the enforcement powers which the reconstruction amendments afforded, Congress in the decade after *Brown v. Board of Education* renewed its attention to civil rights legislation. Notwithstanding Justice Holmes' observation that "relief from a great political wrong" must come from the legislature, Congress was a generally unproductive source with respect to civil rights. Such inaction and inattention reflected the grip of southern legislators who, under the seniority system, dominated key leadership and committee positions in Congress. As the legislative branch finally began to respond to the law's new direction charted by *Brown*, new enactments secured civil and voting rights. Pursuant to its commerce power and authority to enforce the Fourteenth Amendment, Congress passed the Civil Rights Act of 1964, which prohibits discrimination in public accommodations and facilities, public schools and employment.[30] The act also expedited certain voting rights cases and prohibited various methods that denied the franchise. The 1964 act was preceded by the Civil Rights Act of 1957,[31] authorizing the Justice Department to seek injunctions against racially inspired interference with voting rights, and by the Civil Rights Act of 1960,[32] providing federal access to local voting records and empowering courts to register voters where they had been systematically disfranchised.

Congress eventually adopted the Voting Rights Act of 1965, which established a clear national interest in and provided for federal monitoring of state and local elections.[33] Among other things, the act empowers the Attorney General to review all changes of election qualifications and procedures in states governed by the law. The statute covered jurisdictions (1) where prior to November 1, 1964, a test or device to determine voting rights had been used, and (2) where less than half of the potential voters were registered on the aforementioned date or actually voted in the 1964 presidential election.

The Court in *South Carolina v. Katzenbach* upheld the 1965 act.[34] In so doing, it construed congressional enforcement power broadly and refused to limit legislative reach to violations of the amendment itself. Drawing on necessary and proper clause standards of review, it determined that if Congress's objective is "legitimate . . . [and] within the scope of the constitution, . . . all means which are appropriate, which are plainly adapted to that end, which are not prohibited, but consist with the letter and spirit of the constitution, are constitutional."[35] Pursuant to its most recent extension in 1982, the Voting Rights Act continues to operate in states that historically denied or impaired the franchise on racial grounds.

Thirteenth and Fifteenth Amendment jurisprudence, although spanning more than a century, has been less copious than Fourteenth Amendment case law. Until fairly recently, it also has been bound by standards that limited the amendments' independent significance or cramped congressional enforcement power. The Fourteenth Amendment, in contrast, has been a source of extensive judicial attention and creativity. From the Court's original sense that the amendment was concerned essentially with securing civil rights and equality for the nation's new citizens, to subsequent premises that countenanced "[m]ere discriminations" and official segregation, and then to modern anti-discrimination and color-blind principles, doctrine concerning race has been plentiful, complex, and often convoluted. The Fourteenth Amendment also has proved multidimensional insofar as it has evolved as a source of fundamental rights unenumerated by the Constitution, unrelated to race, and beyond the original vision of the framers. The balance of this chapter will focus on seminal reading and development of the Fourteenth Amendment. Subsequent chapters will cover official segregation, the desegregation mandate and anti-discrimination principles, and race-conscious remediation.

Just as the antebellum Supreme Court had to reckon with the unfinished business of the original framing process, the Court during the latter decades of the nineteenth century had to account for loose ends in the Fourteenth Amendment's creation. Seminal review reflected many of the same tensions and conflicts over redistribution of government power that had been evident during the amendment's drafting stage. Competing against vindication of the new national interest was abiding reverence for the states and for the traditions of federalism. Eventually, the national interest represented by the Fourteenth Amendment was acknowledged and with respect to non-racial concerns actually magnified by the Court. Although its immediate response was to trim some significant documental threads, the Court soon began fashioning a constitutional design created in large part from fabric it supplied and stitched.

Predictive of the Fourteenth Amendment's future elasticity and malleability, the Court's initial interpretive exercise did not pertain to the provision's race-dependent concern. The *Slaughter-House Cases* arose from challenges to a Louisiana law prohibiting all but one slaughterhouse in New Orleans.[36] Even if the litigation seemed to distance principle from race, contemporary reality emphasized the association. The day before the Court rendered its judgment was memorable for the Colfax Massacre in Grant Parish, Louisiana, where a dispute over political power culminated in a white-led attack upon a black-defended courthouse. What followed was what the media described as a "Horrible Massacre" in which multitudes of blacks were shot or burned to death and some whites were killed.[37]

Although obligated to rent space to any butcher who applied, the state-created monopoly at issue in the *Slaughter-House Cases* elicited claims that it interfered with the right to pursue a trade and thus compromised the Fourteenth Amendment. A lower court decision, authored by Justice Bradley sitting as a circuit judge, responded favorably to arguments for a broadly defined set of rights. Bradley described the privileges and immunities clause as comprehending personal freedom "to adopt and follow such lawful industrial pursuit" and affording protection "in the possession and enjoyment of [one's] property."[38] Although conceding that these rights were subject to reasonable regulation pursuant to state police powers, he found the monopoly at odds with the Fourteenth Amendment.[39]

Bradley's expansive interpretation failed to carry a majority of the Supreme Court. In a 5–4 decision authored by Justice Miller, the Court maintained that the Fourteenth Amendment was concerned with establishing "the freedom of the slave race, the security of and firm establishment of that freedom, and the protection of the newly-made free man and citizen from the oppressions of those who had formerly exercised unlimited dominion over him."[40] Despite acknowledging the amendment's concern, the Court construed it in a way that significantly blunted its potential to protect the rights of blacks. The majority opinion reflected an exercise in resistance to expanded federal power. Its characterizations of state and national citizenship were, respectively, generous and parsimonious.

In reading the Fourteenth Amendment, the Court focused initially on the first sentence of Section 1 which "opens with a definition of citizenship—not only citizenship of the United States, but citizenship of the States."[41] Recognizing that the provision introduced the new concept of national citizenship, which further invalidated the *Scott* decision, the Court determined that the primary and indisputable purpose of the clause was "to establish the citizenship of the negro."[42] From the phrase "citizens of the United States and of the State wherein they reside," the Court discerned a concept of citizenship that was bifurcated rather than integrated or intertwined. It found "quite clear, then, that there is a citizenship of the United States and a citizenship of a State, which are distinct from each other and which depend upon different characteristics or circumstances in the individual."[43]

The distinction between national and state citizenship preordained effective and enduring devitalization of the privileges and immunities clause. In further dissecting the provision, the Court determined that the clause "speaks only of the privileges and immunities of citizens of the United States, and does not speak of those of citizens of the several States."[44] Such a reading proved fatal to the plaintiffs' claim, which assumed that the two types of citizenship were the same and the interests secured also were identical.[45] Focusing specifically on language that "[n]o State shall make or enforce any law which shall abridge the privileges or immunities of the citizens of the United States," the Court found it

a little remarkable, if this clause was intended as a protection to the citizen of a State against the legislative power of his own State, that the words "citizen of the State" should be left out when it is so carefully used, and used in contra-distinction to "citizens of the United States" in the very sentence which precedes it. It is too clear for argument that the change in phraseology was adopted understandingly and with a purpose.[46]

The assertion, that the significance of separately referenced citizenships was "too clear for argument," was challenged by the Court's own division. Especially for being only a few years removed from the extensive and well-covered debates over the Fourteenth Amendment, review seemed to reflect a dubious inquiry into the amendment's meaning. Given the manifest intention of the framers to transfer at least the guarantees of the Civil Rights Act of 1866 to the privileges and immunities clause, the exercise suggested more an evasion of than a search for actual purpose.

The Court thus imputed to the framers an intent to place only the privileges and immunities of national citizenship under the protection of the Constitution; those of state citizenship, "whatever they may be, are not intended to have any additional protection by this paragraph of the [Fourteenth] Amendment."[47] Having distinguished between privileges and immunities of federal and state citizenship, the Court concluded that "the latter must rest for their security and protection where they have heretofore rested."[48] The practical intimation was that states, which traditionally had defined the incidents of state citizenship and whose abuses established the need for amendment, were minimally affected by constitutional change.

The majority's interpretation so eviscerated the meaning of the privileges and immunities clause that it remains an insignificant factor in Fourteenth Amendment jurisprudence.[49] As previously noted, the framers contemplated a more profound constitutional retooling. Although the Court's understanding reflected a concern expressed by many congressional supporters of the amendment, judicial reaction was excessive. It had been a commonly articulated aim that the restructuring of federal power not be so comprehensive or intrusive that it displaced or eclipsed the general affairs and interests of the states. Supporters and detractors alike, however, recognized how the Fourteenth Amendment altered the relationship between federal and state government insofar as necessary to account for a specified national interest. Typifying original understanding among congressional supporters was the sense that the amendment "plac[ed] personal liberty and personal rights . . . in the keeping of the nation."[50] Critics complained that it would enable Congress to enact "a civil and criminal code for every state in the Union [and thereby afford it] power to occupy the whole domain of local and state legislation."[51] Even if the warning was exaggerated and unwarranted, the Court responded to it.

Having established two variants of citizenship, which were independently significant, the Court considered the nature of their respective incidents. To determine the content of state privileges and immunities, it referred to Article IV, Section 2, which provides that "[t]he Citizens of each State shall be entitled to all Privileges and Immunities of Citizens in the several States."[52] Because this provision does not itemize what those incidents are, reference to it constituted an analytical departure rather than end point. The Court thus examined an antecedent in the Articles of Confederation and a federal court interpretation of Article IV, Section 2. The Articles of Confederation offered some specifics to the effect that "free inhabitants of each of these States . . . [had] all the privileges and immunities of free citizens in the several States; . . . free ingress and egress to and from any other State, and . . . all the privileges of trade and commerce, subject to the same duties, impositions and restrictions as the inhabitants thereof respectively."[53] Looking to Justice Washington's decision in *Corfield v. Coryell*, the Court found that the "privileges and immunities of citizens of the several States . . . [are those] which are *fundamental*; which belong of right to the citizens of all free governments, and which have at all times been enjoyed by citizens of the several States which compose this Union."[54] Detailing what those rights were would have been a treacherous exercise, because disagreement existed then as now over the nature and breadth of fundamental rights and liberties. The Court, therefore, merely restated the observation in *Corfield* that their enumeration

would be more tedious than difficult . . . [but] may all, however, be comprehended under the following general heads: protection by the government, with the right to acquire and possess property of every kind, and to pursue and obtain happiness and safety, subject, nevertheless, to such restraints as the government may prescribe for the general good of the whole.[55]

The depiction of privileges and immunities incidental to state citizenship specifically identified interests in property and personal security and intimated concern with material self-development. It thus tracked what was staked out originally by the Civil Rights Act of 1866 and by architects of the Fourteenth Amendment. As noted in the preceding chapter, their core concern was with contract and property rights, personal mobility and security, and standing before the law. The 1866 act and the Fourteenth Amendment supposedly had established a new federal accountability for those interests. The judicially crafted distinction between federal and state citizenship, however, effectively delimited the federal zone of interest. The Constitution's preexisting privileges and immunities clause had been understood to mean that whatever rights a state afforded its own citizens, "the same . . . shall be the measure of the rights of citizens of other States within your jurisdiction."[56] It descended from a like provision in the Articles of Confederation intended to ensure "mutual friendship and intercourse among the people of the different States."[57] The Fourteenth Amendment established an interest in equal rights not of citizens from different states but of citizens within the same state. Denial of that achievement delayed the actual shift in power contemplated by the framers and transformed the new privileges and immunities clause into a veritable redundancy.

To its own question, as to whether the Fourteenth Amendment by virtue of the privileges and immunities clause was "to transfer the security and protection of all the civil rights we have mentioned, from the States to the Federal Government," the Court answered negatively.[58] If a contrary conclusion were reached, it warned, state legislative power would be usurped by the Congress and the federal judiciary.[59] At least from the *Slaughter-House* majority's perspective, control of the incidents of citizenship was an all-or-nothing proposition, and it refused to preside over a transfer of the incidents of citizenship from state to federal authority.

By so perceiving the question and its role, the Court failed to recognize that the redistribution already had been ordained and the judiciary itself was impeding implementation. It essentially failed or refused to acknowledge an increased federal role in ensuring rights previously protected exclusively by the states. The Court could have acknowledged the federal interest and, because no question of race had been presented, reached the same result. Instead of a sensitive appraisal that recognized conjunctivity, the Court responded in disjunctive terms that also reflected evasion or misunderstanding. Despite a manifest intention to redefine governmental powers, the Court refused to admit it "in the absence of language which expresses such a purpose too clearly to admit of doubt."[60]

Characterization of the privileges and immunities at issue as incidents of state citizenship[61] predetermined a narrow reading of the meaning of federal citizenship. As depicted by the Court, the privileges and immunities of federal citizenship were notable for their relative lack of profundity. Although not purporting to provide an exhaustive recitation, the Court suggested that federal privileges and immunities included the right

"to come to the seat of government to assert any claim he may have upon that government, to transact any business he may have with it, to seek its protection, to share its offices, to engage in administering its functions...of free access to [the nation's] seaports,...to the sub-treasuries, land-offices, and courts of justice in the several States."...to demand the care and protection of the Federal Government over his life, liberty and property when on the high seas or within the jurisdiction of a foreign government....to peaceably assemble and petition for redress of grievances,...[to assert] the writ of *habeas corpus*....to use the navigable waters of the United States...and all rights secured to our citizens by treaties with foreign nations...[to] become a citizen of any State of the Union by a *bona fide* residence therein....To these may be added the rights secured by the 13th and 15th articles of amendment, and by the other clause of the fourteenth....[62]

Having already determined that the right asserted was an incident of state citizenship, the Court considered it unnecessary to pursue an extensive inquiry into federal privileges and immunities and their significance. The Court nonetheless identified some incidents of federal citizenship if only to defeat possible perception that it recognized none. In acknowledging the reality of federal privileges and immunities, however, the *Slaughter-House* Court further diminished them.

After finishing with the privileges and immunities provision, the Court turned its attention to the due process and equal protection clauses. It specifically rejected any notion that the due process guarantee might operate as a check on state legislative power. Noting that the clause paralleled a like provision in the Fifth Amendment, and was "found in some form of expression in the constitutions of nearly all the States,"[63] the Court refused to enhance due process beyond its traditional function as a guarantor of procedural fairness. It concluded that the due process clause had no new meaning "except so far as the [Fourteenth] Amendment may place the restraining power over the States in this matter in the hands of the Federal Government."[64] Even if reflecting a cautious explication, the Court acknowledged a federal interest in procedural fairness. It repudiated the intimation of *Scott v. Sandford* that the due process guarantee also operated substantively as a check upon legislative power. As the Fourteenth Amendment later evolved and became a source of unanticipated rights and liberties, the general vision of Taney rather than of Justice Miller would inspire the meaning of due process.

With respect to the equal protection clause, the Court had no difficulty discerning its central concern with the nation's new citizens and with devices such as the Black Codes that confounded their status. It observed that "[t]he existence of laws in the States where the newly emancipated negroes resided, which discriminated with gross injustice and hardship against them as a class, was the evil to be remedied by this clause, and by it such laws are forbidden."[65] The Court further acknowledged Congress's power to enforce the guarantee by suitable legislation.[66] It thus recognized a federal interest in prohibiting racially discriminatory legislation. The extent of that concern, however, was not amplified. Rather, the Court merely emphasized the narrow focus of equal protection and related its doubt as to "whether any action of a State not directed by way of discrimination against the negroes as a class, or on account of their race, will ever be held to come within the purview of this provision."[67] The development of equal protection jurisprudence from the middle of the twentieth century onward, invalidating classifications based on gender, alienage, and the marital status of parents and acts impacting fundamental rights, would have been a source of astonishment to the *Slaughter-House* majority. Such results have prompted the observation that "(t)he notion of equal protection as it spreads out tends to lift all to the level of the most favored."[68]

Viewing the Fourteenth Amendment as a whole, the Court asserted that from the republic's inception a line had separated federal and state power and, although never well defined, "continued from that day to this."[69] It noted that the first eleven amendments to the Constitution reflected a dominant concern with the exercise of federal power and that the Civil War revealed "the true danger to the perpetuity of the Union" presented by the states.[70] From that backdrop, Justice Miller gleaned an overarching principle "that the existence of the States with powers for domestic and local government, including the regulation of civil rights—the rights of person and of property—was essential to the perfect working of our complex form of government."[71] In a single paragraph, therefore, Miller disclosed the majority's failure or refusal to acknowledge the constitutional reality that had transpired.

Justice Field may have better perceived, but he still distorted the original vision of the Fourteenth Amendment. In his dissent, Field recognized that the amendment had established federal interests that previously were an exclusive concern of the states. He maintained that the privileges and immunities clause

recognizes in express terms, if it does not create, citizens of the United States, and it makes their citizenship dependent upon the place of their birth, or the fact of their adoption, and not upon the Constitution or laws of any State or the condition of their ancestry. A citizen of a State is now only a citizen of the United States residing in that State. The fundamental rights, privileges and immunities which belong to him as a free man and a free citizen, now belong to him as a citizen of the United States, and are not dependent upon his citizenship of any State.[72]

Field recognized the redistributive nature of the Fourteenth Amendment in securing rights against abridgment by the states.[73] Rather than identifying the designation and scope of civil rights as a state function unaffected by the Fourteenth Amendment, Field would have incorporated into the privileges and immunities clause the Civil Rights Act of 1866.[74] Instead of the mostly immaterial and peripheral concerns itemized by the majority, the incidents of federal citizenship as understood by Field included the right "to make and enforce contracts, to sue, be parties and give evidence; to inherit, purchase, lease, sell, hold, and convey real and personal property, and to full and equal benefit of all laws and proceedings for the security of person and property."[75] He also would have included as federal privileges and immunities the itemizations in *Corfield v. Coryell*, which the majority regarded as accoutrements of state citizenship.[76]

Insofar as he would have invalidated the slaughterhouse monopoly as a violation of the Fourteenth Amendment, Field offered an expansive sense of the provision that was as misplaced as the majority's narrow view. As construed by Field, the amendment was a proper source of the municipal law, which the majority feared.[77] Although acknowledging that states could enact reasonable regulation based on their police powers, his failure to defer to the nuisance considerations prompting the challenged law evidenced support for extensive displacement of traditional state concerns.

Justice Bradley, who had authored the lower court opinion, joined Field's dissent but also wrote separately to express his disagreement with the majority. Bradley offered an even more expansive listing of the privileges and immunities of federal citizenship that he considered protected by the Fourteenth Amendment. Referring to the Declaration of Independence, he asserted that the "[r]ights to life, liberty and the pursuit of happiness are equivalent to the rights of life, liberty and property ... [which] are fundamental ... [and] can only be taken away by due process of law."[78] For Bradley, the federal privileges and immunities secured by the Fourteenth Amendment included the Bill of Rights.[79]

Both Bradley and Field were prepared to extend the Fourteenth Amendment beyond its original concern with race. Despite the absence of race-related state action, Field would have found the challenged monopoly an invasion of a federally secured privilege.[80] Bradley suggested violations of the due process guarantee, which he viewed in substantive terms, and of the equal protection clause.[81] The conclusions represented analysis as profound in its overreaching as the majority's was in its narrowness.

The competition of ideas reflected by the divergent opinions in the *Slaughter-House Cases* continues to characterize and influence Fourteenth Amendment jurisprudence to this day. Although Justices Field and Bradley were in the minority, their opinions predicted in significant part the Fourteenth Amendment's eventual meaning. Consistent with the dissenters' position, the Court soon recognized and protected economic rights unrelated to racial considerations. Because the privileges and immunities clause had been eviscerated, however, such reckoning was pursuant to Bradley's concept of due process rather than Field's notion of federal privileges.[82] Later in the twentieth century, the liberty component of the due process clause became the source of substantive personal rights including those of privacy and personal autonomy.[83] Equal protection, although largely ignored until the middle of the twentieth century, eventually functioned as a significant proscription against racial and other classifications.[84]

The dissenting justices thereby previewed the Fourteenth Amendment's future utility in accounting for interests beyond the framers' original expectation. Justice Miller emphasized the provision's central concern with race. By diminishing the privileges and immunities clause's essential significance, and leaving responsibility for civil rights and their enforcement with the states, the Court effectively delimited the possibility of federal remedies for state-caused deprivations. Between the dissenters' expansive interpretation that diluted attention to race and the majority's hypertechnical and restrictive reading, many racially based deprivations of basic rights subsequently escaped constitutional radar. Such a result may not have been disturbing to a society whose interest in racial justice had diminished in inverse proportion to its enhanced attention to national reunification and economic development. Subsequent decisions reflected the altered priorities but, like the *Slaughter-House* ruling, slighted the concerns of an amended constitution. Not until the middle of the twentieth century was the Fourteenth Amendment activated in terms that meaningfully reckoned with its core agenda. Until then, jurisprudence would reflect the distortions of the *Slaughter-House* majority and minority opinions which respectively complicated the quest for racial justice and established embryonic concepts of economic and other unenumerated liberties.

The Supreme Court in 1877 provided further doctrinal impetus to the eventual transformation of the Fourteenth Amendment into a guarantor of economic liberty. In *Munn v. Illinois*, it upheld a state law regulating the rates of grain elevators.[85] Despite upholding the enactment, the Court noted that it accounted for a special public interest and stressed that "in mere private contracts, . . . what is reasonable must be ascertained judicially."[86] The *Munn* decision thus previewed the future direction of substantive due process review, which by the early twentieth century had sanctified liberty of contract. A year before *Munn*, however, the Court disclosed how the Fourteenth Amendment's significance to issues of race would diminish in inverse proportion to the attention afforded general economic rights.

Jurisprudential minimization of the Fourteenth Amendment's significance with respect to race became manifest as pertinent claims for relief emerged. In *United States v. Cruikshank*, the Court vitiated Congress's power to enact laws making interference with another person's civil rights a criminal offense.[87] The *Cruikshank* case resulted from the afore-mentioned racially inspired Colfax Massacre.[88] Despite the backdrop of brutality and the absence of state control or intervention, the Court found that the interest at issue was a state rather than a federal concern.[89] It described the Fourteenth Amendment as a guarantee that "adds nothing to the rights of one citizen as against another . . . [but] simply furnishes an additional guaranty against any encroachment by the States upon the fundamental rights which belong to every citizen as a member of society."[90] Depreciation of a federal interest in criminal activity, as it related to Fourteenth Amendment considerations, reflected a sense that the provision was concerned only with state action and that regulation of crime was a local concern. The decision had profound consequences to the extent it eliminated any official check during ensuing decades on the terrorism and official segregation that would define racial reality especially in the South.

Several years later, in *United States v. Harris*, the Court considered a challenge to the Civil Rights Act of 1871.[91] The act was the basis for federal prosecution of state law enforcement officials charged with conspiracy to deny equal protection of the laws to a person who, while in custody, had been beaten to death.[92] Citing to *Cruikshank*, the Court reasserted that "[t]he duty of protecting all citizens in the enjoyment of an equality of rights was originally assumed by the States, and it remains there."[93]

The Fourteenth Amendment's imminent but selective devolution was not apparent in the first racially significant examination of its substantive meaning. To the contrary, its decision in *Strauder v. West Virginia* suggested the amendment had meaningful potential to reckon with discrimination.[94] In *Strauder*, the Court considered the constitutionality of a state law excluding blacks from juries.[95] That law directly implicated the Fourteenth Amendment, which, the Court observed, "cannot be understood without keeping in view the history of the times when [it] was adopted, and the general objects they plainly sought to accomplish."[96] According to Justice Strong, who wrote the majority opinion, the amendment was enacted to protect the interests of an exploited and disadvantaged race, which required special attention in order to prevent further oppression. Referring to experience immediately following abolition, Strong noted that

it required little knowledge of human nature to anticipate that those who had long been regarded as an inferior and subject race would, when suddenly raised to the rank of citizenship, be looked upon with jealousy and positive dislike, and that state laws might be enacted or enforced to perpetuate the distinctions that had before existed. Discriminations against them had been habitual. It was well known that, in some States, laws making such discriminations then existed, and others might be well expected. The colored race, as a race, was abject and ignorant, and in that condition was unfitted to command the respect of those who had superior intelligence. Their training had left them mere children, and as such they needed the protection which a wise government extends to those who are unable to protect themselves. They especially needed protection against unfriendly action in the States where they were resident. It was in view of these considerations the Fourteenth Amendment was framed and adopted.[97]

The *Strauder* Court thus discerned an original purpose to ensure equal enjoyment of civil rights and to provide "the protection of the general government, in that enjoyment, whenever it should be denied by the States."[98] This perception of the Fourteenth Amendment comported with the *Slaughter-House* Court's depiction of its "one pervading purpose" as accounting for "the freedom of the slave race."[99] The Court further determined that, given the amendment's remedial purpose, "it is to be construed liberally, to carry out the purposes of its framers."[100] Focusing specifically on the equal protection clause, Justice Strong construed it as "declaring that the law in the States shall be the same for the black as for the white; that all persons, whether colored or white, shall stand equal before the laws of the States."[101] Consistent with its standard of liberal construction, the Court found that equal protection not only operated as a prohibition against state action but also afforded "a positive immunity, or right, most valuable to the colored race."[102] It adduced "the right to exemption from unfriendly legislation against them distinctively, as colored; exemption from legal discriminations, implying inferiority in civil society, lessening the security of their enjoyment of the rights which others enjoy, and discriminations which are steps towards reducing them to the condition of a subject race."[103]

Official exclusion of blacks by law from juries resulted in the first finding of a racially significant violation of the Fourteenth Amendment.[104] Because the statute in question excluded citizens on the basis of race, the Court perceived it as "practically a brand upon [black persons], affixed by the law, an assertion of their inferiority, and a stimulant to that race prejudice which is an impediment to securing to individuals of the race that equal justice which the law aims to secure to all others."[105]

The *Strauder* decision represented the first invalidation of a racially discriminatory law under the Fourteenth Amendment specifically and under the Constitution in general. In a companion case, *Ex parte Virginia*, the Court determined that equal protection operated not only against legislative classifications but also against discrimination by state officials.[106] It thus discerned a constitutional violation when blacks were excluded from juries as a function of a judge's determination rather than of statutory prescription. The Court specifically determined that no agency of the State, or of the officers or agents by whom its powers are exerted, shall deny to any person within its jurisdiction the equal protection of the laws. Whoever, by virtue of public position under a State government deprives another of property, life, or liberty without due process of law, or denies or takes away the equal protection of the laws, violates the constitutional inhibition; and as he acts in the name and for the State, and is clothed with the State's power, his act is that of the State.[107]

As a consequence of *Ex parte Virginia*, equal protection operated not just against legislatures, whose enactment of the Black Codes had identified the need for the guarantee, but also against the states generally. The *Strauder* decision in particular suggested that the Fourteenth Amendment provided a direct action against racial discrimination. It acknowledged not only a proper federal interest but also a need on the part of the nation's new citizens for special constitutional attention. The Court also established a standard of review that, although soon moribund, eventually would provide a premise for defeating official segregation. The determination that categorical exclusion of blacks from juries "impl[ied] inferiority" anticipated the principle, subscribed to in 1954, that official segregation communicated a diminished worth and thus was inherently unequal.[108]

In the decades between *Strauder* and *Brown*, courts would be generally insensitive to racially significant connotations of official policy and actions. Special legislative or jurisprudential concern for the nation's new citizens also would be repudiated a few years hence. Even contemporaneous with *Strauder* and *Ex parte Virginia*, the Court disclosed that Fourteenth Amendment review would be qualified by significant limiting principles.

In *Virginia v. Rives*, the Court considered the indictments and convictions of two black defendants by all-white juries.[109] Unlike *Strauder* and *Ex parte Virginia*, evidence did not establish that the absence of black jurors was attributable to state law or action. It was argued that no black ever had served on a jury in the county.[110] Nevertheless, the Court distinguished between protection against actual discrimination and "a right to have the jury composed in part of colored men."[111] It thus established a significant qualification of the *Strauder* premise, not unlike what would limit the anti-discrimination principle that would evolve in the middle of the twentieth century. For the *Rives* Court, discrimination did not present a constitutional concern unless it was officially prescribed by law or official policy. Although acknowledging that a formal statute would implicate the Fourteenth Amendment, if denial of access to the judicial process was racially inspired, it refused to attach the same significance to ministerial acts of "subordinate officer[s]."[112] The Court failed to probe beyond outward appearances of racial neutrality. Because the law on its face did not discriminate and by its terms allowed and even required blacks to serve on juries,[113] the Court refused to inquire further into motive or effect.

The *Rives* case imposed on plaintiffs the heavy burden of demonstrating that discrimination was the actual function of official action. Because a tradition of exclusion and disproportionate impact was rejected as grounds for establishing discrimination, the result presaged the problem that would confound the desegregation mandate and the anti-discrimination principle a century later. As discussed in Chapters 5 and 6, modern discriminatory purpose criteria have cramped the equal protection guarantee in a similar fashion. The problem now, as then, is that wrongful intent may be hidden, and only the most obvious variants of discrimination are subject to identification. The *Rives* decision thus related a lesson that would become pertinent again a century later. Not until the late twentieth century did the Court finally reckon with tactics that continued to operate effectively in excluding blacks from juries.[114]

The *Strauder* decision, although contemporaneously qualified by *Rives*, made a forceful statement on the federal interest represented by the Fourteenth Amendment and the provision's special concern. It was reinforced by the observation, in *Ex parte Virginia*, that the Thirteenth and Fourteenth Amendments "were intended to be, . . . [and] really are, limitations of the power of the States and enlargements of the power of Congress."[115] Racial jurisprudence over the next three-quarters of a century, however, seldom reflected that fundamental realignment. Three years after finding the exclusion of black jurors unconstitutional, the Court rendered a decision challenging not the actual letter but the general spirit of *Strauder*. At issue in the *Civil Rights Cases* was the constitutionality of the Civil Rights Act of 1875,[116] which prohibited discrimination in public venues including "accommodations, advantages, facilities, and privileges of inns, public conveyances on land or water, theaters and other places of public amusement."[117] The cases concerned exclusions of black persons from hotels, theaters, and rail cars. Neither the decision nor the method of review reflected the liberal standard of interpretation advanced in *Strauder*. Rather, the reasoning and result disclosed a growing sense of fatigue with the demands of the Thirteenth and Fourteenth Amendments.

The *Civil Rights Cases* implicated squarely the nature and extent of Congress's enforcement power. In reviewing congressional authority to enact legislation pursuant to the Fourteenth Amendment, the Court determined that legislative power was bound by the terms of Section 1.[118] Noting that the first section of the amendment concerned itself only with state action, it concluded that congressional power was coextensive and thus limited to legislation correcting the effects of state law or action.[119] It did not include authority to create a code of municipal law for the regulation of private rights; but to provide modes of redress against the operation of state laws, and the action of state officers executive or judicial, when these are subversive of the fundamental rights specified in the Amendment.... [L]egislation must ... be predicated upon ... state laws or state proceedings, and be directed to the correction of their operation and effect.[120]

The Court's definition of congressional power thus disclosed the same reluctance, evidenced in the *Slaughter-House* decision, to sanction the redistribution of power provided for by the Fourteenth Amendment. Unlike the *Slaughter-House* Court, which expressed general resistance to the transfer, the *Civil Rights* Court's counteraction was selective. To the extent Fourteenth Amendment doctrine was evolving to account for general interests such as economic liberty, the limitation of legislative power effectively repudiated the amendment's central meaning.

The emerging double standard of Fourteenth Amendment review was denoted not only by contrasting analytical criteria but also by authorship of the majority opinion. As noted previously, Justice Bradley in the *Slaughter-House Cases* had advanced the most expansive vision of the Fourteenth Amendment. In contrast to the broad understanding he had articulated a decade before, Bradley's opinion for the Court in the *Civil Rights Cases* expressed concerns reminiscent of those that influenced the *Slaughter-House* majority. He warned that the legislation at issue, if approved, would

establish a code of municipal law regulative of all private rights between man and man in society. It would be to make Congress take the place of the State Legislatures and to supersede them.... In fine, the legislation which Congress is authorized to adopt in this behalf is not general legislation upon the rights of the citizen, but corrective legislation ... as may be necessary and proper for counteracting such laws as the States may adopt or enforce, and which, by the Amendment, they are prohibited from making or enforcing, or such acts and proceedings as the States may commit or take, and which, by the Amendment, they are prohibited from committing or taking.[121]

The articulated concern that Congress would create a comprehensive body of municipal law was overblown, as indicated by the Court's own observation that the Fourteenth Amendment proscribed only "state action of a particular character."[122] The circumscription of congressional power seemed at odds with settled criteria. Necessary and proper standards, purportedly employed, normally result in accommodation rather than limitation of congressional power.[123] The case for liberal construction was supported not only by *Strauder*'s command for a flexible rather than a technical interpretation but also by the constitutional assignment to Congress of an "affirmative power, by *legislation*, to *enforce* an express prohibition upon the States."[124] Still, the Court concluded that the law was fatally defective because it invaded "the domain of local jurisprudence" and was at odds with "the Tenth Amendment . . . which declares that powers not delegated to the United States by the Constitution, nor prohibited by it to the States, are reserved to the States respectively or to the people."[125]

Not only the Fourteenth Amendment itself but also congressional power to enforce it were restricted to instances of state action. The Court emphasized that

[t]he wrongful act of an individual, unsupported by any such authority, is simply a private wrong, or a crime of that individual; an invasion of the rights of the injured party, it is true, whether they affect his person, his property or his reputation; but if not sanctioned in some way by the State, or not done under state authority, his rights remain in full force, and may presumably be vindicated by resort to the laws of the State for redress. An individual cannot deprive a man of his right to vote, to hold property, to buy and to sell, to sue in the courts or to be a witness or a juror; he may, by force or fraud, interfere with the enjoyment of the right in a particular case; he may commit an assault against the person, or commit murder, or use ruffian violence at the polls, or slander the good name of a fellow citizen; but, unless protected in these wrongful acts by some shield of state law or state authority, he cannot destroy or injure the right; he will only render himself amenable to satisfaction or punishment; and amenable therefor to the laws of the State where the wrongful acts are committed.[126]

Because the federal law extended primarily and directly to activities within the traditional concern of the state, the Court determined that Congress had exceeded its constitutional grasp and wrongly arrogated powers not belonging to it. The Court's reasoning manifested continuing reservations over the extension of federal powers to areas of traditional state concern. Such resistance, however, did not reflect its evolving disposition toward displacement of state power affecting general economic activity. Critical to the increasingly bifurcated standard of review was a detectable sense of diminishing patience with the problems that had necessitated the Reconstruction amendments. Although perhaps less palpable in the Court's Fourteenth Amendment reasoning, race weariness was manifest in its Thirteenth Amendment analysis.

In considering whether passage of the Civil Rights Act of 1875 was justified under Thirteenth Amendment enforcement power, the Court acknowledged that Congress had authority to enact legislation necessary and proper for eradicating slavery and its badges and incidents.[127] It concluded, however, that national legislative power under the amendment did not extend to racial discrimination in public accommodations.[128] As the Court observed, "[i]t would be running the slavery argument into the ground, to make it apply to every act of discrimination which a person may see fit to make."[129] The point emphasized the Court's disinterest in the Thirteenth Amendment as a means for reckoning not only with slavery but also with its immediate legacy.

Although denying Congress the power to reach private discrimination, the Court suggested that a different result would be reached if the exclusion were a product of "unjust discrimination" by the states.[130] The distinction between private and official discrimination, however, was less precise than the Court may have assumed. As modern civil rights legislation has assumed, differentiation between sources of discrimination has less practical significance when the venue itself is public in nature. Even if the Court had been willing to forego the dubious distinction, it is doubtful that it was prepared to recognize a basis for constitutional attention. Reflecting society's general disposition toward the unfinished business of racial justice, the Court expressed its impatience and diminished interest. It accordingly observed that

[w]hen a man has emerged from slavery, and by the aid of beneficent legislation has shaken off the inseparable concomitants of that state, there must be some stage in the progress of his elevation when he takes the rank of a mere citizen, and ceases to be the special favorite of the laws, and when his rights, as a citizen or a man, are to be protected in the ordinary modes by which other men's rights are protected.[131]

This comment effectively indicated that, at least from the Court's perspective, the process of Reconstruction was finished, and the time for special attention had passed.

Compounding the impression of fatigue and impatience that the opinion disclosed was a sense that the contested exclusionary policies and practices simply were not significant. Noting that "thousands of free colored people" prior to abolition enjoyed basic rights, and "no one . . . thought" them compromised by discrimination in public accommodations or denial of certain privileges afforded whites,[132] the Court characterized the racial classifications as "[m]ere discriminations."[133] The depiction presaged the Court's insensitivity to the significance of exclusionary policies that would evidence themselves more profoundly a decade later when official segregation was challenged. Reduction of the contested policies and practices to a level of constitutional insignificance revealed that, even if basic civil rights and equality had been enshrined in the nation's charter document, society in general and the Court in particular had yet to pursue seriously the type of inquiry that would reveal the cultural impediments to meaningful application of the Fourteenth Amendment.

If left to Justice Harlan, who dissented from the judgment and opinion, Congress's enforcement power would have been delineated consistent with the liberal reading suggested by *Strauder* and eventually accepted by the Court in the late 1960s. Harlan regarded the burdens and disabilities of slavery broadly and as a legitimate object of congressional attention. Because slavery was what prompted the Thirteenth Amendment, and the institution was grounded in presumptions of racial inferiority, he argued that newly delineated freedoms were empty without immunity against and protection from all discrimination burdening civil rights.[134] Harlan argued that Congress, pursuant to its enforcement power, could enact laws protecting persons against "deprivation, *because of their race*, of any civil rights granted to other freemen in the same State."[135]

Significant for Harlan, at least with respect to the reach of congressional power, was the context of the challenged discriminatory policies and practices. From his perspective, distinguishing between public and private discrimination in the contexts at issue was an essentially procrustean exercise. He observed that railroads were created for a public purpose and access to them was critical to exercising personal liberty, which included "the power of locomotion, of changing situation or removing one's person . . . without restraint."[136] To the extent the right was impaired by racial discrimination, regardless of its source, Harlan perceived an imposition "which lay at the very foundation of the institution of slavery."[137] He described an innkeeper's function as "*quasi* public employment . . . [which] forbids him from discriminating against any person . . . on account of the race or color of that person."[138] With respect to regulated places of public amusement, Harlan maintained that government licensing "imports, in law, equality of right, at such places, among all members of that public."[139] To conclude otherwise would mean "that the common municipal government of all the people may, in the exertion of its powers, conferred for the benefit of all, discriminate or authorize discrimination against a particular race, solely because of its former condition of servitude."[140]

Harlan's inquiry into the nature of public carriers, inns, and theaters suggested that distinctions between state and private action were not especially significant. His insight was particularly relevant for future Fourteenth Amendment analysis, which, unlike Thirteenth Amendment analysis, requires determination of whether a challenged action is public or private. Jurisprudence eventually would comport more with Harlan's view, although even contemporary case law has refused to regard mere licensing or regulation as grounds for state action.[141] While suggesting that congressional power could reach quasi-public action, Harlan stopped short of the modern view that enables Congress to reach purely private conduct.[142]

Given Harlan's understanding that Congress could prohibit discrimination in public venues under the Thirteenth Amendment, his willingness to allow legislation pursuant to the "enlarged power under the Fourteenth Amendment" followed logically.[143] In delineating what he considered the proper ambit of legislative power, Harlan referred to the specific and unprecedented congressional charge "to enforce '*the provisions of this article*' of Amendment... — *all* of the provisions — affirmative and prohibitive."[144] Given this express assignment of legislative authority, he considered it unnecessary to correlate the enforcement powers of Section 5 to the substantive scope of Section 1. The charge to Congress indicated to him a broad mandate for enforcement "by means of legislation, operating throughout the entire Union, to guard, secure, and protect that right."[145]

Harlan offered a competing understanding of the Fourteenth Amendment in general. For him, the concept of privileges and immunities established constitutional security against racial discrimination. In considering the privileges and immunities conferred by the amendment, he maintained that

[t]here is one, if there be no other: exemption from race discrimination in respect of any civil right belonging to citizens of the white race in the same State.... Citizenship in this country necessarily imports at least equality of civil rights among citizens of every race in the same State. It is fundamental in American citizenship that, in respect of such rights, there shall be no discrimination by the State or its officers, or by individuals or corporations exercising public functions or authority, against any citizen because of his race or previous condition of servitude.[146]

Harlan thus related a constitutional vision that would not be actualized for several more decades. He also criticized the majority's cramped reading of congressional power and consequently "anomalous result."[147]

In accommodating slavery prior to the Civil War, Congress had enacted and the Court had upheld laws that operated directly on states and private persons. Fugitive slave legislation, discussed in Chapter 1, was sustained as a legitimate exercise of an implied albeit dubious power. As Harlan put it:

why shall the hand of Congress be tied, so that — under an express power, by appropriate legislation, to enforce a constitutional provision granting citizenship — it may not... bring the whole power of this Nation to bear upon States and their officers, and upon such individuals and corporations exercising public functions as assume to abridge, impair, or deny rights confessedly secured by the supreme law of the land?[148]

Finally, Harlan took issue with the Court's perception that the nation's new citizens no longer merited special legal attention.[149] He found the majority's sense of favoritism inapt, insofar as the civil rights legislation at issue protected "citizens of every race and color."[150] To the extent they might experience discrimination, Harlan noted, the law also accounted for them.[151] It would not be for nearly another century, as discussed in Chapter 6, that claims of reverse discrimination would clarify in the Court's mind that equal protection interests can cut in more than one way. For several decades after the *Civil Rights Cases*, however, courts largely refused to take seriously Harlan's admonition that "there cannot be, in this republic, any class of human beings in practical subjection to another class, with power in the latter to dole out to the former just such privileges as they may choose to grant."[152]

The *Civil Rights Cases* decision disclosed an enduring but increasingly convoluted tension in the Fourteenth Amendment's early operation. The majority opinion, like the *Slaughter-House Cases* decision, reflected fidelity to traditional premises and understandings of government power in the federalist system. It expressed discomfort with and resistance to a constitutional assignment of power perceived as the step toward a congressionally crafted "code of municipal law for the regulation of private rights."[153] Such reluctance to allow inroads into traditional state responsibilities and functions, when the context was racially significant, contrasted with the Court's evolution toward doctrine that displaced general state economic regulation. The federal interest reflected by the Fourteenth Amendment thus was defined expansively, but not broadly enough to reckon with racial discrimination and the consequent compromise of civil status and rights.

The first decade of racial jurisprudence pursuant to a revised constitution limited federal interest to discrimination that was indisputably official and gross. The possibility of establishing a Fourteenth Amendment violation would diminish further when, as discussed in the following chapter, official segregation was found reasonable and constitutional. The next seventy years would confirm the pertinence of Harlan's query as to whether "the recent Amendments be splendid baubles, thrown out to delude those who deserved fair and generous treatment at the hands of the Nation."[154]

NOTES

1. Civil Rights Cases, 109 U.S. 3, 25 (1883). The Court also determined that the legislation was not supported by the Fourteenth Amendment. *See infra* notes 116–54 and accompanying text.

2. *Id.* at 25.

3. *See* Hodges v. United States, 203 U.S. 1 (1906).

4. Jones v. Alfred H. Mayer Co., 392 U.S. 409 (1968).

5. *Id.* at 439–41.

6. Griffin v. Breckenridge, 403 U.S. 88 (1971).

7. *Id.* at 103–04.

8. *Id.* at 105–06.

9. *See id.* at 92–95 (citing Collins v. Handyman, 341 U.S. 651, 661 (1951)).

10. *Id.* at 104–06.

11. Runyon v. McCrary, 427 U.S. 160 (1976).

12. *Id.* at 170–71, 179.

13. *Id.* at 170–71.

14. 109 S. Ct. 2363 (1989).

15. *Id.* at 2370–72.

16. *Id.* at 2372–73.

17. Memphis v. Greene, 451 U.S. 100, 128–29 (1981).

18. *Id.* at 126–27.

19. General Building Contractors Association, Inc. v. Pennsylvania, 458 U.S. 375, 391 (1982).

20. 16 Stat. 170, 433 (1870).

21. *See* United States v. Cruikshank, 92 U.S. (2 Otto) 542 (1876); United States v. Reese, 92 U.S. (2 Otto) 214 (1876).

22. Giles v. Harris, 189 U.S. 475, 488 (1903).

23. *Id.*

24. *Id.*

25. *E.g.,* Breedlove v. Suttles, 302 U.S. 277 (1937).

26. Guinn v. United States, 238 U.S. 347 (1915).

27. *See* Nixon v. Herndon, 273 U.S. 536 (1927).

28. *See* Nixon v. Condon, 286 U.S. 73 (1932).

29. *See* Terry v. Adams, 345 U.S. 461 (1953); Smith v. Allwright, 321 U.S. 649 (1944); United States v. Classic, 313 U.S. 299 (1941).

30. Civil Rights Act of 1964, 42 U.S.C. §§ 2000a to 2000b–3 (public accommodations and facilities); §§ 2000d to 2000d–6(d) (public education); §§ 2000e to 2000e–2(j) (employment).

31. 71 Stat. 634.

32. 74 Stat. 86.

33. 42 U.S.C. § 1973 to 1973dd–6.

34. South Carolina v. Katzenbach, 383 U.S. 301 (1966).

35. *Id.* at 326 (quoting McCulloch v. Maryland, 17 U.S. (4 Wheat.) 316, 321 (1819)).

36. Slaughter-House Cases, 83 U.S. (16 Wall.) 36 (1873).

37. *See* C. Fairman, VII History of the Supreme Court of the United States, Reconstruction and Reunion, pt. 2, at 261–62 (1987).

38. Live-Stock Dealers & Butchers Association v. Crescent City Live-Stock Landing & Slaughterhouse Co., 15 Fed. Cas. 649, 652 (C.C.D. La. 1870).

39. *Id.* at 652–53.

40. Slaughter-House Cases, 83 U.S. (16 Wall.) at 71.

41. *Id.* at 72.

42. *Id.* at 73.

43. *Id.* at 74.

44. *Id.*

45. *Id.*

46. *Id.*

47. *Id.*

48. *Id.* at 75.

49. The privileges and immunities clause was relied on to invalidate a state law in Colgate v. Harvey, 296 U.S. 404 (1935). Even that single usage was repudiated, however, in Madden v. Kentucky, 309 U.S. 83 (1940).

50. Cong. Globe, 39th Cong., 1st Sess. (1866) (Rep. Garfield).

51. *Id.* at 1414–15 (Sen. Davis).

52. Slaughter-House Cases, 83 U.S. (16 Wall.) at 76–77; U.S. Const. art. IV, § 2, cl. 1.

53. Slaughter-House Cases, 83 U.S. (16 Wall.) at 75 (quoting Articles of Confederation, art. IV).

54. *Id.* at 76 (quoting Corfield v. Coryell, 6 F. Cas. 546, 551 (1823)) (emphasis in Slaughter-House opinion).

55. *Id.* (*quoting* Corfield v. Coryell, 6 F. Cas. at 551–52).

56. *Id.* at 77.

57. *Id.* at 75.

58. *Id.* at 77.

59. *Id.* at 77–78.

60. *Id.*

61. *Id.* at 80.

62. *Id.* at 79–80.

63. *Id.*

64. *Id.*

65. *Id.* at 81.

66. *Id.*

67. *Id.*

68. C. Fairman, *supra* note 37, at 134.

69. Slaughter-House Cases, 83 U.S. (16 Wall.) at 81–82. As a provision for that race and that emergency, the Court emphasized that "a strong case would be necessary for its application to any other." *Id.*

70. *Id.* at 82.

71. *Id.*

72. *Id.* at 95 (Field, J., dissenting).

73. *Id.* at 95–96 (Field, J., dissenting).

74. *Id.* at 96–97 (Field, J., dissenting).

75. *Id.* at 96 (Field, J., dissenting) (quoting Civil Rights Act of 1866, § 1).

76. *Id.* at 97 (Field, J., dissenting).

77. *Id.* at 77–78 (majority opinion).

78. *Id.* at 116 (Bradley, J., dissenting).

79. *Id.* at 118–19 (Bradley, J., dissenting).

80. *Id.* at 105–06 (Field, J., dissenting); *id.* at 122 (Bradley, J., dissenting).

81. *Id.* (Bradley, J., dissenting).

82. *E.g.,* Lochner v. New York, 198 U.S. 45 (1905).

83. *E.g.,* Zablocki v. Redhail, 434 U.S. 374 (1978); Moore v. City of East Cleveland, 431 U.S. 494 (1977); Roe v. Wade, 410 U.S. 113 (1973); Griswold v. Connecticut, 381 U.S. 479 (1965).

84. *See* Chapter 5.

85. Munn v. Illinois, 94 U.S. (4 Otto) 113 (1877).

86. *Id.* at 134.

87. United States v. Cruikshank, 92 U.S. (2 Otto) 542, 555 (1876).

88. *See supra* note 37 and accompanying text.

89. United States v. Cruikshank, 92 U.S. (2 Otto) at 555.

90. *Id.* at 554.

91. United States v. Harris, 106 U.S. 629 (1883).

92. *Id.* at 632.

93. *Id.* at 639 (quoting United States v. Cruikshank, 92 U.S. (2 Otto) at 555).

94. Strauder v. West Virginia, 100 U.S. (10 Otto) 303 (1879).

95. *See id.* at 304–05.

96. *Id.* at 306.

97. *Id.*

98. *Id.*

99. *Id.* at 307.

100. *Id.*

101. *Id.*

102. *Id.* at 307–08.

103. *Id.* at 308.

104. *See id.* at 310–12.

105. *Id.* at 308.

106. *Ex parte* Virginia, 100 U.S. (10 Otto) 339 (1879).

107. *Id.* at 347.

108. Brown v. Board of Education, 347 U.S. 483, 495 (1954) (discussed in Chapter 5).

109. Virginia v. Rives, 100 U.S. (10 Otto) 313 (1879).

110. *See id.* at 322.

111. *See id.* at 322–23.

112. *Id.* at 321–22.

113. *See id.* at 320–21.

114. *See* Batson v. Kentucky, 476 U.S. 79 (1986) (prosecutor may not use peremptory challenges in racially discriminatory fashion).

115. *Ex parte* Virginia, 100 U.S. (10 Otto) at 345.

116. *See* Civil Rights Cases, 109 U.S. 3 (1883).

117. *Id.* at 9–10.

118. *Id.* at 11.

119. *Id.* at 11–12.

120. *Id.* at 11.

121. *Id.* at 13–14.

122. *Id.* at 11.

123. *See* McCulloch v. Maryland, 17 U.S. (4 Wheat.) 316 (1819).

124. Civil Rights Cases, 109 U.S. at 45 (Harlan, J., dissenting) (emphasis in original).

125. *Id.* at 15 (majority opinion)

126. *Id.* at 17.

127. *Id.* at 20.

128. *Id.* at 21.

129. *Id.* at 24.

130. *Id.* at 25.
131. *Id.*
132. *Id.*
133. *Id.*
134. *Id.* at 36 (Harlan, J., dissenting).
135. *Id.* (Harlan, J., dissenting) (emphasis in original).
136. *Id.* at 39 (Harlan, J., dissenting) (quoting W. Blackstone).
137. *Id.* (Harlan, J., dissenting).
138. *Id.* at 41 (Harlan, J., dissenting).
139. *Id.* (Harlan, J., dissenting).
140. *Id.* (Harlan, J., dissenting).
141. *See* Jackson v. Metropolitan Edison Co., 419 U.S. 345 (1974); Moose Lodge No. 107 v. Irvis, 407 U.S. 163 (1972).
142. *See* United States v. Guest, 383 U.S. 745 (1966).
143. Civil Rights Cases, 109 U.S. at 43 (Harlan, J., dissenting).
144. *Id.* at 46 (Harlan, J., dissenting) (emphasis in original).
145. *Id.* at 47 (Harlan, J., dissenting).
146. *Id.* at 48 (Harlan, J., dissenting).
147. *Id.* at 53 (Harlan, J., dissenting).
148. *Id.* (Harlan, J., dissenting).
149. *Id.* at 61 (Harlan, J., dissenting).
150. *Id.* (Harlan, J., dissenting).
151. *Id.* at 62 (Harlan, J., dissenting).
152. *Id.* (Harlan, J., dissenting).
153. *Id.* at 11 (majority opinion).
154. *Id.* at 48 (Harlan, J., dissenting).

Chapter 4

Separate But Equal

Segregation by law has been a defining societal feature for the better half of the Fourteenth Amendment's existence. Official segregation of persons on the basis of race represented the formalization and institutionalization of social preferences that the Supreme Court had passed off in the *Civil Rights Cases* as "[m]ere discriminations."[1] State-mandated segregation, unlike the private action previously adjudicated, directly implicated government in the racial classification process. The *Strauder* Court, as discussed in Chapter 3, had indicated discriminations implying inferiority would merit constitutional attention. A few years later, in the *Civil Rights Cases*, the Court found private racial distinctions insignificant and consistent with societal norms. As jurisprudence evolved into the twentieth century, it became evident that the radiations of the *Civil Rights Cases* would be more predictive of segregation's constitutionality than would the intimations of *Strauder*.

Official segregation, as discussed in Chapter 1, was not an invention of the South. Prior to *Scott v. Sandford*, racial segregation of Boston public schools had been upheld.[2] Several years after the *Scott* decision, and consistent with the North's selective repudiation of Taney's opinion, the Ohio legislature also provided for racially separate schooling.[3] Although a northern creation, segregation was well suited to the needs of the South after the eradication of slavery and the displacement of the Black Codes. Florida enacted the first Jim Crow law in 1887, requiring racial separation in public transportation. By the end of the century, official segregation had become comprehensively established in and a defining feature of the South.

In *Plessy v. Ferguson*, the Supreme Court considered the constitutionality of state-enforced segregation.[4] The case presented a challenge to a Louisiana law, enacted in 1890, requiring racially separate rail cars. Specifically, the statute provided

that all railway companies carrying passengers in their coaches in this state shall provide equal but separate accommodations for the white and colored races, by providing two or more passenger coaches for each passenger train, or by dividing the passenger coaches by a partition so as to secure separate accommodations.
. . . [5]

The petitioner in the case was described as a person of "seven eighths Caucasian and one eighth African blood . . . [and in whom] the mixture of colored blood was not discernible."[6]

The Court in *Plessy* rejected contentions that the law violated the Thirteenth and Fourteenth Amendments. Disclosing what a dead letter the Thirteenth Amendment had become, it observed that the provision's inaptness was "too clear for argument."[7] The Court depicted the amendment as concerned with involuntary servitude, only in the limited sense of "a state of bondage; the ownership of mankind as a chattel, or at least the control of the labor and services of one man for the benefit of another, and the absence of a legal right to the disposal of his own person, property, and services."[8] Having limited the Thirteenth Amendment's potential to reckon with the aftereffects of slavery, the Court concluded that

laws implying merely a legal distinction between the white and colored races—a distinction which is founded in the color of the two races, and which must always exist so long as white men are distinguished from the other races by color—has no tendency to destroy the legal equality of the two races, or reestablish a state of involuntary servitude.[9]

The Court's reading of the Thirteenth Amendment validated original concerns that its actual or potential reach was too limited. In the event any doubt remained, the *Plessy* decision confirmed that the amendment extended only to slavery and its most proximate incidents.

Turning to the Fourteenth Amendment, the Court acknowledged a purpose "to enforce the absolute equality of the two races before the law."[10] It maintained, however, that the amendment did not "intend to abolish distinctions based upon color, or to enforce social, as distinguished from political equality, or a commingling of the two races upon terms unsatisfactory to either."[11] The *Strauder* Court had suggested that official classifications implying inferiority were precluded by the Fourteenth Amendment.[12] With respect to laws requiring racial separation in public venues, the *Plessy* Court found that they did not connote inferiority and were "generally, if not universally, recognized as within the competency of the state legislature in the exercise of their police power."[13] As evidence of settled practice, the Court referred to officially sanctioned school segregation in the North and congressionally mandated racial separation in District of Columbia schools.[14]

The constitutionality of official segregation hinged for the Court on whether the state had exercised its police power reasonably, in good faith, and for the public good, rather than "for the annoyance or oppression of a particular class."[15] The majority, however, was unable to discern or unwilling to acknowledge that racial separation by law failed to satisfy those demands. Although finding the case reducible to whether the law was "a reasonable regulation," it determined that "with respect to this, there must necessarily be a large discretion on the part of the legislature."[16] Confirming how deferential its standard of review was, the Court noted that the state was "at liberty to act with reference to the established usages, customs, and traditions of the people, and with a view to the promotion of their comfort, and the preservation of the public peace and good order."[17] It thus accommodated and effectively validated the culture, including its racist conventions and impulses, of official segregation.

Responsive to the possibility that its decision was at odds with *Strauder*, the Court characterized as fallacious "the assumption that the enforced separation of the races stamps the colored race with a badge of inferiority."[18] Any such perception, it suggested, was "not by reason of anything found in the act, but solely because the colored race chooses to put that construction on it."[19] Further militating against displacement of state law was the Court's articulated sense that social prejudices were not to be defeated by legislation; nor would equal rights be secured "by an enforced commingling of the two races."[20] In closing, the Court emphasized what it considered to be the imprudence of tampering with what it previously had characterized as distinctions "in the nature of things."[21] It thus stressed that

legislation is powerless to eradicate social instincts or to abolish distinctions based upon physical differences, and the attempt to do so can only result in accentuating the difficulties of the present situation. If the civil and political rights of both races are equal, one cannot be inferior to the other civilly or politically. If one race is inferior to the other socially, the Constitution of the United States cannot put them on the same plane.[22]

Official segregation had been objected to, albeit unsuccessfully, on the grounds it was a methodology of race-dependent degradation, harass-

ment, and humiliation. The next several decades would demonstrate
that segregation responded to and facilitated precisely the evils disregarded or discounted in *Plessy*. In an essentially legalistic exercise, the
Court nonetheless satisfied itself with the appearance of neat racial symmetry and blamed segregation's victims for any misunderstanding of the
law. As critics have noted, it was the Court that failed to understand the
meaning of segregation and avoided its constitutional significance. Official segregation was a cornerstone of white supremacy, and the notion
that "blacks were inherently inferior was a conviction being stridently
trumpeted by white supremacists from the press, the pulpit, and the
platform, as well as from the legislative halls of the South."[23] Racial
separation as a function of state decree communicated an official sense
of unfitness for full civil status that effectively mocked the terms of
Strauder.

The true nature and significance of official segregation were sensed
and depicted by Justice Harlan, who warned in his dissent that the
majority's decision eventually would prove "as pernicious as the decision
made . . . in the *Dred Scott Case*."[24] For him, the law in question was at
odds "not only with that equality of rights which pertains to citizenship,
national and state, but with the personal liberty enjoyed by every one
within the United States."[25] Harlan pierced segregation's veil of symmetry by stating the obvious. As he put it, "every one knows . . . its origin
and the purpose was not so much to exclude white persons from railroad
cars occupied by blacks, as to exclude colored people from coaches occupied or assigned to white persons."[26] From Harlan's perspective, and
despite the majority's command that classifications must not be unreasonable, official segregation once established had no logical ending point.
If the state could separate the races on rail coaches, he suggested, it
could assign them to opposite sides of the street and distinguish also
between "native and naturalized citizens . . . or . . . Protestants and Roman
Catholics."[27]

Although a former slave owner, Harlan had reached the conclusion
that "the destinies of the two races, in this country, are indissolubly linked
together, and the interests of both require that the common government
of all shall not permit the seeds of race hate to be planted under the
sanction of law."[28] Challenging the majority's sense that official segregation promoted public harmony and order, he asserted that racial
hatred and distrust were compounded by state laws premised on the
notion "that colored citizens are so inferior and degraded that they
cannot be allowed to sit in public coaches occupied by white citizens."[29]
Harlan dismissed the notion that racial separation was a reasonable exercise of state police power, and asserted "the sure guarantee of the
peace and security of each race is the clear, distinct unconditional rec-

ognition . . . of every right that inheres in civil freedom, and of the equality before the law of all citizens . . . without regard to race."[30]

Harlan's dissent effectively portrayed official segregation as a mechanism for protecting a dominant class and as a scheme that stigmatized blacks and fostered stereotypes. His own racial chauvinism nonetheless manifested itself in the observation that whites were "the dominant race in this country . . . in prestige, in achievements, in education, in wealth, and in power."[31] Furthermore, he "doubt[ed] not, it will continue to be for all time, if it remains true to its great heritage and holds forth to the principles of constitutional liberty."[32] Still, Harlan maintained that under the Constitution, "there is in this county no superior, dominant, ruling class of citizens . . . [and] no caste."[33] Rather, he emphasized, "our Constitution is color-blind."[34]

The *Plessy* Court, having denied that official segregation operated as a stamp of inferiority, fixed its imprimatur on legally mandated racial separation. The majority had depicted the Louisiana law somewhat euphemistically as "equal but separate." The next several decades would demonstrate that "separate but equal" was a more apt description and even then an exaggeration of reality. In *Plessy* itself, the Court deferred to formalized racial separation. What remained to be seen was whether it would insist on meaningful implementation of the equalization requirement. Within a few years, it became evident that, doctrinal appearances aside, official segregation was not subject to significant qualification.

The first test of the *Plessy* premise, in *Cumming v. Board of Education*, disclosed how thoroughly jurisprudence had revamped the Fourteenth Amendment into an instrumentality of the dominant culture.[35] In *Cumming*, the Court permitted a school board to close a black high school, even though it provided secondary education to whites.[36] Citing economic reasons, the board had shut the black school but continued to maintain a high school for white girls and helped fund a private high school for white boys.[37] From the board's perspective, closing the school may have seemed a sensible response to fiscal pressures and a societal context that did not afford black graduates meaningful opportunity to use their education. The decision, however, translated into an instance of inequality so profound as to constitute total deprivation.

Despite his dissent in *Plessy*, Harlan wrote for a unanimous Court and determined that allocation of tax monies was not governed by the Constitution and, in any event, "it is impracticable to distribute taxes evenly."[38] Instead of directing itself to the question of equality, the Court employed a balance-of-harm analysis favoring the school board. Officials had argued and Harlan agreed that if they were required to "maintain a separate school for the sixty children who wished to have a high school education," primary education would have to be denied to 300 black children.[39] The manifest inequality essentially was ignored. The holding instead was referenced to general utilitarian principles of being "in the interest of the greater number of colored children."[40]

The *Cumming* decision revealed the transparency of the separate but equal doctrine. It also fulfilled Harlan's prophecy, expressed in *Plessy*, that racial classifications eventually would be used to mete out and regulate rights and benefits.[41] The *Plessy* Court had conditioned separate on the requirement of equal. Even if the concepts were mutually exclusive, the qualifying principle still was constitutionally significant. Because the Court did not consider alternatives to closure, including a racially mixed school if no other options were practical, it was evident that standards were attuned primarily, and in *Cumming* exclusively, to the interest of segregation. The effective message was that doctrine would be more accommodating to separation than demanding of equality.

During the first decade of the twentieth century, the Court upheld official segregation in private colleges and public transportation. In *Berea College v. Kentucky*, it upheld a state law prohibiting corporations and persons from operating racially integrated schools.[42] Justice Harlan criticized the decision as evasive and hypocritical. Specifically, he considered "[t]he right to impart instruction" a protected liberty interest under the Fourteenth Amendment and meriting the same sentience the Court by then was affording general notions of economic freedom.[43] The *Berea College* decision illuminated the evolving duality of Fourteenth Amendment standards and how official management of race relations could be pervasive and intrusive without constitutional affront.

In *McCabe v. Atchison, Topeka & Santa Fe Railway Co.*, the Court again upheld separate train accommodations.[44] The *McCabe* case differed from *Plessy* to the extent it was necessary to consider whether dedicated eating and sleeping accommodations had to be provided in the absence of black patronage. The Court held that, regardless of demand or usage considerations, separate sleeping and dining cars had to be furnished.[45] The effect of its determination was diluted by the further conclusion that injunctive relief could not be ordered because the complainants themselves had never traveled on the railroad or specifically been denied service.[46] While an underused rail car may have been eloquent testimony of how thoroughly official racism denied opportunities to exercise basic rights secured by the Fourteenth Amendment, the *McCabe* decision merely polished the doctrinal veneer of equality.

During the first few decades of official segregation, the Court identified one instance in which state law was unreasonable and thus unconstitutional. In *Buchanan v. Warley*, it invalidated a municipal ordinance "requiring, as far as practicable, the uses of separate blocks for residences, places of abode and places of assembly by white and colored people respectively."[47] Although cast as a regulation to maintain public peace and promote the general welfare, the Court found it a "direct violation of the fundamental law enacted in the 14th Amendment of the Constitution preventing state interference with property rights except by due process of law."[48] Unlike in the *Berea College* case, in which blacks were not denied an education, the Court apprehended in *Buchanan* the deprivation of a fundamental right.

The *Buchanan* decision presented a significant irony and disclosed how substantially the Fourteenth Amendment had been transformed since its origin. Seminal jurisprudence had emphasized the amendment's concern with affording "a race recently emancipated, a race that through many generations had been held in slavery, all the civil rights that the superior race enjoy."[49] Soon after the *Plessy* decision, the Court developed and amplified the Fourteenth Amendment's meaning in a context entirely unrelated to race. Resultant court decisions enunciated principles of general economic liberty in expansive terms, as doctrine pertaining to the amendment's central concern cramped and contracted.

In *Allgeyer v. Louisiana*, one year after the *Plessy* decision, the Court advanced substantive due process theory to defeat a state law prohibiting the operation of insurance policies not issued in compliance with legislative requirements.[50] Construing the Fourteenth Amendment as a source of substantive rights and liberties, the Court found that due process guaranteed that a person may use "all his faculties . . . [and was] free to use them in all lawful ways."[51] The *Allgeyer* decision extended previously qualified Fourteenth Amendment concepts, jurisprudentially introduced in the *Slaughter-House* dissents, to circumstances unrelated to race. It prefaced the *Lochner* era of substantive due process review which, although now criticized as an exercise in rampant activism,[52] nonetheless offered a convoluted way of finding some segregation unreasonable. The Court's decision in *Buchanan* reflected a sense of constitutional offense premised less on the law's racial significance than on its invasion of general contractual liberty. Such animation of the due process guarantee in substantive fashion, driven by rights designated by the judiciary rather than the Constitution itself, was the essence of Lochnerism.

In *Lochner v. New York* itself,[53] the Court elevated liberty of contract to the status of a fundamental right and for three decades persistently invoked it to thwart economic and social welfare legislation. The episode is widely regarded as a primary example of unrestrained subjectivism and judicial overreaching. The legacy of substantive due process analysis is so profoundly negative that, half a century after its repudiation, contemporary efforts to breathe life into the Fourteenth Amendment almost invariably engender allegations of Lochnerism.[54] Close attention to general economic liberty was especially dubious insofar as doctrine simultaneously retreated from the Fourteenth Amendment's original imperatives. The Supreme Court itself has repudiated Lochnerism on the grounds that the legitimacy of judicial review is contingent upon precepts clearly tied to constitutional text or design.[55] Even assuming the misdirected nature of Fourteenth Amendment analysis, invalidation of officially mandated segregation in *Buchanan* was connected albeit inartfully to the amendment's original but qualified concern with opportunity for material self-development. The opinion relied upon principles of embellishment and convenience to reach the same result that would have been dictated by attention to obvious design. Such analytical circuity thus offered a paradoxical example of how distorted doctrine had become.

As noted in Chapter 2, contractual liberty initially was regarded as an essential incident of citizenship. Considerations of economic freedom which influenced original understanding of civil rights, however, were consumed by more expansive and nonspecific notions of marketplace liberty. As the Supreme Court moved into the twentieth century, its composition was influenced significantly by Presidents Harrison, Cleveland and Taft, who were dedicated to advancing laissez-faire principles and used the judicial appointment process to facilitate broad notions of economic freedom.[56] Consistent with such inspiration, the Court tended vigorously to marketplace freedom[57] and interested itself in racial discrimination only when it intersected that liberty.

Contemporary criticism of Lochnerism focused less on its deviation from racially significant concerns than upon its function in achieving convenient results and impairing the operation of competing and democratically preferred philosophies of governance.[58] The *Lochner* decision itself, which found regulation of working hours at odds with liberty of contract,[59] identified no real nexus to the Fourteenth Amendment's inspiring concerns. In asserting that it would not "substitut[e] the judgment of the Court for that of the legislature,"[60] the Court suggested a standard of review akin to the deferential criteria of *Plessy*. The transparency of its claim and constitutional double standard were revealed, however, by the further pronouncement that "[w]e do not believe in the soundness of the views which uphold this law."[61]

What is especially striking about the Fourteenth Amendment's redirection is how vigorously the new agenda was pursued and how unfinished original business remained. If given a fraction of the jurisprudential consideration afforded economic liberty interests, the separate but equal doctrine at least might have accounted for equalization as well as separation. Lochnerism itself expired in the late 1930s, after political challenges to the Court's authority[62] and as a consequence of personnel changes.[63] The Court eventually announced that "[w]hether the legislature takes for its textbook Adam Smith, Herbert Spenser, Lord

Keynes or some other is no concern of ours."[64] Official segregation would survive, however, for nearly two more decades.

One measure of the difference between separate but equal in theory and in practice was the gross disparity in funding of black and white public schools. South Carolina in 1915, for example, spent ten times more money per white student than per black student.[65] Even by 1954, when southern states were pumping funds into black schools in an effort to rescue the separate but equal doctrine, the average expenditures were $165 per white student and $115 per black student.[66] Such discrepancies confirmed the acuity of Harlan's foresight in *Plessy* that endorsement of official segregation

will not only stimulate aggressions, more or less brutal and irritating, upon the admitted rights of colored citizens, but will encourage the belief that is possible, by means of state enactments, to defeat the beneficent purposes which the people of the United States had in view when they adopted the recent amendments of the Constitution, by one of which the blacks of this country were made citizens of the United States and of the states in which they respectively reside and whose privileges and immunities, as citizens, the states are forbidden to abridge.[67]

Official segregation and the jurisprudentially formulated separate but equal doctrine proved mutually reinforcing for more than half a century. The Supreme Court's deference to state legislative judgment contrasted with its standards of review that cramped congressional power to enforce the Fourteenth Amendment. Pertinent constitutional principle thus seemed largely consonant with antebellum understanding of federal and state interests. The Court's inclination to avoid confronting race-dependent practices and policies was acutely evidenced in the Fifteenth Amendment context, when officials in an Alabama community refused to register black voters.[68] Despite obvious state action at odds with the Fifteenth Amendment's indisputable mandate, the Court refused to intervene. In *Giles v. Harris*, it explained its inaction on the grounds that an injunction would be ignored by the white majority and its elected agents and so would be "pointless."[69] As Justice Holmes observed:

the court has little practical power to deal with the people of the State in a body. The bill imports that the great mass of the white population intends to keep the blacks from voting. To meet such an intent something more than ordering the plaintiff's name to be inscribed upon the [voting] lists ... will be needed.[70]

The Court advised that "relief from a great political wrong, if done, or alleged by the people of a state and the state itself, must be given them by the legislature and the political department of the United States."[71] Such a possibility was remote to say the least, because the state was the cause of deprivation rather than a source of amelioration. Congress within the preceding decade, moreover, had repealed voting rights legislation and blacks generally were unrepresented in a political process entirely unresponsive to their interests.

Although decided on Fifteenth Amendment grounds, the *Giles* case tested the Court's willingness to confront discrimination. The result was discouraging not only for specific equality interests associated with the Fifteenth Amendment but general equality concerns of the Fourteenth Amendment. The possibility of equal protection as a significant doctrinal source was further diminished by Justice Holmes' characterization of it as "the last resort of constitutional arguments."[72] Further evidencing the settled nature of segregation doctrine were how seldom it was challenged and the way it was contested. In *Gong Lum v. Rice*, a student of Chinese descent in Mississippi argued not that official segregation was wrong but that she was denied equal protection in being classified as "colored."[73] The case effectively illustrated how racial separation was a unique interest of whites. The Court found "that the question is [not] any different, or that any different result can be reached, assuming the cases to be rightly decided, where the issue is between white peoples and the peoples of the yellow race."[74]

Despite the entrenched status of official segregation, as a result of legislative enactment and judicial accommodation or endorsement, a legal strategy to defeat it eventually materialized. In the 1930s, Thurgood Marshall commenced the National Association for the Advancement of Colored People's two-decade long challenge of the separate but equal doctrine. The attack, under the litigative direction of Thurgood Marshall, targeted both the operation and the underlying premises of the *Plessy* principle. Marshall's aim was to contest segregation initially on grounds that equalization requirements were being slighted or ignored and ultimately on the basis that separate and equal were mutually inconsistent. Educating the courts with respect to that fundamental inconsonance would require nearly two decades. Given the embedded nature of policy and judicial doctrine, Marshall favored "an attack against the segregation system by law suits seeking absolute and complete equalization of curricula, faculty and physical equipment in white and black schools."[75] The tactical focus reflected a sense "that the extreme cost of maintaining two equal systems would eventually destroy segregation."[76]

The first opportunity to test the strategy before the Supreme Court was presented by *Missouri ex rel. Gaines v. Canada*.[77] The case arose when the state of Missouri denied a black applicant admission to its only public law school.[78] Because the state did not provide a separate institution for black students, it offered to fund a legal education elsewhere.[79] In spite of the offer to pay out-of-state tuition, the Court found a default of the Fourteenth Amendment obligation to maintain "the equality of legal rights to the enjoyment of the privilege which the state has set up."[80] The constitutional duty, as the Court put it, could not "be cast by one state upon another, and no state can be excused from performance by what another state may do."[81] Having considered whether the state had provided legal privileges for whites and denied them to blacks, the Court identified a discrimination that "if not relieved ... would [be] a denial of equal protection."[82] Absent a state law school for black students, it found that the "petitioner was entitled to be admitted to the law school of the state university."[83]

The *Gaines* case represented the first successful challenge, at least in federal court,[84] to official segregation's underpinnings. It reflected a litigative strategy predicated on the assumption that while the separate but equal doctrine would not be displaced immediately, it would wither from persistent demonstration of its illogic. Reality at the time was that the *Plessy* principle was the norm, *Gaines* was the exception, and significant time and energy would have to be invested in showing that official segregation imprinted on its victims "a badge of inferiority."[85] By focusing on graduate and professional education, the NAACP targeted an accurately perceived point of vulnerability in the system of official segregation. Because the venues and numbers of persons affected were relatively small, deviations from the general rule of segregation seemed more achievable than if primary or secondary educational policy was challenged. As Marshall observed:

the university level was the best place to begin a campaign that had as its ultimate objective the total elimination of segregation in public institutions in the United States. In the first place, at the university level no provision for negro education was a rule rather than the exception. Then, too, the difficulties incident to providing equal educational opportunities even within the concept of the "separate but equal" doctrine were insurmountable. To provide separate medical schools, law schools, engineering schools, and graduate schools with all the variety of offerings available at most state universities would be an almost financial impossibility.[86]

The strategy in sum was that if segregation was pushed to the test of satisfying equal as well as separate, the policy eventually would implode as a result of its own weight.

Progress toward that ultimate objective was delayed by judicial caution and insensitivity to the realities of discrimination and by the determination of states to accept the challenge of equalization. In *Sipuel v. Board of Regents*, the Court considered the constitutional claim of a black student denied admission to the University of Oklahoma Law School and afforded no in-state opportunity for legal education.[87] The case essentially replayed the circumstances of *Gaines*. Unlike in the earlier litigation, however, the NAACP sought to demonstrate that a racially separate legal education was inherently unequal.[88] Marshall thus argued that

"segregation in public education helps to preserve a caste system which is based upon race and color. It is designed and intended to perpetuate the slave tradition. . . . 'Separate' and 'equal' can not be used conjunctively in a situation of this kind; there can be no separate equality."[89]

The argument in *Sipuel* previewed the premise that the Court eventually would subscribe to in 1954.[90] In *Sipuel* itself, however, the Court left the separate but equal doctrine intact. Because Oklahoma had neglected the equalization component, the Court demanded that it either provide a separate law school or allow blacks to enroll at the state university.[91]

The state's response was to cordon off a section of the state capitol building and characterize it as a law school.[92] As a manifest avoidance of meaningful equality, this act prompted another constitutional challenge. The Court in *Fisher v. Hurst* declined the invitation to reconsider the separate but equal doctrine's validity.[93] In refusing to find the separate arrangements constitutionally deficient, the Court also indicated a reluctance to manage the interests of equality. Inroads into the separate but equal doctrine thus did not advance beyond the relatively limited accomplishment of *Gaines*. From the NAACP's perspective, the result even suggested regression. If a state was obligated to provide a separate institution, but not to invest significant resources in it, a black student actually might be better off accepting a state's offer to fund his or her education elsewhere. The *Gaines* decision had indicated that the separate but equal principle at least had to live up to its stated premise. The *Sipuel* and *Fisher* rulings appeared consonant, however, with the doctrine's less demanding tradition.

Given the result in *Sipuel*, the NAACP refocused on the deficiencies of separate graduate education and attempted to enhance the Court's sensitivity to those realities. In *Sweatt v. Painter*[94] and *McLaurin v. Oklahoma State Regents for Higher Education*,[95] expert testimony was presented to the effect that segregated education would remain unequal even if tangible differences were eliminated. Given the nature of the challenge to established law and the promise of states to equalize within the context of segregation, the constitutional issue inevitably was reducing itself to the separate but equal doctrine's general fitness. The *Sweatt* and *McLaurin* cases thus represented the most significant challenge yet of the *Plessy* principle.

The *Sweatt* case concerned the University of Texas' refusal to admit a black law student.[96] Unlike the circumstances in *Gaines* and *Sipuel*, the school's decision was based on the availability of a black institution.[97] Despite the separate opportunity and the state's assurance that it promptly would equalize any deficiencies in physical facilities, the Court found the school unequal for constitutional purposes.[98] By directing the university to admit the petitioner,[99] it effectively integrated the school.

The Court's reasoning indicated that, at least in the context of graduate or professional education, it considered separate inimical to equal. The Court noted that the white school had a stronger faculty, a better library, a larger student body, and more extensive student activities.[100] Its analysis did not terminate, however, with identification of physical or readily palpable differences. Rather, the Court identified intangible factors, such as faculty reputation, alumni position and influence, institutional traditions and prestige, and linkage to professional opportunities,[101] which were "incapable of objective measurement."[102]

Consideration of factors disproving the validity of separate but equal prompted like results in the *McLaurin* decision. The case arose when a state university admitted a black applicant to an all-white graduate program, pursuant to court order, but segregated him within the institution itself. Initially, the student was required to attend classes in a side room, study at a desk on the library's upper floor, and use a designated section of the cafeteria at a special time.[103] The rules were altered in the course of litigation so that he could sit in the classroom, albeit in a special row; use the main floor of the library; and eat at regular hours, although at a special table.[104] The Court concluded that the racially determined arrangements impaired the "ability to study, to engage in discussions, and exchange views with other students, and in general, to learn [one's] profession."[105] To the extent it impeded the "pursuit of effective graduate instruction," such internal segregation was found constitutionally impermissible.[106]

The *Sweatt* and *McLaurin* decisions represented significant movement toward general doctrinal upheaval. In *McLaurin*, the Court considered but was unimpressed by arguments that, even without state-mandated restrictions, racial separation would persist. Of particular significance to future rulings, it distinguished between official proscription of commingling and refusal to associate as a function of personal preference.[107] The Court in both decisions emphasized intangible factors that could never be equalized. Although the separate but equal doctrine's broad operation was not reassessed or invalidated, the Court's analysis prefaced its finding a few years later that such "considerations apply with added force to children in grade and high schools."[108] The *Sweatt* and *McLaurin* decisions had immediately significant consequences but were doubly profound insofar as they previewed the impending demise of official segregation in *Brown v. Board of Education*.[109]

Wholesale reformulation of equal protection doctrine had to await the transformation of the Vinson Court into the Warren Court. Although having animated the separate but equal doctrine so that equalization interests were no longer entirely dismissed, the Vinson Court had evidenced its reluctance to jettison the *Plessy* principle altogether. The appointment of Earl Warren as chief justice altered institutional dynamics and resulted in leadership more receptive to the possibility of doctrinal redesign. A challenge to segregated primary and secondary education required not exception from but vitiation of the general rule. As Marshall recognized, elementary and high schools were distinguishable from graduate and professional "specialized institutions with national or even statewide reputations."[110]

Further complicating a challenge to segregated education was the reality that Fourteenth Amendment history seemed to support the established order. An examination of the record reveals that the framers did not contemplate the prospect of racially mixed education.[111] Precisely the opposite intent was suggested insofar as District of Columbia schools were segregated by the same Congress that adopted the Fourteenth Amendment. What history denied eventually would be reclaimed (1) by social science data indicating that official segregation stigmatized black students and denied them equality of educational opportunity, and (2) by a sense that public schooling was more crucial to Fourteenth Amendment interests in 1954 than in 1868.[112]

The Court's eventual repudiation of official segregation, although largely a responsive to the NAACP's challenge, was attributable also to a general evolution of equal protection theory. In the late 1920s, the Court had dismissed the equal protection guarantee as the tool of a desperate litigant.[113] At the same time, it was vitalizing the due process guarantee in substantive terms that created a panoply of basic liberties unspecified by the Constitution. In contrast to its uncharitable readings of equal protection, the Court at the apex of Lochnerism identified fundamental rights and freedom in terms that included not only

freedom from bodily restraint, but the right of the individual to contract, to engage in any of the common occupations of life, to acquire useful knowledge, to marry, to establish a home and bring up children, to worship God according to the dictates of his own conscience, and generally to enjoy those privileges long recognized ... as essential to the orderly pursuit of happiness by free men.[114]

In closing out the *Lochner* era in 1937, the Court announced a major change in Fourteenth Amendment thinking. In *West Coast Hotel v. Parrish*, it depicted substantive due process analysis as a deviation "from the true application of the principles governing the regulation by the State of the relation of employer and employed."[115] The next year, in *United States v. Carolene Products Co.*, the Court advanced a revised, albeit preliminary, view of future Fourteenth Amendment analysis.[116] Although allowing that "the existence of facts supporting ... legislative judgment are to be presumed, for regulation affecting ordinary commercial transactions,"[117] it suggested that special circumstances might justify stricter review. The Court specifically noted that more rigorous examination may be apt when legislation implicates a specific constitutional prohibition "such as those of the first ten amendments."[118] For equal protection purposes, the Court found it unnecessary to inquire "whether prejudice against discrete and insular minorities may be a special condition, which tends seriously to curtail the operation of those political processes ordinarily to be relied upon to protect minorities, and which may call for a correspondingly more searching judicial inquiry."[119]

The *Carolene Products* decision, if not actually setting a new equal protection standard when racial discrimination was at issue, at least ventured the possibility that the Fourteenth Amendment might be animated in terms more responsive to its original purpose. The reality of a new analytical model was evidenced when the Court reviewed an equal protection challenge to the relocation of Japanese Americans during World War II.[120] For reasons of national security, President Roosevelt had authorized their detention in remote camps.[121] In examining the plan, the Court introduced a standard to the effect

that all legal restrictions which curtail the civil rights of a single racial group are immediately suspect. That is not to say that all such restrictions are unconstitutional. It is to say that courts must subject them to the most rigid scrutiny. Pressing public necessity may sometimes justify the existence of such restrictions; racial antagonism never can.[122]

The notion that racial classifications were suspect and thus must be strictly scrutinized by the courts, although not disruptive of the wartime relocation scheme, eventually would prove critical to dismantling the nation's system of official discrimination.

Equal protection until the middle of the twentieth century was reviewed by the courts on the basis of reasonableness standards,[123] which largely translated as judicial deference to legislative judgment. Strict scrutiny, as conceived in *Korematsu v. United States*, provided analytical weaponry for identifying the "racial antagonism" underlying official segregation. Before such rigorous review eventuated, the separate but equal doctrine survived pursuant to outward appearances of symmetrical application. The appearance of parallelism was perhaps best projected by the Supreme Court's allowance of state prohibitions against interracial intimacy or marriage. The Court in 1875 had upheld a state law that enhanced the penalties for fornication if the offenders were of different races and prohibited miscegenation altogether. Reviewing the provision in *Pace v. Alabama*, the Court found no constitutionally significant discrimination because the law applied equally to both races.[124] Not until 1967 did it fully repudiate the notion that equal application of the law was not necessarily synonymous with equal protection of the law. In *Loving v. Virginia*, the Court recognized that antimiscegenation laws were an extension of racist ideology and impaired the freedom to marry.[125]

Arrival at that point of understanding represented a significant passage from the notion that official racial classifications were reasonable and could be considered harmful only if misunderstood. Erosion of the separate but equal doctrine in response to the NAACP's challenge to official segregation suggested that the principle was living on borrowed time. General reconstruction of Fourteenth Amendment standards in the post-*Lochner* era afforded analytical methodology for closely examining the nature, premises, and effects of segregation. When leadership of the Court changed in 1953, circumstances had ripened for what has been described as the "Second American Revolution."[126]

NOTES

1. Civil Rights Cases, 109 U.S. 3, 25 (1883).
2. Roberts v. City of Boston, 59 Mass. (5 Cush.) 198 (1850).
3. State v. McCann, 21 Ohio St. 198 (1872).
4. Plessy v. Ferguson, 163 U.S. 537, 540 (1896).
5. *Id.* at 540–41 (*quoting* Louisiana statute).
6. *Id.* at 541.
7. *Id.* at 542.
8. *Id.*
9. *Id.* at 543.
10. *Id.* at 544.
11. *Id.*
12. Strauder v. West Virginia, 100 U.S. (10 Otto) 303, 308 (1880).
13. Plessy v. Ferguson, 163 U.S. at 544.
14. *See id.* at 544–45.
15. *Id.* at 550.
16. *Id.*
17. *Id.*
18. *Id.* at 551.
19. *Id.*
20. *Id.*
21. *Id.* at 544.
22. *Id.* at 551–52.
23. Levy, *Plessy v. Ferguson*, in Civil Rights and Equality 174 (K. Karst ed. 1989).
24. Plessy v. Ferguson, 163 U.S. at 559 (Harlan, J. dissenting).
25. *Id.* at 555 (Harlan, J., dissenting).
26. *Id.* at 557 (Harlan, J., dissenting).
27. *Id.* at 558 (Harlan, J., dissenting).
28. *Id.* at 560 (Harlan, J., dissenting).
29. *Id.* (Harlan, J., dissenting).

30. *Id.* (Harlan, J., dissenting).

31. *Id.* at 559 (Harlan, J., dissenting).

32. *Id.* (Harlan, J., dissenting).

33. *Id.* (Harlan, J., dissenting).

34. *Id.* (Harlan, J., dissenting).

35. Cumming v. Board of Education, 175 U.S. 528 (1899).

36. *Id.* at 544–45.

37. *Id.* at 530–33.

38. *Id.* at 542.

39. *Id.* at 544.

40. *Id.*

41. *See* Plessy v. Ferguson, 163 U.S. at 562–63 (Harlan, J., dissenting).

42. Berea College v. Kentucky, 211 U.S. 45, 57–58 (1908).

43. *Id.* at 67–68 (Harlan, J., dissenting). The jurisprudentially enhanced breadth of the Fourteenth Amendment, at least when race was not concerned, is discussed *infra* at notes 50–64 and accompanying text.

44. McCabe v. Atchison, Topeka & Santa Fe Railway Co., 235 U.S. 151, 163–64 (1908).

45. *Id.* at 161–62.

46. *Id.* at 161–63.

47. Buchanan v. Warley, 245 U.S. 60, 70 (1917).

48. *Id.* at 82.

49. Strauder v. West Virginia, 100 U.S. (10 Otto) at 306.

50. Allgeyer v. Louisiana, 165 U.S. 575, 592–93 (1897).

51. *Id.* at 589.

52. For a general discussion of the *Lochner* era of substantive due process review and criticisms of it, see L. Tribe, American Constitutional Law 567–86, 769–72 (2d ed. 1988).

53. 198 U.S. 45 (1905).

54. *See, e.g.,* Zablocki v. Redhail, 434 U.S. 374, 407 (1978) (Rehnquist, J., dissenting) (criticizing recognition of fundamental right to marry); Vlandis v. Kline, 412 U.S. 441, 467–68 (1973) (Rehnquist, J., dissenting) (criticizing recognition of fundamental right to travel); Griswold v. Connecticut, 381 U.S. 479, 514–15 (1965) (Black, J., dissenting) (criticizing recognition of fundamental right of privacy). Justice Brennan noted that the lesson of Lochnerism for the Court was that it could "actively intrude into...economic and policy matters only if ...prepared to bear enormous institutional and social costs." United States Trust Co. v. New Jersey, 431 U.S. 1, 62 (1978) (Brennan, J., dissenting).

55. *See, e.g.,* Bowers v. Hardwick, 478 U.S. 186, 194 (1986).

56. *See* A. Mason, William Howard Taft—Chief Justice 157–58 (1964).

57. *See id.*

58. Lochner v. New York, 198 U.S. at 74–76 (Holmes, J., dissenting).

59. *Id.* at 53.

60. *Id.* at 56–57.

61. *Id.* at 61.

62. For a discussion of President Roosevelt's Court-packing plan, *see* H. Abraham, Justices and Presidents 292–93 (1974).

63. *See id.*

64. Ferguson v. Skrupa, 372 U.S. 726, 731–32 (1963).

65. *See* A. Lewis, Portrait of a Decade: The Second American Revolution 29 (1964).

66. *See id.*

67. Plessy v. Ferguson, 163 U.S. at 560 (Harlan, J., dissenting).

68. *See* Giles v. Harris, 189 U.S. 475, 482 (1903).

69. Id. at 488.

70. *Id.*

71. *Id.*

72. Buck v. Bell, 274 U.S. 200, 208 (1927).

73. Gong Lum v. Rice, 275 U.S. 78, 80 (1927).

74. *Id.* at 87.

75. Marshall, *An Evaluation of Recent Efforts to Achieve Racial Integration in Education through Resort to the Courts*, 21 J. Negro Educ. 316, 318 (1952).

76. *Id.*

77. 305 U.S. 337 (1938).

78. *Id.* at 342.

79. *Id.* at 346.

80. *Id.* at 349–50.

81. *Id.* at 350.

82. *Id.* at 345.

83. *Id.* at 352.

84. A similar order, requiring admission of a black student to the only public law school in Maryland, had been achieved in state court litigation. *See* Pearson v. Murray, 182 A. 590, 594 (Md. 1936).

85. Brown v. Board of Education, 347 U.S. 483, 494 (1954).

86. Marshall, *supra* note 75, at 319.

87. *See* Sipuel v. Board of Regents, 332 U.S. 631, 632 (1948).

88. *See* K. Ripple, Constitutional Litigation § 4–4, at 127 (1984).

89. *Id.* (quoting Brief for Appellant as quoted in R. Kluger, Simple Justice 259 (1975)).

90. *See* Chapter 5.

91. Sipuel v. Board of Regents, 332 U.S. at 633.

92. *See* K. Ripple, *supra* note 88, at 127.

93. *See* Fisher v. Hurst, 333 U.S. 147 (1948).

94. 339 U.S. 629 (1950).

95. 339 U.S. 637 (1950).

96. *See* Sweatt v. Painter, 339 U.S. at 631.

97. *See id.* at 633.

98. *See id..* at 635.

99. *Id.* at 635–36.

100. *Id.* at 632–34.

101. *Id.* at 634.

102. *Id.*

103. McLaurin v. Oklahoma State Regents for Higher Education, 339 U.S. at 640.

104. *See id.*

105. *Id.* at 641.

106. *Id.*

107. *Id.* 641–42.

108. Brown v. Board of Education, 347 U.S at 494.

109. 347 U.S. 483 (1954).

110. Marshall, *supra* note 75, at 322.

111. *See* Chapter 2.

112. *See* Brown v. Board of Education, 347 U.S. at 494 and n.11.

113. *See* Buck v. Bell, 274 U.S. at 208, discussed *supra* at note 72 and accompanying text.

114. Meyer v. Nebraska, 262 U.S. 390, 399 (1923).

115. West Coast Hotel v. Parrish, 300 U.S. 379, 397 (1937).

116. United States v. Carolene Products Co., 304 U.S. 144 (1938).

117. *Id.* at 152.

118. *Id.* at 152 n.4.

119. *Id.*

120. Korematsu v. United States, 323 U.S. 214, 219 (1944).

121. *Id.* at 218.

122. *Id.* at 216.

123. *See* Plessy v. Ferguson, 163 U.S. at 550–51.

124. Pace v. Alabama, 106 U.S. 583, 585 (1882).

125. Loving v. Virginia, 388 U.S. 1, 11–12 (1967).

126. A. Lewis, *supra* note 65.

Chapter 5

Desegregation and the Anti-Discrimination Principle

Displacement of official segregation represented a fundamental redirection of equal protection jurisprudence. In both its formulation and its operation, however, the principle that separate inherently was unequal reflected abiding tension between the imperatives of civil equality and societal reality. Dramatic as it was in nature, the desegregation mandate was cautiously introduced. The Supreme Court heard initial arguments in *Brown v. Board of Education* in its 1952 term, invited reargument for its 1953 term, rendered a decision in 1954, and ordered relief in 1955. Within two decades, the desegregation mandate was qualified by limiting principles that significantly reduced its potential for securing equal educational opportunity. From the mid-1950s to early 1970s, however, the Court activated the equal protection guarantee in forceful and unprecedented terms.

The *Brown* decision itself resolved four cases consolidated for purposes of review that challenged segregated public education in Kansas, Delaware, Virginia, and South Carolina. The lower courts had upheld official segregation with varying degrees of enthusiasm. Although the separate but equal doctrine was sustained in Delaware, for instance, educational disparities prompted an order requiring white schools to admit black students.[1]

The South Carolina case[2] was especially notable insofar as it involved two personalities whose careers, before and after *Brown*, symbolized the emerging and dying orders. Thurgood Marshall, who argued the plaintiffs' case, would be appointed to the Supreme Court in another decade.

John J. Parker, who as Chief Judge of the U.S. Court of Appeals for the Fourth Circuit authored the district court panel's split decision upholding segregation, had narrowly missed appointment to the Supreme Court in 1930.[3] Critical to the Senate's rejection of his nomination by one vote was a perception that Parker was anti-labor and anti-black.[4] Refusal to confirm him thus was influenced by a sense that he was "obviously incapable of viewing with sympathy the aspirations of those who are aiming for higher and better places in the world."[5]

As a member of the three-judge panel hearing the challenge to South Carolina's segregated schools, Parker diverted the challenge to the *Plessy* principle into an assessment of whether facilities at black and white schools were being equalized.[6] Consequent analysis led to the conclusion that segregation was "grounded in reason and experience" and consistent with the Fourteenth Amendment.[7] A dissenting opinion criticized the Court for "avoid[ing] the primary purpose of the suit."[8] It objected to a "method of judicial evasion" that would ensure that "these very infant plaintiffs . . . will probably be bringing suits for their children and grandchildren decades . . . hence."[9] Subsequent events confirmed the accuracy of that forecast. After the desegregation mandate was rendered, Judge Parker was prominent in resisting it. Among other things, he asserted that the Constitution, even if forbidding official discrimination, "does not require integration."[10] Such reasoning accepted new doctrine in a legalistic sense only, as it repudiated the need to dismantle segregation. The "frustrating effects"[11] of such analysis reflected a persisting challenge to the federal interest in civil rights and equality and a doctrinal twist calculated to preserve the established order.

The Supreme Court in *Brown* squarely confronted the issue of whether segregated schools were or ever could be made equal for purposes of the Fourteenth Amendment. Having requested and heard reargument on the question of what the framers had contemplated, the Court concluded that the purpose of Congress and the ratifying states was indeterminate.[12] Depiction of the historical record as uncertain is at least debatable. Although inquiry into motive can be a treacherous exercise, since official intent can represent the convergence of varying purposes or be concealed,[13] the actions and aims of the framers were not equivocal. A general consensus existed, as noted in Chapter 2, that the Fourteenth Amendment accounted for a narrow range of rights and equality. Especially pertinent to the question of whether racially mixed schools were contemplated was the fact that the same Congress responsible for the Fourteenth Amendment also provided for segregated schools in the District of Columbia.[14] Some ratifying states, moreover, mandated segregation of public schools or prohibited education of blacks altogether.

As the Court properly noted, public education in the immediate post-Civil War period was a nonexistent or underdeveloped reality in many states.[15] Public schooling, although eventually considered crucial to economic opportunity and personal development, was not so regarded when the Fourteenth Amendment was conceived. The Court concluded that "it is not surprising that there should be so little in the history of the Fourteenth Amendment relating to its intended effect on public education."[16] Such a determination may have been misleading insofar as it suggested an empty record, but it was apt in indicating that education had become connected to original aims in a way the framers themselves never had an opportunity to contemplate.

Having resolved that original intent was essentially unfathomable, the Court allowed that it could not in any event "turn the clock back to 1868 when the Amendment was adopted, or even to 1896 when *Plessy v. Ferguson* was written."[17] Characterizing education as "perhaps the most significant function of state and local governments," the Court stressed its "present place in American life" and its "importance . . . to our democratic society."[18] It thus noted that education

is required in the performance of our most basic public responsibilities, even service in the armed forces. It is the very foundation of good citizenship. Today it is a principal instrument in awakening the child to cultural values, in preparing him for later professional training, and in helping him to adjust normally to his environment. In these days, it is doubtful that any child may reasonably be expected to succeed in life if he is denied the opportunity of an education.[19]

The Court's analysis thus proceeded from the premise that original purpose was not discernible or pertinent but that education was critical for individual development and opportunity. Having identified that nexus, the Court considered the effect of segregation on public education.[20] In assessing the consequences of segregated elementary and secondary schools, it determined that the impairments identified a few terms earlier with respect to graduate education applied with even greater force.[21] The Court found that separation of children solely because of race "generates a feeling of inferiority as to their status in the community that may affect their hearts and minds in a way unlikely ever to be undone."[22] Quoting findings of the Kansas court, which considered itself bound by *Plessy*, the Court reiterated that

[s]egregation of white and colored children in public schools has a detrimental effect upon the colored children. The impact is greater when it has the sanction of the law; for the policy of separating the races is usually interpreted as denoting the inferiority of the negro group. A sense of inferiority affects the motivation of a child to learn. Segregation with the sanction of law, therefore, has a tendency to [retard] the educational and mental development of Negro children and to deprive them of some of the benefits they would receive in a racial[ly] integrated school system.[23]

Sensing the insufficiency of original support for racially mixed schools, the NAACP had introduced extensive social science data confirming the effect of segregation on black children. The extent to which such evidence influenced the *Brown* decision remains uncertain. The Court itself observed that, regardless of the nature or extent of psychological knowledge in 1896, the harmful effects of segregation were now amply documented, and any contrary indications in *Plessy* were inapplicable.[24] The notion that perceptions of inferiority were the fault of the victim[25] rather than the law thus was repudiated. Reference to social science research has engendered criticism that the *Brown* decisions rest on an unacceptable predicate.[26] Despite the opinion's reference to such data, Chief Justice Warren later would deny that it was the actual premise for the ruling.[27]

The thrust of the decision, regardless of the considerations influencing it, was certain and direct. The Court concluded

that in the field of public education the doctrine of "separate but equal" has no place. Separate educational facilities are inherently unequal. Therefore, we hold that the plaintiffs and others similarly situated for whom the actions have been brought are, by reason of the segregation complained of, deprived of the equal protection of the laws guaranteed by the Fourteenth Amendment.[28]

The challenge to segregated public schools had been presented on equal protection and due process grounds. Because the Court discerned an equal protection violation, analysis of the due process claim was bypassed.[29] Although irrelevant to *Brown*, due process considerations were critical to defeating segregation in the District of Columbia.

The Fifth Amendment, unlike the Fourteenth Amendment, does not include an explicit equal protection guarantee. If not subject to identical constitutional demands, federally segregated schools in the District of Columbia might have survived the desegregation mandate as a legal anomaly. In *Bolling v. Sharpe*, the Court concluded that concepts of equal protection and due process emanate from the "American ideal of fairness."[30] It depicted the equal protection guarantee as "a more explicit safeguard of prohibited unfairness" and, for purposes of decisional analysis, subsumed by the due process clause.[31] Operating from the premise that racial classifications must be scrutinized closely, the Court found school segregation in the District of Columbia "not reasonably related to any proper governmental objective and . . . an arbitrary deprivation of . . . liberty in violation of the Due Process Clause."[32]

The determination that separate education was inherently unequal represented a bold jurisprudential stroke but, compared to the challenge of implementation, a relatively simple step. The desegregation principle required radical cultural change and moral redefinition. Recognizing the unsettling demands it was making and the potential for resistance, the Court's consideration of relief was characterized by caution and appeals for state and local cooperation. It immediately sought to dispel concern that constitutional imperatives would be the function of autocratic and inflexible standards for relief. The Court accordingly observed that the decision had "wide applicability" in a "great variety of local conditions" and that the formulation of relief presented "problems of considerable complexity."[33] The decision thus stopped at the point of determining that segregation in public schools was constitutionally impermissible. Determination of relief was postponed for another term. Consistent with the Court's objective of minimizing opposition and securing cooperation, it invited the input of affected states for purposes of assisting in the fashioning of appropriate relief.[34]

In its next term, the Court delineated the terms for relief and remanded the cases to the lower courts for implementation.[35] Reflecting further an effort to secure the support of state and local officials, the ruling was couched somewhat deferentially. The Court acknowledged that school authorities had primary responsibility for solving educational problems.[36] To further minimize its role in the process, the Court vested federal district courts with the responsibility of determining whether desegregation was being effected in "good faith."[37] The charge recognized the district courts' "proximity to local conditions," and presumed they could better assess remedial needs and options.[38] Although the Court had announced a uniform constitutional demand, the implementation process was to be inspired by local calculation and influence.

For purposes of actually framing decrees, the lower courts were reminded of their traditional equitable powers. In exercising that authority, they were to be mindful of the plaintiffs' interests in obtaining relief as soon as practicable and the public's interest in eliminating "obstacles in a systematic and effective manner."[39] At minimum, the Court insisted on "a prompt and reasonable start toward full compliance" and imposed on states the burden of showing that additional time was necessary for effective remediation.[40] Jurisdiction for purposes of assessing the adequacy of desegregation plans thus was assigned to local federal courts. They were directed, however, to ensure that the affected schools developed racially nondiscriminatory admissions policies "with all deliberate speed."[41]

The sharing of remedial duties represented a strategy calculated to defuse resistance and minimize repudiation. The tactic reflected sensitivity to the historically sharp and unsettled dispute over the zones of federal and state interest under the Fourteenth Amendment. Although the Court announced a uniform constitutional demand that cut deeply into established state law, custom, and power, its assignment of primary responsibility for implementation at least appeared to cushion the impact and created a basis for self-determined cooperation.

Reaction to the desegregation mandate was "electric."[42] In states and communities manifestly affected by *Brown*, it also was decidedly negative. In spite of the Court's effort to make desegregation a collaborative enterprise, the general response was characterized by widespread resistance, evasion, and delay. Typical desegregation plans were shams, subterfuges, or inactions that effectively maintained segregation as a function of custom rather than official dictate. Some states passed laws intended to preclude actual desegregation or at least cripple the process.

Arkansas, for instance, enacted legislation intended to free students from compulsory attendance at biracial schools. The statute was rooted in a state constitutional amendment requiring the legislature to approve "in every Constitutional manner the Unconstitutional desegregation decisions . . . of the United States Supreme Court."[43] It eventually was struck down, as discussed later, although desegregation itself required intervention by federal armed forces.[44] The state of Virginia, attempting to deter litigative initiative, activated a regulation providing for disbarment of attorneys representing groups with no pecuniary interest in the litigation.[45] Enforcement was directed primarily at the NAACP but eventually defeated as offensive to the First Amendment.[46] Deferring to local idiosyncrasies, sensing the need for grass-roots support, and aiming to minimize the divisive potential of its decision, the Court originally structured desegregation with an eye to enhancing its acceptability. Reality, however, quickly defeated anticipation. The Court, which had calibrated implementation in terms designed to distance itself from the process, thus was forced to reformulate its strategy.

The first major test of the *Brown* principle presented itself in Little Rock, Arkansas. Although local authorities had devised a desegregation plan, the state legislature, as previously noted, enacted a law purporting to relieve students from compulsory attendance at racially mixed schools.[47] When the governor summoned the National Guard to prevent black students from entering the city's all-white high school,[48] President Eisenhower responded by dispatching federal troops to enforce desegregation.[49] The intensity of public reaction to the events prompted the school board to move for a delay in the implementation of its plan.[50] In support of postponement, the board cited impairment of the educational process attributable to demonstrable tension and conflict. Although acknowledging that the educational process might suffer, and without doubting the board's good faith, the Court in *Cooper v. Aaron* denied the requested delay.[51]

The *Cooper* case was an extension of the persisting debate over federal and state interests reckoned with in *Brown* but for practical purposes still unresolved. Commencing with the premise that the Constitution is supreme and the judiciary has the power to "say what the law is,"[52] the Court characterized the desegregation mandate as "the supreme law of the land and binding on the states."[53] The self-drawn profile of function and effect continues to elicit criticism as an example of judicial over-reaching. For purposes of determining the supreme law of the land, detractors would distinguish between the Constitution itself and the Court's interpretation of it.[54] The decision in *Cooper* was prompted by the sense that "[t]he constitutional rights of respondents are not to be sacrificed or yielded to the violence and disorder which have followed upon the actions of the Governor and Legislature."[55] Given the linkage between official action and public antagonism in Little Rock, the Court determined that "law and order are not here to be preserved by depriving the Negro children of their constitutional rights."[56] It also warned that the desegregation mandate was not to be compromised either directly by legislative, executive, or judicial officers or indirectly by official eva-sion.[57]

In spite of the Court's insistence that constitutional duties were not to be avoided, desegregation plans commonly evolved in terms that appeared to comport with the *Brown* mandate but actually skirted it. Common methods of evasion included policies of gradual implementation, school closures, freedom of choice, gerrymandering of district lines, and remedial limitations. In *Rogers v. Paul*, the Court considered a desegregation plan that expanded at the rate of one grade per year.[58] Because it effectively denied relief to the plaintiffs, who would graduate before desegregation reached their level, the Court determined that the policy did not satisfy constitutional demands.[59]

Some school districts, instead of desegregating, simply stopped operating. To the extent such action was combined with public financial assistance to private schools, however, the Court discerned a constitutional failure. In *Griffin v. County School Board of Prince Edward County*, it determined that the schools were closed solely to avoid desegregation.[60] Supporting that finding was the fact that the public education system had been shut down and a system for funding private schools established after the county had been ordered to desegregate.[61]

Freedom of choice plans projected the image of racial neutrality by enabling students to select the school they would attend. In *Green v. County School Board of New Kent County, Virginia*, however, the Court determined that such a scheme did not satisfy the requirement of "admission to the public schools on a nonracial basis."[62] Significant factors influencing the determination of constitutional infirmity were the plan's adoption after *Brown*, the absence of any white applicants seeking admission to the previously all-black school, and the scarcity of black students seeking transfer to the traditionally all-white school.[63] From those circumstances, the Court inferred an effort to avoid rather than comply with the desegregation mandate.[64] It did not foreclose the possibility that freedom of choice plans might be permissible in other contexts but characterized them generally as ineffective and "unacceptable . . . if there are reasonably available other ways . . . promising speedier and more effective conversion to a unitary, nonracial school system."[65]

The Court in the aftermath of *Brown* also foiled manipulation of school district lines calculated to evade desegregation. In *Wright v. City Council of Emporia*, it found a school district's subdivision to be an impermissible scheme for insulating a predominantly white community from constitutional demands.[66] The Court also invalidated the partition of a single school district into two districts.[67] The suspect nature of both schemes was enhanced by the timing of the boundary changes, which occurred immediately after the prospect of desegregation arose.[68]

The success of the *Brown* principle ultimately was dependent on its effective enforcement. While state and local officials resisted and evaded the mandate, federal action in the mid–1960s significantly bolstered the cause and process of desegregation. By authorizing the United States attorney general to bring desegregation actions, Congress expanded the possibility of constitutional challenges beyond the range of private and often limited resources. The Department of Health, Education, and Welfare, moreover, promulgated rules denying federal funding to districts not complying with the imperatives of *Brown*.

States nonetheless persisted with strategies and devices designed to cramp operation of the desegregation mandate. Obstructionist efforts resulted in laws that did not contest the validity of *Brown* but curtailed the nature and scope of remedies for effecting desegregation. In *North Carolina State Board of Education v. Swann*, the Court struck down a state law precluding pupil assignments on the basis of race and prohibiting busing.[69] Its ruling was grounded on the supremacy clause, requiring "state policy [to] give way when it operates to hinder vindication of federal constitutional guarantees."[70]

In subsequent years, anti-busing measures were upheld to the extent they were not perceived as an evasion of *Brown*. The Court, in *Crawford v. Board of Education*, determined that a California constitutional amendment denying state courts any option to order busing except to remedy official and purposeful segregation, did not offend the Fourteenth Amendment.[71] In *Washington v. Seattle School District No. 1*, it found that redistribution of the power to make race-dependent assignments or to order busing effected a substantial and unique racial burden.[72] The pertinent law, approved by voters, transferred such authority from local school boards to the state legislature. Arguably, such a removal of power had been effected when state court authority was reduced. The Court in *Crawford*, however, did not find the circumstances comparable.

By the end of the 1960s, the changes contemplated by *Brown* had bypassed an entire generation of public school students. The Court was thus prompted to reexamine the premises for effectuating the *Brown* mandate. Reality was that conditions in the region most affected by the desegregation principle for practical purposes had remained largely unchanged. One of the districts subject to the original desegregation order in *Brown* remained "totally segregated" a decade later.[73] Given such unvaried circumstances, compounded by persisting evasion and intransigence, the Court eventually asserted that "[t]he time for mere 'deliberate speed' has run out."[74] It accordingly demanded that school boards come forward with a desegregation "plan that promises realistically to work, and promises realistically to work *now*."[75]

Movement from a standard of "all deliberate speed" to one of immediate relief fortified the Court's role in the desegregation process. The *Griffin* decision had suggested that equitable powers might be used prohibitively and affirmatively to halt public funding of private schools and to reopen and operate public schools.[76] In *Swann v. Charlotte-Mecklenburg Board of Education*, the Court elaborated on the subject of remedial authority and defined the possibilities for relief expansively.[77]

As the *Swann* opinion noted, a district court's power to prescribe the terms of desegregation was broad and extensive but conditioned on proof of a constitutional violation and failure of school officials to adopt an effective plan.[78] In *Green*, the Court had defined "an affirmative duty to take whatever steps might be necessary to convert to a unitary system in which racial discrimination would be eliminated root and branch."[79] Consistent with that premise, the *Swann* Court identified eradication of all official discrimination as a school board's first duty.[80]

Perceiving that faculty assignments could effect swift and meaningful change in a segregated system, the Court approved fixed ratios of white and black teachers.[81] Such allowance, as jurisprudence in other remedial contexts has disclosed, was a rare departure from the Court's usual animus toward quotas.

The Court regarded construction policies as critical in maintaining or undoing school segregation. Because school siting prior to *Brown* had been rooted in segregation, and since 1954 had been used to avoid desegregation, the Court warned that patterns of building and abandonment would be "a factor of great weight."[82] Local courts thus were to be attentive to the possibility that "construction and abandonment are not used and do not serve to perpetuate or re-establish [a] dual system."[83]

With respect to student assignments, the Court contemplated and accepted the possibility of "bizarre" results, inconvenience, and burden as an inevitable but necessary incident of desegregation.[84] It observed that "[a]ll things being equal," assignment of students to schools nearest their homes was sensible, but further noted that "all things are not equal in a system that has been deliberately constructed and maintained to enforce racial segregation."[85] Attendance policies thus were to be the function of discretionary judgment, checked only by the requirement that relief must be keyed toward the objectives of dismantling a dual school system.[86]

In reviewing the district court's demand for racial balance among students, the Court rejected the notion of fixed quotas as a constitutional imperative.[87] This limitation was a preview of standards that, as discussed in Chapter 6, eventually defined analysis of affirmative action and other remedial policies. In *Swann*, the Court refused to translate the desegregation principle into a command "that every school in every community must always reflect the racial composition of the school system as a whole."[88] Although required to purge their districts of discrimination, authorities were not subject to a "per se rule" against one-race schools.[89] As a departure point in the process of remediation, but not an inflexible requirement, the Court approved the limited use of numerical ratios as a legitimate exercise of a court's discretion.[90]

Despite refusing to provide rigid student transportation guidelines, the Court recognized that busing "has been an integral part of the public education system for years."[91] It thus endorsed busing for desegregation purposes,[92] at least to the extent travel time and distance were not so excessive that they presented a health risk to students or impaired the educational process.[93]

The *Swann* ruling represented the desegregation mandate's apex but also prefaced its devolution. Even before the decision was rendered, signs of popular discomfort with the implications of *Brown* had appeared on the political landscape. Widespread opposition to busing translated into significant support during 1968 for the presidential candidacy of George Wallace. An ardent segregationist at the time, Wallace attracted significant backing in the North and West, where major cities appeared vulnerable to the desegregation mandate's extension. A central theme in Richard Nixon's campaign was the reconstruction of the Supreme Court with personnel who not only would be responsive to law and order concerns but also would blunt the operation of the equal protection guarantee. Nixon won with less than a majority of the total vote. His appeal, coupled with Wallace's, suggested renewed tension akin to what characterized public sentiment in the decade after the Fourteenth Amendment was enacted. Although the amendment reflected a commitment to racial justice, its potential soon was qualified by societal resistance and fatigue. Mounting discomfort with the desegregation mandate suggested a like conflict between general aims and inclination to persevere with and accept the consequences of doctrinal change. Actual delimitation of the desegregation principle was prefaced by the *Swann* Court's observation that once a unitary school system was established, barring resegregation as a function of official action, constitutional responsibilities had been fulfilled.[94] The *Swann* decision, while delineating desegregative remedial powers in broad terms, thus established a foundation for doctrinal limitation.

Consistent with invalidation of dual school systems in 1954, the Court in quick order had struck down official segregation in numerous public venues.[95] Within several years, judicial output pursuant to *Brown* had exceeded the volume of cases decided over six decades of separate but equal jurisprudence. Given the aforementioned political trends of the late 1960s, it is not surprising that when the Warren Court became the Burger Court, equal protection jurisprudence soon began to reflect equivocation.

Central to *Brown* was the objective of abolishing racially identifiable schools. The Court perceived racial separation as a system which officially connoted inferiority and adversely affected the self-image and educational opportunities of its victims. Consistent with the Court's understanding are observations that formal segregation causes psychological injury "by assaulting a person's self-respect and human dignity, and [by] brand[ing]...with a sign that designates inferior status to others."[96] Without belittling the significance of *Brown*, it is necessary to recognize what the Court accomplished in 1954 and how the principle then enunciated was later qualified. The desegregation mandate, as it evolved, required liquidation of educational systems segregated by law or by overtly discriminatory official action.[97] Left unaffected by constitutional demands, however, has been pervasive and extensive segregation in the North and West attributable to patterns of residential settlement. Critics have asserted that whether a "child perceives his separation as discriminatory and invidious, he is not...going to make fine distinctions about the source of particular separation."[98] Whatever concern originally existed for the impact of segregation on self-image and opportunity therefore was lost in the translation of the doctrine in the 1970s.

The desegregation mandate was articulated at the same time society was experiencing unprecedented individual mobility and significant demographic changes. Enhanced opportunities for personal movement coalesced with suburban development to expand and redefine metropolitan areas. By the 1970s, new school districts had been established in communities that recently had not even existed. Given their lack of history, identifying a record of overt, much less subtle, discrimination was a virtual impossibility. As Justice Powell observed, "[t]he type of state-enforced segregation that *Brown I* properly condemned no longer exists in this country."[99] Notwithstanding the opportunity to craft doctrine that would reach segregation regardless of cause, the Court, instead of reckoning with the underlying dynamics of racially separate education, stopped at elimination of its overt manifestations.

As the 1970s unfolded, it became apparent that the outer limits of equal protection had been reached. Confinement of the *Brown* mandate to instances where segregative intent was identified checked the process of desegregation as it threatened to expand into heavily populated areas of the North and West.[100] Reflecting dominant public concern with the potential scope of desegregation, the Court invalidated a remedial plan covering a major northern city and its suburbs.[101] Having demarcated the spatial scope of desegregation remedies, the Court next fixed temporal limitations on desegregation obligations. It held that resegregation of a school district, following implementation of a desegregation decree, was not constitutionally offensive absent proof of discriminatory motive.[102] The trilogy of limiting principles, enunciated in three separate decisions, preserved opportunities for white flight and effectively immunized suburban communities from the demands of *Brown*.

The first qualification of the desegregation principle, in *Keyes v. School District No. 1*, conditioned the duty to desegregate on demonstration of officially discriminatory action.[103] For a constitutional responsibility to exist, it was necessary to establish first a *prima facie* case of segregative intent, which authorities had the opportunity to rebut.[104] To the extent segregation could be attributed to factors other than what the Court would consider purposeful state action, no duty to desegregate would exist. Desegregation thus would be a selective rather than a comprehensive duty, imposed only when a formal system of segregation had existed or a palpable discriminatory intent could be identified.

By failing to acknowledge a link between government action and housing patterns, the Court overlooked or discounted the legacy of official policies and practices that facilitated residential segregation. As the Court noted, "the differentiating factor between *de jure* segregation and so-called *de facto* segregation . . . is *purpose* or *intent* to segregate."[105] The line between the two concepts, however, is more illusory than real. Segregated housing was a function in many communities of officially enforced restrictive covenants.[106] Racially separated neighborhoods were an extension of not only state but national policy. The Federal Housing Administration's lending policies, for instance, protected residential loans from "adverse influences" that included the mixing of "inharmonious racial groups."[107] Further contributing to racially discrete neighborhoods have been decisions concerning the construction and closing of schools, employment of faculty and staff, assignment of students, siting of public housing, and distribution of urban development funds.[108]

Rather than exploring those ties to state action, the Court opted for bright but not necessarily precise boundaries between permissible and impermissible segregation. The consequent dividing line formally distinguishes race-dependent and race-neutral action but is useful in discerning and defeating overt rather than subtle discrimination. Even if officially determined racial separation was more evident in the South, where it was patently systematized, segregation in education was a pervasive national phenomenon.[109] Arguably, it was more insidiously rooted in the North where racial segregation became more spatial than ceremonial.[110] Despite required change in the South, as Justice Powell observed, no comparable progress would be realized in the North and West because "of the *de jure–de facto* distinction."[111] Powell suggested a hypocrisy in the Court's formulation insofar as it was "accepted complacently by many of the same voices which denounced the evils of segregated schools in the South."[112] Characterizing the severability of segregation as "a legalism rooted in history rather than present reality," which also was irrational insofar as cause did not alter adverse effect on such educational opportunity, he would have abolished the *de jure/de facto* distinction.[113]

The differentiation survived Powell's challenge and profoundly diminished the Court's responsiveness to and concern with modern segregation. It announced or at least prefaced a reluctance to adjust equal protection doctrine to the new demographic realities of the post-*Brown* era. Comprehensive realization of equal educational opportunity and elimination of all racially identifiable schools were placed beyond the reach of the desegregation mandate. Motive-referenced criteria thus exempted from constitutional attention much racially separate and unequal education.

The duty to desegregate, as limited by the *de jure* requirement, imposed a substantial burden upon plaintiffs seeking to establish a constitutional violation. That a school system was intentionally segregated could be easily proved insofar as the law spoke for itself, as it did during the Jim Crow era. Discriminatory purpose when not overt may be elusive, however, and its discernment a "tortuous effort."[114] Even the most routine decisions, as Powell noted, may affect segregation. A panoply of opportunities exists for influencing the racial mix of public schools, including

action or nonaction with respect to school building construction and location; the timing of building new schools and their size; the closing and consolidation of schools; the drawing or gerrymandering of student attendance zones; the extent to which a neighborhood policy is enforced; the recruitment, promotion and assignment of faculty and supervisory personnel; policies with respect to transfers from one school to another; whether, and to what extent, special schools will be provided, where they will be located, and who will qualify to attend them; the determination of curriculum, including whether there will be "tracks" that lead primarily to college or to vocational training, and the routing of students into these tracks; and even decisions as to social, recreational and athletic policies.[115]

Further complicating the inquiry is the problem of varying, mixed or disguised motive.[116] In those parts of the country which did not have laws requiring dual schools, proof of segregation was elusive or non-existent. Segregation of primary and secondary education in the North and West, not surprisingly, remains more profound and resistant than in the South.[117]

The *de jure* principle operates in effect as a liability-limiting concept akin to the tort principle of proximate cause. The standard, which requires a nexus between act and injury that is not too attenuated, ensures that liability for a negligent act will not be limitless. Although the cutoff point is not precisely defined, responsibility for consequential harm abates as actual injury becomes more distant and less foreseeable. Like the concept of proximate cause, the *de facto* notion is vulnerable to subjective perceptions that influence the etching of legally significant dividing lines. The liability-reducing criteria, chosen to qualify the desegregation principle, seem notable more for their capacity to restrain than for their precision.

Investment in such limiting principles for desegregation provoked sharp debate within the Court itself. As noted previously, Justice Powell would have avoided the *de jure/de facto* distinction altogether. Justice Marshall observed that school district boundaries yielding racially distinct systems, whether proximately or more remotely caused by official action, communicate the same negative message that concerned the *Brown* Court. The premise that a child's constitutional rights are not implicated because he or she is "born into a *de facto* society"[118] struck Marshall as facile and capricious.[119] To the extent racial separation suggests a systematic pattern, breeds a sense of inferiority, and impairs educational development and opportunity, causation-based distinctions from his perspective seemed more a function of convenience than principle. This perception conformed with Powell's sense that causation-referenced limiting principles serve no purpose other than to "perpetuate a legalism rooted in history rather than present reality."[120]

Further bounding the duty to desegregate was the Court's determination that, in the event of purposeful segregative design, any remedy must be tailored to the scope of the constitutional violation. Such a qualification radiated from the *de facto* distinction and ensured that demands would not be imposed in communities where official wrong was not discernible. As demonstrated by the circumstances from which *Milliken v. Bradley* arose, the limiting principle precluded interdistrict remedies in major urban centers.[121] Even if the city school system itself had a history of discrimination, any attempt to desegregate was a generally vain exercise if a court order could not reach adjacent and mostly white suburban communities that had evolved in the meantime.

In the *Milliken* case, it was established that the Detroit school board purposely had created and maintained a segregated system.[122] The trial court determined that the state had contributed significantly to that result. With respect to the city's role, the trial court specifically found that the school board had created and maintained optional attendance zones, bused students to distant schools for purposes of perpetuating segregation, and gauged construction policies to minimize mixing.[123] It determined that the state had facilitated segregation by nullifying a voluntary desegregation plan, overseeing construction, implementing a transportation program that was racially steered and unequally funded, and sanctioning race-dependent attendance plans.[124]

Despite the trial court's findings, the Supreme Court disagreed with the nature and extent of illegal state action. Although not foreclosing the use of interdistrict remedies as a matter of theory, the Court limited their operation to constitutional violations transcending a single district. Area-wide relief was unavailable as a practical matter, therefore barring a finding that district lines had been established or adjusted to foster segregation or that the racially discriminatory acts of one district had a segregative effect in another.[125] Without such a determination, the Court found that the scope of relief exceeded the nature of the constitutional violation.[126]

In emphasizing local autonomy in education and minimizing the possibilities for cross-district relief, the Court effectively shielded most metropolitan areas from constitutional demands. As Justice White saw it, however, deliberate segregative acts and consequences were left unremedied, and similar results would follow elsewhere to the extent states vested "sufficient power over [their] public schools in [their] local school districts."[127] He thus emphasized findings "that over a long period of years those in charge of the Michigan public schools engaged in various practices calculated to effect the segregation of the Detroit school system."[128] Even if the state was implicated in fostering segregation, the Court was unwilling to impute the wrong to specific suburban districts.

The desegregation principle, having been circumscribed in *Keyes* by the *de jure/de facto* distinction, thus was narrowed further in *Milliken*. Reversal of the trial court decision communicated an attitude contrary to what the Court had radiated for nearly two decades. Federal courts, which had been rebuked for not going far enough in facilitating desegregation, were admonished for going too far. In contrast to the demand in *Green* for plans that work now, the circumscription of remedial potential in *Milliken* suggested the possibility that effective relief might not even be an option.

Exemption of suburban districts from remedial obligations reflected another significant doctrinal change. Previously, the Court had insisted on elimination of the vestiges of segregation, "root and branch."[129] Without the possibility of interdistrict relief, it was evident that eradication

processes might be partial rather than comprehensive. Such consequences have elicited criticism on the grounds that the Court has not only
relaxed remedial obligations but also disregarded *Brown*'s concern with
equal educational opportunity. As Justice Marshall put it, the denial of a
meaningful remedy afforded "no remedy at all ... guaranteeing that Negro children ... will receive the same separate and inherently unequal
education in the future as they have been unconstitutionally afforded
in the past."[130]

The *Keyes* and *Milliken* decisions showed the Court's reluctance to
adapt the desegregation principle to diverse circumstances of racial separation. Further indicating that the *Brown* mandate would not be a doctrine for all segregative seasons was a third limiting principle
emphasizing that the duty to desegregate was not enduring. In *Milliken*,
the Court had determined that constitutional obligations were subject
to spatial restrictions. Its decision in *Pasadena City Board of Education v.
Spangler* established qualifications also with respect to duration.[131]

In *Spangler*, the Court determined that desegregation duties abated
when a unitary system was established.[132] "[H]aving once implemented
a racially neutral attendance pattern in order to remedy ... perceived
constitutional violations," new duties would not be imposed simply as a
function of demographic change.[133] Termination of remedial obligations, upon severance of the linkage between official act and segregative
result was presented as an extension of the *de facto* concept. Further
constitutional responsibility would not be imposed absent a showing of
segregative action attributable to state or local authorities.[134] The indi-
cation of *Spangler* was that when a system becomes unitary, barring
evidence of official tampering, school officials need not respond if the
community resegregates. It is not a universally accepted premise, however, that population redistribution after a desegregation order is constitutionally insignificant. The Court in *Spangler* attributed demographic
consequences affecting the racial composition of schools to the "quite
normal pattern of human migration."[135] Despite that characterization,
it has been argued that a connection to official action exists, which the
Court simply ignores. Justice Marshall maintained that insofar as a state
has "created a system where whites and Negroes were intentionally kept
apart so that they could not become accustomed to learning together,
[it] is responsible for the fact that many whites will react to the dismantling of that segregated system by attempting to flee to the suburbs."[136]

The limiting principle enunciated in *Spangler* denied any such responsibility. To the extent resegregation follows desegregation efforts
and a linkage to official action is not discerned, equal protection is not
implicated. The promise of "a unitary school system in which racial
segregation [was] eliminated root and branch"[137] thus does not operate
as a permanent guarantee of racially mixed education. Removal of re-

segregation from a chain of events commenced by discriminatory practices and policies was consistent with the liability-limiting nature of the *de facto* concept itself and likewise reminiscent of how proximate causation principles operate. The practical consequence was further expansion of constitutionally permissible segregation. Desegregation in such cities as Boston, Detroit, Dayton, and San Francisco was followed by declining white enrollment at rates ranging from 15 to 22 percent during the implementation years themselves.[138] Such an exodus, without the opportunity for interdistrict remedies, has helped make meaningful desegregation in urban centers a mathematical impossibility.

Further diminishing the potential of the desegregation principle was the determination that education was not a fundamental right. The *Brown* Court had described education as "importan[t]...to our democratic society," and at least intimated that it was of fundamental significance.[139] That impression was reinforced in *Bolling v. Sharpe*, when the Court referred to a "deprivation of...liberty."[140] In *San Antonio Independent School District v. Rodriguez*, however, the Court declared that education was not a fundamental right and thus rejected the proposition that it must be equally funded in all of a state's districts.[141] The irony of the *Rodriguez* decision was that disparities in educational quality, which theoretically might have been repaired pursuant to the separate but equal doctrine, were no longer subject to constitutional regulation.

For some, the devolution of the desegregation mandate in the 1970s was reminiscent of Fourteenth Amendment jurisprudence a century earlier. Responding to what he perceived as unwarranted doctrinal retreat, Justice Marshall reminded that "[d]esegregation is not and was never expected to be an easy task."[142] What he saw in principles limiting *Brown*'s operation was a general sense that the desegregation process "ha[d] gone far enough."[143] Such an observation hints that, as in the *Civil Rights Cases*,[144] constitutional principle had reached the margins of societal tolerance and interest had given way to fatigue. The narrowing of the desegregation principle also suggests that, at least with respect to its premise that the law "is powerless to eradicate social instincts,"[145] the *Plessy* Court did not entirely miscalculate.

The Court, especially during the late 1950s and throughout the 1960s, invoked the equal protection guarantee. Such jurisprudence was contrary to doctrinal antecedents notable for accommodation of state power and cultural norms. As equal protection doctrine assumed the risk of social disruption, abiding tensions associated with the Fourteenth Amendment invariably were exacerbated. Justice Powell thus observed that "in city after city [forced integration has fostered]...[t]he process of resegregation, stimulated by resentment against judicial coercion."[146] For many years, the Court refused to factor in resentment of and resistance to desegregation as mitigating considerations in the crafting of constitutional policy.[147] Yet it was the Court itself during the 1970s that, while not overtly deferring to separatist instincts, afforded them constitutional living space.

Powell also characterized modern school segregation as the consequence of "familiar segregated housing patterns . . . caused by social, economic, and demographic forces for which no school board is responsible."[148] This depiction reflects perceived limits of constitutional responsibility and suggests perhaps that residential segregation is normative. Consistent with that vision is Justice Rehnquist's observation that "[e]ven if the Constitution required it, and it were possible for federal courts to do it, no equitable decree can fashion an 'Emerald City' where all races, ethnic groups, and persons of various income levels live side by side."[149]

The desegregation mandate originally assumed that educational policy should be race-neutral rather than race-dependent. It is ironic but perhaps not surprising, given lingering race-consciousness, that interest in preserving constitutional gains has induced contemporary policy attentive to race. Burdens imposed on minorities to maintain integration, however, have refocused attention on the feasibility of *Brown*'s aims in a society that, if no longer segregated as a matter of law, nonetheless remains functionally disposed toward racial separation.

Preserving the accomplishments of *Brown* thus has presented a challenge to school boards, which, in attempting to avoid resegregation, have reverted to policies that previously would have been unthinkable. In the name of integration maintenance, school boards have discontinued or substantially modified busing plans and reintroduced neighborhood school concepts that would have been unacceptable during the first decade of *Brown*. Contrary to the original aim of eliminating racially identifiable schools, single-race facilities define some modern integration maintenance plans. Such reversion reflects an official sense that controls on racial mixing are necessary to stem an otherwise accelerated movement of white students from public schools.[150]

In Brooklyn, New York, for instance, where the white student population had declined from 94.2% in 1957 to 36.4% in 1981, school officials adopted a freedom of choice plan, which allowed students from an all-minority high school to attend other high schools in Queens and later anywhere in New York.[151] Because white students continued to exit city schools and thereby destabilize desegregation efforts, official policy increasingly factored in white sensitivities.[152] The pursuit of racial balance thus became hostage to white perceptions that, if sensing too much or too quick of a minority increase, might prompt further disenrollment.[153]

By imposing controls on the rate and extent of racial change at critical schools, officials contemplated metered minority transfers that would minimize white flight and resegregation.[154] Restricted entry into racially diverse schools, however, effectively locked many minorities into racially identifiable schools. Black and Hispanic students were not allowed to enroll in schools where their attendance would cause white enrollment to drop below 50 percent.[155] The plan thus assumed the continuation of at least some single-race schools and established a system of racial preferences that effectively burdened minorities to preserve a semblance of racial balance.[156]

A system of racially identifiable schools also was central to an integration maintenance plan adopted in Norfolk, Virginia.[157] Unlike New York, where school integration was mandated by state policy, Norfolk schools had been desegregated by judicial decree in 1971—fifteen years after litigation had commenced.[158] Four years after being ordered to desegregate, the school system was declared unitary.

Consistent with the experience of other cities forced to desegregate, the population of Norfolk itself diminished and white enrollment in the school system declined substantially. To minimize white flight, the school board reestablished neighborhood schools for elementary students[159] in anticipation that they eventually would be fed into racially mixed junior and senior high schools.[160] The trial court noted that public sentiment could not obstruct or dilute the obligation to dismantle an officially segregated dual school system.[161] Nonetheless, it concluded that white flight might be factored into voluntary efforts to improve racial balance.[162] Concern for the dominant race's reaction, which was a source of the *Plessy* principle[163] but unacceptable as a basis for evading desegregation responsibilities,[164] thus was reintroduced as a predicate for integration maintenance. Constitutional achievement accordingly had been reduced to a determination that limited segregation was needed to preserve some racial diversity.

The desegregation process by the 1990s resembled to some extent a ritual performed as a condition for reversion to the societal norm. Consistent with such imagery, the Court in *Board of Education of Oklahoma City Public Schools v. Dowell* emphasized that school desegregation decrees "are not intended to operate in perpetuity."[165] In so doing, the Court distinguished permanent decrees in the antitrust context where a "continuing danger of unlawful[ness] still existed"[166] and modification was impermissible if litigative aims "have not been fully achieved."[167] Despite the reemergence of racially identifiable schools, even if ultimately chargeable to past, albeit abandoned, discriminatory policy,[168] the *Dowell* Court reiterated that inquiry will be confined to whether school officials have "complied in good faith with [a] desegregation decree . . . , and whether the vestiges of past discrimination hav[e] been eliminated to the extent practicable."[169] As for the tension that still defines Fourteenth Amendment jurisprudence, the resolution is more accommodating than disruptive of a society functionally disposed toward, if no longer officially governed by, racial distinctions.

General equal protection doctrine since 1954 has mirrored changes in the desegregation principle. Consistent with the *de jure* requirement grafted on the *Brown* principle, constitutional reckoning during the 1970s became captive to the "discriminatory purpose" standard. The Court determined that claims of disproportionate impact in employment, housing, and criminal justice were constitutionally insignificant because disproportionate impact by itself did not satisfy the requirement of purposeful discrimination.[170] Motive-based inquiry, as noted previously, is notoriously unfavorable to constitutional claims because subjective intent is easily concealed or otherwise difficult to discern.[171] For precisely such reasons, the Court has refused to apply purpose criteria in the freedom of speech context.[172] Motive-referenced inquiry was inapt, it observed, because constitutional "stakes are sufficiently high . . . to eschew guesswork."[173]

Despite its repudiation and futility in other constitutional contexts, purpose criteria have been jurisprudentially established for equal protection purposes. As explained by the Supreme Court, a focus on disproportional impact alone would disrupt the political process by jeopardizing "a whole range of tax, welfare, public service, regulatory, and licensing statutes."[174] Critics maintain that such concern is overblown because the Court must attend only to effects that have racial significance.[175] Investment in discriminatory purpose criteria for practical purposes has established an effective foil to equal protection claims. Although the Court has suggested a historical pattern of segregation would count as evidence that an illegal motive infected a challenged action, it turned a blind eye to substantial disparities in the operation of a state's death penalty and the legacy of a dual justice system. Research offered in *McCleskey v. Kemp* showed that Georgia prosecutors "sought the death penalty in 70% of the cases involving black defendants and white victims; 32% of the cases involving white defendants and white victims; 15% of the cases involving black defendants and black victims; and 19% of the cases involving white defendants and black victims" during a ten-year period.[176] Georgia courts, moreover, assessed the death penalty "in 22% of the cases involving black defendants and white victims; 8% of the cases involving white defendants and white victims; 1% of the cases involving black defendants and black victims; and 3% of the cases involving white defendants and black victims."[177] Responding to those disparities, the Court dismissed duality in capital punishment as a mere "discrepancy that appears to correlate with race . . . [and] an inevitable part of our criminal justice system."[178] Such a conclusion, as Justice Brennan suggested, was possible only to the extent the Court ignored the history of a dual criminal justice system and the different advice an attorney would be obligated to provide white and black clients.[179] Even if probably not understood by the Court as constitutionally significant, an execution in 1991 represented the first time in nearly half a century that a white defendant was put to death in the United States for a crime against a black victim.[180]

Consistent with its forceful expoundment of the equal protection guarantee during the 1960s, the Court simultaneously read Congress's power to enforce the Fourteenth Amendment in broad terms. As a consequence, post-*Brown* civil rights legislation prohibiting discrimination in employment, education, voting, housing, and public contracting became possible.[181] As equal protection jurisprudence approached the final decade of the twentieth century, however, the Court narrowed the operative reach of two legislative enactments.

In *Wards Cove Packing Co. v. Atonio*, it increased the burden upon claimants alleging discrimination under Title VII of the Civil Rights Act of 1964.[182] Plaintiffs consequently were obligated, in establishing a *prima facie* case, to identify the specific employment practice allegedly responsible for any observed statistical disparities.[183] A previous requirement, that an employer justify a challenged practice by showing "business necessity," was relaxed in favor of "a reasoned review" of its justification.[184]

The Court in *Patterson v. McLean Credit Union* narrowed 42 U.S.C. §1981, the modern descendant of the Civil Rights Act of 1866, so that it prohibited racial discrimination in contracts but did not cover post-formation harassment.[185] Responding to concern about its direction, the Court observed that "[n]either our words nor our decisions should be interpreted as signaling one inch of retreat from...forbid[ding] discrimination in the private, as well as the public sphere."[186]

Both decisions, however, delimited the scope of anti-discrimination standards. The *Patterson* decision retreated from even the early command of *Strauder* that remedial legislation was to be construed liberally and flexibly.[187] The Court's drift prompted some justices to "wonder whether the majority still believes that race discrimination—or, more accurately, race discrimination against nonwhites—is a problem in our society, or even remembered that it ever was."[188]

Even though eventually qualified, the *Brown* decision remains unsettling to some legal theorists still unable to square it with principles of judicial restraint. Perceptions of the desegregation mandate as an essentially anti-democratic exercise are rooted in an original record that did not contemplate racially mixed schools. Some critics endeavor to reconcile the desegregation principle with apolitical demands by suggesting that the *Brown* case required investment in methodology disfavored by the Fourteenth Amendment's framers or abandonment of equal protection altogether.[189] The notion that the Court was caught between two alternatives, each at odds with original understanding, may be a somewhat procrustean and unnecessary effort at reconciling the imperatives of review with the requirements of democratic consent. The same history that discloses early provision for racially segregated schools also reveals original flexibility in accounting for civil rights. When the Fourteenth Amendment was framed, for instance, it was considered politically suicidal to advocate black suffrage. What was unrealistic in 1868 proved not only feasible but also essential in 1869 when Republicans, concerned with the influence of a politically resurgent South and seeking security for recently established civil status and rights, championed the notion. The redirection of policy showed an inclination to reexamine and even abandon an initial position if necessary to realize overarching aims. It at least is credible if not certain that, upon recognizing how closely related education would be to economic opportunity, the framers might have made similar adjustments in their thinking.

The devolution of *Brown* has disclosed a coursing of the law to a point that actually may be closer to initial expectations than the either-or choice identified by many professed originalists. Distinctions between *de jure* and *de facto* segregation and consequent constriction of the duty to desegregate, compounded by reversion of judicial review from strict scrutiny to mere rationality when discriminatory purpose is not established, indicate repudiation of a broadly defined anti-discrimination principle. Such qualification at least comports with the reality that original equalization concerns themselves were limited. As discussed in Chapter 7, however, resultant doctrine still underserves original and consensual expectations.

NOTES

1. *See* Brown v. Board of Education, 347 U.S. 483, 486 n.1 (1954) (citing Gebhart v. Belton, 87 A.2d 862 (Del. 1952)).
2. Briggs v. Elliott, 98 F. Supp. 529 (E.D.S.C. 1951).
3. *See* Lively, *The Supreme Court Appointment Process: In Search of Constitutional Roles and Responsibilities*, 59 S. Cal. L. Rev. 551, 567–72 (1986).
4. *See id.* at 567.
5. 72 Cong. Rec. 8,037 (1930) (Sen. Wagner).
6. *See* Briggs v. Elliott, 98 F. Supp. at 538–40 (Waring, J., dissenting).
7. *Id.* at 536.
8. *Id.* at 540 (Waring, J., dissenting).
9. *Id.* (Waring, J., dissenting).
10. Briggs v. Elliott, 132 F. Supp. 776, 777 (E.D.S.C. 1955).
11. United States v. Jefferson County Board of Education, 372 F.2d 836, 863 (5th Cir. 1966), *corrected*, 380 F.2d 385 (5th Cir.), *cert. denied*, 389 U.S. 840 (1967).
12. Brown v. Board of Education, 347 U.S. at 489.
13. *See supra* notes 17–19 and accompanying text.

14. *See* Chapter 2, note 30 and accompanying text.

15. Brown v. Board of Education, 347 U.S. at 489–90.

16. *Id.* at 490.

17. *Id.* at 492.

18. *Id.* at 492–93.

19. *Id.* at 493.

20. *Id.*

21. *Id.* at 494.

22. *Id.*

23. *Id.*

24. *Id.*

25. See Plessy v. Ferguson, 163 U.S. 537, 551 (1896), discussed in Chapter 4.

26. *See, e.g.,* R. Bork, The Tempting of America 82–83 (1990).

27. *See* R. Kluger, Simple Justice 706 (1976).

28. Brown v. Board of Education, 347 U.S. at 495.

29. *See id.*

30. Bolling v. Sharpe, 347 U.S. 497 (1954).

31. *Id.* at 499.

32. *Id.* at 500.

33. Brown v. Board of Education, 347 U.S. at 495.

34. *Id.* at 495–96.

35. Brown v. Board of Education, 349 U.S. 294 (1955).

36. *See id.* at 299.

37. *Id.*

38. *Id.*

39. *Id.* at 300.

40. *Id.*

41. *Id.* at 301.

42. A. Mason, The Supreme Court from Taft to Warren 207–08 (1968).

43. Ark. Const. amend. 44 (quoted in Cooper v. Aaron, 358 U.S. 1, 8–9 (1958)).

44. *See* Cooper v. Aaron, 358 U.S. at 12.

45. NAACP v. Button, 371 U.S. 415, 422 (1963).

46. *Id.* at 444–45.

47. *See* Cooper v. Aaron, 358 U.S. at 8–9.

48. *See id.* at 11.

49. *See id.* at 12.

50. *See id.* at 12–13.

51. *Id.* at 16–17.

52. Marbury v. Madison, 5 U.S. (1 Cranch) 137, 177 (1803).

53. Cooper v. Aaron, 358 U.S. at 18.

54. *See, e.g.,* R. Bork, *supra* note 26, at 120, 176; Meese, *The Law of the Constitution,* 61 Tul. L. Rev. 979, 982 (1987).

55. Cooper v. Aaron, 358 U.S. at 16.

56. *Id.*

57. *Id.* at 18.

58. Rogers v. Paul, 382 U.S. 198 (1965).

59. *Id.* at 200.

60. Griffin v. County School Board of Prince Edward County, 377 U.S. 218, 232 (1964).

61. *See id.* at 225.

62. Green v. County School Board of New Kent County, Virginia, 391 U.S. 430 (1968).

63. *See id.* at 438, 441.

64. *Id.* at 438.

65. *Id.* at 441.

66. Wright v. City Council of Emporia, 407 U.S. 451 (1972).

67. United States v. Scotland Neck City Board of Education, 407 U.S. 484 (1972).

68. Wright v. City Council of Emporia, 407 U.S. at 456; United States v. Scotland Neck City Board of Education, 407 U.S. at 486–87.

69. North Carolina State Board of Education v. Swann, 402 U.S. 43 (1971).

70. *Id.* at 45.

71. Crawford v. Board of Education, 458 U.S. 527 (1982).

72. Washington v. Seattle School District No. 1, 458 U.S. 457, 484 (1982).

73. A decade after *Brown*, barely two percent of black students in southern states attended schools where they were not in a racial majority. *See* Bureau of the Census, U.S. Dept. of Commerce, Statistical Abstract of the United States 124 (1974).

74. Green v. County School Board of New Kent County, Virginia, 391 U.S. at 438 (quoting Griffin v. County School Board of Prince Edward County, 377 U.S. at 234.

75. *Id.* at 439 (emphasis in original).

76. *See* Griffin v. County School Board of Prince Edward County, 377 U.S. at 233–34.

77. Swann v. Charlotte-Mecklenburg Board of Education, 402 U.S. 1 (1971).

78. *See id.* at 15–16.

79. Green v. County School Board of New Kent County, Virginia, 391 U.S. at 437–38.

80. Swann v. Charlotte-Mecklenburg Board of Education, 402 U.S. at 15.

81. *Id.* at 19–20.

82. *Id.* at 21.

83. *Id.*

84. *Id.* at 28.

85. *Id.*

86. *Id.* at 28–29.

87. *Id.* at 24.

88. *Id.*

89. *Id.* at 26.

90. *Id.* at 25.

91. *Id.* at 29.

92. *Id.* at 29–30.

93. *Id.* at 30–31.

94. *Id.* at 31–32.

95. *E.g.,* New Orleans City Park Improvement Association v. Detiege, 358

U.S. 54 (1958) (parks); Gayle v. Browder, 352 U.S. 903, 903 (1956) (buses); Mayor and City Council of Baltimore City v. Dawson, 350 U.S. 877, 877 (1955) (beaches).

96. Lawrence, *The Id, the Ego and Equal Protection: Reckoning with Unconscious Racism*, 39 Stan. L. Rev. 317, 350–51 (1987).

97. Columbus Board of Education v. Penick, 443 U.S. 449, 458–60 (1979).

98. A. Bickel, The Supreme Court and the Idea of Progress 119 (1970).

99. Columbus Board of Education v. Penick, 443 U.S. at 481 (Powell, J., dissenting).

100. *See* Keyes v. School District No. 1, 413 U.S. 189 (1973).

101. *See* Milliken v. Bradley, 418 U.S. 717 (1974).

102. *See* Pasadena City Board of Education v. Spangler, 427 U.S. 424 (1976).

103. Keyes v. School District No. 1, 413 U.S. at 208.

104. *Id.* Put simply, a *prima facie* case exists when a plaintiff establishes facts that, absent any contradictory evidence, would entitle him or her to prevail.

105. *Id.* (emphasis in original).

106. *See id.* at 216 (Douglas, J., concurring).

107. *See* P. Jacobs, Prelude to Riot: A View of Urban America from the Bottom 140 (1967).

108. Keyes v. School District No. 1, 413 U.S. at 216 (Douglas, J., concurring).

109. *See* U.S. Department of Health, Education and Welfare, School Enrollment Survey (1971), 118 Cong. Rec. 563–66 (1972).

110. G. Myrdal, An American Dilemma 621 (1944).

111. Keyes v. School District No. 1, 413 U.S. at 218–19 (Powell, J., concurring and dissenting).

112. *Id.* at 219 (Powell, J., concurring and dissenting).

113. *Id.*

114. *Id.* at 234–35 (Powell, J., concurring and dissenting).

115. *Id.* at 234–35; *see* Goodman, *De Facto School Segregation: A Constitutional and Empirical Analysis*, 60 Calif. L. Rev. 275, 284–85 (1972).

116. *See* Edward v. Aguillard, 482 U.S. 578, 636–37 (1987) (Scalia, J., dissenting); United States v. O'Brien, 391 U.S. 367, 383–84 (1969); Lawrence, *supra* note 96, at 319.

117. *See* U.S. Commission on Civil Rights, Desegregation of the Nation's Public Schools: A Status Report 18–27 (1979).

118. Cisneros v. Corpus Christi Independent School District, 467 F.2d 142, 148 (5th Cir. 1972) (en banc) (quoting United States v. Jefferson County Board of Education, 380 F.2d at 397 (Gewin, J., dissenting)).

119. Milliken v. Bradley, 418 U.S. at 782, 804–05 (Marshall, J., dissenting).

120. Keyes v. School District No. 1, 413 U.S. at 219 (Powell, J., concurring and dissenting).

121. Milliken v. Bradley, 418 U.S. at 717.

122. *Id.* at 725–26.

123. *Id.*

124. *Id.* at 734–35 n.16; *id.* at 770–71 (White, J., dissenting).

125. *Id.* at 746–47.

126. *Id.*

127. *Id.* at 763 (White, J., dissenting).

128. *Id.* at 762 (White, J., dissenting).

129. Green v. County School Board, 391 U.S. at 438.

130. Milliken v. Bradley, 418 U.S. at 782 (Marshall, J., dissenting).

131. Pasadena City Board of Education v. Spangler, 427 U.S. at 437.

132. *Id.* at 436.

133. *Id.* at 436–37.

134. *Id.* at 435–36. *See* Swann v. Charlotte-Mecklenburg Board of Education, 402 U.S. at 32 (absent showing of deliberate official action to manipulate demographics and thereby affect racial composition of schools, further judicial action unnecessary).

135. 427 U.S. at 436.

136. Milliken v. Bradley, 418 U.S. at 806 (Marshall, J., dissenting).

137. Swann v. Charlotte-Mecklenburg Board of Education, 402 U.S. at 15 (*quoting* Green v. County School Board of New Kent County, 391 U.S. at 437–38).

138. Marek, *Education by Decree*, New Perspectives, Summer 1985, at 36, 39.

139. Brown v. Board of Education, 347 U.S. at 492–93.

140. Bolling v. Sharpe, 347 U.S. at 500.

141. San Antonio Independent School District v. Rodriguez, 411 U.S. 1, 33–37 (1973).

142. Milliken v. Bradley, 418 U.S. at 814 (Marshall, J., dissenting).

143. *Id.* (Marshall, J., dissenting).

144. In striking down federal civil rights legislation prohibiting racial discrimination in public accommodations, as discussed in Chapter 3, the Court observed that "there must be some stage in the progress of [one's] elevation when he takes the rank of a mere citizen, and ceases to be the special favorite of the laws, and when his rights . . . are to be protected in the ordinary mode by which other men's rights are protected." Civil Rights Cases, 109 U.S. 3, 25 (1883).

145. Plessy v. Ferguson, 163 U.S. at 551.

146. Columbus Board of Education v. Penick, 443 U.S. at 483 (Powell, J., dissenting).

147. *See, e.g.,* Alexander v. Holmes County Board of Education, 396 U.S. 19, 20 (1969); Cooper v. Aaron, 358 U.S. at 16.

148. Columbus Board of Education v. Penick, 443 U.S. at 483 (Powell, J., dissenting).

149. Cleveland Board of Education v. Reed, 445 U.S. 935, 938 (1980) (Rehnquist, J., dissenting from denial of certiorari).

150. *See, e.g.,* Riddick v. School Board of Norfolk, 784 F.2d 521, 527 (4th Cir.), *cert. denied,* 479 U.S. 938 (1986); Parent Association of Andrew Jackson High School v. Ambach, 598 F.2d 705 (2d Cir. 1979).

151. *See* Parent Association of Andrew Jackson High School v. Ambach, 598 F.2d at 710–11.

152. Parent Association of Andrew Jackson High School v. Ambach, 738 F.2d 574, 576 (2d 1984).

153. *Id.*

154. *Id.*

155. *Id.* at 577.

156. *Id.* at 581 n.9.

157. *See* Riddick v. School Board of Norfolk, 627 F. Supp. 814 (E.D. Va. 1984), *aff'd*, 784 F.2d 521 (4th Cir.), *cert. denied*, 479 U.S. 938 (1986).

158. *Id.* at 816–17.

159. *Id.* at 818.

160. *Id.*

161. *Id.* at 823.

162. *Id.* at 824.

163. *Id.* Segregation, as discussed in Chapter 4, was upheld on the grounds that it reflected established custom, promoted public comfort, and preserved peace and order.

164. *See supra* note 147 and accompanying text.

165. Board of Education of Oklahoma City Public Schools v. Dowell, 111 S. Ct. 630, 632 (1991).

166. *Id.* at 636.

167. *Id.* (quoting United States v. United Shoe Machinery Corp., 391 U.S. 244, 248 (1968)).

168. *Id.* at 644 (Marshall, J., dissenting).

169. *Id.* at 638.

170. *See* McCleskey v. Kemp, 481 U.S. 279, 298 (1987) (death penalty); Village of Arlington Heights v. Metropolitan Housing Development Corporation, 429 U.S. 252, 265 (1977) (housing); Washington v. Davis, 426 U.S. 229, 240 (1976) (public employment).

171. *See supra* note 116 and accompanying text.

172. *See* United States v. O'Brien, 391 U.S. at 383–84.

173. *Id.* at 384.

174. Washington v. Davis, 426 U.S. at 248.

175. *See* Lawrence, *supra* note 96, at 355–58.

176. McCleskey v. Kemp, 481 U.S. at 287.

177. *Id.* at 286.

178. *Id.* at 312.

179. *Id.* at 321, 329 (Brennan, J., dissenting).

180. *See* Rarity for U.S. Executions: White Dies for Killing Black, New York Times, Sept. 7, 1991, § 1, at 1, col. 1.

181. *See* Civil Rights Act of 1964, 42 U.S.C. §§2000a to 2000b–3 (public accommodations and facilities); §§2000d to 2000d–6(d) (public schools); § 2000e to 2000e–2(j) (employment).

182. Wards Cove Packing Co. v. Atonio, 109 S. Ct. 2115 (1989).

183. *Id.* at 2124.

184. *Id.* at 2126.

185. Patterson v. McLean Credit Union, 109 S. Ct. 2363, 2373 (1989).

186. *Id.* at 2379.

187. Strauder v. West Virginia, 100 U.S. 303 (1879).

188. Wards Cove Packing Co. v. Atonio, 109 S. Ct. at 2136 (Blackmun, J., dissenting, joined by Brennan and Marshall, J.J.).

189. R. Bork, *supra* note 26.

Chapter 6

Color Blindness Revisited

The concept of a color-blind Constitution was introduced by Justice Harlan in the late nineteenth century.[1] Harlan's assertion that "[t]here is no caste here"[2] essentially was dismissed by the *Plessy* Court pursuant to distinctions between civil and social equality. Eventual determination that separate was inherently unequal in education and in other public contexts reflected investment in color blindness as a broad spectrum principle of equal protection. The subsequent addition of discriminatory purpose criteria, however, effectively narrowed and confounded the possibilities of establishing constitutional violations. By requiring proof of illegal motive and discounting the significance of disproportionality, the Supreme Court fashioned doctrine responsive to overt discrimination but poorly adapted to recognizing and accounting for subtle or unconscious prejudice.

As equal protection jurisprudence coursed toward the end of the twentieth century, traditional manifestations of discrimination, such as prescriptive segregation, essentially had been eradicated. Racism and discrimination primarily had become unconscious or a function of hidden motive.[3] To the extent patently race-conscious policies existed, they generally manifested themselves as initiatives or programs accounting for past discrimination. For modern purposes, therefore, color-blind criteria have become more instrumental in defeating the remediation rather than the reality of discrimination against minorities.

Affirmative action is a concept susceptible to diverse understandings that are not always clarified before debate commences. The notion, for instance, may include institutional initiatives to identify impediments to minority recruiting, advancement or retention. It also may denote an effort to seek out qualified minority candidates and thus broaden a selection pool. Affirmative action also may describe a program of minority preferences. Such policies, especially in employment and education contexts, have been the source of significant constitutional controversy.

The debate over racial preferences discloses abiding tension between society's commitment to racial justice and its willingness to absorb associated costs. The Court first reckoned substantively with the issue of minority set asides in 1978. A few years earlier, in *De Funis v. Odegaard*, it had denied review of a preferential admission program at a state-supported law school.[4] Dismissal of the action as moot elicited criticism that the Court was "transform[ing] principles of avoidance of constitutional decisions into devices for side-stepping resolution of difficult cases."[5] The denial of review also prompted dissenting justices to note the pressing nature of the issue and that "few constitutional questions in recent history have stirred as much debate."[6] The controversy magnified rather than abated, and the Court a few years later rendered its lengthiest and most fractionated decision on race since *Scott v. Sandford*.

In *Regents of the University of California v. Bakke*, the Court examined a preferential admissions program at a state medical school.[7] The institution had established criteria which set aside positions for designated racial or ethnic minorities. The respondent, a white male, maintained that he was denied admission as a consequence of the policy.[8] The California Supreme Court, finding the program at odds with the state constitution, Title VI of the Civil Rights Act of 1964, and equal protection, accordingly ordered the school to admit the respondent.[9] The U.S. Supreme Court affirmed the decision[10] but did so on grounds that did not conclusively answer the constitutional question. Four justices determined that the special admissions program breached neither the equal protection guarantee nor Title VI of the Civil Rights Act of 1964.[11] Four justices avoided the constitutional issue altogether and discerned a violation of Title VI.[12] Justice Powell concluded that the program was generally at odds with the equal protection guarantee and Title VI.[13] Unlike the four justices who discerned a statutory violation, Powell maintained that neither Title VI nor the Constitution barred all race-conscious programs.[14] His refusal to foreclose such classifications entirely was significant because it was the one constitutional point in the decision that commanded majority support.[15]

On the critical question of what the appropriate standard of review should be, Powell refused to join the four justices who found the program constitutionally permissible. Instead of a bifurcated level of review contingent on the nature of the classification, he asserted that any racial favoritism, even if characterized as benign, should be subject to strict review.[16] The level of judicial scrutiny employed in evaluating a policy or action is critical to the outcome of a case. To the extent a mere rationality standard operates, as in the assessment of general economic regulation, review is highly deferential and the contested law generally is upheld. When the Court engages in strict scrutiny, the challenged enactment or provision must be justified by compelling reasons and must minimally burden constitutional interests. Such exacting review, characterizing analysis of racial classifications, tends to be unforgiving. In between strict and rationality criteria is an intermediate standard of review, used when gender and other classifications are implicated, which is reducible to a balancing of constitutional and governmental interests. In advocating rigorous judicial scrutiny of the special admissions program, Powell did not make clear whether he meant review that, as applied since 1954, was "strict in theory, and fatal in fact."[17] Confusing the issue somewhat was his mixing of "compelling interest" language of an intermediate standard.[18] Because a less rigorous level of review was urged by other justices whom he did not join, it may be logical to infer that Powell intended all racial classifications to be reviewed pursuant to the most exacting standards.

Having identified what he considered the appropriate level of scrutiny, Powell determined whether a compelling reason existed for the special admissions program. The university had offered four justifications that included enrolling a minimum number of students from certain racial or ethnic groups, eliminating discrimination, improving health care in disadvantaged communities, and maintaining a diverse student body.[19] Powell considered each point seriatim. First, he determined that the objective of admitting a fixed proportion of designated minorities, whether identified in terms of quotas or goals, was "facially invalid."[20] Although acknowledging a valid state interest in accounting for "identified discrimination," he concluded that remediation requires legislative or judicial findings of prior wrongdoing by the pertinent institution or program.[21] Such determinations had not been made, nor did he consider the school itself authorized to make them on its own.[22] Third, Powell criticized the assumption that minority students necessarily would practice in and thereby improve the quality of health care in disadvantaged communities.[23] Even if that goal might reflect a profound interest, he found no evidence that the "special admissions program is either needed or geared to promote that goal."[24] Finally, Powell determined that the aim of general diversification represented a compelling interest. Although disapproving of diversification based on racial or ethnic considerations exclusively, he concluded that "students with a particular background—whether it be ethnic, geographic, culturally advantaged or disadvantaged—may bring to a professional school of medicine experiences, outlooks and ideas that enrich the training of its student body and better equip its graduates to render with understanding their vital service to humanity."[25]

Given four votes for a manifestly race-conscious policy and Powell's approval of race as a factor within a general diversification policy,[26] majority support existed at least for the latter premise. The Court did not exempt any racial classification from close scrutiny for compliance but left open the possibility of limited consideration of race. Although the policy itself was deficient under the Fourteenth Amendment, the state had a constitutional "interest that legitimately may be served by a properly devised admissions program involving the competitive consideration of race and ethnic origin."[27]

Justice Brennan, joined by Justices White, Marshall, and Blackmun, urged a more relaxed standard of review on the grounds that the Court should not impede initiatives calculated to eliminate discrimination against minorities.[28] For Brennan, the process defect rationale of strict scrutiny was inapt because whites were neither traditionally excluded from nor underrepresented in the political process and their interests were thus unlikely to be slighted.[29] Because even benign-appearing classifications might stereotype or stigmatize a discrete group, and because race constituted an immutable characteristic, Brennan did not advocate entirely deferential review.[30] Rather, he proposed an intermediate standard that would have required a careful examination of but a more favorable disposition toward racial preferences. As Brennan put it:

to justify such a classification an important and articulated purpose for its use must be shown. In addition, any statute must be stricken that stigmatizes any group or that singles out those least well represented in the political process to bear the brunt of a benign program. Thus our review under the Fourteenth Amendment should be strict—not " 'strict' in theory and fatal in fact," because it is stigma that causes fatality—but strict and searching nonetheless.[31]

Brennan thus proposed a version of "strict" review friendlier to remedial policy and aims but not insensitive to possible abuse or misuse of racial classifications. Specifically, any preferential policy would have to be justified by an important interest outweighing its burdens and narrowly tailored to avoid stigmatizing consequences. From Brennan's perspective, remediation of societal discrimination was a significant interest that outweighed any harm to members of the majority race.[32] Nor did he consider the special admissions policy a source of stigma insofar as the respondent would not "in any sense [be] stamped as inferior by [his] rejection."[33]

In a separate opinion, Justice Marshall noted the nation's legacy of racial discrimination, which from his viewpoint justified race-dependent attention.[34] Noting that the Court a century earlier had foreclosed "several affirmative action programs after the Civil War," he expressed his "fear that we have come full circle."[35] Justice Blackmun maintained that racial discrimination could not be effectively reckoned with absent policies that directly and explicitly confronted its consequences. He accordingly observed that "[i]n order to get beyond racism, we must first take account of race."[36]

A third analysis was provided by a plurality of four justices who, focusing solely on the statutory permissibility of the program, asserted that federal law required strict neutrality.[37] In an opinion joined by Chief Justice Burger and Justices Rehnquist and Stewart, Justice Stevens opined that Title VI and its legislative history required strict colorblindness.[38]

Justice Blackmun had expressed the hope that the "time will come when an 'affirmative action' program is unnecessary ... [and] ... we could reach this stage within a decade at the most."[39] It has become evident after nearly two decades of litigation that, to say the least, Blackmun was overly optimistic. Two years after the *Bakke* case, the Court confronted the question of federal set-asides for minority contractors in public works projects. The resultant decision in *Fullilove v. Klutznick* reflected further fragmentation of opinion.[40] The program at issue, requiring 10 percent minority participation in all covered work, was upheld. Three justices, in an opinion written by Chief Justice Burger, found it a proper exercise of congressional power.[41] Three others, headed by Justice Marshall, advocated a standard of review akin to what Brennan had asserted in *Bakke*.[42] Justices Stewart and Rehnquist articulated absolute opposition to all racial classifications,[43] and Justice Stevens expressed his general disfavor of them.[44]

Burger specifically avoided any of the analytical formulas advanced in *Bakke*.[45] His opinion did not disclose clearly, however, what standard of review was appropriate. He considered whether the program's objectives were within Congress's power and found sufficient authority under the commerce, spending, and necessary and proper clauses and the Fourteenth Amendment.[46] Burger, however, did not indicate whether legislative means must be justified by an important or a compelling interest and thus whether scrutiny should be rigorous or relaxed. Further muddying the standard of review was his observation that deference must be extended to congressional policy choices, but that legislative means must be subject to "careful judicial evaluation."[47] It appears that, because the program implicated congressional authority, Burger favored judicial inquiry of "limited scope."[48] He also found the policy reasonably designed to accomplish its end.[49] Contributing to the program's reasonableness, at least from Burger's perspective, were the absence of fixed quotas, its remedial operation in a prospective fashion, the availability of waivers for contractors who could not secure minority participation despite their best efforts, and safeguards against participation by front groups and firms unaffected by discrimination.[50]

Justice Powell in a concurring opinion reasserted his previously articulated strict scrutiny standard and concluded that the set-aside program passed constitutional muster. In his view, the policy represented remediation of specific discrimination identified by a body capable of making such findings.[51] Redressing the effects of discrimination, at least to the extent such practice was established, represented to Powell a compelling interest.[52] He also recognized the Thirteenth and Fourteenth Amendments as sources of authority affording Congress discretion to choose a suitable remedy for redressing racial discrimination.[53]

Also concurring were Justices Marshall, Brennan, and Blackmun. They found the policy constitutional because it repaired the effects of discrimination and thus was substantially related to achieving an important governmental objective.[54]

Justice Stewart, joined by Justice Rehnquist, authored a dissent that invoked Harlan's depiction of the Constitution as color-blind. Stewart maintained that "any official action that treats a person differently on account of his race or ethnic origin is inherently suspect."[55] Whether Harlan actually would have endorsed such an undifferentiating presumption against all racial classifications is unclear. His vision of a color-blind constitution was articulated in response not to remedial initiatives but to classifications favoring a "dominant race—a superior class of citizens."[56] Regardless of how Harlan actually would have regarded modern affirmative action programs, adopted by democratic processes to account for consequences of historical discrimination against minorities, Stewart and Rehnquist insisted that racial classifications generally should be prohibited, regardless of whom they benefited and why.

Justice Stevens was willing to "assume that the wrong committed against the Negro class is both so serious and so pervasive that it would constitutionally justify an appropriate classwide recovery measured by a sum certain for every member of the injured class."[57] Stevens, however, found Congress's interest in support of "favored access . . . a plainly impermissible justification for this racial classification."[58] With respect to the historical realities of the construction industry, he discerned inadequate evidence of past discrimination against any particular minority.[59] Unlike Stewart and Rehnquist, Stevens indicated that preferential policies may be apt for "victims of unfair treatment in the past" or for groups less able to compete in the future.[60]

The *Bakke* and *Fullilove* decisions established a limited constitutional tolerance for remedial classifications. Still uncertain, however, were standards of review and adequate justification. By the mid-1980s, even though a majority position had yet to evolve, at least two trends had manifested themselves. First, it was evident that remedial classifications would elicit enhanced judicial attention. Second, general societal discrimination, despite its reality and legacy, would not be a permissible reference point for race-conscious remedies. Such truths manifested themselves when the Court invalidated a preferential layoff scheme for teachers in *Wygant v. Jackson Board of Education.*[61]

The policy at issue in *Wygant* had been collectively bargained for and adopted following a history of racial tension and problems in the affected school system. It responded specifically to the underrepresentation of minority faculty members, reflected a sensed need for minority role models, and was described by the court of appeals "as an attempt to alleviate the effects of societal discrimination."[62] A plurality of four, in an opinion written by Justice Powell, determined that societal discrimination by itself was "too amorphous a basis for imposing a racially classified remedy."[63] Even a limited remedial policy could not survive, pursuant to the plurality position, absent "some showing of prior discrimination by the governmental unit involved."[64] Also rejected was the role model theory as a justification for preferential status. As Powell put it:

[t]he role model theory allows the Board to engage in discriminatory hiring and layoff practices long past the point required by any legitimate remedial purpose. ... [B]ecause the role model theory does not necessarily bear a relationship to the harm caused by prior discriminatory hiring practices, it actually could be used to escape the obligation to remedy such practices by justifying the small percentage of black teachers by reference to the small percentage of black students. Carried to its logical extreme, the idea that black students are better off with black teachers could lead to the very system the Court rejected in [1954].[65]

The plurality cautioned that before implementing an affirmative action program, a public official or entity "must have sufficient evidence to justify the conclusion that there has been prior discrimination . . . so that remedial action is warranted."[66] Such an inquiry was crucial, from Powell's perspective, for purposes of eliminating vestiges of discrimination and avoiding new racial distinctions.[67] Without specific evidence of past discrimination, at least as indicated by four justices, policy was bound by principles of racial neutrality.

The plurality also determined that the "reasonableness" test used by the court of appeals was the wrong standard of review.[68] Strict scrutiny, which had been advocated singularly by Powell in *Bakke*, thereby attracted broader support in *Wygant*. As described by Powell, strict review required that "the means chosen to accomplish the state's asserted purpose must be specifically and narrowly framed to accomplish that purpose."[69] Although advocating rigorous review, the plurality did not foreclose all race-conscious remedies. It acknowledged "that in order to remedy the effects of prior discrimination, it may be necessary to take race into account. As part of this Nation's dedication to eradicating racial discrimination, innocent persons may be called upon to bear some of the burden of the remedy."[70]

Concern with what were indentified as innocent victims, and the context in which burdens were imposed as a consequence of remedial policies, was significant to the outcome in *Wygant*. Powell distinguished preferential hiring and layoff provisions on the grounds that the latter resulted in more profound harm.[71] He observed that

[i]n cases involving valid *hiring* goals, the burden to be borne by innocent individuals is diffused to a considerable extent among society generally. Though hiring goals may burden some innocent individuals, they simply do not impose the same kind of injury that layoffs impose. Denial of a future employment opportunity is not as intrusive as loss of an existing job.[72]

Because the impact of preferential layoffs was considered too severe, and because less burdensome remedies such as hiring goals were available, the plurality concluded that the policy could not "satisfy the demands of the Equal Protection Clause."[73]

Justice O'Connor wrote separately to emphasize that a finding of prior discrimination should not be an absolute prerequisite for voluntary affirmative action plans by public employers.[74] Although noting that such a finding ensures policy responsive to identified illegality, rather than general societal discrimination, she cautioned that the requirement "would severely undermine public employers' incentive to meet voluntarily their civil rights obligations."[75] Despite the divergence of opinions and the absence of a clear majority position, O'Connor suggested that significant common ground existed among the various justices. She thus ventured that

the Court is at least in accord in believing that a public employer, consistent with the Constitution, may undertake an affirmative action program which is designed to further a legitimate remedial purpose and which implements that purpose by means that do not impose disproportionate harm on the interests, or unnecessarily trammel the rights, of innocent individuals directly and adversely affected by a plan's racial preference.[76]

Even if suggesting an evolving majority position, O'Connor's sentiment did not represent a consensus.

In a dissenting opinion, Justice Marshall criticized the Court for disregarding key facts and circumstances and for relying on an underdeveloped factual record.[77] Although agreeing that "layoffs are unfair," he distinguished the harm from constitutional injury.[78] Marshall suggested that dislocation was a function of economic realities rather than the challenged process.[79] From his perspective, a general proscription of preferential layoffs denied the community of "hard-won benefits of its integration efforts" and elevated seniority to a fundamental and indefeasible status.[80] He further noted that the prioritization of seniority was selective because qualifications and needs unrelated to race traditionally have been allowed to trump it.[81]

Marshall was influenced by the source of the layoff provision and manner in which it had been established. The policy had emerged from the collective bargaining process and, as he described it, thus had been "forged in the crucible of clashing interests.... [in which] the economic powers of the predominantly white teachers' union were brought to bear against those of the elected Board, and the process yielded consensus."[82] Given a procedure described as "a legitimate and powerful vehicle for the resolution of thorny problems," over which the judiciary normally exercises "minimal supervision," he suggested that

[t]he perceived dangers of affirmative action being misused, therefore, are naturally averted by the bilateral process of negotiation, agreement, and ratification. [When] an elected school board and a teachers' union collectively bargain a layoff provision designed to preserve the effects of a valid minority recruitment plan by apportioning layoffs between two racial groups, as a result of a settlement achieved under the auspices of a supervisory state agency charged with protecting the civil rights of all citizens, that provision should not be upset by this Court on constitutional grounds.[83]

Justice Stevens offered a separate dissent and an alternative line of inquiry. Instead of debating whether such classifications could be justified by general or specific discrimination in the past, Stevens advocated a forward-looking perspective. He thus suggested attention to whether promoting "the public interest in educating children for the future... justifies any adverse effects on the disadvantaged group."[84] At least for purposes of public education, he concluded that

one of the most important lessons that the American public schools teach is that the diverse ethnic, cultural, and national backgrounds that have been brought together in our famous "melting pot" do not identify essential differences among the human beings that inhabit our land. It is one thing for a white child to be taught by a white teacher that color, like beauty, is only "skin deep"; it is far more convincing to experience that truth on a day-to-day basis during the routine, ongoing learning process.[85]

He thus found "a rational and unquestionably legitimate basis" for recruiting and retaining minority teachers.[86]

Stevens also suggested that the trend toward race-neutral standards, regardless of a classification's purpose, was misdirected. Unlike the plurality, he advocated distinguishing between policies that excluded minorities and those that were designed to include them. As Stevens related it, an

exclusionary decision rests on the false premise that differences in race, or in the color of a person's skin, reflect real differences that are relevant to a person's right to share in the blessings of a free society. As noted, that premise is "utterly irrational," and repugnant to the principles of a free and democratic society. Nevertheless, the fact that persons of different races do, indeed, have differently colored skin, may give rise to a belief that there is some significant difference between such persons. The inclusion of minority teachers in the educational process inevitably tends to dispel that illusion whereas their exclusion could only tend to foster it. The inclusionary decision is consistent with the principle that all men are created equal; the exclusionary decision is at war with that principle. One decision accords with the Equal Protection Clause of the Fourteenth Amendment; the other does not. Thus, consideration of whether the consciousness of race is exclusionary or inclusionary plainly distinguishes the Board's valid purpose in this case from a race-conscious decision that would reinforce assumptions of inequality.[87]

Stevens acknowledged that preferential policies may cause constitutionally unacceptable harm. Instead of the generally prohibitive standards established by the majority to protect innocent victims, however, Stevens proposed a two-part inquiry into whether consequent burdens were excessive or inimical to the public interest. Such analysis would focus first on the procedures used to establish the classification and second on the nature and extent of the actual harm.[88] Looking at the first consideration, Stevens described the collective bargaining procedure as "scrupulously fair."[89] He noted that the union representing all teachers "negotiated the provision and agreed to it; the agreement was put to a vote of the membership, and overwhelmingly approved."[90] Stevens characterized the injury itself as the consequence of economic conditions and the policy of preserving the faculty's integrated character.[91] Such harm to him was indistinguishable from the results of a decision to protect a teacher with special skills.[92] Because the layoff provision effected "a valid public purpose," was the output of "fair procedures," had "a narrow breadth," transcended "the harm to petitioners," and represented a step toward eliminating "entirely from governmental decision-making such irrelevant factors as a human being's race," Stevens discerned no constitutional offense.[93]

Justice Powell's opinion in *Bakke* had disclosed an animus toward racial quotas that for practical purposes since has defined the possibilities for affirmative action. A plurality decision supported by Powell departed from that general rule, however, in a case characterized by exigent circumstances. At issue in *United States v. Paradise* was a lower court order requiring the Alabama state police to set aside for qualified black troopers at least fifty percent of the promotions to the rank of corporal.[94] The quota system was framed as a temporary remedy and had been preceded by twelve years of noncompliance, litigation, and delay.[95]

The plurality opinion, authored by Justice Brennan, did not set a specific standard of review but determined that the order was narrowly tailored to effect a compelling government interest and at least would survive strict scrutiny.[96] The compelling justifications included the elimination of past and present discrimination and the enforcement of federal court judgments.[97] Given the need for flexible and temporary relief, the ineffectiveness of alternative remedies, the availability of waiver provisions, the relationship of the numerical goals to the relevant labor market, and the impact of relief on the rights of third parties, the plurality apprehended a sufficiently tight fit between the means and the ends.[98]

The Brennan plurality also found that the 50 percent standard did not impose undue burdens on innocent persons. Rather,

the temporary and extremely limited nature of the requirement substantially limits any potential burden on white applicants for promotion.... Nor has the Court imposed an "absolute bar" to white advancement.... The one-for-one requirement does not require the layoff and discharge of white employees and therefore does not impose burdens of the sort that concerned the plurality in Wygant.... Because the one-for-one requirement is so limited in scope and duration, it only postpones the promotions of qualified whites.[99]

Although joining the opinion, Justice Powell separately emphasized the "persistent violation of constitutional rights and repeated failure to carry out court orders," which, if unaccounted for, would have subverted the judiciary's remedial power.[100] Referring also to the state's past and persistent disobedience, Justice Stevens suggested that it should have the burden of proving that relief exceeded the bounds of reasonableness.[101]

Justice O'Connor, joined by Chief Justice Rehnquist and Justice Scalia, dissented. They maintained that evidence did not support "such an extreme quota" because it "far exceeded the percentage of blacks in the trooper force," was prompted solely by "in terrorem" considerations, and thus could not "survive strict scrutiny."[102] She also suggested several alternatives, such as the appointment of a trustee to develop promotion procedures and the issuance of citations, fines, or other penalties for contempt of court decrees.[103] O'Connor emphasized that racial classifications "must fit with greater precision than any alternative remedy," and concluded that the order failed strict scrutiny.[104]

The first decade of affirmative action jurisprudence was characterized by doctrinal competition and uncertainty. In *City of Richmond v. J. A. Croson Co.*, analysis was substantially clarified and hardened against race-conscious remedies.[105] For the first time, a majority agreed not only that societal discrimination was an inapt premise but also that remedial policies should be subject to strict scrutiny.[106] Justice Scalia urged an especially rigorous model of review that would translate into a virtually absolute proscription of all racial classifications.[107] Dispute within the majority thus was reducible to whether strict scrutiny should be exacting or unforgiving.

At issue in *Croson* was a municipal set-aside program for minority contractors that essentially replicated the policy adopted by Congress and upheld in the *Fullilove* case.[108] Local government officials had based the program on congressional findings of nationwide discrimination in the construction industry and on a local study. The latter showed that while blacks constituted 50 percent of Richmond's population, minority businesses received only .67 percent of the city's building contracts.[109] Despite the congruence with congressional action, Justice O'Connor distinguished state and local remedial initiatives on the grounds that they are not a function of the "specific constitutional mandate to enforce the dictates of the Fourteenth Amendment."[110] Characterizing the equal protection guarantee as an explicit check on state power, the Court resolved the tension in favor of a proscriptive constitutional interest. At least in the context of remediation, the Court diverted from a Fourteenth Amendment legacy of deference to state concern.

Forceful use of the equal protection guarantee to curb state authority, as demonstrated in preceding chapters, is not a historical norm. Except for a short interval commencing with *Brown* and expiring with the introduction of motive-based criteria, equal protection review largely has yielded to state interests and imperatives. The Court in *Croson*, however, maintained that "[t]o hold otherwise would be to cede control of the [guarantee] to the 50 state legislatures and their myriad political subdivisions."[111] Nor was remedial latitude affected by the nature of the classification. As the Court noted:

[t]he mere recitation of a benign or compensatory purpose for the use of a racial classification would essentially entitle the States to exercise the full power of Congress under §5 of the Fourteenth Amendment and insulate any racial classification from judicial scrutiny under §1. We believe that such a result would be contrary to the intentions of the Framers of the Fourteenth Amendment, who desired to place clear limits on the States' use of race as a criterion for legislative action, and to have the federal courts enforce those limitations.[112]

Turning to the operative standard of review, O'Connor asserted that racial classifications, regardless of how they are characterized, must be closely examined. She maintained that

[a]bsent searching judicial inquiry into the justification for such race-based measures, there is simply no way of determining what classifications are "benign" or
"remedial" and what classifications are in fact motivated by illegitimate notions
of racial inferiority or simple racial politics. Indeed, the purpose of strict scrutiny
is to "smoke out" illegitimate uses of race by assuring that the legislative body
is pursuing a goal important enough to warrant use of a highly suspect tool.
The test also ensures that the means chosen "fit" this compelling goal so closely
that there is little or no possibility that the motive for the classification was
illegitimate racial prejudice or stereotype.[113]

Refusal to differentiate among classifications, regardless of "the race
of those burdened or benefited,"[114] reflected a sense that group-
referenced policies are categorically pernicious. O'Connor accordingly
observed that remedial "[c]lassifications based on race carry a danger of
stigmatic harm. Unless they are strictly reserved for remedial settings,
they may in fact promote notions of racial inferiority and lead to a politics
of racial hostility."[115] In repudiating a more relaxed standard of review
proposed by the dissent, she emphasized that "without first engaging in
an examination of the factual basis for [the] enactment and the nexus
between its scope and that factual basis," it would be impossible to determine whether a classification was truly remedial.[116] What O'Connor
depicted as a "watered-down version of equal protection review," from
her perspective, would ensure "that race will always be relevant in American life."[117] Further militating in favor of close scrutiny, at least for
O'Connor, was the fact that blacks constituted half of the city's population
and held a majority of the council seats.[118] Such political dynamics suggested to her a possibility that the legislative process might be misused
and a need for exacting review of its output.

Also fatal to the set-aside plan were what O'Connor considered inadequate findings of actual discrimination in the local construction industry. Although acknowledging "the sorry history of both private and
public discrimination in this country," O'Connor renounced the notion
that societal discrimination by itself was sufficient to support a race-
dependent policy.[119] Without a showing of actual discrimination, she
asserted, a legislative body could not determine the precise scope of the
injury it needed to redress.[120] Amorphous claims, O'Connor cautioned,
would engender policies with no logical stopping point.[121] Noting that
the remedial policy at issue defined "minority" in broad terms, including
Aleuts and Eskimos, who probably never even resided in Richmond, she
discerned a "gross overinclusiveness...[which] strongly impugns the
city's claim of remedial motivation."[122]

Characterizing the plan as insufficiently linked to identified discrimination, O'Connor suggested that it was impossible to assess whether it
was narrowly tailored to remedy past wrongs.[123] She nonetheless found
no evidence that race-neutral methodologies, such as city financing of

small firms, had been considered.[124] Consistent with the Court's general hostility toward fixed quotas, at least absent exigent circumstances, O'Connor opined that the plan could not be tailored to achieve any goal other than unadorned racial balancing.[125] Despite acknowledging that legislative factfinding ordinarily is accorded a presumption of regularity and usually deferred to, she concluded that mere recitation of a benign purpose, generalized reference to remedial goals, and identification of disparities were inadequate to survive strict scrutiny.[126]

Although having foreclosed the possibility of race-conscious remedies in response to general societal discrimination, O'Connor noted that "[n]othing we say today precludes a state or local entity from taking action to rectify the effects of identified discrimination within its jurisdiction."[127] As possibilities for an adequate remedial premise, she suggested significant statistical disparity between the number of qualified minority contractors willing and able to perform and the number of them actually engaged by the city or its prime contractors.[128] In an extreme case, she acknowledged that "some form of narrowly tailored racial preference might be necessary to break down patterns of deliberate exclusion."[129] O'Connor reminded, however, that

[p]roper findings in this regard are necessary to define both the scope of the injury and the extent of the remedy necessary to cure its effects. Such findings also serve to assure all citizens that the deviation from the norm of equal treatment of all racial and ethnic groups is a temporary matter, a measure taken in the service of the goal of equality itself.[130]

In closing, O'Connor further repudiated the notion, already rejected by the *Wygant* plurality, that remediation might be referenced to general historical reality. She warned that

[t]o accept Richmond's claim that past societal discrimination alone can serve as the basis for rigid racial preferences would be to open the door to competing claims for "remedial relief" for every disadvantaged group. The dream of a Nation of equal citizens in a society where race is irrelevant to personal opportunity and achievement would be lost in a mosaic of shifting preferences based on inherently unmeasurable claims of past wrongs.... We think such a result would be contrary to both the letter and spirit of a constitutional provision whose central command is equality.[131]

Discerning no sufficient basis for remediation, O'Connor determined that the city's "treatment of its citizens on a racial basis violates the dictates of the Equal Protection Clause."[132]

Justice Stevens, concurring separately and in part, reiterated his preference for the criteria he advanced in *Wygant*. He found the Richmond program deficient because it (1) made "no claim that the public interest in the efficient performance of its construction contracts will be served by granting a preference to minority-business enterprises," (2) represented a legislative rather than judicial remedial effort, and (3) was a function of racial stereotyping.[133]

Justice Scalia, concurring only in the judgment and thus not the reasoning supporting it, challenged "the Court's dicta suggesting that... state and local government may in some circumstances discriminate on the basis of race...."[134] Scalia proposed a standard that, absent extraordinary circumstances unrelated to remediation, would prohibit any official racial classification. He observed that

[t]he difficulty of overcoming the effects of past discrimination is as nothing compared with the difficulty of eradicating from our society the source of those effects, which is the tendency—fatal to a nation such as ours—to classify and judge men and women on the basis of their country of origin or the color of their skin. A solution to the first problem that aggravates the second is no solution at all.[135]

For Scalia, color blindness was a fixed rule that could be deviated from only to dismantle an officially segregated school system or to deal with "a social emergency rising to the level of imminent danger to life and limb."[136] As an example of exigent circumstances sufficient to justify a departure from strict neutrality, he suggested a prison riot necessitating temporary segregation.[137] Expressing further his general antipathy toward remedial classifications, he asserted that "[w]here injustice is the game,... turn-about is not fair play."[138] From Scalia's perspective, and excepting school desegregation processes, policy designed to undo the effects of identifiable discrimination would have to be race-neutral.

Resistance to race-conscious remedies, even in response to specifically identified discrimination, distinguished Scalia's position from that of the O'Connor plurality. He stressed, however, that nothing precluded a state from implementing a racially neutral remedial "preference to identified victims of discrimination. While most of the beneficiaries might be black, neither the beneficiaries nor those disadvantaged by the preference would be identified *on the basis of their race*."[139]

Although acknowledging "that in our society blacks have suffered discrimination immeasurably greater than any directed at other racial groups," Scalia maintained that race-dependent policy reinforces "a manner of thinking by race that was the source of the injustice and that will, if it endures within our society, be the source of more injustice still."[140] In closing, he cautioned that

racial preferences appear to "even the score" (in some small degree) only if one embraces the proposition that our society is appropriately viewed as divided into races, making it right that an injustice rendered in the past to a black man should be compensated for by discriminating against a white. Nothing is worth that embrace. Since blacks have been disproportionately disadvantaged by racial discrimination, any race-neutral remedial program aimed at the disadvantaged *as such* will have a disproportionately beneficial impact on blacks. Only such a program, and not one that operates on the basis of race, is in accord with the letter and the spirit of our Constitution.[141]

The alternative of policy focused on general rather than racial disadvantage has elicited criticism that it diverts attention from the unique harm of racial discrimination and is unresponsive to its legacy. Proponents of race-conscious measures maintain that, if remediation was referenced to need rather than historical discrimination, indigent whites would receive most of the benefits.[142] Justice Marshall, joined by Justices Brennan and Blackmun, authored an especially strident dissent, depicting the decision as "a deliberate and giant step backward in this Court's affirmative action jurisprudence."[143] Marshall noted the significance of the majority investment in strict scrutiny but found it ironic that the decision "second guess[ed]" the judgment of a city which as "the former capital of the Confederacy... knows what racial discrimination is."[144]

Marshall criticized the Court for "down-play[ing] the fact that the City Council had before it a rich trove of evidence that discrimination in the Nation's construction industry had seriously impaired the competitive position of businesses owned or controlled by members of minority groups."[145] He would have shifted the presumption in favor of remediation because Richmond had not demonstrated itself to be an exception to the comprehensive pattern of exclusion identified by Congress. From the Court's opinion, Marshall apprehended a sense of "cynicism" responsible for "a grapeshot attack on race-conscious remediation," blindness to the reality of national discrimination, and, a consequent lack of perspective infecting its analysis of the entire case.[146]

Marshall discerned two interests sufficient to justify the set-aside program. The first was the city's general aim of eradicating the effects of racial discrimination.[147] The second premise was "the prospective one of preventing the city's own spending decisions from reinforcing and perpetuating the exclusionary effects of past discrimination."[148] Contrary to O'Connor's reading of the record, Marshall was satisfied that extensive evidence existed to establish a record of discrimination. He referred specifically to presidential and congressional studies, the miniscule proportion of city contracts awarded to minority enterprises, and the absence of any testimony challenging the reality of pervasive racial discrimination.[149] Such reference points, Marshall maintained, were "a far cry from the reliance on generalized 'societal discrimination' which the majority decries as a basis for remedial action."[150] For him, the

Court's failure to apprehend a real history of specifically identifiable discrimination "simply blinks credibility"[151] and reflected "an unwillingness to come to grips with why construction contracting was" essentially a whites-only enterprise.[152]

Pursuing further his critique of the Court's pluralistic sensitivity, Marshall described invalidation of the set-aside program as a function of the majority's "armchair cynicism."[153] He suggested that if it had

paused for a moment on the facts of the Richmond experience, it would have discovered that the city's leadership is deeply familiar with what racial discrimination is. The members of the Richmond City Council have spent long years witnessing multifarious acts of discrimination, including, but not limited to, the deliberate diminution of black residents' voting rights, resistance to school desegregation, and publicly sanctioned housing discrimination. Numerous decisions of federal courts chronicle this disgraceful recent history.[154]

Marshall also objected to the lack of significance attached to findings by the federal government. To the extent that state and local authorities could not rely on such data, he perceived an onerous and formalistic documentary obligation even when "the reality of past discrimination was apparent."[155] Marshall intimated that the Court's hard line against remedial classifications, although couched in vigorous equal protection terms, actually forestalled a reckoning with discrimination.

In place of strict scrutiny, Marshall suggested a standard of review that would be attentive to abuse or misuse of classifications but also function more hospitably toward race-conscious remedies. For him it was sufficient that the program at issue was (1) substantially related to the city's aims of remedying past discrimination and (2) narrowly tailored insofar as it afforded waivers, did not interfere with vested interests, and operated prospectively.[156]

Although claiming that he "would ordinarily [end] his analysis at this point," the majority's investment in strict scrutiny "compelled [him] to add more."[157] Marshall observed that

[t]oday, for the first time, a majority of this Court has adopted strict scrutiny as its standard of Equal Protection Clause review of race-conscious remedial measures. This is an unwelcome development. A profound difference separates governmental actions that themselves are racist, and governmental actions that seek to remedy the effects of prior racism or to prevent neutral governmental activity from perpetuating the effects of such racism.[158]

He thus found troubling the Court's refusal to differentiate racial classifications for constitutional purposes.[159] For him, a sensible distinction existed between classifications reflecting a presumption of racial inferiority and those designed to remedy the effects of discrimination.

Marshall expressed concern that, just as many communities were elect-
ing minority leaders inclined to rectify past discrimination, the Court
was harnessing them in a "strict scrutiny straitjacket."[160] Failure to accommodate remedial initiatives, he suggested, evaded or discounted "the
tragic and indelible fact that discrimination against blacks and other
racial minorities in this Nation has pervaded our Nation's history and
continues to scar our society."[161] Marshall's sense was that the *Croson*
decision compounded rather than deviated from a jurisprudential legacy
that largely had accommodated discrimination. He expressed concern
that

[i]n concluding that remedial classifications warrant no different standard of
review under the Constitution than the most brute and repugnant forms of state-
sponsored racism, a majority of this Court signals that it regards racial discrimination as largely a phenomenon of the past, and that government bodies need
no longer preoccupy themselves with rectifying racial injustice. I, however, do
not believe this Nation is anywhere close to eradicating racial discrimination or
its vestiges. In constitutionalizing its wishful thinking, the majority today does a
grave disservice not only to those victims of past and present racial discrimination
in this Nation whom government has sought to assist, but also to this Court's
long tradition of approaching issues of race with the utmost sensitivity.[162]

As depicted by Marshall, the Court's response was reminiscent of sentiment a century before that victims of discrimination should "cease[ ]
to be the special favorite of the laws . . . [and] be protected in the ordinary
modes by which other men's rights are protected."[163]

Finally, Marshall regarded the Court's invigoration of the equal protection guarantee as an exercise in convenience rather than principle.
The selective significance of equal protection, at least for him, was evidenced by doctrine that confounded policies for reckoning with discriminatory realities.[164] Such analysis struck Marshall as procrustean and
inconsistent with the original concern "that States would *not* adequately
respond to racial violence or discrimination against newly freed
slaves."[165] For him, interpretation of the Reconstruction amendments in
a way that cramps remedial attention "turns the[m] . . . on their heads."[166]
He argued that "nothing in the Amendments themselves, or in our long
history of interpreting or applying those momentous charters, suggests
that States, exercising their police power, are in any way constitutionally
inhibited from working alongside the Federal Government in the fight
against discrimination and its effects."[167] His suggestion that the Court
had transformed the original meaning of the Fourteenth Amendment
was notable because the premises he challenged were fashioned by justices closely associated with concepts of judicial restraint and fidelity to
framer's intent.

Justice Marshall, who had helped guide the Court out of the separate but equal era, offered pointed criticism for what he perceived as doctrinal regression. In so doing, he illuminated an ironic spin of equal protection jurisprudence. A century earlier, the Court had deferred to the exercise of state police power and effectively accommodated the white majority.[168] In the affirmative action context, Marshall objected because the Court had curbed state power but again accommodated the dominant culture.[169] Compounding Marshall's message of despair was Blackmun's expression of disappointment that "this Court, the supposed bastion of equality, ... [had acted] as though discrimination had never existed or was not demonstrated."[170] His perception, like Marshall's, was that "the Court today regresses."[171]

Subsequent jurisprudence has disclosed that, even if constitutional standards have hardened against racially preferential policies, they are not yet entirely proscriptive or necessarily limited to the narrow premises approved in *Croson*. In *Metro Broadcasting, Inc. v. Federal Communications Commission*, the Court upheld the policies that afforded minorities an advantage in comparative broadcast licensing proceedings and offered an incentive for financially distressed licensees to sell their radio or television properties to minorities.[172] The Federal Communications Commission, prompted by Congress, had adopted both policies on the grounds that minorities were underrepresented in broadcasting and that increased minority participation would enhance programming diversity.[173]

The Court, in reviewing the policies, determined that they did not offend the Fifth Amendment. It assigned overarching significance to the fact that the minority ownership programs had been not only congressionally approved but mandated.[174] The Court determined, moreover, that the preferences were permissible without regard to whether they were remedial or not. Specifically, it

h[e]ld that benign race-conscious measures mandated by Congress—even if those measures are not "remedial" in the sense of being designed to compensate victims of past governmental or societal discrimination—are constitutionally permissible to the extent that they serve important governmental objectives within the power of Congress and are substantially related to the achievement of those objectives.[175]

The Court concluded that the provisions were within Congress's power and sufficiently related to important aims.[176]

More specifically, it determined that enhancement of broadcast diversity constituted at least "an important governmental objective."[177] Justice Brennan, who wrote the majority opinion, analogized the challenged preferences to the "constitutionally permissible goal on which a race-conscious university admissions program may be based."[178] Promotion of program diversity in particular, he noted, "serves important First Amendment values."[179]

In finding the policies substantially related to permissible governmental aims, the Court referred to "long study and painstaking consideration of alternatives"[180] that established the policies as "critical means of promoting broadcast diversity" and to which it "must give great weight."[181] It anticipated

that expanded minority ownership of broadcast outlets will, in the aggregate, result in greater broadcast diversity. A broadcasting industry with representative minority participation will produce more variation and diversity than will one whose ownership is drawn from a single racially and ethnically homogeneous group. The predictive judgment about the overall result of minority entry into broadcasting is not a rigid assumption about how minority owners will behave in every case but rather is akin to Justice Powell's conclusion in *Bakke* that greater admission of minorities would contribute, on average, "to the robust exchange of ideas."[182]

Besides agreeing with the policies' premises, the Court rejected arguments that the preferences ran afoul of established equal protection doctrine.[183] It thus was unpersuaded that the challenged policies would result in impermissible stereotyping.[184] Responding to contentions that the rules would create unending preferences based on race, the Court found them "appropriately limited in extent and duration, and subject to reassessment and revaluation by Congress prior to any extension or re-enactment."[185] The majority also depicted the provisions as means rather than ends, which would expire on their own when the goal of diversification had been realized.[186] With respect to arguments that the preferences victimized nonminorities, the Court found that the burden upon them was "slight."[187] Contributing to the Court's sense of insubstantial injury was the broadcast licensing process itself, which offers no settled expectation that an application will be granted without consideration of multiple public interest factors that include minority ownership.[188]

Justice O'Connor, joined by Chief Justice Rehnquist and Justices Scalia and Kennedy, dissented on the grounds that the policy impermissibly distributed "benefits and burdens among individuals based on the assumption that race or ethnicity determines how they act or think."[189] O'Connor perceived a policy rooted in stereotype and at odds with what she considered the settled demands of strict scrutiny. Because the Court did not require a compelling justification for the preferences, she found a "renewed toleration of racial classifications and a repudiation of our recent affirmation that the Constitution's equal protection guarantees extend equally to all citizens."[190] Although she acknowledged broad congressional latitude in the exercise of remedial power under the Fourteenth Amendment, O'Connor maintained that such power was not implicated by a federal program, as opposed to a congressional "act respecting the States."[191] She found the policies constitutionally defective because they were inadequately grounded in the Fourteenth Amendment, not pitched toward remedying identified past discrimination, and indefensible pursuant to strict scrutiny.[192] For O'Connor, the policies represented neither a proper remedial purpose nor a proper exercise of power.[193] In sum, she found the standard of review too relaxed, the justification too insubstantial and impertinent, and the rules inadequately tailored.

Justice Kennedy wrote a separate dissent, suggesting that the relaxed standard of review ignored the lessons of earlier jurisprudential ignominies. He warned that "a fundamental error of the *Plessy* Court was its similar confidence in its ability to identify "benign discrimination."[194] Referring to South African apartheid law's disclamation of any unflattering premises, Kennedy noted that "[p]olicies of racial separation and preference are almost always justified as benign, even when it is clear to any sensible observer that they are not."[195] He concluded that

perhaps the Court can succeed in its assumed role of case-by-case arbiter of when it is desirable and benign for the Government to disfavor some citizens and favor others based on the colors of their skin. Perhaps the tolerance and decency to which our people aspire will let the disfavored rise above hostility and the favored escape condescension. But history suggests much peril in this enterprise, and so the Constitution forbids us to undertake it. I regret that after a century of judicial opinions we interpret the Constitution to do no more than move us from "separate but equal" to "unequal but benign."[196]

In response to the warning, the majority expressed its inability to "understand how Justice Kennedy can pretend that examples of 'benign' race-conscious measures include South African apartheid, the 'separate but equal' law at issue in *Plessy v. Ferguson,* and the internment of American citizens of Japanese ancestry upheld in *Korematsu v. United States.*"[197] The Court voiced "confiden[ce] that an 'examination of the legislative scheme and its history' . . . will separate benign measures from other types of racial classifications."[198]

The *Metro Broadcasting* decision commanded the narrowest possible majority. It galvanized four dissenting justices into an opposing position that seemed especially unbending. Respectively authoring and supporting the judgment and opinion were Justices Brennan and Marshall. Given their subsequent resignations and replacement by Justices Souter and Thomas, the future vitality of the ruling is uncertain.

The debate over racial preferences, in the course of its evolution, has enkindled increasingly sharp and at times ill-tempered argument on both sides. The case against affirmative action is forcefully stated in the *Croson* decision and the *Metro Broadcasting* dissents, which identify concerns about limitless racial preserves, harm to innocent victims, stereotyping and stigmatization, racial politics, and judicial ineptitude in distinguishing harmful from benign classifications.[199] Such reasoning has elicited criticism from both within and beyond the Court. Doctrinal resistance to racial preferences comports with dominant attitudes, which strongly disfavor them.[200] It also reflects the persisting dilemma of the Fourteenth Amendment, which, although framed primarily with a systematically disadvantaged minority in mind, historically has been implemented in terms that accommodate majoritarian priorities. Principles unfriendly to race-conscious remediation thus have been criticized as convenient rationalizations rather than convincing rationales.

Concern that advantages granted to racial minorities will be overbroad and operate indefinitely, for instance, has been characterized as unfounded.[201] Because a popular majority elects the personnel who formulate and implement preferential programs, critics maintain that resultant policy is vulnerable to and conditioned anyway by the limits of self-sacrifice.[202] Consistent with the argument is the challenge of a preferential layoff policy that was collectively bargained for but contested when its terms were implemented.[203] Such reaction suggests a remedial policy susceptible to inherent limits of self-denial and to superseding interest.

The Court also has been criticized for exaggerating the risk of racial stigmatization presented by affirmative action programs. Preferential policies, it is argued, do not label minorities as incompetent or unable to succeed without special help. Rather, racial stereotypes derive from cultural perceptions deeply rooted in the society's history. A successful program might even defeat stigma, if it followed that white males no longer were perceived as having achieved success against limited competition. Social science data exist for the proposition that hiring preferences actually may be effective in defeating minority stereotypes. The premise is that, as institutions become culturally diversified, uninformed perceptions vanish. Race-conscious remedies also have been described as a response to rather than the cause of stereotypes.

Harm to innocent victims constitutes a reference point that candidly identifies societal aversion to or reserve in assuming the burdens of remediation. Critics of affirmative action maintain that, regardless of how structured, preferential policies cause discernible harm to white males who themselves are blameless.[204] A counterpoint is that individual innocence is illusory because whites as a group have benefited from advantages obtained and accumulated at the expense of minorities.[205] A similar point, expressed less provocatively and without implications of blame, may be that innocence is irrelevant when advantage has compounded from a profound wrong and thus should not be a bar to its undoing.

The Court's emphasis upon the risks of racial polarization has been faulted on grounds it reflects a selective and belated jurisprudential concern. Race was a central factor in the distribution of civil and political rights when the republic was founded and when the Fourteenth Amendment was fashioned.[206] Long after the Reconstruction amendments were adopted, race-dependent policies minimized black influence in the political process.[207] Even now, race is a significant determinant of voting patterns.[208] Tribal politics also characterized the debate over the Civil Rights Act of 1990, which Congress passed and the president vetoed. Opponents of the bill, particularly the chief executive, were criticized for exploiting white resentment of minorities with misleading claims that it would require hiring quotas.[209] Racial antagonism is a crucial factor in modern politics because, as one political consultant noted, it is an "issue [that] moves numbers."[210] Given a well-established history of racial politics, concern that affirmative action will fuel or foster such tribalism attaches unique significance to a common and durable phenomenon. Disapproving references to racial politics, in a society still inclined toward race-specific classifications and governed by competing interest groups, thus elicit criticism for their selective focus.

Factional favoritism is an undeniable feature of a political system that is defined by interest groups and that routinely dispenses special advantages. Congress, for instance, has awarded benefits to workers dislocated from industries adversely affected by government regulation.[211] The Court itself has upheld veterans' benefits programs against challenges of overbreadth and intrinsic unfairness which have ensnared race-conscious remediation.[212] Because legislatively conferred group advantage is the norm, foreclosure of racial preferences may be susceptible to argument that the preclusion is race-dependent itself.

Efforts to reckon with the nation's legacy of discrimination confront daunting impediments attributable to modern standards of review. Discriminatory purpose requirements, as discussed in Chapter 5, confound proof of an equal protection violation. Despite its reality, general societal discrimination has been precluded as a permissible basis for remediation. Accounting for discrimination, absent congressional action pursuant to adequate findings, is limited to rare provable instances of specific discrimination. Even when permitted, therefore, racially focused remediation is bound by the prerequisite of proving discriminatory motive. The net consequence for modern purposes is doctrine that is inapt at discerning subtle or unconscious discrimination against minorities but usually fatal to policies that would reckon with it.

When detached from the context of race and its historical tendency to distort perception, remedial accounting for a particular group or interest is recognizable as a common and generally uncontroversial political phenomenon. When economic opportunity is impaired by systemic dysfunction, for instance, intervention to undo excessive accumulations of power and advantage and open up or maximize opportunity is a regulatory norm. Antitrust laws, for instance, originated from a sense that the

system of production and of exchange is having that tendency which is sure at some not very distant day to crush out all small men, all small capitalists, all small enterprises. This is being done now. We find everywhere over our land the wrecks of small, independent enterprises thrown in our pathway. So now the American Congress and the American people are brought face to face with this sad, this great problem. Is production, is trade, to be taken away from the great mass of the people and concentrated in the hands of a few men who... have been enabled to aggregate to themselves large, enormous fortunes.[213]

Even without constitutional direction akin to the equal protection decree, Congress and the judiciary have directly fashioned redistributive doctrine calculated to optimize the allocation of economic power.[214] The breakup of American Telephone and Telegraph Company disclosed a willingness to restructure the nation's central communications system out of concern with accumulated advantage, dominance, and influence.[215] Refashioning of the industry was characterized by repudiation of rationales often used to defeat race-conscious remediation. Relief was neither foreclosed nor delayed by concerns that special relief or attention would stigmatize or stereotype AT&T's competitors. Enhanced economic opportunity was regarded as a legitimate objective.[216] Nor were consequent restrictions on the dominant company regarded as harm to an innocent victim. Rather, the district court emphasized that it may be necessary to "pry open to competition a market that has been closed" by illegal action.[217] Consequent restrictions were imposed despite a possible argument that AT&T was blameless in having acquired its preeminent position.[218]

Claims that innocent parties were victimized surfaced in a comparable context, when the Federal Communications Commission ordered persons or entities owning a daily newspaper and broadcasting station in the same community to divest one or the other property.[219] Cross-ownership was a function of prior Commission policies encouraging publishers to acquire radio and television properties.[220] Despite such inducement and consequent reliance, "innocent" publishers were obligated to surrender their holdings in the interest of enhanced opportunity and diversity.[221]

Because remediation of dysfunction and redistribution of advantage are policy norms in the economic marketplace, the Court's resistance to preferential policies continues to elicit criticism as being exaggerated and misplaced. Even if the objections are accepted as apt, the case against race-conscious remediation is not without cogent reason. Contrary to the Court's sense that racial preferences are dangerously potent, such programs have been characterized as too feeble insofar as they account mainly for interests of a relatively elite and qualified subgroup.[222] Consequent concern that such policy diverts attention from more profound disadvantage to the interests of persons likely to succeed without special attention is reducible to an inexpensive and relatively low impact form of racial justice, and may foster a self-subverting sense of victimization.[223] Even if societal discrimination were allowed as a permissible reference point for remedial initiative, the argument is that a policy of favoritism would not be substantially related to its declared aim. A counterpoint is that affirmative action need not operate to the exclusion of other methodologies for effecting racial justice.[224] Given a history bereft of policy calculated to account comprehensively for racial disadvantage, however, reality may favor identifying and emphasizing options with maximum potential. In a culture generally hostile to the notion of racial preferences, the case against affirmative action might profit from enhanced attention to whether remediation actually achieves its stated aims.[225]

Such review would demonstrate that the challenge for equal protection, now as in 1868, is to actualize doctrine that accounts effectively for original concern with race-dependent impediments to opportunity. The desegregation mandate was successful only in securing a consensus for the principle that palpable official discrimination is constitutionally unacceptable. The primary value of group-referenced remedial concepts thus may relate less to actual results than as a reminder of and leverage point for attention and progress necessary for effectuating genuine color blindness.

Given the difficulties of proving purposeful discrimination, and thus a constitutional violation, doctrinal resistance to remediation of societal discrimination strikes critics as selective and misplaced.[226] Judicial decisions unrelated to race, but nonetheless implicating profound constitutional concerns, disclose that standards of review are not always unrelenting and may even be accommodating to state interests. The Court has noted, for instance, that "[f]rom the beginning of civilized societies, legislators and judges have acted on various unprovable assumptions . . . [that] underlie much lawful state regulation."[227] Even when protection has been sought for trenchant constitutional interests, the Court has adhered to the principle that "unprovable assumptions about what is good for the people [are] not a sufficient reason to find [a statute] unconstitutional."[228] If viewed as general economic or social policy, remediation would merit a deferential judicial response.[229] Because racial classifications have had such disabling consequences over the course of the nation's history, few would argue for an entirely relaxed review of them. Still, undifferentiated evaluation of racial classifications risks criticism that the Court, like its predecessor a century ago, is more interested in formal imagery than the underlying realities of discrimination.

Typifying such reproval of modern equal protection jurisprudence is the report of a national civil rights organization headed by the former chair of the U.S. Commission of Civil Rights. The study criticized judicial performance during the 1980s as "appearing increasingly hostile toward civil rights advocates."[230] Judicially crafted standards that complicate proof of discrimination, except when remediation is at issue, were characterized as the product of an "overwhelmingly white, conservative, wealthy and male...federal court bench."[231] Such outcomes are attributed to the Reagan administration, which followed the well-established tradition of court packing and, as a result of detailed screening and opportunities to appoint judges, was successful in securing its agenda.[232] By 1991, the Reagan and Bush administrations had appointed 70 percent of the nation's federal judges.[233]

The report essentially complained of a federal judiciary that has reverted toward insensitivity to or fatigue with racial realities. It objects specifically to nascent standards of constitutional color blindness "rest[ing] on the notion that America no longer has a duty to act affirmatively in order to overcome the legacy of slavery and government sanctioned segregation...[but] ignor[ing] the well-documented realities of continuing discrimination and its effects."[234] The study concluded that "a major segment of the nation's minority population continues to suffer the legacy of years of oppression and discrimination."[235] As constitutional theories and standards continue to be debated, such observations afford a reminder of how unfinished the business of 1787, 1868, and 1954 remains.

NOTES

1. Plessy v. Ferguson 163 U.S. 537, 559 (1896) (Harlan, J., dissenting).

2. *Id.*

3. *See* Lawrence, *The Id, the Ego and Equal Protection: Reckoning with Unconscious Racism*, 39 Stan. L. Rev. 317, 339–44 (1987).

4. De Funis v. Odegaard, 416 U.S. 312 (1974).

5. *Id.* at 350 (Brennan, J., dissenting). The principle of mootness operates when the facts and circumstances generating a claim no longer present an actual case or controversy. In *De Funis*, the claimant was nearing the end of his legal education and the law school had indicated it would allow him to graduate. The Court determined that a judgment would not have affected the parties' legal relationship, and thus the controversy was considered academic. *See id.*

6. *Id.*

7. Regents of the University of California v. Bakke, 438 U.S. 265 (1978).

8. *Id.* at 277–78.

9. 18 Cal.3d 34, 132 Cal. Rptr. 680, 553 P.2d 1152 (1976).

10. Regents of the University of California v. Bakke, 438 U.S. at 320 (Powell, J.); *id.* at 421 (Stevens, J., Burger, C.J., Stewart and Rehnquist, J. J., concurring and dissenting).

11. *Id.* at 324–79 (Brennan, White, Marshall, and Blackmun, J.J., concurring and dissenting). Title VI of the Civil Rights Act of 1964, 42 U.S.C. §§ 2000d to 2000d–7, prohibits racially based exclusion from "any program or activity receiving Federal financial assistance." *Id.,* § 2000d.

12. *Id.* at 408–21 (Stevens, J., Burger, C.J., Stewart and Rehnquist, J.J., concurring and dissenting).

13. *Id.* at 272–320 (Powell, J.).

14. *Id.* at 320 (Powell, J.).

15. *See id.* at 325–26 (Brennan, White, Marshall, and Blackmun, J.J., concurring and dissenting).

16. *Id.* at 291 (Powell, J.).

17. Gunther, *Foreword: In Search of Evolving Doctrine on a Changing Court: A Model for a Newer Equal Protection,* 86 Harv. L. Rev. 1, 8 (1972).

18. *See* Regents of the University of California v. Bakke, 438 U.S. at 305 (Powell, J.).

19. *Id.* at 306 (Powell, J.).

20. *Id.* at 307 (Powell, J.).

21. *Id.* at 307–09 (Powell, J.).

22. *Id.* at 309–10 (Powell, J.).

23. *Id.* at 310–11 (Powell, J.).

24. *Id.* at 310 (Powell, J.).

25. *Id.* at 314 (Powell, J.).

26. *Id.* at 311–15 (opinion of Powell, J.); *id.* at 362 (Brennan, White, Marshall, and Blackmun, J.J., concurring and dissenting).

27. *Id.* at 320 (opinion of Powell, J.).

28. *Id.* at 355 (Brennan, White, Marshall, and Blackmun, J.J., concurring and dissenting).

29. *Id.* at 357 (Brennan, White, Marshall, and Blackmun, J.J., concurring and dissenting).

30. *Id.* at 361–62 (Brennan, White, Marshall, and Blackmun, J.J., concurring and dissenting).

31. *Id.* (Brennan, White, Marshall, and Blackmun, J.J., concurring and dissenting).

32. *Id.* at 362 (Brennan, White, Marshall, and Blackmun, J.J., concurring and dissenting).

33. *Id.* at 375 (Brennan, White, Marshall, and Blackmun, J.J., concurring and dissenting).

34. *Id.* at 387–96 (Marshall, J., concurring and dissenting).

35. *Id.* at 402 (Marshall, J., concurring and dissenting).

36. *Id.* at 407 (Blackmun, J., concurring and dissenting).

37. *Id.* at 416–18 (Stevens, J., Burger, C.J., Stewart and Rehnquist, J.J., concurring and dissenting).

38. *Id.* at 418 (Stevens, J., Burger, C.J., Stewart and Rehnquist, J.J., concurring and dissenting).

39. *Id.* at 403 (Blackmun, J., concurring and dissenting).

40. Fullilove v. Klutznick, 448 U.S. 448 (1980).

41. *Id.* at 456–92 (plurality opinion). A plurality opinion is one that receives more votes than any concurrence, but falls short of attracting a majority necessary for precedential significance.

42. *Id.* at 517–22 (Marshall, Brennan, and Blackmun, J.J., concurring).

43. *Id.* at 522–32 (Stewart and Rehnquist, J.J., dissenting).

44. *Id.* at 532–54 (Stevens, J., dissenting).

45. *Id.* at 492 (plurality opinion).

46. *Id.* at 472–80 (plurality opinion).

47. *Id.* at 480 (plurality opinion).

48. *Id.* at 480–81 (plurality opinion).

49. *Id.* at 480 (plurality opinion).

50. *Id.* at 481–82 (plurality opinion).

51. *Id.* at 502 (Powell, J., concurring).

52. *Id.* at 508 (Powell, J., concurring).

53. *Id.* (Powell, J., concurring).

54. *Id.* at 520–21 (Marshall, J., concurring).

55. *Id.* at 523 (Stewart, J., dissenting).

56. Plessy v. Ferguson, 163 U.S. at 560.

57. Fullilove v. Klutznick, 448 U.S. at 537 (Stevens, J., dissenting).

58. *Id.* at 542 (Stevens, J., dissenting).

59. *Id.* at 538–41 (Stevens, J., dissenting).

60. *Id.* at 553 (Stevens, J., dissenting).

61. 476 U.S. 267 (1986).

62. *Id.* at 274 (plurality opinion).

63. *Id.* at 276 (plurality opinion).

64. *Id.* at 274 (plurality opinion).

65. *Id.* at 275–76 (plurality opinion) (citations omitted).

66. *Id.* at 277 (plurality opinion).

67. *Id.* at 277–78 (plurality opinion).

68. *Id.* at 279 (plurality opinion).

69. *Id.* at 279–80 (plurality opinion).

70. *Id.* at 280–81 (plurality opinion).

71. *Id.* at 280–81 (plurality opinion).

72. *Id.* at 282–83 (plurality opinion) (emphasis in original).

73. *Id.* at 284 (plurality opinion).

74. *Id.* at 286 (O'Connor, J., concurring).

75. *Id.* at 290 (O'Connor, J., concurring).

76. *Id.* at 287 (O'Connor, J., concurring).

77. *Id.* at 295 (Marshall, J., dissenting).

78. *Id.* at 296, 307 (Marshall, J., dissenting).

79. *Id.* at 307 (Marshall, J., dissenting).

80. *Id.* at 307–08 (Marshall, J., dissenting).

81. *Id.* at 308 (Marshall, J., dissenting).

82. *Id.* at 310 (Marshall, J., dissenting).

83. *Id.* at 312 (Marshall, J., dissenting).

84. *Id.* at 313 (Stevens, J., dissenting).

85. *Id.* at 315 (Stevens, J., dissenting).

86. *Id.* at 315–16 (Stevens, J., dissenting).
87. *Id.* at 316–17 (Stevens, J., dissenting).
88. *Id.* at 317 (Stevens, J., dissenting).
89. *Id.* at 318 (Stevens, J., dissenting).
90. *Id.* (Stevens, J., dissenting).
91. *Id.* at 318–19 (Stevens, J., dissenting).
92. *Id.* at 319 (Stevens, J., dissenting).
93. *Id.* at 320 (Stevens, J., dissenting).
94. United States v. Paradise, 480 U.S. 149 (1987).
95. *Id.* at 163 (plurality opinion).
96. *Id.* at 185–86 (plurality opinion).
97. *Id.* at 167 (plurality opinion).
98. *Id.* at 171–86 (plurality opinion).
99. *Id.* at 182–83 (plurality opinion) (citations omitted).
100. *Id.* at 186 (Powell, J., concurring).
101. *Id.* at 193 (Stevens, J., concurring).
102. *Id.* at 198–99 (O'Connor, J., dissenting).
103. *Id.* at 200 (O'Connor, J., dissenting).
104. *Id.* at 199 (O'Connor, J., dissenting).
105. 109 S. Ct. 706 (1989).
106. *Id.* at 723–24 (plurality opinion); *id.* at 735 (Scalia, J., concurring).
107. *Id.* at 735 (Scalia, J., concurring).
108. *Id.* at 712–14 (plurality opinion).
109. *Id.* at 714 (plurality opinion).
110. *Id.* at 719 (plurality opinion).
111. *Id.* (plurality opinion).
112. *Id.* (plurality opinion).
113. *Id.* at 721 (plurality opinion).
114. *Id.* (plurality opinion).
115. *Id.* (plurality opinion).
116. *Id.* (plurality opinion).
117. *Id.* at 722 (plurality opinion).
118. *Id.* (plurality opinion).
119. *Id.* at 724 (plurality opinion).
120. *Id.* (plurality opinion).
121. *Id.* (plurality opinion).
122. *Id.* at 728 (plurality opinion).
123. *Id.* (plurality opinion).
124. *Id.* (plurality opinion).
125. *Id.* (plurality opinion).
126. *Id.* at 723–24 (plurality opinion).
127. *Id.* at 729 (plurality opinion).
128. *Id.* (plurality opinion).
129. *Id.* (plurality opinion).
130. *Id.* at 730 (plurality opinion).
131. *Id.* at 727 (plurality opinion).
132. *Id.* at 730 (plurality opinion).
133. *Id.* at 731–32 (Stevens, J., concurring).

134. *Id.* at 735 (Scalia, J., concurring).

135. *Id.* (Scalia, J., concurring).

136. *Id.* (Scalia, J., concurring).

137. *Id.* (*citing* Lee v. Washington, 390 U.S. 333 (1968) (Black, Harlan, and Stewart, J.J., concurring)).

138. *Id.* at 737 (Scalia, J., concurring).

139. *Id.* at 738 (Scalia, J., concurring) (emphasis in original).

140. *Id.* at 739 (Scalia, J., concurring).

141. *Id.* (Scalia, J., concurring) (emphasis in original).

142. *See* Rowan, Thomas hearings split blacks along class lines, Detroit *Free Press*, Sep. 24, 1991, §A, at 13, cols. 1–3.

143. *Id.* at 740 (Marshall, J., dissenting).

144. *Id.* at 739–40 (Marshall, J., dissenting).

145. *Id.* at 740 (Marshall, J., dissenting).

146. *Id.* at 740–43 (Marshall, J., dissenting).

147. *Id.* at 743 (Marshall, J., dissenting).

148. *Id.* at 744 (Marshall, J., dissenting).

149. *Id.* at 746 (Marshall, J., dissenting).

150. *Id.* (Marshall, J., dissenting).

151. *Id.* (Marshall, J., dissenting).

152. *Id.* (Marshall, J., dissenting).

153. *Id.* at 749 (Marshall, J., dissenting).

154. *Id.* at 748 (Marshall, J., dissenting).

155. *Id.* at 750 (Marshall, J., dissenting).

156. *Id.* (Marshall, J., dissenting).

157. *Id.* at 752 (Marshall, J., dissenting).

158. *Id.* (Marshall, J., dissenting) (citations omitted).

159. *Id.* (Marshall, J., dissenting).

160. *Id.* at 753 (Marshall, J., dissenting).

161. *Id.* at 752 (Marshall, J., dissenting).

162. *Id.* (Marshall, J., dissenting).

163. Civil Rights Cases, 109 U.S. 3, 25 (1883). *See generally* City of Richmond v. J. A. Croson Co., 109 S. Ct. at 740 (Marshall, J., dissenting).

164. City of Richmond v. J. A. Croson Co., 109 S. Ct. at 754–57 (Marshall, J., dissenting).

165. *Id.* at 756 (Marshall, J., dissenting) (emphasis in original).

166. *Id.* (Marshall, J., dissenting).

167. *Id.* at 757 (Marshall, J., dissenting).

168. *See* Plessy v. Ferguson, 163 U.S. at 550.

169. City of Richmond v. J. A. Croson Co., 109 S. Ct. at 756–57 (Marshall, J., dissenting).

170. *Id.* at 757 (Blackmun, J., dissenting).

171. *Id.* (Blackmun, J., dissenting).

172. Metro Broadcasting, Inc. v. Federal Communications Commission, 110 S. Ct. 2997 (1990).

173. *See id.* at 3004–05.

174. *Id.* at 3008.

175. *Id.* at 3008–09.

176. *Id.* at 3009.

177. *Id.* at 3010.

178. *Id.*

179. *Id.*

180. *Id.* at 3019.

181. *Id.* at 3016.

182. *Id.* at 3016–17.

183. *Id.* at 3016–27.

184. *Id.* at 3016.

185. *Id.* at 3024.

186. *Id.* at 3025.

187. *Id.* at 3026.

188. *Id.*

189. *Id.* at 3029 (O'Connor, J., dissenting).

190. *Id.* (O'Connor, J., dissenting).

191. *Id.* at 3030 (O'Connor, J., dissenting).

192. *Id.* at 3030–32 (O'Connor, J., dissenting).

193. *Id.* at 3031–3041 (O'Connor, J., dissenting).

194. *Id.* at 3046 (Kennedy, J., dissenting).

195. *Id.* (Kennedy, J., dissenting).

196. *Id.* at 3047 (Kennedy, J., dissenting).

197. *Id.* at 3008 n.12 (majority opinion).

198. *Id.*

199. *See* Metro Broadcasting, Inc. v. Federal Communications Commission, 110 S. Ct. at 3032–43 (O'Connor, J., dissenting); *id.* at 3044–46 (Kennedy, J., dissenting); City of Richmond v. J. A. Croson Co., 109 S. Ct. at 721.

200. When asked "Do you believe that because of past discrimination against black people, qualified blacks should receive preference over equally qualified whites in such matters as getting into college or getting jobs?" 72 percent of whites and 42 percent of blacks answered negatively. *Newsweek Poll of April 23–25, 1991*, Newsweek, May 6, 1991, at 24, col. 3.

201. *See, e.g.*, Ely, *The Constitutionality of Reverse Discrimination*, 41 U. Chi. L. Rev. 723, 735–36 (1974).

202. *See id.*

203. *See supra* notes 61–93 and accompanying text.

204. *See* F. Lynch, Invisible Victims: White Males and the Crisis of Affirmative Action (1989).

205. *See* Ross, *Innocence and Affirmative Action*, 43 Vand. L. Rev. 297, 301 (1990).

206. *See* Chapters 1 and 2.

207. *See* Chapters 3 and 4.

208. *See* Pinderhughes, *Legal Strategies for Voting Rights: Political Science and the Law*, 28 How. L.J. 515, 531 (1985).

209. *Panel Attacks Bush on Civil Rights Work*, Miami Herald, April 18, 1991, at 17A, cols. 1–2.

210. *The New Politics of Race*, Newsweek, May 6, 1991, at 22, col. 1.

211. The Clean Air Act, for instance, provides for compensation for workers displaced by increased regulation. *See* 42 U.S.C. §§ 7621–22 (1977).

212. *See* Personnel Administrator v. Feeney, 442 U.S. 256, 280–81 (1979).

213. 21 Cong. Rec. 2548 (1870) (Sen. George).

214. *See* Northern Pacific R.R. v. United States, 356 U.S. 1, 4 (1956); Sherman Act, 15 U.S.C. §§ 1–2 (1890).

215. *See* United States v. American Telephone & Telegraph Co., 552 F. Supp. 131 (D.D.C. 1982), *aff'd*, 460 U.S. 1001 (1983).

216. *See id.* at 149.

217. *Id.* at 150 (quoting International Salt Co. v. United States, 332 U.S. 392, 401 (1947)).

218. *See* P. Areeda & L. Kaplan, Antitrust Analysis 527 (1988).

219. *See* Federal Communications Commission v. National Citizens Committee for Broadcasting, 436 U.S. 775, 787 (1978).

220. *See id.* at 782–83.

221. *See id.* at 783–84.

222. *See* W. Wilson, The Declining Significance of Race 110 (1978).

223. *See* S. Carter, Reflections of an Affirmative Action Baby (1991); S. Steele, The Content of Our Character (1990); W. Wilson, *supra* note 222.

224. *See, e.g.*, Kennedy, *Persuasion and Distrust: A Comment on the Affirmative Action Debate*, 99 Harv. L. Rev. 1327, 1333–34 (1986).

225. Criticism of the premises of affirmative action are detailed, for instance in T. Sowell, Civil Rights: Rhetoric or Reality? (1984).

226. *See* Kennedy, *supra* note 224, at 1334–36.

227. Paris Adult Theater I v. Slaton, 413 U.S. 49, 61 (1973).

228. *Id.* at 62.

229. *See* City of New Orleans v. Dukes, 427 U.S. 297, 303 (1976).

230. *Panel Attacks Bush on Civil Rights Work, supra* note 209.

231. *Id.*

232. *See* Lively, *The Supreme Court Appointment Process: In Search of Constitutional Roles and Responsibilities*, 59 S. Cal. L. Rev. 551, 564 (1986).

233. *See There Goes the Judge*, Newsweek, April 22, 1991, at 31, cols. 2–3.

234. *Panel Attacks Bush on Civil Rights Work, supra* note 208.

235. *Id.*

Chapter 7

Original Imperatives and Doctrinal Possibility

The legacy of slow, delayed, and incomplete responses to the imperatives of the Fourteenth Amendment has created a constitutional distortion that perverts not only the law but also critical response to it. Failure to account fully for the amendment's central aims results in justifiable frustration, as commitment to civil rights and equality redundantly is articulated, only to be qualified by subsequent limiting principles. Critical review of equal protection jurisprudence reveals a history of doctrinal potential and incomplete actualization. Although analytical failures may be apparent as evidenced by the limited reach, effect and unwinding of the desegregation mandate and by contemporary intent standards which thwart equal protection claims, the possibility of viable alternative premises is confounded by theories that tend to be disputable and thus unserviceable. Much of the Fourteenth Amendment's original business in the meantime remains unfinished and lost between cramped jurisprudence and overly grand or novel response. Given the amendment's existence as an extension of supreme democratic will and the consequent indefeasibility of its core aims, a redirection of attention to original meaning might help ameliorate the abiding tension between doctrinal possibility and actuality.

Even if measured according to the expectations of its framers,[1] the Fourteenth Amendment has been a qualified success at best. The rights to travel without inordinate constraint;[2] to own, possess, and convey property;[3] and to make contracts,[4] for instance, have been secured in varying degree. Even so, jurisprudence continues to struggle with and shrink from those core interests of the Fourteenth Amendment. In recognizing that Congress has secured the right to contract, for instance, the Supreme Court refused to extend the federal interest to post-formation harassment.[5] Such analysis in 1989 disregarded the general principle, enunciated more than a century before, that remedial legislation is to be construed not restrictively but liberally and flexibly to realize its corrective aims.[6] Although the formality of a dual system of criminal justice has been erased, moreover, the Court accepts "[a]pparent discrepancies in sentencing [as] an inevitable part of our criminal justice system,"[7] even when the disparities are pronounced.

Whether evaluated by the minimal demands of original intent contemplating accommodation of "[m]ere discriminations" or by criteria more ambitiously accounting for a discriminatory legacy, the Fourteenth Amendment in general and equal protection in particular have been substantially underachieved. Because standards have been calibrated so that they reach only obvious discrimination, constitutional radar is as defective now as it was more than a century ago when the Court in *Virginia v. Rives* refused to reckon with discrimination that did not overtly disclose its true character.[8] During the 1980s, the Court identified only three instances in which racial minorities were or may have been denied equal protection. In *Batson v. Kentucky*, it determined that a prosecutor may not use peremptory challenges in a racially discriminatory fashion to remove potential jurors and thereby overturned a contrary holding from the past.[9] The Court also found in *Washington v. Seattle School District No. 1* that a ballot initiative, transferring power to order busing from school boards to the state legislature,[10] constituted a breach of equal protection. What was perceived as an impermissible, race-dependent transfer of power in *Washington* did not influence review in *Crawford v. Board of Education*, which upheld voter ratification of a constitutional amendment prohibiting busing absent *de jure* segregation.[11] An equal protection deprivation also was recognized in *Hunter v. Underwood*,[12] when the Court invalidated a state criminal law enacted nearly a century earlier for patently discriminatory reasons.[13] The decisional significance of *Hunter* is minimized by the fact that the law at issue was a relic of official segregation and thus did not present the modern problem of proving wrongful intent. The decision also left open the possibility that the law might be reenacted pursuant to a racially neutral purpose.[14]

Such limited constitutional yield reflects the Court's reticence to probe the implications of egregious racial disparities in settings descending directly from official dualism[15] and contrasts with sharply increased attention and hostility to affirmative action during the same period.[16] Pursuant to modern criteria, the equal protection guarantee affords no meaningful way of confronting and accounting for sophisticated or subtle practices that in modern times deny equal opportunity and connote inferiority as effectively, and perhaps even more insidiously, than did the overt methods of the past. Contemporary analysis as a consequence falls short not only of the potential *Brown* but also of *Strauder*.[17]

Fourteenth Amendment jurisprudence over the course of its existence has disclosed a persistent and as yet unresolved conflict. While acknowledging the interests generally established by the Fourteenth Amendment, the Court seldom and only sporadically has accounted meaningfully for them. Case law in large part consists of statements of principle qualified by limiting or conditioning precepts, which retard doctrinal operation or efficacy. The Court initially held the Fourteenth Amendment captive to narrow state action concepts and perceptions of "mere" and "reasonable" discrimination. Not until 1954 did the Court activate equal protection in a way that made serious demands for societal change. The anti-discrimination phase proved unique in its initial dictate but ultimately became normative as its final contours were narrowed and its demands were reduced. The consequent emergence of motive-based standards and undifferentiating color-blind criteria effectively has resulted in a judiciary that is minimally interventionist when minorities press their claims but more aggressive when the majority complains. Forceful actualization of the federal interest underlying the Fourteenth Amendment, rarely evidenced except for a relatively brief interval from the 1950s to 1970s, ironically did not materialize until state and local governments endeavored to repair rather than maintain a discriminatory heritage.

The formulation of and investment in Fourteenth Amendment doctrine that is inchoate or a step behind the realities of racial injustice has proved more common than exceptional. It is evidenced not only by qualification of the anti-discrimination principle[18] but also by resistance to more remedy-friendly doctrine. Not surprisingly, such performance has resulted in critical attention to theories and principles that might reckon more directly and effectively with the nation's legacy of discrimination. Consistent with the Court's own sense that motive-based inquiry should be avoided when constitutional "stakes are [too] high,"[19] for instance, it has been suggested that review should assess not the intent but the racial significance of a challenged action.[20] Such a focus has been touted for its utility in reaching modern variants of subtle, unconscious, and otherwise constitutionally insignificant racism.[21] Instead of performing a predictably vain search for intent, the Court would assess whether an official action could be perceived as racially stigmatizing.[22]

The notion that equal protection results would vary if standards were simply retooled and made more sensitive to the nature of contemporary racial realities probably represents a false lead. Recognition of societal wrongdoing already is apparent in constitutional renderings that acknowledge "the sorry history of both private and public discrimination in this country."[23] Operative standards, despite such perception, are notable for their capacity to avoid accountability that would significantly contest societal norms or demand substantial revision of the established order. Anticipation of different results pursuant to alternative standards disregards a central lesson provided by two centuries of racial jurisprudence. Despite an understanding of the nation's legacy of discrimination, the Court, except during the desegregation era, has refrained from doctrine that would challenge established practice or custom.

Reality is that even the discriminatory purpose test could establish constitutional offense if facts and circumstances were examined in a more rigorous and sensitive fashion.[24] Continuing adherence to criteria that are largely unresponsive to minority discrimination claims, and disowned in other constitutional circumstances,[25] suggests that they endure because their deficiencies actually are strengths. Jurisprudence that articulates a broad commitment to eliminating all vestiges of discrimination[26] trades in false imagery insofar as the Constitution itself has not been regularly interpreted in such terms. National policy, which has hedged between support of anti-discrimination principles and inadequate enforcement or remedial efforts, offers a more accurate reflection of a societal determination qualified by competing priorities. Even if doctrine was redirected to account for racially significant events or policy, the standard still would be susceptible to qualifying standards that would limit or negate its utility. History thus suggests the improbability that substantially different equal protection results would eventuate from a simple recasting of analytical criteria.

Evidence that equal production unproductivity is not simply a function of technical standards comes from a variety of constitutional contexts where cultural significance is a pertinent consideration. In *City of Memphis v. Greene*, for example, a traffic barrier between black and white neighborhoods was challenged as a "badge of slavery" at odds with the Thirteenth Amendment.[27] The Court's failure to recognize the barrier's manifest racial significance showed that review was no more discerning than if performed pursuant to Fourteenth Amendment standards.

Modern establishment clause review further demonstrates that the Court may not necessarily discern or acknowledge the cultural significance of a challenged state action. Like Thirteenth Amendment analysis, which considers whether government action has racial significance, establishment clause review inquires into religious significance.[28] Findings that nativity scenes,[29] references to God on coinage,[30] and legislative prayer[31] do not have such meaning suggest that the results are less the function of operative standards than of an unresponsiveness to minority perceptions or a disinclination to probe imagery or practices that reflect cultural norms.

In the freedom of speech and press contexts, where sensitivity to diversity is indispensable, the Court has been criticized for an "acute ethnocentric myopia . . . and depressing inability to appreciate that in our land of cultural pluralism, there are many who think, act and talk differently from the Members of this Court, . . . and who do not share their [fragile] sensibilities."[32] In finding that commonly used profanities were unfit for general public consumption via the airwaves,[33] the Court disregarded or discounted the significance of expression with culturally specific meaning at odds with its own perceptions.[34] As Justice Brennan noted, "The words . . . [found] so unpalatable may be the stuff of everyday conversations in some, if not many, of the innumerable subcultures that compose this Nation."[35] He thus alluded to academic evidence that "[w]ords generally considered obscene . . . are considered neither obscene nor derogatory in the [black] vernacular except in particular contextual situations and when used with certain intonations."[36] Judicial insensitivity to that reality has manifested itself in a ruling that, instead of examining rap music in its cultural context, found certain lyrics obscene pursuant to general community standards.[37] Such analysis reinforces a sense that results would not change if racial significance rather than discriminatory purpose was the touchstone. Development of new theories to animate equal protection may generate intellectual attention and even acclaim, but the exercise is purely academic if the societal norms and priorities defining equal protection do not accommodate their implications.

A final reckoning with equal protection requires appreciation of the disparity between formal appearance and real achievement. The *Brown* decision is commonly regarded as a monument to racial equality. The desegregation mandate and consequent anti-discrimination principle present powerful rhetorical imagery, but, pursuant to subsequent limiting principles, actual performance has not lived up to its billing. Qualification of the desegregation requirement, as noted in Chapter 5, effectively exchanged "separate but equal" for "separate and unequal." The original decision in *Brown* delayed relief in hopes of securing popular acceptance. As desegregation demands narrowed and weakened, deferral in large part translated into denial.

A fundamental tenet of *Brown* was that desegregation was essential for equal educational opportunity and thus was a means rather than a mere end in itself. The Court thus characterized education as "the most important function of state and local governments. . . . the very foundation of good citizenship. . . . succe[ss] in life. . . . [and] a right which must be made available to all on equal terms."[38] Post-*Brown* jurisprudence largely has foreclosed the possibility of equal educational opportunity as a function of constitutional imperative. By concluding that education is not a fundamental right,[39] wealth classifications are not suspect[40] and

racially disproportionate impact by itself is insufficient to establish constitutional responsibility,[41] the Court has more than repudiated *Brown's*
potential. It also has recalibrated standards to the point that constitutional capability may be even less than under the separate but equal
principle. Implicit in the delay of immediate relief was the prospect of
more profound long-term constitutional results. The narrowing of standards and accommodation of functional racial separation and distinction,
however, have diminished if not defeated that possibility. The desegregation thesis, suggesting enhanced Fourteenth Amendment performance, thus has proved subject to antithesis in a dialectic that arguably
has yielded doctrinal regression.

The jurisprudence of race over two centuries has consistently frustrated initiatives and theories that might animate the Constitution in a
way that would significantly account for minority interests. Rejection of
color-blind criteria a century ago when segregation was challenged, and
subscription to such standards as race-conscious remediation has become
a prominent issue, illustrate the adaptability of rationales in forging
constitutional results consonant with dominant impulses. The influence
of cultural norms and priorities upon equal protection's coursing has
been well-understood by those who have sought to redirect it. In *Brown*
itself, the constitutional challenge stressed how segregation harmed not
only minorities but the entire society. Argument thus was offered that
desegregation would enhance the image of the United States as it vied
for international favor during the early phases of the Cold War.[42] Considerations of international image, when the North was courting international favor during the Civil War, influenced emancipation. Modern
arguments for remediation have referred to a general interest in maximizing human resources to enhance global competitiveness. Equal protection's adaptability in constitutionalizing concerns unrelated to race[43]
denotes further a guarantee not fixed by a transcendent limiting principle but animated selectively by priority.

With or without judicial inspiration, equal protection over the course
of its existence has not amounted to much more than cultural norms will
allow. Under any circumstances when minority concerns are being
pressed and doctrine propounded without clear charter sanction, judicial
renderings are susceptible to allegations of usurping legislative power.
Crucial to an effective equal protection guarantee therefore is a clear
sense of what is truly vulnerable to charges of anti-democratic functioning. Ideological output concerning the proper limits of judicial review is
extensive. Theories of restraint account for concepts of literalism,[44] originalism,[45] and neutrality,[46] which collectively vie with non-interpretive
notions that the Constitution realistically cannot be vitalized without reference to external values.[47] Debate over the general role of the judiciary
is compounded in the equal protection context, where intervention on

behalf of minorities clearly confronts majoritarian rule, by premises competing to minimize and to enhance the guarantee's vitality.

A survey of pertinent literature discloses no shortage of alternatives to modern equal protection theory. Paul Brest argues that courts should construe the equal protection clause as an anti-discrimination principle directed toward race-dependent practices.[48] Owen Fiss maintains that courts should focus on group disadvantage because proving discrimination is problematic and strains judicial resources.[49] Charles Lawrence suggests analysis that considers the cultural significance of government action to determine if it is racially stigmatizing or implies inferiority.[50] Bruce Ackerman proposes an equal protection jurisprudence that moves beyond process defect theory and formulates "a legally cogent set of higher-law principles."[51] Such theories contrast with the minimalist views that would narrowly delineate equal protection's operation. Chief Justice Rehnquist, for instance, has favored an equal protection guarantee responsive only to racial discrimination and would limit close scrutiny to instances in which wrongful intent is established.[52]

No matter how artfully framed and persuasively justified, equal protection doctrine is unlikely to be widely accepted if it evokes charges that it is anti-democratic. Without clear and well-accepted constitutional grounding, courts that confront the political process and threaten to retool legislative output more favorably toward minority interests invite resistance prompted or at least referenced to anti-democratic perceptions. History reveals, despite some prominent exceptions, that jurisprudence generally has avoided disruptive consequences even at the expense of constitutional imperative.

Maximizing not just the potential but also the actual efficacy of equal protection doctrine requires understanding and accepting institutional resistance to unsettling consequences. It also is essential to realize that theory not clearly tied to manifest constitutional concern can be attacked by competing perspectives and perverted as a result of altered circumstance. Doctrine premised on political science, as discussed later, has been victimized by its own creativity and uncertain linkage to constitutional design. Although a reference point for racial jurisprudence of the past half century,[53] the concept of process dysfunction as a basis for equal protection animation is largely anachronistic. The right to vote is largely secured, and actual representation is defined by the extent of electoral participation.[54] If contemporary exclusion from the legislative process is a function of self-determination rather than official discrimination, concern with systemic distortion exaggerates the significance of an increasingly irrelevant factor, while inviting unnecessary resistance to modern political output. Attention to process defects resulted in strict scrutiny of racial classification. Judicial review itself has become distorted and the original theory perverted, however, to the extent exacting review now is reserved primarily for remedial policies enacted by democratically elected agents. Rigorous review detached from its original justification thus has evolved as accounting methodology for persons who never have been excluded from the political process or part of a historically disadvantaged group.

Doctrine that feeds anti-democratic perceptions risks defiance and evasion if jurisprudential demands are substantial and underwrites constitutional torpor or incongruity if the Court lacks the resolve to make meaningful demands. Modern equal protection doctrine is especially unsatisfactory to the extent it offers unacceptable options and ultimately confounds constitutional reckoning. A choice between high conflict/high risk doctrine and avoidance/abdication is especially remiss when basic and indisputable aims of the Fourteenth Amendment remain unsatisfied.

Jurisprudence may challenge or displace legislative enactment and popular sentiment, but, to the extent clearly referenced to original intent or consensual understanding, it is safe from allegations of anti-democratic tendencies. Failure to mine fully the possibilities of originalism may be due to an awareness of the overtly racist sentiment and limited aims that inspired the Fourteenth Amendment. A consequent motivation for more exotic doctrine may be a sense that work influenced by such attitudes and aspirations itself is infected or spoiled. For all the sophisticated theories competing to animate doctrine more aggressively and expansively, they are pragmatically doomed to the extent they would unsettle cultural norms and be objected to as fundamentally anti-democratic.

Equal protection for practical purposes is reducible to the art of the possible within a framework now, as always, limited but not without significant opportunity for achievement. Society and its governing agents are bound by constitutional baselines that reflect the paramount explications of democratic consent. As noted in Chapter 2, the central and consensual aims of the Fourteenth Amendment were to ensure basic economic opportunity for material self-development and to provide for strict parity within the legal system, regardless of race. The implications of these core interests and the existence of less certain concerns might be debated—and avoided to the extent that clear reference points did not exist. Because the essential agenda is so indisputable, equal protection vitality would be enhanced by identifying and effectuating the logical radiations of original design, which remain pertinent to a legacy of discrimination more than a century after the Fourteenth Amendment's introduction. Consequent doctrine closely tied to facilitating elemental opportunity and equality of legal status would begin with the significant advantage of immunity to anti-democratic perceptions and debate that respectively cripple and enervate other alternatives.

Movement toward theory and consequent standards that are rooted

in original soil but more productive in their yield necessitates a reexamination of some old shibboleths. Modern notions of suspect classifications and strict scrutiny evolved from the sense that discrete and insular
minorities traditionally were excluded from or underrepresented in the
legislative process and thus merited special judicial attention.[55] Review
of racial classifications evolved to the point that it was characterized as
"strict in theory and fatal in fact."[56] Such scrutiny may have been pro-
democratic rather than anti-democratic insofar as it accounted for defects in the representative process. It was especially apt when enactments
that implied inferiority, perpetuated privilege, or denied opportunity
were at issue. As traditionally disadvantaged minorities have enhanced
their political identity and influence, in a system predicating success on
effective coalition building and brokering among interest groups, special
jurisprudential attention is more difficult to justify on the grounds of
process defect. Evidence suggests that blacks in recent years have increased their influence in the political system. The Civil Rights Act of
1991,[57] passed by Congress in response to restrictive Supreme Court
readings of civil rights laws, illustrates how a group that was once entirely
excluded from the legislative process now participates in alliances that
yield political accomplishments.[58] Congress, in the previous year, failed
to override a presidential veto of a similar enactment.[59] The experience
suggests at least on the federal level that a previously outcast group no
longer is entirely disabled by prejudice and, like other non-dominant
groups, may prevail in some proportion to its actual numerical strength.

   Jurisprudence that justified special constitutional attention when the
political system was grossly distorted actually may imperil the representative process when it has become more responsive to all citizens. As
localities with a long and pervasive history of discrimination have attempted to reckon with their past, the Court has confounded their efforts. Constitutional impedance is a function of strict scrutiny, deriving
from now misplaced assumptions of exclusion from or unrepresentation
in the political process. The consequent anomaly is that the harshest
standard of review, for practical purposes, has been reserved primarily
for constitutional claims by the dominant racial group. It is ironic that
the Court, which vitalized the equal protection guarantee with notions
of suspect classification and strict scrutiny when the political process was
perceived as dysfunctional is cramping the system as it approaches the
ideal that the Court identified. Analytical standards introduced to repair
process defect thus may be responsible for its aggravation.

   Even with its limited aspirations, the Fourteenth Amendment was
supported by a significant sense of obligation to account for racial disadvantage. The notion that race never can be a factor in official action
may represent a desirable ideal and may afford neat symmetry to the
extent it touts general color blindness, but it denies the methodology for

a constitutionally sanctioned reckoning. By making race unmentionable, even though its presence and implications are pervasive and selectively unattended to, jurisprudence seriously confounds even the limited aims of the Fourteenth Amendment. The Court actually may impede progress toward real color blindness insofar as premature insistence on neutrality may deter morally inspired initiatives intended to remedy the consequences of past policy and practice. Categorical prohibition of racially referenced policy, to the extent premised upon legal criteria of color blindness, establishes a constitutional standard incongruent with the reality of persisting color-consciousness. It thus leaves the Court vulnerable to criticism that it has fast-tracked legal standards beyond society's actual moral development. Even worse, such legal principles project imagery of societal development that may engender complacency and actually deter individual or collective attention to moral reality.

Equal protection's potential has been constrained by a sense of the judiciary in competition with the representative process and thus the consent of the governed. The indisputable albeit limited aims of the Fourteenth Amendment, however, are a supreme extension of rather than a challenge to popular will. No higher expression of democratic consent exists than what the Constitution itself ordains. Doctrine neither should be cast in terms of creative theory, therefore, nor should it negate credible initiatives aimed at transforming ideals into reality. Rather, equal protection theory and principle should maximize the possibilities of linkage to cognizable and incontrovertible interests and present themselves with the certainty that constitutional aims and democratic imperatives are coextensive and essentially the same. Original design may not support the most expansive or exotic notions of equality, but it affords the opportunity for confident enunciation of assertive and meaningful standards for interests that still await a full accounting.

Pragmatic vitalization of the Fourteenth Amendment favors divesting anachronistic and uncertain theories and attending instead to the amendment's credible emanations. Such review essentially would be a function of how closely related a claimed interest is to original or consensual goals of the Fourteenth Amendment. As the relationship between modern policy and original or consensual agenda becomes less fathomable, scrutiny of a challenged circumstance or action should intensify. Correlatively, as the nexus becomes more discernible, scrutiny should be less rigorous. Review would be in inverse proportion to the close or distant association with the original agenda and consensual glosses on it. As amended by subsequent experience, constitutional concern would extend to any form of official racial discrimination or stigmatization manifestly inimical to equal protection criteria established in 1954.

Fourteenth Amendment analysis thus should focus upon (1) whether a challenged policy or action implicates a clear original or consensual concern and (2) whether the policy or action credibly conforms with or contravenes amplified original interest. Race-conscious policies advancing basic elements of the amendment's historical agenda should be subject to less than strict scrutiny. Conversely, when the relationship between central aims and a challenged action is attenuated or uncertain, review should be more rigorous. Such a sliding scale would calibrate judicial concern not to secondary or peripheral matters—including motive, process defect, cultural significance, and even disputable implications of a classification—but rather to more justifiable constitutional concerns.

The efficacy of the equal protection guarantee consequently would be enhanced but not to the point it would be an uncontrollable peril to all legislation that classifies or has disparate effects. The parade of horribles, referred to by the Court in justifying motive-based inquiry,[60] would never materialize. General tax legislation that routinely classifies, for instance, would not implicate original or consensual concern and thus not be subject to serious equal protection challenges.[61] Similarly a reduction in public benefits that disproportionately affects the poor may not be proximately related to cognizable Fourteenth Amendment concerns, even if it affects one racial group more than another.[62] Disparate impact would have constitutional significance to the extent it related to venues and circumstances close to acknowledged Fourteenth Amendment concerns with basic opportunity and a fair system of justice. Although probity would diminish as ties to the original agenda became more distant, it would not be categorically discounted.

A fortified jurisprudence of original design should closely examine disproportionality not only in employment and business venues but also in areas that are critical to economic opportunity, such as education. Instead of limiting principles that gloss the funding differentials among racially identifiable schools that are not officially segregated, a constitutional duty would exist to provide quality education. To the extent a traffic barrier between black and white neighborhoods does not impede basic opportunity, it would survive equal protection review. Attention to original aims, however, might engender more sensitive Thirteenth Amendment analysis that recognized how such official acts may be consistent with reducing a particular group to the status of a subject race. Disparities in the criminal justice system's operation would be closely scrutinized pursuant to original concern with equal status before the law.

Initiatives to facilitate equal economic opportunity for racial minorities should be constitutionally permissible if they effectuate core Fourteenth Amendment aims and if their adoption is not procedurally irregular.[63] Standards of review should be receptive to voluntary efforts to integrate the educational system or the workplace as policies legitimately tied to Fourteenth Amendment aims. Presumptively valid would be a diversification scheme, such as the plan defeated in *Wygant v. Jackson Board of*

Education, designed to facilitate basic opportunity and subscribed to without procedural aberration.[64] Attention to the link between policy and original aim, unlike an entirely deferential mode of review, would enable the Court to identify and invalidate schemes that were inadequately rooted in original design. The possibility that a locally powerful minority might enact policy to secure unfair advantage, which worried the Court in *City of Richmond v. J. A. Croson Co.*,[65] still could be discerned pursuant to a credibility standard. Even if such a program fit within a clear concern of the original agenda, it would fail if not accounting for a legitimate interest under the circumstances and if proper procedures were not followed. The inquiry should remain fixed, however, on whether the plan credibly reckoned with a persisting discriminatory legacy of recognizably constitutional significance.

Even if affirmative action presents some of the negatives and risks that the Court has catalogued,[66] judicial intervention is unjustified when the representative process is not dysfunctional but rather is effectively accounting for original imperatives. Holding society and its legislative agents to an as yet unrealized standard, in the form of color blindness, detaches law from morality without compelling justification. It also represents social engineering and micromanagement, which proponents of restraint supposedly condemn, and defines and limits policies that may compete for moral subscription.

Jurisprudence that speaks in idealistic flourishes and then manipulates doctrine so that the results comport with actual moral circumstance is the preface for an Orwellian legacy. Society has not evolved to the point that racial distinctions are no longer pertinent or prominent. Race-dependent attitudes and judgments always have been and remain rooted in the nation's traditions and conscience as defining societal characteristics. Review that suggests a deep and broad spectrum commitment to erasing discrimination, even as it effectively avoids the task, not only transcends original vision. It also is delusionary and obstructive to society's own confrontation with and even consciousness of racial reality. A culture indulged by constitutional imagery, suggesting a higher state of moral development than actually exists, is the victim of an especially insidious form of judicial activism insofar as its incentive for real moral growth is diminished.

The jurisprudence of race now, as over the course of two centuries, is reducible to a doctrine of affordability. Slavery was accommodated at the republic's inception after factoring in the toll otherwise to a viable political and economic union. The separate but equal doctrine calculated the cost of insisting that society abandon its established traditions and attitudes. Curtailment of the anti-discrimination principle generally, and the desegregation mandate particularly, likewise reflects a sense that jurisprudence cannot impose demands that are too unsettling or in conflict with higher priorities. Standards as they have evolved so far denote the reality of a society not disposed toward absorbing fully the cost of accounting for racial discrimination. What remains affordable and serviceable, but largely neglected, is doctrine that would achieve the central and consensual aims of the Fourteenth Amendment. The interests of constitutional productivity point not to doctrinal creativity that will be disputed and defeated but to maximization of an original agenda that affords an irrefutable constitutional baseline for policy and review. The alternative is constitutional law presuming a society that is mythical rather than real and a source of disputable theories instead of real accomplishments.

NOTES

1. *See* Chapter 2.
2. Civil Rights Act of 1964, 42 U.S.C. § 2000a to 2000b (1964), precludes discrimination in public accommodations and facilities that otherwise limited eating and shelter options appurtenant to travel. *See, e.g.*, Katzenbach v. McClung, 379 U.S. 294, 304 (1964); Heart of Atlanta Motel v. United States, 379 U.S. 241, 258 (1964).
3. For instance, the Court has held that racially restrictive covenants violate both the Thirteenth and Fourteenth Amendments. *See* Shelley v. Kraemer, 334 U.S. 1, 20–21 (1948).
4. *See, e.g.*, Patterson v. McLean Credit Union, 109 S. Ct. 2363, 2370 (1989) (42 U.S.C. § 1981 precludes racial discrimination with respect to making and enforcing contracts).
5. The Court held that Section 1981 does not reach racial harassment that occurs after formation of an employment contract. *See* Patterson v. McLean Credit Union, 109 S. Ct. at 2373–74. The dissent argued that the majority failed to recognize that racial harassment during employment "denie[s] the right to make an employment contract on [an equal] basis." *Id.* at 2393 (Brennan, J., dissenting).
6. In striking down a state law excluding blacks from juries, the Court emphasized that the Fourteenth Amendment was to be interpreted in a way that implemented its remedial purpose. Strauder v. West Virginia, 100 U.S. (10 Otto) 303, 307 (1880). Such interpretive philosophy characterizes the review of modern federal regulation in general. The federal securities laws, for instance, are to "be construed 'not technically and restrictively, but flexibly to effectuate [their] remedial purposes.'" Herman & McLean, Inc. v. Huddleston, 459 U.S. 375, 386–87 (1983) (quoting Securities and Exchange Commission v. Capital Gains Research Bureau, Inc., 375 U.S. 180, 195 (1963)).
7. McCleskey v. Kemp, 481 U.S. 279, 312 (1987).
8. Virginia v. Rives, 100 U.S. (10 Otto) 313 (1879).
9. Batson v. Kentucky, 476 U.S. 79 (1986).
10. Washington v. Seattle School District No. 1, 458 U.S. 457 (1982).
11. Crawford v. Board of Education, 458 U.S. 527 (1982).
12. 471 U.S. 222 (1985).

13. *Id.* at 233.

14. *Id.*

15. *See* McCleskey v. Kemp, 481 U.S. at 279, 329–33, 343–44 (Brennan, J., dissenting).

16. *See* Martin v. Wilks, 109 S. Ct. 2180 (1989); City of Richmond v. J. A. Croson Co., 488 U.S. 469 (1989); United States v. Paradise, 480 U.S. 149 (1986); Local 28, Sheet Metal Workers International Association v. EEOC, 478 U.S. 421 (1986); Local No. 93, International Association of Firefighters v. Cleveland, 478 U.S. 501 (1986); Wygant v. Jackson Board of Education, 476 U.S. 267 (1986); Firefighters Local Union No. 1784 v. Stotts, 467 U.S. 561 (1984); Minnick v. California Department of Corrections, 452 U.S. 105 (1981); Fullilove v. Klutznick, 448 U.S. 448 (1980).

17. The *Strauder* Court, as noted in Chapter 3, intimated that the Fourteenth Amendment was concerned with discrimination "implying inferiority." Strauder v. West Virginia, 100 U.S. (10 Otto) at 308.

18. See Chapter 5.

19. United States v. O'Brien, 391 U.S. 367, 384 (1968).

20. *See* Lawrence, *The Id, the Ego and Equal Protection: Reckoning with Unconscious Racism*, 39 Stan. L. Rev. 317, 355–62 (1987).

21. *See id.* at 349–50.

22. *See id.* at 354–55.

23. City of Richmond v. J. A. Croson Co., 109 S. Ct. at 706, 724.

24. Cases involving grossly disparate applications of the death penalty and state-facilitated segregation of city and suburban schools appear on their face to be constitutionally violative, even under a rigorous discriminatory intent test. Yet, the Court explained away duality in the death penalty context as a mere "discrepancy that appears to correlate with race . . . [and] an inevitable part of our criminal justice system." McCleskey v. Kemp, 481 U.S. at 312. The Court set aside a trial court's findings of fact in a school segregation case in order to avoid ordering intermunicipal desegregation. *See* Milliken v. Bradley, 418 U.S. 717, 745–47 (1974).

25. *See, e.g.*, United States v. O'Brien, 391 U.S. at 383–84.

26. *E.g.*, Columbus Board of Education v. Penick, 443 U.S. 449, 459 (1979).

27. City of Memphis v. Greene, 451 U.S. 100, 124 (1981). The city had a long and pervasive history of official segregation, as well as traditions connoting racial inferiority. *See id.* at 137 (Marshall, J., dissenting). The city erected the barrier at the request of residents in the white neighborhood. *See id.* at 135 (Marshall, J., dissenting).

28. *See* Lawrence, *supra* note 20, at 319.

29. *See* Lynch v. Donnelly, 465 U.S. 668, 685 (1984).

30. *See id.* at 676.

31. *See* Marsh v. Chambers, 463 U.S. 783, 795 (1983).

32. Federal Communications Commission v. Pacifica Foundation, 438 U.S. 726, 775 (1978) (Brennan, J., dissenting).

33. The specific language contained in a broadcast satire of social usage and response to certain words is reproduced in the appendix to the court's opinion. *See id.* at 751–55.

34. *See id.* at 750 (characterizing broadcast of language at issue as equivalent to "a pig [in the] parlor").

35. *Id.* at 776 (Brennan, J., dissenting).

36. *Id.* (quoting Bins, *Toward an Ethnography of Contemporary African American Oral Poetry*, in Language and Linguistics Working Papers No. 5, at 82 (1972)).

37. *See* Skywalker Records, Inc. v. Navarro, 739 F. Supp. 578 (S.D. Fla. 1990).

38. Brown v. Board of Education, 347 U.S. 483, 493 (1954). In mandating desegregation of federal schools in the District of Columbia, despite the absence of an explicit equal protection provision in the Fifth Amendment, the Court reinforced the notion that education was a fundamental right. *See* Bolling v. Sharpe, 347 U.S. 497, 499–500 (1954).

39. *See* San Antonio Independent School District v. Rodriguez, 411 U.S. 1, 36 (1973).

40. *See id.* at 28–29.

41. *See id.*

42. *See, e.g.*, Amicus Curiae Brief for American Civil Liberties Union at 28–31, Brown v. Board of Education, 347 U.S. 483 (1954); Amicus Curiae Brief for American Federation of Teachers at 25–26, Brown v. Board of Education, 347 U.S. 483 (1954).

43. Modern equal protection addresses classifications based on gender, alienage, and illegitimacy and also covers discriminatory acts impacting on fundamental rights. It thus would be a source of surprise to early observers who "doubt[ed] . . . very much whether any action of a State not directed . . . against the negroes . . . will ever be held to come within the purview of this provision." Slaughter-House Cases, 83 U.S. (16 Wall.) 36, 81 (1872).

44. Strict constructionism is predicated on the notion that "the Court has no power to add or subtract from the procedures set forth by the Founders." In re Winship, 397 U.S. 358, 377 (1970) (Black, J., dissenting). The doctrine directs courts to construe the Constitution "in a straightforward manner . . . paying close attention to its words and avoid twisting or stretching their meanings [so] there will be few occasions for controversies that can be manipulated." L. Tribe, God Save This Honorable Court 41 (1985). Given the inadequacy of a purely textual approach to construing the many critical open-ended terms of the Constitution, it is not surprising that strict constructionists constitute "a very unpopulated subgroup." G. Gunther, Constitutional Law 518 n.11 (1991).

45. Originalism requires that courts confronted with vague or indeterminate constitutional provisions construe those provisions with reference to the subjective intent of the framers of the Constitution. *See* D. Lively, Judicial Review and the Consent of the Governed: Activist Ways and Popular Ends 56–59 (1990). The theory is susceptible to the same criticisms leveled against the Court's motive-based Fourteenth Amendment inquiry.

46. Neutrality calls on courts to employ objective interpretive principles that favor no particular group, even when the interpretation proves subjectively unsatisfying. *See* Bork, *Neutral Principles and Some First Amendment Problems*, 47 Ind. L.J. 1, 6–7 (1971); Tushnet, *Following the Rules Laid Down: A Critique of Interpretivism and Neutral Principles*, 96 Harv. L. Rev. 781, 805–06 (1983); Wechsler, *Toward Neutral Principles of Constitutional Law*, 73 Harv. L. Rev. 1, 11–12, 15 (1959). The neutral principles model suffers from a misplaced assumption that

a singular principle links serial decisions and that factors invariably can be advanced, as in the case of affirmative action, to distinguish circumstances from the general rule.

47. *See, e.g.*, Grey, *Do We Have an Unwritten Constitution?*, 27 Stan. L. Rev. 703, 706 (1975); Tushnet, *supra* note 46.

48. *See* Brest, *Foreword: In Defense of the Antidiscrimination Principle*, 90 Harv. L. Rev. 1, 6 (1976).

49. *See* Fiss, *Groups and the Equal Protection Clause*, 5 Phil. & Pub. Aff. 107, 153–54 (1976).

50. *See* Lawrence, *supra* note 20, at 355–62.

51. Ackerman, *Beyond Carolene Products*, 98 Harv. L. Rev. 713, 744 (1985).

52. Sugarman v. Dougall, 413 U.S. 634, 649–57 (1973) (Rehnquist, J., dissenting).

53. The Court's strict scrutiny of racial classifications is rooted in the premise that prejudice against discrete and insular minorities may distort the political process otherwise relied upon for protection. *See* United States v. Carolene Products Co., 304 U.S. 144, 152 n.4 (1938).

54. The Voting Rights Act of 1965, 42 U.S.C. § 1973 (1988), continues to secure voting rights and political participation in states that historically denied or impaired the franchise on racial grounds. In the 1988 presidential election, 50.2 percent of the voting age population actually cast ballots. Statistical Abstract of the United States 258 (table 433) (1989). During the 1986 congressional election, 46 percent of the eligible population voted. Statistical Abstract of the United States 249 (table 418) (1988).

55. *See* United States v. Carolene Products Co., 304 U.S. at 152 n.4. The concepts of suspect classification and rigid scrutiny made their literal debut in Korematsu v. United States, 323 U.S. 214, 216 (1944).

56. Gunther, *Foreword: In Search of Evolving Doctrine on a Changing Court: A Model for a Newer Equal Protection*, 86 Harv. L. Rev. 1, 8 (1972).

57. *See* S. 1745, 102nd Cong., 1st Sess. (Nov. 1991) (Lexis, Genfed Library, Bills File). The law, among other things, curtails belated challenges to consent decrees incorporating affirmative action plans, places upon employers the burden of showing that practices having a racially disparate impact are justified by business necessity, and extends protection against racial discrimination in employment contracts to post-formation harassment. The enactment thus displaces case law discussed *supra* at notes 4–6 and accompanying text, and in Chapter 5, notes 182–86 and accompanying text.

58. Unlike other interest group efforts, organized initiatives toward securing racial justice are qualified by standards prohibiting a remedial focus that is race-conscious. *See* City of Richmond v. J.A. Croson Co., 109 S. Ct. 721.

59. *See* 136 Cong. Rec. S 16,562, S 16,589 (Oct. 24, 1990).

60. The Court has reasoned that without a discriminatory intent standard for the Fourteenth Amendment, "a whole range of tax, welfare, public service, regulatory, and licensing statutes" would be endangered. Washington v. Davis, 426 U.S. 229, 248 (1976).

61. A tax that without adequate justification singled out an interest protected by the equal protection guarantee, however, would be susceptible to constitutional challenge. *Cf.* Minneapolis Star & Tribune Co. v. Minnesota Commissioner

of Revenue, 460 U.S. 575, 585 (1983). Although not directly referring to the equal protection guarantee, the Court cited to authority for the proposition that such regulation, even if unrelated to suppression of expression, would be "presumptively unconstitutional." *Id.* (citing Police Department of Chicago v. Mosley, 408 U.S. 92, 95 (1972)).

62. Denial of government funds for abortions thus would not be likely to present an equal protection claim under the proposed standards. *See, e.g.*, Harris v. McRae, 448 U.S. 297, 326 (1980); Maher v. Roe, 432 U.S. 464, 469–70 (1977).

63. Judicial scrutiny to determine whether laws were enacted in conformance with procedural norms would be intended to ensure that any preferential scheme emerged from a fair process. *See* Wygant v. Jackson Board of Education, 476 U.S. 267, 317 (1986) (Stevens, J., dissenting).

64. *See id.*

65. *See* City of Richmond v. J. A. Croson Co., 109 S. Ct. at 722.

66. *See id.* at 721. The Court's objections to affirmative action are examined in Chapter 6.

Bibliography

BOOKS

Abraham, H., Justices and Presidents (1974).

Allen, R., The Life and Experience and Gospel Labors of the Rt. Rev. Richard Allen (1960).

Areeda, P., & Kaplan, L., Antitrust Analysis (1988).

Baer, J., Equality under the Constitution: Reclaiming the Fourteenth Amendment (1983).

Bell, D., And We Are Not Saved (1987).

Bell, D., Race, Racism and American Law (1973).

Berger, R., Government by Judiciary (1977).

Bickel, A., The Supreme Court and the Idea of Progress (1970).

Black, C., Jr., Structure and Relationship in Constitutional Law (1969).

Bork, R., The Tempting of America (1990).

Carter, S., Reflections of an Affirmative Action Baby (1991).

Cover, R., Justice Accused (1975).

Du Bois, W.E.B., The Suppression of the African Slave-Trade to the United States of America, 1638–1870 (1896).

Dunham, A., & Kurland, P., eds., Mr. Justice (1964).

Elliot, J., ed., The Debates in the Several State Conventions of the Adoption of the Federal Constitution (1901).

Fairman, C., History of the Supreme Court of the United States, Reconstruction and Reunion (1971) (1987).

Farrand, M., ed., The Records of the Federal Convention of 1787 (1937).

Fehrenbacher, D., The Dred Scott Case (1978).

Finkelman, P., An Imperfect Union (1981).

Goldwin, R., & Kaufman, A., eds., The Constitution, Equality and Race (1988).

Graham, H., Everyman's Constitution (1968).

Gunther, G., Constitutional Law (1991).

Hall, K., ed., The Law of American Slavery (1987).

Higginbotham, A., Jr., In the Matter of Color (1978).

Hyman, H., A More Perfect Union (1973).

Hyman, H., & Wiecek, W., Equal Justice under the Law (1982).

Jacobs, P., Prelude to Riot: A View of Urban America from the Bottom (1967).

Jordan, W., White over Black: American Attitudes Toward the Negro (1968).

Kaczorowski, R., The Politics of Judicial Interpretation: The Federal Courts, Department of Justice and Civil Rights, 1866–1876 (1985).

Karst, K., Belonging to America (1989).

Karst, K., ed., Civil Rights and Equality (1989).

Kettner, J., The Development of American Citizenship, 1608–1870 (1978).

Kluger, R., Simple Justice (1975).

Kurland, P., Politics, the Constitution, and the Warren Court (1970).

Lewis, A., Portrait of a Decade: The Second American Revolution (1964).

Lively, D., Judicial Review and the Consent of the Governed: Activist Ways and Popular Ends (1990).

Lynch, F., Invisible Victims: White Males and the Crisis of Affirmative Action (1989).

Lynd, S., Class Conflict, Slavery and the United States Constitution (1967).

Mason, A. The Supreme Court from Taft to Warren (1958).

Mason, A. William Howard Taft—Chief Justice (1964).

Myrdal, G., An American Dilemma (1944).

Nelson, W., The Fourteenth Amendment: From Political Principle to Judicial Doctrine (1988).

Phillips, U., American Negro Slavery (1918).

Ripple, K., Constitutional Litigation (1984).

Sowell, T., Civil Rights: Rhetoric or Reality? (1984).

Steele, S., The Content of Our Character (1990).

Story, J., Commentaries on the Constitution (1905).

ten Broek, J., Antislavery Origins of the Fourteenth Amendment (1951).

Tribe, L., American Constitutional Law (1988).

Tribe, L., God Save This Honorable Court (1985).

Tushnet, M., The American Law of Slavery (1981).

Wiecek, W., The Sources of Antislavery Constitutionalism in America, 1760–1848 (1977).

Wilson, W., The Declining Significance of Race (1978).

Woodward, C., The Burden of Southern History (1960).

ESSAYS

Ackerman, *Beyond Carolene Products*, 98 Harv. L. Rev. 713 (1985).

Bins, *Toward an Ethnography of Contemporary African American Oral Poetry*, in Language and Linguistics Working Papers No. 5 (1972).

Bork, *Neutral Principles and Some First Amendment Problems*, 47 Ind. L.J., 1 (1971).

Brest, *Foreword: In Defense of the Antidiscrimination Principle*, 90 Harv. L. Rev. 1 (1976).

Ely, *The Constitutionality of Reverse Discrimination*, 41 U. Chi. L. Rev. 723 (1974).

Fehrenbacher, *Slavery, the Framers, and the Living Constitution*, in Slavery and Its Consequences: The Constitution, Equality and Race (R. Goldwin & A. Kaufman eds. 1988).

Finkelman, *Prigg v. Pennsylvania and Northern State Courts*, in The Law of American Slavery (R. Hall ed. 1987).

Fiss, *Groups and the Equal Protection Clause*, 5 Phil. & Pub. Aff. 107 (1976).

Goodman, *De Facto School Segregation: A Constitutional and Empirical Analysis*, 60 Calif. L. Rev. 275 (1972).

Graham, The Early Antislavery Backgrounds of the Fourteenth Amendment, 1950 Wis. L. Rev. 610 (1950).

Grey, *Do We Have an Unwritten Constitution?*, 27 Stan. L. Rev. 703 (1975).

Gunther, *Foreword: In Search of Evolving Doctrine on a Changing Court: A Model for a Newer Equal Protection*, 86 Harv. L. Rev. 1 (1972).

Kennedy, *Persuasion and Distrust: A Comment on the Affirmative Action Debate*, 99 Harv. L. Rev. 1327 (1986).

Lawrence, *The Id, the Ego and Equal Protection: Reckoning with Unconscious Racism*, 39 Stan. L. Rev. 317 (1987).

Levy, *Plessy v. Ferguson*, in Civil Rights and Equality (K. Karst ed. 1989).

Lively, *The Supreme Court Appointment Process: In Search of Constitutional Roles and Responsibilities*, 59 S. Cal. L. Rev. 551 (1986).

Lively & Plass, *Equal Protection: The Jurisprudence of Denial and Evasion*, 40 Am. U.L. Rev. 1307 (1991).

Marek, *Education by Decree*, New Perspectives, Summer 1985, at 36.

Marshall, *An Evaluation of Recent Efforts to Achieve Racial Integration in Education through Resort to the Courts*, 21 J. Negro Education 316 (1952).

Meese, *The Law of the Constitution*, 61 Tul. L. Rev. 979 (1987).

Pinderhughes, *Legal Strategies for Voting Rights: Political Science and the Law*, 28 How. L.J. 515 (1985).

Ross, *Innocence and Affirmative Action*, 43 Vand. L. Rev. 297 (1990).

Sandalow, Constitutional Interpretation, 79 Mich. L. Rev. 1033 (1981).

Sullivan, *Sins of Discrimination: Last Term's Affirmative Action Cases*, 100 Harv. L. Rev. 78 (1986).

Tushnet, *Following the Rules Laid Down: A Critique of Interpretivism and Neutral Principles*, 96 Harv. L. Rev. 781 (1983).

Wechsler, *Toward Neutral Principles of Constitutional Law*, 73 Harv. L. Rev. 1 (1959).

Index

About the Author

DONALD E. LIVELY is Professor of Law at the University of Toledo College of Law. He is the author of *Modern Communications Law* (Praeger, 1991) and *Essential Principles of Communications Law* (Praeger, 1991).